Credo

Credo

The Catechism Of The Old Catholic Church

The Old Catholic Church of the United States

iUniverse, Inc.

New York Lincoln Shanghai

Credo
The Catechism Of The Old Catholic Church

iUniverse books may be ordered through booksellers or by contacting:

iUniverse
2021 Pine Lake Road, Suite 100
Lincoln, NE 68512
www.iuniverse.com
1-800-Authors (1-800-288-4677)

ISBN: 0-595-34066-0

Printed in the United States of America

Nihil Obstat: ✠ Andre' J. W. Queen, SCR, Vicar-General, D.D., S.T.D.
Imprimatur: ✠ Robert Matthew Gubala, SCR, Archbishop-Metropolitan, D.D., Ph.D.
The Old Catholic Church of the United States

Visit us at: http://www.oldcatholic.us

Specific chapters and appendix materials were adapted and expounded upon from *Old Catholic: History, Ministry, Faith & Mission,* by Bishop Andre' Queen, SCR, used by permission. The Chapter, *The Ecumenical Councils & The Early Church Fathers,* was provided by Fr. Jerome D. Kwasek, Episcopal Vicar for the Diocese of California. Certain historical vignettes and historical information were provided, by permission, by The Archives of the American Congregation of St. Benedict through Bishop Donald Pierce Weeks, OSB, Abbot-Ordinary. The *Foundational Catechism* was provided by the Old Catholic Church of America, through His Eminence, Archbishop-Metropolitan James E. Bostwick. Special thanks also goes to Archbishop Denis M. Garrison, for allowing the reproduction of his *Treatise on the Married Episcopate, An Argument From Tradition For Ordaining Married Priests To The Episcopate of the Orthodox Catholic Church.* Quotations of early Church Fathers not cited are from the Christian Classics Ethereal Library Collection, and are in the public domain, as are quotations denoted "CCEL".

This Catechism was approved by the English-speaking Churches of the **International Synod of Old Catholic Churches** (ISOCC). Reviewed by: Archbishop Robert M. Gubala, SCR, Archbishop James Bostwick, Archbishop Robert McBride (Ret.), Bishop Andre' Queen, SCR, Bishop David Bowler, SSB, Bishop Howard Weston-Smart and Bishop Sherman Mosley.

In Memory of Archbishop Arnold Harris Mathew &

Archbishop Joseph Renee Vilatte,

Your Sacrifice Will Not Be Forgotten.

"Now I rejoice in what was suffered for you, and I fill up in my flesh what is still lacking in regard to Christ's afflictions, for the sake of his body, which is the church" (Col. 1: 24).

And We Will Hear Your Words.

"Almighty and everlasting God, Whose only begotten Son, Jesus Christ the Good Shepherd, has said, 'Other sheep I have that are not of this fold: them also I must bring, and they shall hear My voice, and there shall be one fold and one shepherd'; let Thy rich and abundant blessing rest upon the Old Roman Catholic Church, to the end that it may serve Thy purpose by gathering in the lost and straying sheep. Enlighten, sanctify, and quicken it by the indwelling of the Holy Ghost, that suspicions and prejudices may be disarmed, and the other sheep being brought to hear and to know the voice of their true Shepherd thereby, all may be brought into full and perfect unity in the one fold of Thy Holy Catholic Church, under the wise and loving keeping of Thy Vicar, through the same Jesus Christ, Thy Son, who with Thee and the Holy Ghost, liveth and reigneth God, world without end. Amen."

—Archbishop Mathew's Prayer for Catholic Unity

Contents

Foreword

From the Archbishop-Metropolitan of
the Old Catholic Church of the United States
His Eminence, The Most Reverend Robert Matthew Gubala, SCR

This published Catechism is a first of it's kind for the Old Catholic Church in General and the "Old Catholic Church of the United States" in particular.

Although a Catechism is one of the most important learning tools of the faith, it is just the beginning, a "first step" in our journey to learning and understanding more about our Faith and our God.

This work is a foundation for all who wish to become part of the Old Catholic Church. It remains true to the beliefs of the early Church and true Catholicism and faithful to the founding Fathers of the Old Catholic movement.

It is my fervent hope and prayer that all who read this Catechism, find it helpful and bring them to a better understanding about who Old Catholics are and what we believe.

Peace and Blessings,

Robertus Matheus

Most Reverend
✠ Robert Matthew Gubala, SCR, D.D., Ph.D.
Archbishop—Metropolitan

Visit us at: www.oldcatholic.us

Preface

His Excellency,
The Most Reverend Andre' J. W. Queen, SCR, D.D., S.T.D.
Vicar General,
The Old Catholic Church of the United States

Because it is critical that both members of this Church and non-members alike are informed as to the teachings of the Church, this work has been undertaken. Not to supplant, but to be supported by, the timeless witness of Christian faith as expressed in Holy Scripture and Sacred Apostolic Tradition, the revelation of Truth, authoritatively taught by the Church, this catechetical work is provided for use in the instruction in the faith. In addition, this authoritatively instituted work can be used to clearly indicate what we, as Old Catholics, believe, and how we come to know God. The journey to becoming part of the Body of Christ is not academic, but spiritual, and the catechetical instruction must be enlivened by an active and healthy prayer life, and instruction is perfected, not in intellectual pursuit, but in prayer, supplication, and the living out of the faith we profess.

Old Catholic Covenant

Covenant of the Old Catholic Churches of Christ
(Full Sacrament)

The Catholic community churches of Christ agree as follows:

We adhere to and profess the faith of the one, holy, catholic and apostolic Church of Christ, as expressed in the Symbol of Nicea, the "Church of the Seven Councils," the "Undivided Church." We adhere to Christ alone, and profess no faith other than that handed over to his holy disciples and Apostles, and handed down even to us in this day.

Knowing the Church is One, and looking forward with the greatest hope to the restoration of all disciples in the unity that Christ desires, we agree to the following standards of conduct between us, the standards of friendship and holy fellowship even the midst of our divisions and confusions:

1. All persons who have received a Trinitarian baptism are by virtue of that Baptism Christians and disciples of Christ.

2. All persons who have received a Trinitarian baptism and adhere to the ancient Catholic faith as expressed by the Symbol of Nicea (Nicea-Constantinople) are Catholics.

3. All persons who adhere to the full Catholic faith as received by the Church until the Great Schism of 1054 A.D. (the "Church of the Seven Councils") are Old Catholics, in the fullness of the Catholic faith.

4. We are unconcerned with theologoumena (theological opinions) beyond the received and accepted faith of the ancient Councils of the Church, provided they do not teach things contrary or inimical to that faith, or Tradition.

5. We profess the right and power of the Catholic Church to bear her witness in the world, and to make even now rulings concerning her faith and practice.

6. As Old Catholics, we are profoundly aware of our unique witness in the Church, and locate ourselves as the Local Church, in the Mystery that is the Church as a whole. We adhere to Christ and to Him alone, and in all things wherein we must differ from others in expressing the Catholic and Apostolic faith or determining our practice of that faith, we appeal to Christ, and to the Church as a whole, in future council

7. We seek only to walk and talk with God, whom we know in Christ Jesus, and as we are guided by the Holy Spirit. We seek Transfiguration, the fullness of our walk with God, in this life, in the here and now

TO THIS END, WE AGREE:

1. That all Christians are disciples of Christ, and are welcome to join us in prayer and fellowship, as their faith allows them.

2. That all persons of any of the Catholic traditions are welcome in prayer and fellowship, as their faith allows them.

3. That all Catholics holding the fullness of the Catholic and Apostolic faith, regardless of their church affiliation, are regarded as being in communion with us, and upon presentation of their bona fides, may be received in fellowship and admitted to the sacraments, and receive any pastoral care.

Pastors shall take care to give letters of good standing, or letters of dismissal, to any person requiring them, and should have set forms for doing so, given the mobility of the population in these times.

Pastors and faithful shall take care to document the sacraments of the Church received, and if possible should have a standard form or dossier that may be carried by the faithful, to document baptism, chrismation, current church standing, and so on.

Holy Things are for the Holy
(the Mysteries of the Church are reserved for those initiated into them)

Holy Communion may be received by:

1. Any person baptized with a Trinitarian baptism, who understands the sacrament in the sense that the Catholic faith has always held concerning the Body and Blood of Christ, present in the sacrament.

    a.   The baptized person should be Chrismated (confirmed) before receiving Communion

2. In accordance with ancient custom, no person (even a priest celebrant) should receive Holy Communion, even in a service of the Pre-Sanctified, without first professing the faith of the Catholic Church, in the form of the Symbol of Faith, the "We believe" of the Church "I believe" of the individual person:

Symbol of Nicea

I believe in one God, the Father Almighty, Maker of heaven and earth, and of all things visible and invisible;
And in one Lord Jesus Christ, the Son of God, the Only-begotten; Light from Light, Very God of Very God; begotten, not made, of one essence with the Father, by whom all things were made:
Who for us [men] and for our salvation came down from heaven, and was incarnate of the Holy Spirit and the Virgin Mary, and was made man;
And was crucified also for us under Pontius Pilate, and suffered and was buried;
And the third day He rose again, according to the Scriptures;
And ascended into heaven, and sits at the right hand of the Father;
And He shall come again with glory to judge the living and the dead, Whose kingdom shall have no end.
And I believe in the Holy Spirit, the Lord and Giver of Life, Who proceeds from the Father, Who with the Father and the Son together is worshipped and glorified, Who spoke by the Prophets;
And I believe in One, Holy, Catholic, and Apostolic Church.
I acknowledge one Baptism for the remission of sins.
I look for the Resurrection of the dead, And the Life of the world to come. Amen.

[Only the Symbol as laid down at Nicea and Constantinople shall be required, without additions or subtractions; but any common translation may be used.]

3. The person shall profess a faith in the Sacrament as Christ instituted it in any acceptable form, but the traditional prayer of faith and confession "I Believe, O Lord, and I Confess…" is highly recommended prior to taking Communion:

I Believe, O Lord, and I Confess

I believe, O Lord, and I confess that you are truly the Christ, the Son of the Living God, who came into the world to save sinners, of whom I am the chief.
And I believe that this is truly your own immaculate Body, and that this is truly your own precious Blood.
Wherefore, I pray you: have mercy on me and forgive my transgressions, both voluntary and involuntary, of word and deed, of knowledge and of ignorance; and make me worthy to partake without condemnation of your immaculate Mysteries, unto remission of my sins and unto life everlasting. Amen.

3. The sacraments of Baptism, Chrismation and Holy Communion are so closely linked and intertwined in the Mystery of Christ and his Church, that no person may receive them unless understanding the Catholic faith, and being initiated into it.

To this end, a clear understanding of the Catechumenate is important, and should be reinstated in the Church as a distinct part of her life.

For infants and adults alike, Baptism, Chrismation and Holy Communion (first Communion) should be given together, or in close proximity of time and place: those baptized should be Chrismated immediately, and Holy Communion should then be given from the Pre-Sanctified.

4. Christians not of the Catholic traditions should not be admitted to Communion and the Sacraments ordinarily, but there may exist over-riding reasons in charity to admit persons to the Sacraments, where they are well-disposed to receive them, and hold them as Christ gave them, or as the Church teaches and administers them.

For, what Christ made the Sacraments to be, that indeed they are.

CHAPTER 1

An Overview of this Catechism

Why Do We Need A Catechism If We Have The Bible?

Sacred Scripture has always been used for further instruction of individuals who are already members of the Church, and not as a lone catechetical (teaching) tool to win over unbelievers. Unbelievers have always come to the faith as a result of the example set by the Church, that is, the people of God. Scripture itself indicates that there are many things in them that are not easily understood, and that the unscrupulous twist and mis-use them to their own benefit. Scripture shows classic examples, such as the eunuch that was reading Hebrew Scripture, when, coming across Paul, exclaimed that he did not understand them, as he had no one to instruct him in the meaning of Scripture. Scripture, inspired by the Holy Spirit, was written *by* the Church, *for* the Church, and is meant to be taught, read and understood *within* the Church. The understanding of what Scripture means to say, rather than the uninformed reader's own individual mores crafting an individual interpretation of Scripture, is the key to unlocking a major part of the rich knowledge and teaching of Christianity. The books of the Bible were never meant to be interpreted apart from the understanding of them that comes from being part of the Church, as either a member of the Nation of Israel in the Old Testament, or as a Christian convert in the New Testament. This Deposit of Faith, found in the written Scriptures and in the living Apostolic Tradition, are authoritatively taught by the Church's Magisterium.

Jesus did not write a book; nor did He command His Apostles to do so. Thus, the written accounts of the life of Jesus and the beginning of the early Church, written by a few of the Apostles and their companions, comprise a major part but not all of the Deposit of Faith. Much, indeed, nearly all of what was taught, was done by word of mouth, the verbal teaching of the Faith which we refer to as the Apostolic Tradition. This Apostolic Tradition, unlike the "traditions of men", was the Gospel, and as such, was (and is) authoritatively equal to the accounts and

1

letters to the local Churches written later. Scripture indicates this, in the Apostle's admonishment to "hold fast" to what the local Church had been taught, "either by letter or by word of mouth", along with numerous other such references to oral teaching. The Apostles taught the "Apostolic Traditions" (i.e. the "Good News"), and they passed on the responsibility for the care and stewardship of this teaching to Elders whom they ordained and appointed to lead the local Churches founded.

Protestant acclamations for the concept of "sola scriptura", is faith in a system that cannot lay claim to being a historically Christian concept believed by anyone, until Wycliff invented it in the 14th century, and then the leaders of the Protestant Reformation, who adopted it (and later re-worked and re-invented it) in the 16th century. For the first three centuries of the existence of the early Church, there was no Bible as we know it today. Even after the canon (table of contents) of Scripture was determined by the Church, early Bibles were made by hand, one character at a time, over many years, and were quite expensive. An entire community would have to pool its financial resources in order to purchase a single Bible, which was usually ornate and richly illustrated. Such great treasures were not immune to theft, and, in many places, were chained to the Church lectern, to be available without being subject to theft. The books of the Bible did not all originally have titles (and of those that did, some are called by different titles now), nor did many identify their authors. None had chapter and verse numbers, as those were *added arbitrarily by book printers* after the invention of the printing press in 1450 A.D. Chapters and verses, although great for the printers, many times inadvertently separated one part of a thought or idea from another, and in so doing, created an artificial "punctuation" of sorts, in which improper or incorrect interpretations of Scripture have developed outside of the Church.

Another fateful reason against "sola scriptura" is that, quite simply, the vast majority of peoples from the establishment of the early Church, until only recently (historically speaking) could not read or write. Most of the faithful got their knowledge of Scripture from attending Mass, and hearing the readings of the Old and New Testament. They also learned through the rich artwork in the Churches, statues, icons, mosaics and tapestries, which visually depicted important events in Christianity. With their ears, they heard, and with their eyes they saw,—for many, *very* many, could not read or write.

The Church does not, and has never, restrict or forbid the individual reading of Scripture, but rather instructs Her members to become steeped in its Holy

Guidance, as understood and interpreted within nearly two thousand years of Christian teaching, *and not apart from it* (indeed, there were several approved versions of the Bible in German, well before Martin Luther's faulty translation, and translations of the Bible into at least a dozen different languages before his birth). This is not a uniquely Old Catholic understanding, it is also the understanding of the interpretation of Holy Scripture of the Roman Catholic Church, as well as the Eastern Orthodox Churches and the Oriental Orthodox Churches as well, both of whom were separate from the Roman Catholic Church well before the Protestant Reformation. This understanding of Scriptural interpretation then, is the rule, *not the exception*, and has been so for the entire history of the Christian faith.

The focus behind the understanding of modern Scriptural interpretation is the human will for individualism, which is rampant today. Such an "absolute individualism", as expressed in having an individual interpretation of Scripture is really a "pulling away" from the communion found within the Church. The Christian faith is a communal faith, and not the faith of sole individuals, each within their own cell, individually (and incorrectly) interpreting Scripture, and refusing to engage in the communal acts of praise, worship, sacrifice and service that we, as Christians, are called to engage in, and refusing to submit themselves to the authority of an orthodox, apostolic Church. As the adage goes, "divide and conquer", Christianity has been, on some levels, nearly conquered, through a completely secular misapplication and interpretation of the concepts of freedom and individuality. To be free of the authority of the Church is to be free of Christ Himself, who founded the Church. Such "freedom", can only lead to man's sorrowful downfall and make him a slave to sin. The Church is the Bride of Christ, the individual members are the "adopted sons and daughters of God", and the Church is familial and communal, *because that is God's plan for it.*

How Is This Catechism Structured?

This Catechism is designed to provide multiple formats of instruction. In a sense, it is several catechisms. As one person may find the "question and answer" format helpful, another may prefer the flowing literary theological presentation. Others may find the instruction of defending the faith in practice the most helpful. Your instructor may even utilize several parts together, as you go through particular aspects of the faith. In every instance, the purpose of this catechism is to provide the catechumen with answers to questions about the Old Catholic faith. This tool is to be used in conjunction with your Bible and both should be present when attending instruction, or contemplative reading of Scripture at home. Your instructor will be able to answer questions as well, in addition to your pastor and assistant pastor.

The authorized translation of the Bible, for catechetical study is the "Revised Standard Version—Catholic Edition" (RSV-CE), and the preferred format is the "Ignatius Study Bible", published by Ignatius Press at a modest cost. Do not bring the large "Family Bible" traditionally used to record significant family events. You will be expected to make notes and underline or highlight text within the Bible you bring, so do not bring the "family heirloom".

Laying A Strong Foundation

There are no shortcuts to a sound knowledge of the Faith. You must take the time to read the materials provided and complete the assigned work your instructor provides. You must take the time to read your Bible, ask questions regarding passages you need clarification on, and most importantly, you must pray regularly. Catechetical instruction is not an intellectual exercise; it is a journey to become a part of God's family, the Bride of Christ, the Church. It is a yearning to grow closer to God, through devout prayer, attendance at Mass and study. There is no greater pursuit, and it is a pursuit that benefits others who come into contact with you as well. As you conform your life to Christ, your entire life becomes a witness of God's love.

One cannot overemphasize the need to study and understand the proper interpretation of Scripture. St. Jerome wrote, "Ignorance of Scripture, is ignorance of Christ". Likewise, the "Christian faith is not a 'religion of the book.' Christianity is the religion of the 'Word' of God, 'not a written and mute word, but incarnate and living"(St. Bernard). A spirit-filled life can only come about through your commitment to God, who provides the grace to come closer to Him yet. Therefore, not one day should pass without prayer, not one day should pass not touched by the living Word of God.

There is no point in this journey, where you are "in", when you "know everything you need to know". Our journey is a lifelong one, in which God continually molds us and fashions us into image of Christ Jesus. So, although catechetical instruction is for a time, we shall always continue to learn and grow closer in prayer, praise, fellowship and worship.

How Long Does It Take To Become A Full Member?

Some people will need more time than others to prepare for the lifetime commitment that comes with membership in the Old Catholic Church. The usual length of preparation is from one to two years. For those already baptized and who seek full communion in the Old Catholic church, the time may also vary. The thing to remember is that it the discernment process proceeds in accordance with where each person is in relation to understanding the faith.

Prospective catechumens or candidates should experience the yearly calendar of Old Catholic practice at least once in order to make an informed decision. It is imperative that all such individuals considering full membership not be rushed, but rather clear and deliberate progress should be preferred to ensure that everyone is properly instructed.

The traditional time for the sacraments of initiation or the rite of reception into the Church, is the Easter Vigil. Lent prepares both catechumens and candidates for new life through baptism, confirmation and the Eucharist.

Am I A Catechumen Or Candidate?

Individuals who are non-baptized persons seeking membership in the Church are designated "Catechumens". Catechumens become full members of the Old Catholic Church by means of Baptism, Confirmation, and the Eucharist, which are referred to as the Sacraments of Initiation.

A validly baptized individual from a Protestant tradition, who is preparing for reception the Old Catholic Church, is a different matter. A baptized person should not be led through the entire catechumenal process or be called a catechumen. Such persons are designated "Candidates". By this we mean that this person is a candidate for the Old Catholic Sacrament of Confirmation and a candidate preparing to receive Holy Communion in the Old Catholic Church, and thus become a full member of the Old Catholic Church.

Likewise, a validly baptized individual from a sacramental, apostolic Church, who is preparing for reception in the Old Catholic Church, is also designated a "Candidate". Instruction for such individuals typically will be shorter than in the first two instances, due to the many commonalities found among the sacramental apostolic churches.

Candidates for membership in the Old Catholic church may find certain elements of the catechumenate process helpful in their own instruction. An understanding of Old Catholic beliefs, the observance of Old Catholic Holy Days of Obligation and Feast Days in the church year and the experiences of the Old Catholic community are all necessary. The differences must be specifically addressed by the candidate and the instructor and parish priest.

Since candidates are already validly baptized, the rites that mark their steps of the formation process are different than those of catechumens. These are rites of reception by the parish, and the recognition of membership by the Bishop, a celebration of the call to continuing conversion and a penitential rite. Reception into the Old Catholic Church takes place with a Profession of Faith, Confirmation and Eucharist. By the "penitential rite" we mean that the person examines his or her own life, examining those things that he has done right and things that he has done wrong, with repentance and a commitment to the Christian life. The Sacrament of Reconciliation is the appropriate means for this individual to turn from sin to grace, from an old life in the world to a new life in Christ, before she or he enters into full communion.

"What Do You Ask of God's Church?"

During Sunday Mass, you hear a knock at the door of the church. The celebrant goes to the door and welcomes a group of people. He invites them to come forward and asks them, "What do you ask of God's Church?" Each person's answer is different but reflects the same desire for faith and community.

This is the first step in the initiation of new adult members into the Church. Each step brings the person closer to being accepted as full members of the Church.

People who are considering joining the Old Catholic Church enter the pre-catechumenate. They are welcomed into the Church and begin to get to know the Old Catholic Church more profoundly. Those who decide to go further initiate a course of preparation known as the catechumenate.

Although not yet full members of the Church, catechumens immediately begin to live the Christ-life life. While being instructed in the Faith, catechumens join the Church in prayer and worship, and participate in the life of the Church.

When the catechumens are ready to respond fully to God's call to conversion and faith, the Church invites them to take the next step in this process of initiation, called the Rite of Election. This ceremony takes place on the first Sunday of Lent and marks the entry of the catechumens into their final forty days of preparation, the origin of the season of Lent. The final stage, complete membership in the Church, takes place during the solemn Vigil of Easter, when the catechumens receive the sacraments of initiation, which are: Baptism, Confirmation, and the Eucharist. This is not an end, but the beginning of their journey in faith as Old Catholics.

Five Steps Towards Full Reception

The Five Steps Are:

1. The Period of Inquiry,
2. Catechumenate,
3. Period of Purification and Enlightenment/Scrutinies,
4. The Paschal Triduum with the Sacraments of Initiation, and
5. Mystagogical Catechesis.

The Period of Inquiry

The Period of Inquiry is a time to become acquainted with the Old Catholic Church, and to hear the good news of salvation from Christ Jesus.

During this period, the Gospel of Jesus is proclaimed, and inquirers look within their own lives to make and mark connections. This reflective process of self-examination becomes a continuing, on-going method used by inquirer and member alike.

This period lasts as long as the individual needs it to last, from a few months to several years, if needed. During this period, some may decide that this is not the right time for them to seek membership in the Old Catholic Church, due to their own life circumstances or because they feel some other Tradition is better for them.

Period of the Catechumenate

The Period of the catechumenate is the first stage of commitment leading to full membership. For a person to enter this phase, they must have already come to believe in Jesus Christ as their Lord and Savior and must sincerely desire to become members of the Old Catholic Church.

During this period, the initial conversion is deepened and strengthened. The individual comes to understand, more and more deeply, the love of God in their own. This period lasts as long as is necessary.

Period of Purification or Illumination

The Period of Purification corresponds to that time known in the Old Catholic Church as Lent, the six-weeks of preparation for Easter become the days of prayerful time for catechumens and candidates, as they prepare for the moment of welcome as full members and are established as such by the Sacraments of Initiation.

This period is begun by the Rite of election, celebrated with the Diocesan Bishop; by this rite they are accepted as candidates for the Sacraments by the Bishop, representing the fact that this decision is not theirs alone. Normally this rite takes place the first week of Lent.

Throughout Lent, special prayers are offered at the Sunday Eucharist for the catechumens and candidates; they are called scrutinies; these prayers for strengthening in grace and virtue and for purification from all past evil and from any bonds which hinder them from experiencing the love of God. Throughout this period, the Elect are invited to join with the whole Church in a deeper practice of works of charity and in the practice of fasting and prayer.

Celebrating the Sacraments of Initiation Paschal Triduum

The Sacraments of Initiation are celebrated at the Easter Vigil, an extended period of prayer, discernment, and hearing the Word of God. By the waters of Baptism, a person is born into the new life of grace and becomes a member of the Body of Christ. Anointing with special holy oil called Chrism seals the initiation by the power of the Holy Spirit, and participation in the Eucharist marks full membership (koinonia [Greek]-communion) in the church.

Period of Mystagogy

The Period of Mystagogy lasts from Easter Sunday until the completion of the Easter season, fifty days later on Pentecost Sunday and completes the initiation process. Those who have just shared in the sacraments of initiation are now called "Neophytes" and during this period they reflect on what they have just gone through and look to the future as to how they can now live out their Old Catholic faith.

Duties and Responsibilities

Every member of this Church has a duty and responsibility to support her through voluntary work, time and financial support. Each member is expected to contribute liberally, each as their own situation allows, and not to the harm or deprivation of family or self. The Church does not require financial compensation for any Sacrament, indeed she shall never ask for any. No one is to be turned away who asks for any sacrament, properly disposed, due to inability to make an offering. Every member has a duty and responsibility to make themselves knowledgeable in the faith, by attending regular Mass, instruction and refresher instruction annually, at least. Members are expected to read the Holy Bible liberally, and learn the age-old meaning of their teaching from Holy Mother Church.

Every member has a responsibility to live the faith, and "walk in faith", particularly in not participating in activities that are contrary to the faith. Every member is expected to receive the sacrament of reconciliation in Confession at least once a year. Likewise, every member is to be careful to not engage in activities that facilitate activities that are contrary or outright sinful. This would include being careful to scrutinize teachers, mentors and elected officials who may state that they are "Christian" in a generic sense, yet their actions betray either a willingness to acquiesce to the will of secular society rather than obey their professed faith, or those who use their church membership as a means to obtain further selfish gains.

St. Clement warned the Church at Corinth about those who do not intend to truly live the faith; "Let us cleave, therefore, to those who cultivate peace with godliness, and not to those who hypocritically profess to desire it. For [the Scripture] says in a certain place, 'This people honors Me with their lips, but their heart is far from Me.' And again: 'They bless with their mouth, but curse with their heart.' And again it says, 'They loved Him with their mouth, and lied to Him with their tongue; but their heart was not right with Him, neither were they faithful in His covenant.' 'Let the deceitful lips become silent,' [and 'let the

Lord destroy all the lying lips,] and the boastful tongue of those who have said, Let us magnify our tongue; our lips are our own; who is lord over us? For the oppression of the poor, and for the sighing of the needy, will I now arise, says the Lord: I will place him in safety; I will deal confidently with him."[1]

Spreading the Faith

Members of this Church are instructed not to engage in attempts to convert members of other Christian communities into this one, but are to be concerned with the unchurched, and those who have fallen away from regular attendance at Mass and worship of God at any Church. Individuals from other Christian communities are to be welcomed, but not proselytized. However, if an individual wishes to become a member of this Church, that person shall not be prevented from doing so, but shall be properly instructed in the faith, be properly initiated into the Church, and enrolled among its numbers.

Visitors are invited to come to Mass and other parish services, attend catechetical instruction and Bible study, and learn as much as possible about the Church. However, only members of this Church, and her duly constituted sister churches in communion with her, may be fully received at the altar rail, and partake of the Precious Body and Blood of Our Lord in the Eucharist. Members of other Christian Communions who have maintained Apostolic Succession, and profess the Real Presence of Christ in the Eucharist, if properly disposed spiritually and in good standing in their own communion, may be admitted to the altar rail and partake in limited situations, when such individuals are unable to receive such sacraments through no fault of their own. No clergy of this communion shall be compelled to administer the sacraments to an individual who does not qualify under these conditions.

All members of this Church are expected to participate and support parish-level activities to spread the faith throughout the local community, using initiatives developed by the local parish. Members engaged in these activities are to be properly instructed in explaining the faith to the unchurched and members of other faiths that they may encounter in the community, so as to properly educate all as to the worship, faith and practice of this Church. It is in the living of our faith that we come to live the Christ-like life. It is the living of our faith that people many times find the stumbling block. But do not hesitate to engage in the difficult or thankless job, for the sake of the Kingdom of God:

"Jesus has always many who love His heavenly kingdom, but few who bear His cross. He has many who desire consolation, but few who care for trial. He finds many to share His table, but few to take part in His fasting. All desire to be happy with Him; few wish to suffer anything for Him. Many revere His miracles; few approach the shame of the Cross. Many love Him as long as they encounter no hardship; many praise and bless Him as long as they receive some comfort from Him. But if Jesus hides Himself and leaves them for a while, they fall either into complaints or into deep dejection. Those, on the contrary, who love Him for His own sake and not for any comfort of their own, bless Him in all trial and anguish of heart as well as in bliss of consolation. Even if He should never give them consolation, yet they would continue to praise Him and wish always to give Him thanks. What power there is in pure love for Jesus—love that is free from all self-interest and self-love!"[2]

On The Mass

The liturgy is rightly understood as the "work of the people". The Mass is the corporate worship of the entire Church. As such, the Mass is never a locally owned or controlled "property" of a particular parish. The Mass must be done properly, with the proper prayers, readings, rubrics and schedules for the particular Rite. Meaning, if a parish is praying the Tridentine Latin Rite, everything about the Mass must be proper to that Rite, without innovation or modification. No individual, no member of laity nor clergy, has the right to modify the Mass or add to it or take anything away from it. Indeed, the laity have the right to a validly and properly administered liturgy. With unauthorized modifications come misinterpretation and misunderstanding about everything from the proper roles of the sacred ministers and the laity, to a proper understanding of the Eucharist (Real Presence) and a lack of a sense of the sacred, which is to be avoided at all times. The prayers and liturgical practices of the Church find their origins in Scripture and Tradition, and are not to be discarded, nor substituted with current trends or faddish ideas.

Regardless of the Rite used, Novus Ordo, the Gul-Mathew or the Tridentine in Latin or the vernacular, the proper rubrics, vestments, readings, prayers and cycles must be followed, without exception. Depending on your status when you began the membership process, you may or may not be able to partake of the Holy Eucharist at Mass for a time. Your instructor or parish priest will go into further detail with you and inform you of your particular status. Regardless of the liturgical rites used by your local parish, we, as one church, profess our faith as one unified voice.

As A New Member

Undoubtedly some of the Church's activities will be new to you. We urge you to acquaint yourself with them as soon as possible, and ask questions as necessary. This is *your* Church, *your* family of faith. You are a member of the Church, the Bride of Christ, and have certain obligations as a result thereof. You will be expected to attend Mass on all Holy Days of Obligation, attend catechetical instruction and proceed through the Rite of Christian Initiation or Rite of Reception of Christian Converts, and be enrolled in the rolls of the parish you are attending.

Your local parish functions only as a result of the hard work of the parishioners. By bringing their professional secular skills, knowledge and ability forward to be used to help build up the parish, it exists and functions. In addition, the tithes and offerings of the individual members pay 100% of the cost of operating the parish, and without this financial support, the parish cannot continue to operate. As taught in the Old Testament, we offer one tenth of the financial blessings bestowed upon us, each month, as an offering to God, and to support the teaching of the Good News and the spread of His Holy Church.

Church Organization

The Church is organized in a hierarchal structure. The smallest organized group is called a "parish", and consists of the local faithful of that community assisted and spiritually fathered by at least one Priest, and usually a Priest who is normally the "Rector", and a Deacon, who assists him. A priest is ordained to serve a particular local Church, and usually remains with that local parish for the duration of his public ministry. Each parish has a "Parish Council" made up of members of that parish who have been elected to assist the Rector in the stewardship and care of the parish. In addition to the Parish Council are many other committees and ministries that various members of the Parish undertake, and everyone is invited to contribute their special skills to the benefit of the Church.

Several parishes in a similar geographic area are organized into a "Diocese", which is cared for by a Bishop of the Church (called an Ordinary), or in some cases by an Episcopal Vicar (Senior Priest) who assists the Bishop. The Bishop will usually ask other members of both the laity and clergy to assist him in the care and administration of the activities of the diocese. Several dioceses in a similar geographic area may be organized into a Province. A Province is cared for by a Bishop who has been appointed by the Archbishop-Metropolitan to the office of "Provincial Ordinary".

Overseeing the national and international activities for the Church is the Vicar-General, or Chancellor. The Vicar-General (or Chancellor) overseers the proper operation of the Church on a large scale and attends to other duties as determined by the Archbishop-Metropolitan.

Periodically, the Church comes together in synod to plan for the future, approve a new bishop-elect, or answer some pressing issue of faith. The synod is composed of the College of Bishops and operates in accordance with the Church's Code of Canon Law.

The Archbishop-Metropolitan is the spiritual head of the Church. Along with the College of Bishops, he is responsible for protecting and defending the faith; ensuring orthodox teaching and doctrine are observed. He presides at all synods of the Church and ultimately approves all church functions either directly or in conjunction with the College of Bishops. From the authority of the Archbishop-Metropolitan are several councils or other bodies authorized to oversee and audit certain aspects of Church operation, to protect the Church and ensure good order and operation.

In addition to the organization just defined, within the Church are Religious Orders consisting of lay members, professed brothers and sisters and ordained clergy, as well as educational institutions, chaplaincy ministries, and much more.

The lay members of the Church are sinew and muscle of this Body, which makes everything the Church undertakes possible. The faithful are they who are served by the clergy, religious and appointed lay ministers of this Church, and who themselves go out into the World to serve and, through their secular lives and work, bring the message and love of Christ to others who do not know Him. Through the faith of the faithful of the Church, the unchurched are drawn to come to know Him. The faithful are, at all levels of the Church, essential to this Church successfully fulfilling her mission.

Our Church is also part of a larger family, called the "International Synod of Old Catholic Churches" (ISOCC). We are part of a worldwide, universal family, with fellow Old Catholics around the world, who profess their faith in union with us.

ENDNOTES FOR CHAPTER ONE

1. St. Clement, *The First Epistle of Clement to the Corinthians*, 97 A.D., Christian Classics Ethereal Library, Public Domain.

2. Thomas, a Kempis, *The Imitation of Christ*, 1400 A.D., Christian Classics Ethereal Library, Public Domain.

CHAPTER 2

A Foundational Catechism

This catechetical format provides a solid foundation for basic instruction as well as offers an opportunity to select specific topics for more detailed study. Certain theological concepts within this catechetical format are amplified to provide a more detailed understanding.

Official Catechism

Preliminary Instruction:

Q. What is a catechism?

A. A Catechism is an instruction in the faith, to be taught to all Christians, to enable them to please God, and save their own souls.

Q. What is the meaning of the word "catechism"?

A. It is a Greek word, signifying instruction, or oral teaching; and has been used ever since the Apostles' times to denote that primary instruction in the Orthodox faith, which is needful for every Christian. **Luke 1:4; Acts 18:25**

Q. What is necessary in order to please God, and save one's own soul?

A. In the first place the knowledge of the true God, and right faith in Him; in the second place, a life according to faith and good works.

Q. Why is faith necessary in the first place?

A. Because, as the word of God testifies, *Without faith it is impossible to please God.* **Heb. 11:6**

Q. Why must a life according to faith, and good works, be inseparable from this faith?

A. Because as the word of God testifies, *faith without works is dead.* James 2:20

Q. What is faith?

A. According to the definition of St. Paul, *Faith is the substance of things hoped for, the evidence of things not seen.* **Heb. 11:1** That is, a trust in the unseen, as though it were seen, in that which is hoped and waited for, as if it were present.

Q. What is the difference between knowledge and faith?

A. Knowledge has for its object things visible and comprehensible; faith, things which are invisible and even incomprehensible. Knowledge is founded on experience, on examination of its object; but faith on belief of testimony to truth. Knowledge belongs properly to the intellect, although it may also act on the heart; faith belongs principally to the heart, although it is imparted through the intellect.

Q. Why is faith and knowledge only necessary in religious instruction?

A. Because the chief object of this instruction is God invisible and incomprehensible, and the wisdom of God hidden in a mystery; consequently, many parts of this learning cannot be embraced by knowledge, but may be received by faith.

Faith, says St. Cyril of Jerusalem, is the eye which enlighteneth every man's conscience; it giveth man knowledge. For as the prophet says, If ye will not believe, ye shall not understand. **Isaiah 7:9, Cyr. Cat. V**

On Divine Revelation:

Q. What is the source of the Catholic Faith?

A. Divine Revelation.

Q. What is meant by the words Divine Revelation?

A. That which God Himself has revealed to men, in order that they might rightly and savingly believe in Him, and worthily honor Him.

Q. Has God given such a revelation to all men?

A. He has given it for all, as being necessary for all alike, and capable of bringing salvation to all: but since not all men are capable of receiving a revelation immediately from God, He has employed special persons as heralds of His revelation, to deliver it to all who are desirous of receiving it.

Q. Who were some of the men who received Divine Revelation?

A. Adam, Noah, Abraham, Moses and other Prophets, received and preached the beginnings of divine revelation; but it was the Incarnate Son of God, our Lord Jesus Christ, who brought it to earth in its fullness and perfection, and spread it over all the world by His disciples and Apostles.

The Apostle Paul says in the beginning of his Epistle to the Hebrews: *God, who at sundry times, and in diverse manners, spoke in times past unto the Fathers by the Prophets, hath in these last days spoken unto us by His Son; Whom He hath appointed heir of all things, by Whom also He made the Worlds.* **I Cor. 11:7; John 1:8; Mat. 11:27**

Q. Can man then have some knowledge of God without a special revelation from Him?

A. Man may have some knowledge of God by contemplation of those things He has created; but this knowledge is imperfect and insufficient, and can serve only as a preparation for faith, or as a help towards the knowledge of God from His revelation. *Rom. 1:20; Acts 27:26-2*

On Holy Tradition and Holy Scripture:

Q. How is Divine Revelation spread among men, and preserved in the true Church?

A. By two channels: Holy Tradition and Holy Scripture.

The early Church is admonished, in Scripture, to hold fast to what they had been taught "either by letter, or by word of mouth".

Q. What is meant by the name of Holy Tradition?

A. By the name Holy Tradition is meant the doctrine of faith, the law of God, and the sacraments, has handed down by the true believers and worshippers of God by word and example from one to another, and from generation to generation.

"Now we command you, brethren, in the name of our Lord Jesus Christ, that you keep away from any brother who is living in idleness and not in accord with the tradition that you received from us." 2 Thess. 3:6

Q. What is the repository of Holy Tradition?

A. All true believers united by holy tradition of the faith, collectively and successively, by the will of God, compose the Church; and She is the sure repository of holy Tradition, or as St. Paul expresses it, *The Church of the living God, the pillar and ground of the truth.* I Tim. 3:15

Q. What is that which you call Holy Scripture?

A. Certain books written by the Spirit of God, through men sanctified by God, called Prophets and Apostles. Theses books are commonly termed the Bible.

Q. What does the word "Bible" mean?

A. It is Greek, and means *The Books.* The name signifies that the sacred books deserve attention before all others.

Q. Which is the more ancient, Holy Tradition, or Holy Scripture?

A. The most ancient and original instrument for spreading Divine Revelation is Holy Tradition. From Adam to Moses there were no sacred books. Our Lord Jesus Christ Himself delivered His Divine doctrine and ordinances to His disciples by word and example, but not in writing. The same method was followed by the Apostles also at first, when they spread abroad the faith and established the Church of Christ. The necessity of tradition is further evident from this, that books can be available only to a small part of mankind, but tradition to all.

Q. Why then was Holy Scripture given?

A. To this end, that Divine Revelation might be preserved more exactly and unchangeably. In Holy Scripture we read the words of the Prophets and Apostles precisely as if we were living with them and listening to them, although the latest of the sacred books were written a thousand and some hundred years before our time.

Luke writes his Gospel [Luke-Acts] to stand beside, and not replace Holy Tradition (Paradosis, Gk) that had been orally transmitted, "It seemed good also to me to write an orderly account for you, most excellent Theophilus, so that you may know the certainty of the things you have been taught."

Q. Must we follow Holy Tradition, even when we possess Holy Scripture?

A. We must follow that tradition which agrees with the Divine Revelation and with Holy Scripture, as is taught is by Holy Scripture itself. The Apostle Paul writes: *Therefore, brethren, stand fast, and hold the traditions which ye have been taught, whether by word or our epistle.* **II Thess. 2:15**

From this, we can understand that Apostolic Teaching was transmitted both orally and later, by letter. Both having come to us from Christ through His Apostles, are of equal spiritual authority. Christ taught orally, and commanded the Apostles to do the same, never Himself committing any of His teaching to written form, although later some of His Apostles and their co-workers did.

Q. Why is Tradition necessary even now?

A. As a guide to the right understanding of Holy Scripture, and for the right ministration of the Sacraments.

Scripture was written by the members of the Church, for the members of the Church, and not as an instructional text for the uninitiated. Thus, it is not possible to correctly interpret and understand Scripture without the guidance of the Church who wrote it. Merely translating words from one language to another does not convey the message adequately—one must know the writer and the intended audience, the unique words and phrases indigenous to that language and people, the culture and issues of the times, the faith and understanding of the faith, and much more. Simply translating the words conveys none of this, and without the proper context provided by the Church with Apostolic Tradition; it is dangerously easy to misinterpret Scripture. Satan himself knows Scripture, and twists it to draw away the uninstructed from the faith, and away from God.

On Holy Scripture in particular:

Q. When were the sacred books written?

A. At different times; some before the birth of Christ, others after.

Key to understanding the Scriptures is the understanding that, although divinely inspired, the written books convey the social and cultural understanding of the world, through the eyes of the inspired writer. We must also understand the writer was writing to a specific audience, and audience that the writer could assume knew certain facts and information that need not be written. Consider also, that these books were written in another language, several thousand years ago, and although we can translate the words into our language, translating what these words truly meant, both to the writer and the intended reader is a task that is far more difficult—impossible for those without the benefit of the Apostolic Tradition found in the Church.

Q. Have not these two divisions of the sacred books each their own names?

A. They have. Those written before the birth of Christ are called the books of the Old Testament; while those written after are called books of the New Testament.

Q. What are the Old and New testaments?

A. In other words: the old and new agreements of God with men.

Q. Of what does the Old Testament consist?

A. That God promised men a Divine Savior, and prepared them to receive Him.

Q. How did God prepare men to receive the Savior?

A. Through gradual revelations, by prophecies and types.

Q. Of what does the New Testament consist?

A. That God has actually given men a Divine Savior, His only-begotten Son, Jesus Christ.

Q. How many books of the Old Testament are there?

A. Forty-seven.

Q. Is there any division of the books of the Old Testament by which you can give a more distinct account of their contents?

A. They may be divided into the four following classes:

1. Books of the Law, which form the basis of the Old Testament.
2. Historical books, which contain principally the history of religion.
3. Doctrinal, which contain the doctrine of religion.
4. Prophetical, which contain prophecies, or predictions of things future, especially of Jesus Christ.

Q. Which are the books of the Law?

A. The five books written by Moses: Genesis, Exodus, Leviticus, Numbers, and Deuteronomy. Jesus Christ Himself, gives to these books the general name of the Law of Moses. **Luke 24:44**

Q. What in particular is contained in the book of Genesis?

A. The account of the creation of the world and of man, and afterwards the history and ordinances of religion in the first ages of mankind.

Q. What is contained in the other four books of Moses?

A. The history of religion in the time of the Prophet Moses, and the Law given through him from God.

Q. Which are the historical books of the Old Testament?

A. The Books of Joshua, the son of Nun, Judges, Ruth, Kings, Chronicles, the books of Esdras, and the books of Nehemiah, Ester, Tobias, Judith, and Maccabees.

Q. Which are doctrinal?

A. The book of Job, The psalms, the books of Solomon.

Q. What should we remark in particular of the book of Psalms?

A. This book, together with the doctrine of religion, contains also allusions to its history, and many prophecies of our Savior Christ. It is a perfect manual of prayer and praise, and on this account is in continual use in the Divine service of the Church.

Q. Which books are prophetical?

A. Those of the Prophets: Isaiah, Jeremiah, Ezekiel, Daniel, the twelve others plus Baruch.

Q. How many books of the New Testament are there?

A. Twenty-seven.

Q. Are there among these any, which answer to the books of the Law, or form the basis of the New Testament?

A. Yes. The Gospel, which consist of the four books of the Evangelists Matthew, Mark, Luke, and John.

Q. What does the word Gospel mean?

A. It is the same word as the Greek word "Evangel", and means good and joyful news.

Q. Of what have we good news in the books called the Gospel?

A. Of the Divinity of our Lord Jesus Christ, of His advent and life on earth, of His miracles and saving doctrine, and finally, of His death upon the cross. Also, His glorious resurrection, and Ascension into heaven.

Q. Why are these books called the Gospel?

A. They are called Gospel because man can have no better or more joyful news than these, of a Divine Savior and everlasting salvation. For the same cause, whenever the Gospel is read in the Church, it is prefaced and accompanied by joyful exclamation: *Glory be to Thee, O Lord. Glory be to Thee.*

Q. Are any of the books of the New Testament historical?

A. Yes. One; the book of the Acts of the Holy Apostles.

Q. Of what does it give an account?

A. Of the descent of the Holy Spirit on the Apostles, and the extension through them of Christ's Church.

Q. What is an Apostle?

A. The word means a messenger. It is the name given to those disciples of our Lord Jesus Christ, whom He sent to preach the Gospel.

Q. Which books of the New Testament are doctrinal?

A. The seven General Epistles; namely, one of the Apostle James, two of Peter, three of John, and one of Jude; and fourteen Epistles of the Apostle Paul: namely, one to the Romans, two to the Corinthians, one to the Galatians, one to the Ephesians, one to the Philippians, one to the Colossians, two to the Thessalonians, two to Timothy, one to Titus, one to Philemon, and one to the Hebrews.

Q. Are there also among the books of the New Testament any prophetical?

A. Such is the book of the Apocalypse, which means Revelation.

Q. What are the contents of this book?

A. A mystical representation of the future destinies of the Christian Church, and of the whole world.

Q. What rules must we observe in reading Holy Scripture?

A. First, we must read it devoutly, as the Word of God, and with prayer to understand it right; secondly, we must read it with a pure desire of instruction in faith, and incitement to good works; thirdly, we must take and understand it in such sense as agrees with interpretation of the Church and the holy fathers.

OFFICIAL CATECHISM

THE FIRST PART: ON FAITH

On the Creed Generally, and on its Origin:

Q. What is the Nicene Creed?

A. The Nicene Creed is a summary of that doctrine which all Christians are bound to believe.

Q. What are the 12 divisions of the Creed?

A. They are as follows:

1. I believe in one God the Father, Almighty, Maker of heaven and earth, and of all things visible and invisible;

2   And in one Lord Jesus Christ, the Son of God, the only-begotten, begotten of the Father before all worlds, Light of Light, very God of very God, begotten, not made of one substance with the Father, by whom all things were made;

3. Who for us men, and for our salvation, came down from heaven, and was incarnate of the Holy Spirit, and of the Virgin Mary, and was made man;

4. And was crucified also for us, under Pontius Pilate, and suffered, and was buried.
   Jesus truly suffered for us, not merely appeared to do so, but physically suffered for us, and died.

5. And rose again the third day according to the Scripture;
   Jesus truly rose from the dead, not metaphorically, but truly and in the flesh.

6. And ascended into heaven, and sitteth on the right hand of the Father;
   Jesus ascended body and soul, into heaven.

7. And He shall come again with glory to judge the living and the dead, whose kingdom shall have no end.

8. And I believe in the Holy Spirit, the Lord, the Giver of Life, who proceedeth from the Father, who with the Father and the Son together is worshipped and glorified, who spoke by the Prophets.

9. I believe one Holy, Catholic, and Apostolic Church.
   All Churches who hold to the faith, as handed down to us from Christ through the Apostles, and maintain it without innovation, omission or modification, are of the one Holy, Catholic, and Apostolic Church.

10. I acknowledge one baptism for the remission of sins.
    Trinitarian baptism is required of us, as we must belief and be baptized, in order to be saved.

11. I look for the resurrection of the dead;

12. And the life of the world to come. Amen.

Q. From whom have we this summary of the Faith?

A. From the Fathers of the First and Second Ecumenical Councils.

Q. What is an Ecumenical Council?

A. An assembly of the Bishops and theologians of the Catholic Church, as far as possible, from the whole world, for the confirmation of true doctrine and practice among Christians.

Q. How many Ecumenical Councils have there been?

A. Seven: 1) Nicea; 2) Constantinople; 3) Ephesus; 4) Chalcedon; 5) The second of Constantinople; 6) The third of Constantinople; 7) The second of Nicea.

Q. What evidence is there in Scripture for holding Ecumenical Councils?

A. From the example of the Apostles, who held a Council in Jerusalem. *Acts 15.* This is grounded also upon the words of Jesus Christ Himself, which give to the decisions of the Church such weight, that whoever disobeys them is left deprived of grace. The means by which the Catholic Church utters her decisions is an Ecumenical Council. **Mat. 28:17**

Q. What were the particular occasions for assembling the First and Second Ecumenical Councils, at which the Creed was defined?

A. The first was held for the confirmation of the true doctrine respecting the Son of God, against the error of Arius; the second for the confirmation of the true doctrine respecting the Holy Spirit, against Macedonius.

On the Articles of the Creed:

Q. What method shall we follow in order the better to understand the Nicene Creed?

A. We must notice its division into twelve articles or parts, and consider each article separately.

Q. What is spoken of in each article of the Creed?

A. The first article of the Creed speaks of God as the prime origin, more particularly of the first Person of the Holy Trinity, God the Father, and of God as Creator of the World;

The second article, of the Second Person of the Holy Trinity, Jesus Christ, the Son of God;

The third article, of the incarnation of the Son of God;

The fourth article, of the suffering and death of Jesus Christ;

The fifth article, of the resurrection of Jesus Christ;

The sixth article, of the Ascension of Jesus Christ into heaven;

The seventh article, of the second coming of Jesus Christ upon earth;

The eighth article, of the third person of the Holy Trinity, the Holy Spirit:

The ninth article, of the Church;

The tenth article, of Baptism, under which are implied the other Sacraments also;

The eleventh article, of the future resurrection of the dead;

The twelfth article, of the life everlasting.

On the First Article:

Q. What does it mean to believe in God?

A. To believe in God is to have a lively belief in His being, His attributes, and worlds; and to receive with all our heart His revealed word for the salvation of men.

Without faith it is impossible to please God; for he that cometh to God must believe that He is, and that He is a rewarder of those that diligently seek Him. **Heb.11:6 Eph. 3:16,17**

Q. What must be the immediate and constant effect of a firm faith in God?

A. The confession of this same faith.

In the confessing of our faith, we also strive to live out our faith in our daily lives. This too, is a "confession" of faith as well, and we become living examples of that faith.

Q. What is the confession of this faith?

A. It is openly to show that we hold the Catholic faith, and this with such sincerity and firmness, that neither force, nor threats, nor tortures, nor death itself, may be able to make us deny our faith in the true God and in our Lord Jesus Christ.

Q. For what reason is the confession of the faith necessary?

A. The Apostle Paul witnesses that it is necessary for salvation. *For with the heart man believeth unto righteousness, and with the mouth confession is made unto salvation.* **Rom. 10:10**

Q. What does Holy Scripture teach us of the unity of God?

A. The very words of the Creed on this point are taken from the following passage of the Apostle Paul: *There is none other God but one. For though there be they that are called gods, whether in heaven or on earth, as there be gods many, and lords many, but to us there is but one God, the Father, of whom are all things, and we in Him: and one Lord Jesus Christ, by whom are all things, and we by Him.* **I Cor. 7:4-6**

Q. Can we know the very essence of God, or God as He is?

A. No. It is above all knowledge, not men only, but of Angels. The apostle Paul says that God *dwelleth in the light, which no man can approach unto, Whom no man hath seen, nor can see.* **I Tim. 6:16**

It is not possible for the created to fully comprehend He who is uncreated. We see and comprehend Him, through His Divine Love, in a limited manner.

Q. What are some of the attributes of God?

A. God is a Spirit, eternal, all-good, all knowing, all-just, almighty, all present, unchangeable, all-sufficing to Himself, all-blessed.

Q. If God is a Spirit, how does Holy Scripture ascribe to Him bodily parts, as heart, eyes, ears, hands.

A. Holy Scripture in this suits itself to the common language of men; but we are to understand such expression in a higher and spiritual sense. For instance, the heart of God means His goodness or his love; eyes and ears mean His omniscience: hands, His almighty power.

Q. If God is everywhere, why do men say that God is in heaven, or in the church?

A. God is everywhere: but in heaven He has a special presence manifested in everlasting glory to the blessed spirits; also in churches He has, through grace and Sacraments, a special presence devoutly recognized and felt by believers, and manifested sometimes by extraordinary signs.

Jesus Christ says: *Where two or three are gathered together in my name, there am I in the midst of them.* **Mat. 28:20**

Q. How are we to understand these words of the Creed, *I believe in one God the Father?*

A. This is to be understood with reference to the mystery of the Holy Trinity; because God is one in substance, but three in persons, the Father, the Son, and the Holy Spirit. *I John 5:7*

Q. Is the Holy Trinity mentioned in the Old Testament also?

A. Yes; only not as clearly. For instance. *By the Word of the Lord were the heavens made, and all the hosts of them by the breath of his mouth.* **Psalm 33:6** *Holy, Holy, Holy is the Lord of Hosts: The whole earth is full of His glory.* **Isaiah 6:3**

Q. How is God one in three Persons?

A. We cannot understand this inner mystery of the Godhead; but we believe it on the infallible testimony of the word of God. *The things of God knoweth no man, but the Spirit of God.* **I Cor. 2:11**

Q. What difference is there between the Persons of the Holy Trinity?

A. God the Father is neither begotten, nor proceeds from any other Person: the Son of God is from all eternity begotten of the Father: the Holy Spirit from all eternity proceeds from the Father.

Q. Are the three Persons of the Most Holy Trinity all of equal majesty?

A. Yes. All are equally God. The Father is true God; the Son equally true God; and the Holy Spirit true God; but in three Persons there is only one God.

Q. Why is God called Almighty?

A. Because He upholds all things by His power and His will.

Q. What is expressed by the words of the Creed, *Maker of heaven and earth, and of all things visible and invisible?*

A. That all was made by God, and that nothing can be without God. The book of Genesis begins thus: *In the beginning God created the heaven and the earth.* The Apostle Paul speaking of Jesus Christ, the Son of God says: *By Him were all things created, that are in heaven, and that are in earth, visible and invisible, whether they be thrones, or dominions, or principalities, or powers; all things were created by Him, and for Him.* **Coloss. 1:16**

Q. What is meant in the Creed by the word invisible?

A. The invisible or spiritual world, to which belong the Angels.

Q. What are the Angels?

A. Angels are Spirits, having intelligence, will, and power, but no material bodies.

Q. What does the name Angel mean?

A. It means a <u>Messenger</u>.

Q. Why are they so called?

A. Because God sends them to announce His will. Thus for instance, Gabriel was sent to announce to the Most Holy Virgin Mary the conception of the Savior.

Q. Which was created first, the visible world or the invisible?

A. The invisible was created before the visible, and the Angels before men. *Who laid the corner-stone thereof? When the stars were created, all My Angels praised Me with a loud voice.* **Job 38:6,7**

Q. Where in Scripture are Guardian Angels mentioned?

A. In Psalm 91: 11: *He shall give His Angels charge over thee, to guard thee in all thy ways.*

Q. Has each one of us a Guardian Angel?

A. Yes. Of this we may be assured from the following words of Jesus Christ: *Take heed that ye despise not one of these little ones: for I say unto you, that in heaven their Angels do always behold the face of my Father, which is in heaven.* **Mat. 18:10**

Q. Are all Angels good and protective?

A. No. There are also evil angels, otherwise called devils.

Q. How did they become evil?

A. They were created good, but they swerved from their duty of perfect obedience to God, and so fell away from Him into self-will, pride, and malice. According to the words of the Apostle Jude, *they are the Angels which kept not their first estate, but left their own habitation.* **Jude 6**

Q. What does the name devil mean?

A. It means slanderer or deceiver.

Q. Why are the evil angels called devils, that is, slanderers or deceivers.

A. Because they are ever laying snares for men, seeking to deceive them, and mislead them with false notions and evil wishes.

Q. What has Holy Scripture revealed to us of the creation of the world?

A. In the beginning God created from nothing the heaven and the earth, and all that they contain. Afterwards God successively produced: on the first day of the world, light; on the second, the firmament or visible heaven; on the third, the gathering together of the waters on the earth, the dry land, and what grows thereupon; on the fourth, the sun, moon, and stars; on the fifth, fishes and birds; on the sixth, four-footed creatures living on the earth, and lastly man. With man the creation finished: and on the seventh day was called the Sabbath, which in the Hebrew tongue means rest. **Gen. 2**

Q. Were the visible creatures created such as we see them now?

A. No. At creation everything was very good; that is, pure, beautiful, and harmless.

Q. Are we not informed of something particular in the creation of man?

A. God in the Holy Trinity said: *Let Us make man in Our image, and after Our likeness,* **Gen. 1:26** *And God made the body of the first man, Adam, from the earth: breathed into his nostrils the breath of life: brought him into Paradise; gave him for food, beside the other fruits of Paradise, the fruit of the tree of life: and lastly, having taken a rib from Adam while he slept, made from it the first woman, Eve.* **Gen 2:22**

Q. What is meant by the image of God?

A. The Image of God consists, as explained by the Apostle Paul, *In righteousness and holiness of truth.* **Eph. 4:24**

Q. What is the breath of life?

A. The soul, a substance spiritual and immortal.

Q. What is Paradise?

A. The word Paradise means garden. It is the name given to the fair and blissful dwelling place of the first man, described in the book of Genesis as like a garden.

Q. Was the Paradise in which man first lived material or spiritual?

A. For the body it was material. A visible and blissful dwelling place; but for the soul it was spiritual, a state of communion by grace with God, and spiritual contemplation of the creatures.

Q. What was the tree of life?

A. A tree, by feeding on whose fruit man would have been, even in the body, free from disease and death.

Q. Why was Eve made from a rib of Adam?

A. To the intent that all mankind might be by origin naturally disposed to love and care for one another.

Q. For what purpose did God create man?

A. That he should know God, love, and glorify Him, and so be happy forever.

Q. What is divine providence?

A. Divine providence is the constant energy of the almighty power, wisdom, and goodness of God, by which He preserves the being and faculties of His creatures, directs them to good ends, and assists all that is good; but the evil that springs by departure from good either cuts off, or corrects it, and turns it to good results in cooperation with the goodwill of men.

Behold the birds of the air, for they sow not, neither do they reap, nor gather into barns, yet your heavenly Father feedeth them. Are ye not much better than they? **Mat. 6:26** From these words is shown at once God's general providence over creatures, and His special providence over man.

On the Second Article:

Q. How are we to understand the name *Jesus Christ, the Son of God*?

A. Son of God is the name of the second person of the Holy Trinity in respect to His Godhead: This same Son of God was called Jesus, when He was conceived and born on earth as man: Christ is the name given Him by the Prophets, while they were as yet expecting His advent upon earth.

Q. What does the name Jesus mean?

A. Savior.

Q. By whom was the name Jesus first given?

A. By the Angel Gabriel.

Q. Why was this name given to the Son of God at His conception and birth on earth?

A. Because He was conceived and born to <u>save</u> men.

Q. What does the name Christ mean?

A. Anointed One.

Q. Is it only Jesus the Son of God who is called Anointed?

A. No. <u>Anointed</u> was in Old Testament times a title of Kings, High Priests, and Prophets.

Q. Why then is Jesus the Son of God called Anointed?

A. Because to His manhood were imparted without measure all the gifts of the Holy Spirit, and so He possesses in the highest degree the knowledge of a Prophet, the holiness of a High Priest, and power of a King.

Q. In what sense is Jesus Christ called Lord?

A. In this sense, that He is truly God; for the name Lord is one of the names of God. *In the Beginning was the Word, and the Word was with God, and the Word was God.* **John 1:1**

For first-century Palestinian Jews, the term "Lord" was used to refer to YHWH (God). In a second sense then, when the early Christian Church stated that Jesus Christ is Lord, they are saying that Jesus Christ is God (YHWH).

Q. Why is Jesus called the Only-begotten Son of God?

A. Because He alone is the Son of God begotten of the substance of God the Father, and so is of one substance with the Father. **John 1:12**

The Word was made flesh, and dwelt among us, and we beheld His glory, the glory as of the Only-begotten of the Father, full of grace and truth. John 1:14. *No man hath seen God at any time: the Only-begotten Son, which is in the bosom of the Father, He hath declared Him.* **ib. 18**

Q. Why in the Creed is it said further of the Son of God that He is "begotten of the Father"?

A. By this is expressed that personal property, by which He is distinguished from the other Persons of the Holy Trinity.

Q. Why is it said that He is begotten before all worlds?

A. That none should think there was ever a time when He was not. In other words, by this is expressed that Jesus Christ is the Son of God from all eternity, even as God the Father is from all eternity.

Q. What do the words *"Light of Light"* mean in the Creed?

A. Under the figure of the visible light they in some manner explain the incomprehensible generation of the Son of God from the Father. When we look at the sun, we see light: from this light is generated the light visible everywhere beneath: but both the one and the other is one light, indivisible and of one nature. In like manner, God the Father is the everlasting Light: **I John 1:5.** Of Him is begotten the Son of God, Who also is the everlasting Light: the God the Father and God the Son are one and the same everlasting Light, indivisible, and of one Divine nature.

Q. What force is there in the words of the Creed, God of God?

A. That the Son of God is called God in the same proper sense as God the Father. *We know that the Son of God is come, and hath given us (light and) understanding, that we may know the true God, and be in Him that is true, in His Son Jesus Christ: This is the true God and eternal life.* **I John 5:20**

Q. Why is it further added of the Son of God in the Creed that he is begotten, not made?

A. This was added against the Arian heresy, which incorrectly taught that the Son of God was made.

Q. What do the words *Of one substance with the Father* mean?

A. They mean that the Son of God is of one and the same Divine being with God the Father. *I and the Father are one.* **John 9:30**

Q. What is shown in the next words in the Creed, *By whom all things were made?*

A. That God the Father created all things by His Son, as by His eternal Wisdom and His eternal Word. *All things were made by Him, and without Him was not any thing made which was made.* **John 1:3**

On the Third Article:

Q. What do we mean when we say that He came down from heaven, seeing that as God He is everywhere?

A. It is true that He is everywhere: and so He is always in heaven, and always on earth; but on earth He was without a human body; afterwards He appeared in the flesh; in this sense it is said that *He came down from heaven. No man hath ascended up to heaven, but He that came down from heaven, even the Son of man, which is in heaven.* **John 3:13**

Q. For what reason did the Son of God come down from heaven?

A. *For us men, and for our salvation,* as it is said in the Creed.

Q. In what sense, is it said that the Son of God came down from heaven for us men?

A. In this sense, that He came upon earth not for one nation nor for some men only, but for us men universally.

Q. From what did Christ wish to save us?

A. From sin, the curse, and death.

Q. What is sin?

A. *Sin is the transgression of the law.* I John 3:8

Q. How did sin pass from the devil to men?

A. The devil deceived Eve and Adam, and tempted them to break God's commandment.

Q. What commandment?

A. God commanded Adam in Paradise not to eat of the fruit of the *Tree of the knowledge of good and evil,* and also told him that if he ate of it, he would die.

Q. Why did it bring death to man to eat of the fruit of the *Tree of the knowledge of good and evil?*

A. Because it involved disobedience to God's will, and so separated man from God and His grace, and alienated him from the life of God.

It was the supernatural and sanctifying grace of God that sustained Adam and Eve. Thus, when they sinned, they lost this grace, and all who came after them were born without this supernatural grace (deprived of sanctifying grace), and it is this state of birth without that grace which we call "original sin".

Q. What is meant by the *Tree of the knowledge of good and evil?*

A. Man through this tree came to know by the act itself what good there is in obeying the will of God, and what evil there is in disobeying it.

Q. How could Adam and Eve listen to the devil against the will of God?

A. God of His goodness, at the creation of man, gave him a will naturally disposed to love God, but still free; and man used this freedom for evil.

We still, today have God's gift of free will, to use to choose what path we will take. Ultimately, in order to benefit from Christ's salvific sacrifice, we must choose and believe in Jesus Christ.

Q. How did the devil deceive Adam and Eve?

A. Eve saw in Paradise a serpent, which assured her that if men ate of the fruit of the tree of the knowledge of good and evil, they would know good and evil, and would become gods. Eve was deceived by this promise and ate of it. Adam ate after her example.

Q. What came of Adam's sin?

A. The curse and death.

Q. What is the curse?

A. The condemnation of sin by God's just judgment, and the evil which from sin came upon the earth for the punishment of men. God said to Adam, *Cursed is the ground for thy sake.* **Gen. 3:17**

Q. What is the death which came from the sin of Adam?

A. It is two fold: Bodily, when the body loses the soul which gives it life; and spiritual, when the soul loses the grace of God, which gives it the higher and spiritual life.

Q. Can the soul then die, as well as the body?

A. It can die, but not in the same way as the body. The body, when it dies loses sense, and is dissolved; the soul, when it dies by sin, loses spiritual light, joy, and happiness, but is not dissolved nor annihilated, but remains in a state of suffering, anguish, and darkness.

Q. Why must all men share the effects of Adam's sin?

A. Because all have descended from Adam, thereby sharing the consequences of sin, and all sin themselves. *By one man sin entered into the world, and death by sin, and so death passed upon all men, for that all have sinned.* **Rom. 5:12**

Each of us has inherited, as a result of Adam's sin, a natural birth not accompanied by supernatural grace. This supernatural grace of God sustained Adam and Eve's bodies and kept them free from decay, sickness and death.

Q. Did men have any hope left for salvation?

A. When our first parents had confessed before God their sin, God, of His mercy, gave them hope for salvation.

Q. What was this hope?

A. God promised, that the *seed of the woman should bruise the serpent's head.* **Gen. 3:15**

This passage of Scripture is the Proto-Evangelium, the first prophecy of the coming of Jesus, the second Adam, who would prevail against the serpent, where the first Adam had failed.

Q. What did that mean?

A. It meant that Jesus Christ should overcome the devil who had deceived men, and deliver them from sin, the curse, and death.

Q. Why is Jesus Christ called *the seed of the woman*?

A. Because he was born on earth without a father from the Most Holy Virgin Mary.

The very term "seed of the woman" is an extremely unusual term. In no other place in Hebrew literature or Scripture is there ever referred to anyone being of the "woman's seed", whereas traditionally the term is used in reference to a male. This prophesizes that the "new Adam" would not be born of an earthly father, but a heavenly one.

Q. What benefit was there in this promise?

A. The benefit was that from the time of the promise men could believe savingly in the Savior that was to come, even as we now believe in the Savior who has come.

Q. Did people in fact from the Old Testament believe in the Savior that was to come?

A. Some did, but the greater part forgot God's promise of a Savior.

Q. Did not God repeat this promise?

A. More than once. For instance, He made to Abraham the promise of a Savior in the following words: *In thy seed all the nations of the earth be blessed.* **Gen 22:18** The same promise He repeated afterwards to David in the following words: *I will set up thy seed after thee, and I will establish His throne for ever.* **II Kings 7:12,13**

Q. What do we understand by the word <u>Incarnation</u>?

A. That the Son of God took upon Himself human flesh without sin, and was made man, without ceasing to be God. *The Word was made flesh.* **John 1:14**

Q. Why in the Creed, after it has been said of the Son of God that He was incarnate, is it further added that He was made man?

A. To the end that none should imagine that the Son of God took only flesh or a body, but should acknowledge in Him a perfect man consisting of body and soul. *There is one Mediator between God and men, the man Christ Jesus.* **I Tim. 2:5**

Q. And so is there only one nature in Jesus Christ?

A. No; there are in Him without separation and without confusion two natures, the Divine and the human, and with these two natures, two wills.

Q. Are there not therefore also two persons?

A. No; One person, God and man together; in one word, a God-man. The Evangelist Luke relates that when the Virgin Mary had asked the Angel, who announced to her the conception of Jesus, *How shall this be, seeing I know not a man?* The Angel replied to her, *The Holy Spirit shall come upon thee, and the power of the highest shall overshadow thee; therefore also that Holy thing which shall be born of thee shall be called the Son of God.* **Luke 1:34,35**

Q. Who was the Virgin Mary?

A. A holy virgin of the ancestry of Abraham and David, from whose line the Savior, by God's promise, was to come; betrothed to Joseph, a man of the same line, in order that he might be her guardian; for she was dedicated to God with a vow of perpetual virginity.

Q. Did Mary remain, in fact, a virgin?

A. She remained a virgin before the birth, during the birth, and after the birth of the Savior; and therefore, is called ever-virgin.

Q. What other great title is there with which the Church honors the Holy Virgin Mary?

A. That of Mother of God.

Q. Can you show the origin of this title in Holy Scripture?

A. It is taken from the following words of the Prophet Isaiah: *Behold, a virgin shall conceive, and bear a Son, and they shall call his name Emmanuel, which being interpreted, is God with us.* **Isaiah 7:14, Mat. 1:23**

So also the righteous Elizabeth calls the Most Holy Virgin *The Mother of the Lord*; which title is all one with that of Mother of God, *Whence is this to me, that the Mother of my Lord should come to me?* **Luke 1:43**

"Lord", in ancient Hebrew usage was specifically used to refer to Yahweh (God), whose name they would not speak.

Q. In what sense is the Most Holy Virgin called Mother of God?

A. Although Jesus Christ was born of her not in His divinity, but of his humanity, still she is rightly called Mother of God, because He that was born of her as a man is nevertheless God.

Q. What thoughts should we have of the exalted dignity of the Most Holy Virgin Mary?

A. As Mother of the Lord she is higher than all created beings in grace and nearness to God.

Q. Give examples of how God prepared His people to know the Saviour when He would be born.

A. The prophet Isaiah foretold that the Saviour should be born of a virgin. **Is. 7:14** The Prophet Micah foretold that the Saviour should be born in Bethlehem; and this prophecy the Jews understood even before they heard of its fulfillment. **Mat. 2:4-6** The Prophet Malachi, after the building of the second temple at Jerusalem, foretold that the coming of the Saviour was drawing near, that He should come to this temple, and that before Him should be sent a forerunner who would be like the Prophet Elias, clearly pointing by this to John the Baptist. **Mal 3:1; 4:5** The Prophet Zachariah foretold the triumphal entry of the Saviour into Jerusalem. **Zach. 9:9** The Prophet Isaiah with wonderful clearness foretold the sufferings of the Saviour. **Is 53** David, in the 23rd Psalm, described the sufferings of the Saviour on the cross itself. And Daniel, 490 years before, foretold the appearance of the Saviour, His death on the cross, and the subsequent destruction of the temple of Jerusalem, and abolition of the Old Testament sacrifices. **Dan. 9**

Q. Did men, in fact, recognize Jesus Christ as the Saviour at the time that He was born and lived upon earth?

A. Many did recognize Him by various ways. The wise men of the East recognized Him by a star, which before His birth appeared in the East. The shepherds of Bethlehem knew of Him from Angels, who distinctly told them that the saviour was born in the city of David. Simeon and Anna, by special revelation of the Holy Spirit, knew Him when He was brought, forty days after His birth, into the temple. John the Baptist, at the river Jordan, at His baptism, knew Him by revelation, by the descent of the Holy Spirit upon Him in the form of a dove, and by a voice from heaven from God the Father; *This is My beloved Son, in Whom I am well pleased; hear Him.* **Mark 9:7** Besides this, very many recognized Him by His preaching, and especially by the miracles which He worked.

Q. What are some of the miracles of Jesus Christ?

A. People suffering under incurable diseases, and possessed by devils, were healed by Him in the twinkling of an eye, by a single word, or by the touch of His hand, and even through their touching His garment. Once with five, and another time with seven loaves He fed in the wilderness several thousand men. He walked on the waters, and by a word calmed the storm. He raised the dead; The son of the widow of Nain, the daughter of Jairus, and Lazarus on the fourth day after his death.

Q. How does Christ save us?

A. By His teaching, His life, His death, and resurrection.

Q. What was Christ's main teaching?

A. The Gospel of the Kingdom of God, or in other words, the doctrine of salvation and eternal happiness. **Mark 1:14,15**

Q. How are we saved by Christ's teachings?

A. When we receive it with all our heart, and walk according to it. For, as the false words of the devil, received by our first parents, became in them the seed of sin and death, so, on the contrary, the true word of Christ, sincerely received by Christians, becomes in them the seed of a holy and immortal life. They are, in the words of the Apostle Peter, *born again, not of corruptible seed, but of incorruptible, by the word of God which liveth and abideth for ever.* **I Pet. 1:23**

Q. How do we receive salvation by Christ's life?

A. When we imitate it. For He says, *If anyone serve Me, let Him follow Me; and where I am, there shall also My servant be.* **John 12:26**

On the Fourth Article:

Q. How did it come to pass that Jesus Christ was crucified when His teaching and works should have moved all to love Him?

A. The elders of the Jews and the scribes, who represent all unrepentant sinners, hated Him because He rebuked their false doctrine and evil lives, and envied Him because the people who heard Him teach and saw His miracles respected Him more than them; and hence they falsely accused Him and condemned Him to death.

Q. Why is it said that Jesus Christ was crucified under Pontius Pilate?

A. To mark the time of when He was crucified.

Q. Who was Pontius Pilate?

A. The Roman governor of Judea, which had become subject to the Romans.

Q. Why is this circumstance worthy of remark?

A. Because in it we see the fulfillment of Jacob's prophecy: *The scepter shall not depart from Judah, nor a lawgiver from between his feet, until Shiloh come: and He is the desire of the nations.* **Gen. 44:10**

Q. Why is it not only said in the Creed that Jesus Christ was crucified, but also added that He suffered?

A. To show that His crucifixion was not only a resemblance of suffering and death, as some have said, but a real suffering and death.

Q. Why is it also mentioned that He was buried?

A. This likewise is to assure us that He really died, and rose again; for His enemies even set a watch at His sepulchre, and sealed it.

Q. How could Jesus Christ suffer and die when He was God?

A. He suffered and died not in His Godhead, but in His manhood; and He did this not because He could not avoid it, but because it pleased Him to suffer for our salvation.

He Himself had said: *I lay down My life, that I may take it again. No man taketh it from Me, but I lay it down for Myself. I have power to lay it down, and I have power to take it again.* **John 10:17,18**

Q. In what sense is it said, that Jesus Christ was crucified for us?

A. That He, by His death on the cross, delivered us from sin, the curse, and death. **Ephes. 1:7; Gal. 3:13; Heb. 2:14,15**

Q. According to Scripture how does the death of Jesus Christ upon the cross deliver us from sin, the curse, and death?

A. *God hath willed to make known to His saints, what is the riches of the glory of this mystery of the Gentiles, which is Christ in you, the hope of glory.* **Col. 1:26,27**

For if by one man's offense death reigned by one, much more they which receive abundance of grace and of the gift of righteousness shall reign in life by one, Jesus Christ. **Rom. 5:17**

There is therefore now no condemnation to them which are in Christ Jesus, who walk not after the flesh but after the spirit. For the law of the spirit of life in Christ Jesus hath made me free from the law of sin and death. For what the law could not do, in that it was weak through the flesh, God sending His own Son in likeness of sinful flesh, and for sin, condemned sin in the flesh; that the righteousness of the law might be fulfilled in us, who walk not after the flesh, but after the spirit. **Rom. 7:1-4**

Q. Did Jesus Christ suffer and die for all men?

A. For His part, He offered Himself as a sacrifice strictly for all, and obtained for all grace and salvation; but this benefits only those of us, who, for our parts, of our own free will, have *fellowship in His sufferings, being made conformable unto His death.* **Philipp. 3:10**

Q. How can we have fellowship in the sufferings and death of Jesus Christ?

A. We have fellowship in the sufferings and death of Jesus Christ through a lively and sincere faith, through the Sacraments, in which is contained and sealed the virtue of His saving sufferings and death, and lastly, through the crucifixion of our flesh with its lusts. **Gal. 2:19,20; Rom. 6:3; I Cor.11:26; Gal. 5:24**

Q. How can we crucify the flesh with its lusts?

A. By doing what is contrary to them. For instance, when anger prompts us to insult an enemy and to do him harm, but we resist the desire, and, remembering how Jesus Christ on the cross prayed for His enemies, pray likewise for ours, we crucify the sin of anger.

On the Fifth Article:

Q. What is the proof given by Jesus Christ, that His sufferings and death have brought salvation to us men?

A. That He rose again, and so laid the foundation for our blessed resurrection. *Now is Christ risen from the dead, and become the first-fruits of them that slept.* **I Cor. 15:20**

Q. What is <u>hades</u> or <u>hell</u> as used in the Creed?

A. Hades is a Greek word, and means a place void of light. In the Creed by this name is understood a spiritual prison, that is, the state of those spirits which are separated by sin from the sight of God's countenance, and from the light and blessedness which it confers. **Jude 1:6**

Q. For what reason did Jesus Christ descend into hell?

A. So that He might there also preach His victory over death, and deliver the souls which with faith awaited His coming. *For Christ also hath once suffered for sins, the just for the unjust, that He may bring us to God, being put to death in the flesh, but quickened in the Spirit: in which also He went and preached unto the Spirits in Prison.* **I Pet. 3:18,19**

Q. What do we mean by the words of the Creed, *and rose again the third day according to the Scripture?*

A. These words were put into the Creed from the following passage in the Epistle to the Corinthians: *For I delivered unto you first of all that which I also received, how that Christ died for our sins, according to the Scripture; and that He was buried, and that He rose again the third day, according to the Scripture.* **I Cor. 15:3,4**

Q. What force is there in these words, *according to the Scripture?*

A. By this is shown that Jesus Christ died and rose again, precisely as had been written of Him prophetically in the books of the Old Testament.

Q. Where for instance, is there anything written of this event?

A. In the 53rd chapter of the book of the Prophet Isaiah, for instance, the suffering and death of Jesus Christ is shown forth with many particular traits; as, *He was wounded for our transgressions, He was bruised for our iniquities; the chastisement of our peace was upon Him; and with His stripes we are healed.* **Isa. 5**

Of the Resurrection of Christ the Apostle Peter quotes the words of the 16th Psalm: *For why? Thou shalt not leave My soul in hell, neither shalt Thou suffer Thy holy one to see corruption.* **Acts 2:27**

Q. Is this also the Scripture of the Old Testament, that Jesus Christ should rise again on the third day?

A. A prophetic type of this was set forth in the Prophet Jonah: *And Jonah was in the belly of the fish three days and three nights.* **John 1:17**

Q. How was it known that Jesus Christ had risen?

A. The soldiers who watched His sepulchre knew this, because an angel of the Lord rolled away the stone which closed His sepulchre, and at the same time there was a great earthquake. Angels likewise announced the Resurrection of Christ to Mary Magdalene and some others. Jesus Christ Himself on the very day of His Resurrection appeared to many; also to the women bringing spices, to Peter, to the two disciples going to Emmaus, and lastly, to all the Apostles in the house, the doors being shut. Afterwards He often showed Himself to them during the span of forty days; and one day, He was seen by more than five hundred believers at one time. **I Cor. 15:6**

Q. What did Jesus Christ after His resurrection continue to teach the Apostles?

A. He continued to teach them the mysteries of the Kingdom of God. **Acts 1:3**

On the Sixth Article:

Q. Is the statement of our Lord's Ascension in the sixth article of the Creed taken from Scripture?

A. It is taken from the following passage of Holy Scripture: *He that descended is the same also that ascended up far above all heavens, that He might fill all things.* **Eph. 4:10**

We have such a High Priest, who is set on the right hand of the throne of the majesty in the heavens. **Heb. 8:1**

Q. Was it in His Godhead or His manhood that Jesus Christ ascended into heaven?

A. In His manhood. In His Godhead He ever was and is in heaven.

Q. How does Jesus Christ *sit at the right hand of God the Father,* seeing that God is everywhere?

A. This must be understood spiritually; that is, Jesus Christ has one and the same majesty and glory with God the Father, humanity having been exalted in His Divinity.

On the Seventh Article:

Q. How does Holy Scripture speak of Christ's coming again?

A. *This Jesus, which is taken up from you into heaven, shall so come in like manner as ye have seen Him go in to heaven.* **Acts 1:2** This was said to the Apostles by angels at the time of our Lord's Ascension.

Q. How does it speak of the future judgment?

A. *The hour is coming, in which all that are in the graves shall hear the voice of the Son of God, and shall come forth; they that have done good, unto the resurrection of life, and they that have done evil, unto the resurrection of damnation.* **John 5:28,29** These are the words of Christ Himself.

Q. How does it speak of His kingdom which is to have no end?

A. *He shall be great, and shall be called the Son of the Highest; and the Lord God shall give unto Him the throne of His father David, and He shall reign over the house of Jacob for ever, and of His kingdom there shall be no end.* **Luke 1:32,33** These are the words of the angel to the Mother of God.

Q. Will the second coming of Christ be like His first?

A. No, it will be different. He came to suffer for us in great humility, but He shall come to judge us *in His glory, and all the holy angels with Him.* **Mat. 25:31**

Q. Will He judge all men?

A. Yes. All without exception.

Q. How will He judge them?

A. The conscience of every man shall be laid open before all, and not only shall all deeds which he has ever done in his whole life upon earth be revealed, but also all the words he has spoken, and all his secret wishes and thoughts.

The Lord shall come, who will bring to light the hidden things of darkness, and will make manifest the counsels of the heart; and then shall every man have praise of God. **I Cor. 4:5**

Q. Will He then condemn us even for evil words and thoughts?

A. Yes, He will, unless we correct them by repentance, faith, and amendment of life. *I say unto you, that every idle word that men shall speak, they shall give account thereof in the day of judgment.* **Mat. 12:36**

Q. Will Jesus Christ soon come to judge the earth?

A. We do not know the day nor the hour. Therefore, we should live so as to be always ready. *The Lord is not slack concerning His promise, as some men count slackness; but is long suffering toward us, not willing that any should perish, but that all should come to repentance. But the day of the Lord will come as a thief in the night.* **II Pet. 3:9,10**

Watch, therefore, for ye know neither the day nor the hour wherein the Son of man cometh. **Mat. 25:13**

Q. What are the signs of the coming of Christ?

A. In the word of God certain signs are revealed, such as the decrease of faith and love among men, the abounding of sin and disasters, the preaching of the Gospel to all nations, and the coming of the Antichrist. **Mat. 24**

Q. What is meant by the <u>Antichrist</u>?

A. An enemy of Christ, who will strive to overthrow Christianity, but instead of doing so, shall himself come to a destructive end. **II Thess. 2:8**

Q. What is Christ's kingdom?

A. Christ's kingdom is, first, the whole world; secondly, all believers upon earth; thirdly, all the blessed in heaven.

The first is called the kingdom of nature, the second the kingdom of grace, the third the kingdom of glory.

Q. Which of these is meant when it is said in the Creed, that of Christ's Kingdom there *shall be no end*?

A. The kingdom of glory.

On the Eighth Article:

Q. In what sense is the Holy Spirit called the Lord?

A. In the same sense as the Son of God; that is, as truly God.

Q. Is it witnessed by Holy Scripture?

A. It is plain from the words spoken by the Apostle Peter to rebuke Ananias: *Why hath Satan filled thine heart, to lie to the Holy Spirit?* and further on, *Thou hast not lied unto man, but unto God.* **Acts 5:3,4**

Q. What are we to understand by this, that the Holy Spirit is called *the giver of life?*

A. That He, together with God the Father and the Son, gives life to all creatures, especially spiritual life to man. *Except a man be born of water and of the Spirit, he cannot enter into the kingdom of God.* **John 3:5**

Q. How do we know that the Holy Spirit proceeds from the Father?

A. This we know from the following words of Jesus Christ Himself: *But when the Comforter is come, whom I will send unto you from the Father, even the Spirit of truth, which proceeds from the Father, He shall testify of Me.* **John 15: 26.**

Q. Does the Doctrine of the procession of the Holy Spirit from the Father admit of any change or supplement?

A. No. First, because the Catholic Church, in this doctrine, repeats the exact words of Jesus Christ; and His words, without doubt, are a precise and perfect expression of the truth. Second, because the second Ecumenical Council, whose chief object was to establish the true doctrine concerning the Holy Spirit, has without doubt correctly set forth the same in the Creed; and the Catholic Church has acknowledged this so decidedly, that the third Ecumenical Council in its seventh canon has forbidden the composition of any new Creed.

Q. By whose authority is it stated that the Holy Spirit is equal *with the Father and the Son,* and *together* with them *is worshipped and glorified?*

A. It appears from this, that Jesus Christ commanded them to *baptize in the name of the Father, and of the Son and of the Holy Spirit.* **Mat. 28:19**

Q. Why is said in the Creed that the Holy Spirit spoke through the prophets?

A. This is said against certain heretics, who taught that the books of the Old Testament were not written by the Holy Spirit.

For prophecy came not in old time by the will of man; but holy men of God spoke as they were moved by the Holy Spirit. **II Pet. 1:12**

Q. Why then is there no mention of the Apostles in the Creed.

A. Because when the Creed was composed none doubted the inspiration of the Apostles.

Q. Was not the Holy Spirit shown forth to men in some very special manner?

A. Yes. He came down upon the Apostles in the form of fiery tongues, on the 50th day after the resurrection of Jesus Christ, the day called Pentecost.

Q. Is the Holy Spirit communicated to men even now?

A. He is communicated to all true Christians. *Know ye not that ye are the temple of God, and that the Spirit of God dwelleth in you?* **I Cor. 3:16**

Q. How may we be made partakers of the Holy Spirit?

A. Through fervent prayer, and through the Sacraments.

If ye then, being evil, know how to give good gifts unto your children how much more shall your heavenly Father give the Holy Spirit to them that ask Him? **Luke 11:13**

But after that the kindness and love of God our Savior toward man appeared, not by works of righteousness which we have done, but according to his mercy He saved us, by the washing of regeneration, and renewing of the Holy Spirit, which He shed on us abundantly through Jesus Christ our Savior. **Titus 3:4-6**

Q. What are the chief gifts of the Holy Spirit?

A. The Chief and more general are, as stated by the Prophet Isaiah, the following seven: the spirit of the fear of God, the spirit of knowledge, the spirit of might, the spirit of counsel, the spirit of understanding, the spirit of wisdom, the spirit of the Lord, or the gift of piety and inspiration and in the highest degree. **Isaiah 11:2**

On the Ninth Article:

Q. What is the Church?

A. The Church is a divinely instituted community of believers united by the catholic faith, the law of God, the hierarchy, and the Sacraments.

It is within the Church, that Christians are to belong, and not kept segregated from one another, nor believing that participation and communion with the other members of the Church is optional or unnecessary. An individualistic concept of Christianity is inherently flawed, for it is as a people that Christ commands us and directs us forward, and as a body of Christians, the "Bride of Christ" that the Church is lead and instructed by the Apostles and their successors.

It is the Church, and not the individual separated from the Church, that Christ said the "gates of hell" would not prevail against. It is as members of the Church, that we wield the greatest of spiritual power against Satan.

Q. What does it mean to *believe in the Church*?

A. It means piously to honor the true Church of Christ, and to obey her doctrine and commandments, from a conviction that grace ever abides in her, and works, teaches, and governs for salvation of men flowing from her One and only eternal Head, the Lord Jesus Christ.

Q. How can the Church, which is visible, be the object of faith, when faith, as the Apostle says, *is the evidence of things not seen*?

A. First, though the Church is visible, the grace of God which dwells in her, and in those who are sanctified in her, is not; and this is what properly constitutes the object of faith in the Church.

Second, the Church, though visible insofar as she is upon earth, and contains all right believing Christians living upon earth, still is at the same time invisible, insofar as she is also in heaven, and contains all those that have departed in true faith and holiness. **Heb. 12:22-24**

Q. How are we assured that the grace of God abides in the true Church?

A. First, that her head is Jesus Christ, God and man in one person, *full of grace and truth,* who fills His body, that is, the Church, with like grace and truth. **John 1:14,17**

Second, that He has promised His disciples the Holy Spirit to *abide with them for ever,* and that, according to this promise, the Holy Spirit appoints the pastors of the Church. **John 14:16; Eph. 1:22,23; Acts 20:28**

Q. How are we assured that the grace of God abides in the Church even to the present, and shall abide in it to the end of the world?

A. We are assured by the following words of Jesus Christ and His Apostles: *I will build my Church, and the gates of hell shall not prevail against it.* **Mat. 16:18** *I am with you always, even unto the end of the world. Amen.* **Mat. 28:20**

Unto Him, God the Father, be glory in the Church by Christ Jesus throughout all ages, world with out end Amen. **Eph. 3:21**

Q. Why is the Church one?

A. Because she is one spiritual Body, has one Head, Christ, and is given life by one Spirit of God. *There is one body and one Spirit, even as ye are called in hope of your calling in one; one Lord, one faith, one baptism; one God and Father of all.* **Eph. 4:4-6; I Cor.3:10,11; II Col.1:24,25**

Q. What duty does the unity of the Church place on us?

A. That of *endeavoring to keep the unity of the Spirit in the bond of peace.* **Eph.4:3**

Q. How does it agree with the unity of the Church that there are many separate and independent Churches, some who are called Western Rite Orthodox and others who are called Eastern Orthodox?

A. These are particular Churches, or parts of the one Catholic Church: the separateness of their visible organization does not hinder them from being spiritually great members of the one body of the Catholic Church, having one Head, Christ, and one spirit of faith and grace. This unity is expressed outwardly by unity of Creed, and by communion in Prayer and Sacraments.

The separate secular body politics that the earthly Church operates within, is not what defines communion within the body of the faithful, but rather the faith we profess. This profession of faith, expressed in the Creed, binds and joins us supernaturally with fellow Christians who profess this same faith in its entirety. Thus Old Catholics, Roman Catholics, Eastern Orthodox, and Oriental Orthodox, all share the same faith, celebrate the same Sacraments, and receive the same grace of God.

Q. Is there also a unity between the church on earth and the Church in heaven?

A. There is, both by their common relation to one Head, our Lord Jesus Christ, and by mutual communion with one another.

Q. What means of communion does the Church on earth have with the Church in heaven?

A. The prayer of faith and love. By the offering of the same Holy Sacrifice of Christ, the faithful who belong to the Church militant upon earth, in offering their prayers to God, call upon at the same time to their aid, the Saints who belong to the Church in heaven; and these standing on the highest steps of approach to God, by their prayers of intercessions purify, strengthen, and offer before God the prayers of the faithful living upon earth, and by the will of God work graciously for and with them, either by invisible virtue, or by distinct apparitions, and in other ways.

We see illustrated in Revelation, how the intercessory prayers of the Saints in Heaven are brought to the sacred altar of God, and thus from Scripture, we understand that the Saints in Heaven pray for us and with us to God, interceding on our behalf.

Q. What is the basis for the rule of the Church upon earth to *invoke in prayer the Saints* of the Church in heaven?

A. The basis is Holy Tradition, the principle of which is to be seen also in Holy Scripture. For instance, when the Prophet David cries out in prayer *O Lord God of Abraham, Isaac, and of Israel our fathers,* he makes mention of Saints in aid of his prayer, exactly as now the Orthodox Catholic Church calls upon *Christ our true God, by the prayers of His most pure Mother and all His Saints.* See **1 Chron. 29:18.**

Just as we ask one another among the Church here on earth to pray for us, and pray with us, so too, can we ask those among the Church in heaven to pray for us, and with us as well. That the saints of God pray for one another, and with one another, does not detract from Christ, but glorifies Him.

Q. Is there any testimony in Holy Scripture to the *mediatory prayer* of the Saints in heaven?

A. The Evangelist John, in the Revelation, saw in heaven an Angel, to whom *was given much incense, that he should offer it, by the prayers of all Saints, upon the golden altar which was before the throne; and the smoke of the incense ascended up by the prayers of the Saints out of the hands of the Angel before God.* **Rev. 8:3,4**

Q. Is there any testimony in Holy Scripture concerning *apparitions of Saints* from heaven?

A. The Evangelist St. Matthew relates, that after the death of our Lord Jesus Christ upon the cross, *many bodies of the Saints which slept arose, and came out of the graves after His resurrection, and went into the holy city, and appeared unto many.* **Mat. 27:52,53** And since a miracle so great could not be without some adequate purpose, we must suppose that the Saints which then arose appeared for this reason, that they might announce the descent of Jesus Christ into hell, and His triumphant resurrection.

Q. What testimonies are there to confirm us in the belief that the Saints, after their departure, work miracles through certain earthly means?

A. 1. The fourth book of Kings testifies that by touching the bones of the Prophet Elisha a dead man was raised to life. **IV Kings 13:21**

   2. The Apostle Paul not only in his own immediate person administered healings and miracles, but the same was done also in his absence by handkerchiefs and aprons taken from his body. **Acts 19:12** By this example we may understand that the Saints, even after their deaths, may in like manner work through earthly means, which have been received from the holy power.

Q. Why is the Church holy?

A. Because she is sanctified by Jesus Christ through His passion, through His teaching, through His prayer, and through the Sacraments.

Christ loved the Church, and gave Himself for it; that He might sanctify it, having cleansed it with the washing of water by the word, that He might present it to Himself a glorious Church, not having spot, or wrinkle, or any such thing, but that it should be holy and without blemish. **Eph. 5:25-27**

In His prayer to God the Father for believers, Jesus Christ said among other things: *Sanctify them through Thy truth: Thy word is truth. And for their sakes I Sanctify Myself, that they also may be sanctified in truth.* **John 17:17-19**

Q. How is the Church holy, when she has in her body many sinners?

A. Men who sin, but purify themselves by true repentance, do not hinder the Church from being holy, but impenitent sinners, either by the visible act of Church authority, or by the invisible judgment of God, are cut off from the body of the Church: and so she is with respect to these also kept holy. *Put away from among yourselves that wicked person.* **I Cor. 5:13** *Nevertheless the foundation of God stands sure, having this seal, the Lord knows them that are His. and let every one that calls on the name of the Lord depart from iniquity.* **II Tim. 2:19**

Q. Why is the Church called <u>Catholic</u>?

A. Because she is not limited to any place, nor time, nor people, but contains true believers of all places, times, and peoples; hence, she is universal.

The very word "Catholic" means "universal", and thus the entire Church, regardless of how she is known or named in a particular place, identifies and professes its belief as the One, Holy Catholic and Apostolic Church.

The Apostle Paul says that *the word of the gospel is in all the world; and brings forth fruit.* **Coloss. 1:5,6** and that in the Christian Church there *is neither Greek nor Jew, circumcision nor uncircumcision, barbarian nor Scythian, bond nor free: but Christ is all, and in all.* **ib. 3:11**

They which be of faith are blessed with faithful Abraham. **Gal. 3:9**

Q. What great privilege has the Catholic Church been given?

A. She alone has the sublime promises *that the gates of hell shall not prevail against her;* that the Lord shall *be with her even to the end of the world;* that in her shall abide *the glory of God in Jesus Christ throughout all generations for ever;* and consequently that she shall never apostatize from the faith, nor sin against the truth of the faith, of fall into error.

Any individual, or group who departs from the faith, by denying some part of it, or refusing to be obedient to the faith, has apostatized and left the Church. This is true for laity and clergy alike, and such individuals are not to be accorded any of the spiritual rights or gifts accorded to the Church unless he or they repent, and are restored by the Sacrament of Reconciliation.

Q. If the Catholic Church contains all true believers in the World, must we not acknowledge it to be necessary for salvation, that every believer should belong to her?

A. Yes. Since Jesus Christ, in the words of St. Paul, *is the Head of the Church, and He is the Saviour of the Body;* it follows that in order to have a participation in His salvation, we must be members of His Body, that is, of the Catholic Church. **Ephes. 5:23**

The Apostle Peter writes that *baptism saves us* after the figure of the *ark of Noah.* All who were saved from the great flood were saved only in the ark; so all who obtain everlasting salvation, obtain it only in the one Catholic Church.

Any individual who, having full knowledge of the faith, refuses to accept the faith and be part of the Church, places their soul in immortal danger. An individual who, through no fault of their own, never having been brought to the fullness of the faith, refuses or rejects the Faith and the Church, may, through God's Divine Love and Mercy, yet be saved, albeit in a way we do not comprehend.

Q. Why is the Church called <u>Apostolic</u>?

A. Because she has from the Apostles without breakage or change both her doctrine and the succession of the gifts of the Holy Spirit, through the laying on of consecrated hands. **Ephes. 2:19,20**

Q. What does the Creed teach us, when she calls the Church Apostolic?

A. It teaches us to hold fast the Apostolic doctrine and tradition, and cast out such doctrine and such teachers, as are not in conformity with the doctrine of the Apostles. **II Thess. 2:15; Titus 3:10; Titus 1:10,11; Mat. 18:17**

Q. What Ecclesiastical Institution is there through which the succession of the Apostolic ministry is preserved?

A. The Hierarchy of Bishops, Priest, and Deacons.

In Acts 1:15–25, we see that the Church understood the position of disciple previously held by Judas, as a holy office. They prayed for guidance to select an individual who would *"take the place in this ministry and apostleship from which Judas turned aside to go to his own place"*. Peter, quoted **Psalm 69:25**, in saying, *"Let his habitation become desolate, and let there be no one to live in it; and 'His office let another take."* This verse, among others, provide clear biblical teaching that the Twelve held special positions as established by Christ, that are correctly understood to be supernatural offices that others would succeed to after they had fallen asleep in Christ. Consider St. Paul's directions and instructions on the qualifications of a bishop, in saying, *"This saying is sure: If anyone aspires to the office of bishop, he desires a noble task."* **1 Tim 3:1**

Q. Where does the Hierarchy of the Orthodox Catholic Church have its beginnings?

A. From Jesus Christ Himself, and from the descent of the Holy Spirit on the Apostles; from which time it has continued in unbroken succession, through the laying on of hands, in the sacrament of Holy Orders.

And He gave some, Apostles, and some, Prophets; and some, Evangelists; and some, Pastors and Teachers; for the perfecting of the Saints, for the work of the ministry, for the edifying of the Body of Christ. **Eph. 4:11, 12**

Q. What is the highest authority in the Catholic Church?

A. An Ecumenical Council.

Q. What is the highest authority of sections of the Catholic Church?

A. An Archbishop and the Synod.

Q. Under what ecclesiastical authority are dioceses and vicariates?

A. Under the authority of Bishops.

Q. If anyone desires to fulfill his duty of obedience to the Church, how may he learn what she requires of her children?

A. This may be learned from Holy Scripture, from the canons of the Holy Apostles, the seven Holy Ecumenical and various Provincial Councils, and the Holy Fathers, and from the Books of Ecclesiastical Canons.

On the Tenth Article:

Q. Why does the Creed mention Baptism?

A. Because faith is sealed by Baptism and the other Sacraments.

Q. What is a Sacrament?

A. A Sacrament is a holy act, through which grace, the saving power of God, works supernaturally upon man, and is instituted by Christ.

Q. How many Sacraments are there?

A. Seven: 1) Baptism; 2) Confirmation/Chrismation; 3) Holy Eucharist; 4) Penance; 5) Holy orders; 6) Matrimony; 7) Anointing of the Sick.

Q. What virtue is there in each of these Sacraments?

A. 1. In Baptism man is born to a new spiritual life.
   2. In confirmation he receives the grace of spiritual growth and strength, and is made a member of the universal priesthood of all believers.
   3. In the Communion, or Holy Eucharist, he is spiritually fed upon the Body and Blood of Christ.
   4. In Penance he is cleansed of spiritual diseases, that is, of sin.
   5. In Holy Orders he receives grace spiritually to regenerate, feed, and nurture others, by doctrine and Sacraments.

6. In Matrimony he receives a grace sanctifying the married life, and the natural procreation and nurture of children.

7. In Anointing of the Sick he has medicine even for bodily diseases, in that he is healed of spiritual ones.

Q. But why does the Creed not mention all these Sacraments, instead of mentioning Baptism only?

A. Because Baptism was the subject of a question, whether some people, as heretics, ought not to be rebaptized; and this required a decision, which so came to be put into the Creed.

On Baptism:

Q. What is baptism?

A. Baptism is a Sacrament in which a believer having his body plunged three times in water, or water poured three times, in the name of God the Father, the Son, and the Holy Spirit, dies to the life of sin, both original and actual, and is born again of the Holy Spirit to a life spiritual and holy. *Except a man be born of water and of the Spirit, he cannot enter into the kingdom of God.* John 3:5

Q. When and how did Baptism begin?

A. First, *John baptized with the baptism of repentance, saying unto the people that they should believe on Him which should come after him, that is, on Christ Jesus.* Acts 19:4 Afterwards, Jesus Christ by His own example sanctified Baptism when He received it from John. After explaining what to a Pharisee Nicodemus, what he must do to in order to enter the Kingdom of God, Jesus and His disciples go into the land of Judea, where He remained with them and baptized. John 3:22 After His resurrection He gave the Apostles the solemn commandment: *Go ye and teach all nations, baptizing them in the name of the Father, and of the Son, and of the Holy Spirit.* Mat.28:19

Q. What is most essential in the administration of Baptism?

A. Threefold immersion in water, or pouring of water, in the name of the Father, and of the Son, and of the Holy Spirit.

Q. What is required of those who seek to be baptized?

A. Repentance, and faith; which is why before Baptism they recite the Creed. *Repent, and be baptized every one of you in the name of Christ Jesus for the remission of sins, and ye shall receive the gift of the Holy Spirit.* **Acts 2:38**

He that believes and is baptized, shall be saved. **Mark 16:16**

Q. But why then are children baptized?

A. Because of the faith of their parents and sponsors, who are also bound to teach them the faith as soon as they are of an age to learn.

Q. How can you show from Holy Scripture that we ought to baptize infants?

A. In the time of the Old Testament infants were circumcised when eight days old; but Baptism in the New Testament takes the place of circumcision; consequently infants should also be baptized.

".but Jesus said, 'Let the children come to me, and do not hinder them; for to such belongs the kingdom of heaven.' And he laid hands on them and went away." **Math. 19:14**

In the conversion of entire households, everyone was baptized, and nowhere does Holy Scripture admit exception of children. A perfect example of this is the conversion of the jailer of St. Paul and Silas, *"And he took them the same hour of the night, and washed their wounds, and he was baptized at once, with all his family."* **Acts 16:33**

Q. Where in Scripture does it state that Baptism takes the place of circumcision?

A. From the following words of the Apostle Paul to believers: *Ye are circumcised with the circumcision made without hands, in putting off the body of the sins of the flesh, by the circumcision of Christ, buried with Him in Baptism.* **Coloss. 2:11,12**

Q. Why are there sponsors at Baptism?

A. In order that they may stand as witnesses before the Church for the faith of the baptized, and after Baptism, if need be, assume the religious education of the child if the parents neglect to do so.

Q. Why before baptizing do we use exorcism?

A. To drive away the devil, who since Adam's fall has had power over men. The Apostle Paul says that all men, without grace, *walk according to the course of this world, according to the prince of the power of the air, the spirit that now works in the children of disobedience.* **Ephes. 2: 2**

Q. What name bears the force of exorcism?

A. The name of Jesus Christ, invoked with prayer and faith. Jesus Christ gave to believers this promise. *In My name shall they cast out devils.* **Mark 16:17**

Q. What force does the sign of the cross have on this and other occasions?

A. What the name of Jesus Christ crucified is when pronounced with faith by motion of the lips, the same is true concerning the sign of the cross when made with faith by motion of the hand, or represented in any other way.

Q. When did the sign of the cross originate?

A. From the times of the Apostles.

Q. What does the white garment, which is put on after Baptism symbolize?

A. The purity of the soul and of the Christian life.

Q. Why do they often place a small cross upon the baptized?

A. As a visible expression and continual remembrance of Christ's command: *If any man will come after me. let him deny himself, and take up his cross, and follow Me.* **Mat. 16:24**

Q. What is symbolized by giving the baptized a candle?

A. Spiritual joy joined with spiritual illumination.

Q. How is this to be understood, that in the Creed we confess one Baptism?

A. That Baptism cannot be repeated.

Q. Why cannot Baptism be repeated?

A. Baptism is spiritual birth: a man is born but once; therefore, he is also baptized but once.

Q. What is the state of those who sin after Baptism?

A. That they are more guilty of their sins than the unbaptized, since they had from God special help to do well, and have cast it away.

For if after they have escaped the pollutions of the world through the knowledge of the Lord and Saviour Jesus Christ, they are again entangled therein and overcome, the latter end is worse with them that the beginning. **II Pet. 2:20**

Q. Is there another way for those who sin after Baptism to obtain pardon?

A. There is; through the Sacrament of Penance.

On Confirmation:

Q. What is Confirmation, or Chrismation?

A. Confirmation/Chrismation, is a Sacrament in which the baptized believer, being anointed with holy chrism in the name of the Holy Spirit, as well as having hands laid on him, receives the gifts of the Holy Spirit for growth and strength in spiritual life, and full membership in the universal priesthood of the laity. **I John 2:20-27; 2 Cor. 1: 21,22**

Q. Is the outward form of anointing with chrism mentioned in Holy Scripture?

A. It may well be supposed that the words of St. John refer to a visible as well as to an inward anointing; but it is more certain that the Apostles, for imparting to the baptized the gifts of the Holy Spirit, used *imposition of hands.* **Acts 7:14-16**

Q. What is to be said of the holy chrism?

A. That its consecration is reserved to the hands of the Hierarchy, as successors of the Apostles, who used the laying on of their own hands to communicate the gifts of the Holy Spirit.

Q. What is signified by anointing the forehead?

A. The sanctification of the mind, which governs the whole person.

On the Holy Eucharist:

Q. What is the Holy Eucharist?

A. The Holy Eucharist is a Sacrament in which the believer, under the forms of bread and wine, partakes of the true Body and Blood of Christ unto everlasting life.

Q. How was this Sacrament instituted?

A. Jesus Christ immediately before His passion consecrated it for the first time, showing in it by anticipation a sign of His sufferings for our salvation. After having administered it to the Apostles, He gave them at the same time the power to perpetuate this Sacrament.

Q. What is to be said of the Sacrament of the Holy Eucharist in regard to Divine Service in the Church?

A. That it forms the chief and most essential part of Divine Service.

Q. What is the name of that Service, in which the Sacrament of the Holy Eucharist is consecrated?

A. The Liturgy or the Mass.

Q. What does the word *Liturgy* mean?

A. Common service.

The liturgy is the work or prayer of the entire Church, it is not owned by any particular local church. Nor is it the right of any part of local church to modify the liturgy. Because of this, the liturgy is not subject to individual or local modification, and the Church only uses that liturgy that is and has been historically used by the Church throughout the ages. Every liturgy then, must be properly done, without local adaptation, omission or modification.

Q. What does the word *Mass* mean?

A. Dismissal, taken from the end of the liturgy, where the Church is sent forth to bear Christ into the world.

Q. What is to be noted about the place where the Liturgy normally is celebrated?

A. It must normally be celebrated in a Church which the Bishop has approved.

Q. What does the word Church mean?

A. An assembly.

Rightly understood then, the Church is the *assembly* or *gathering of the faithful,* and not the building which houses them. And if the Church *is* an *assembly,* then an individual who refuses to be a part of the gathering of the faithful, is refusing to be part of the Church. Thus, an individualistic, "sola scriptura" declaration of faith, is fundamentally flawed and incorrect. The Catholic faith is a social, communal faith, requiring one to live out one's faith among others, both within the Church and for those outside of it as well.

Q. Why is the table on which the Liturgy or Mass is celebrated called an altar?

A. Because on it Jesus Christ, as King, is mystically present and offered.

Q. What are the two major divisions of the Mass?

A. First, the Mass of the Catechumens, or instructional part; second, the Mass of the Faithful or the Eucharist proper.

Q. What are the divisions of the Mass of the Catechumens?

A. 1.   Confession of sin.
    2.   Praise.
    3.   Prayer.
    4.   Epistle.
    5.   Gospel.
    6.   Sermon (Homily)

Q. What are the major Divisions of the Mass of the Faithful?

A. 1.   Offering of bread and wine
    2.   The Eucharistic Prayer or Canon.
    3.   The Invocation of the Holy Spirit and the Words of Institution. **Mat. 26:26-28**

4. Prayers for the Living and the Dead.

5. The Lord's Prayer.

6. Breaking of the Sacred Bread.

7. The Communion Rite.

8. The Thanksgiving.

9. The Blessing and Dismissal.

Q. Why is the bread used in the Mass sometimes called the Lamb or Host?

A. Because it is the figure of Jesus Christ suffering, as was in the Old Testament *the Paschal Lamb,* and because He is the Victim (Hostia) or Host of the Sacrifice.

Q. What was the Paschal Lamb?

A. The lamb which the Israelites, by God's command, killed and ate in memory of their deliverance from destruction in Egypt; it was offered in sacrifice.

Q. Why is the wine for the Mass or Liturgy mixed with water?

A. Because the whole of this celebration is ordered so as to show forth the sufferings of Christ; and when He suffered there flowed from His pierced side blood and water.

Q. What happens at the moment of Invocation—Consecration in the Mass?

A. At the moment of this act, the bread and wine are changed, or transubstantiated, into the Body and Blood of Christ.

Q. How are we to understand the word *transubstantiation?*

A. That the bread truly, really, and substantially becomes the true Body of the Lord, and the wine the true Blood of the Lord. It is a mystery, which the mind cannot understand, but it is received in faith.

As a mystery of our faith, we do not know, nor can we explain how it happens, nor do we attempt to do so. We do however, boldly state that the bread and wine are transformed and become Christ Jesus, Body, Blood, Soul and Divinity; and are made present for us to partake of, as did His Apostles, as He presented them, by His declaration, His Body and Blood. We do not, then, seek to explain how it occurs, we seek to faithfully profess that it does occur. Any word used to describe this true Mystery of our faith will be inadequate, and fall short of describing God's Love, Grace and Supernatural Will involving in this great Sacrament, also rightly understood as a sacramentum (oath), and much more.

Q. What is required of everyone who approaches the Sacrament of Holy Communion?

A. Each one is required to examine his conscience before God, to confess one's sins, to seek absolution, and to fast according to the laws of the Church. **I Cor. 11:28, 29**

Q. What benefit does one receive who communicates in the Body and Blood of Christ?

A. He is in the closest manner united to Jesus Christ Himself, and, in Him, is made partaker of everlasting life. **John 6:56; 5:54**

Q. Should we communicate often in the Holy Mysteries of Christ.

A. The primitive Christians communicated every Lord's Day. The Church calls on all who would live religiously to confess before their heavenly Father, and communicate in the Body and Blood of Christ whenever they attend Mass or are ill, but requires all without exception to receive It at least once a year during the Easter time.

Having that great spiritual blessing available, we should avail ourselves of this great Supernatural Gift as often as possible, insofar as we are in a state of grace and disposed by the Church to do so.

Q. What part do they have in the Liturgy or the Mass who only hear it without receiving Holy Communion.

A. They may and should take part of the Liturgy by prayer and faith, and especially by continual remembrance of our Lord Jesus Christ, who expressly has commanded us *to do this in remembrance of Him.* **Luke 22:19**

Q. What should we remember at the time in the Liturgy when the Gospel is proclaimed?

A. That Jesus Christ is present to preach the Gospel. Therefore, we should have the same attention and reverence, as if we saw and heard Jesus Christ in the flesh.

Q. What should we remember at the time in the Liturgy when the bread and wine are offered?

A. That Jesus Christ is going to suffer voluntarily as a victim to the slaughter.

Q. What should we remember at the moment of the consecration of the bread and wine?

A. The Last Supper of Jesus Christ himself with His Apostles, and also His suffering, death, burial, resurrection, Ascension, and that He will come again to His people.

Q. Will the Sacrament of the Holy Eucharist continue forever in the true Church of Christ?

A. Yes, it will continue until Christ's coming again, as the Apostle Paul testified: *For as often as ye eat this bread, and drink this cup, ye do show forth the Lord's death, till He come.* **I Cor. 11:26**

On the Sacrament of Penance:

Q. What is Penance?

A. Penance is a Sacrament in which he who confesses receives, through the absolution of the Priest, forgiveness of his sins by Jesus Christ Himself. **Mark 1:4,5; Mat. 18:18; John 20:22,23**

"On the evening of that day, the first day of the week, the doors being shut where the disciples were, for fear of the Jews, Jesus came and stood among them and said to them, 'Peace be with you.' When he had said this, he showed them his hands and his side. Then the disciples were glad when they saw the Lord. Jesus said to them again, 'Peace be with you. As the Father has sent me, even so I send you.' And when he had said this, he breathed on them and said to them, 'Receive the Holy Spirit. If you forgive the sins of any, they are forgiven; if you retain the sins of any, they are retained." **John 20:–22**

Q. What is required of the Penitent.

A. Contrition for his sins, with full purpose of amendment of life, faith in Jesus Christ, and hope in His mercy. **II Cor. 7:10; Ezek. 33:19**

A confession that is not accompanied by contrition, cannot obtain for the confessor the Sacrament of Penance.

Q. In what ways can we prepare for the Sacrament?

A. By fasting, prayer, examination of conscience, and by penance.

Q. What is meant by the term *penance?*

A. The word means contrition. See **2 Cor. 2:6.**

On the Sacrament of Holy Orders:

Q. What is Holy Orders?

A. Holy Orders is a Sacrament in which the Holy Spirit, through the laying on of the bishop's hands, ordains those who are chosen to administer the sacraments, and to feed the flock of Christ. *Let a man so account of us, as of the ministers of Christ, and stewards of the Mysteries of God.* **I Cor. 4:1**

Take heed therefore unto yourselves, and to all the flock, over which the Holy Spirit has made you overseers, to feed the Church of God, which He has purchased with His own Blood. **Acts 20:28**

Q. What does it mean to feed the Church?

A. It means to instruct the people in faith, piety, and good works.

Q. How many necessary degrees are there of Holy Orders?

A. Three: those of Bishop, Priest, and Deacon.

Q. What difference is there between them?

A. The Deacon serves at the altar; the Priest administers the Sacraments in dependence upon the Bishop; the Bishop not only administers the Sacraments himself, but has power also to ordain to others, by laying on of his hands, the office of Deacon, Priest, and Bishop.

Of the Episcopal power the Apostle Paul writes to Titus: *For this cause I Left thee in Crete, that thou should set in order the things that are wanting. and ordain elders in every city.* **Titus 1:5**

And to Timothy: *Lay hands suddenly on no man.* **I Tim. 5:22**

On the Sacrament of Matrimony:

Q. What is Matrimony?

A. Matrimony is a Sacrament in which, on the free promise of the man and woman before the Priest and the Church to be true to each other, their union is blessed to be an image of Christ's union with the Church, and grace is asked for them to live together in love and honesty, and for the procreation and Christian upbringing of children.

Q. From what source do we know that Matrimony is a Sacrament?

A. From the following words of the Apostle Paul: *A man shall leave his father and mother, and shall be joined unto his wife, and they two shall be one flesh. This mystery is great; but I speak concerning Christ and the Church.* **Eph. 5:31,32**

Q. Is it the duty of all to marry?

A. No. Virginity is another way in which to serve Christ. **Mat. 19:11,12; 1 Cor: 7:8,9,32,33,38**

One may become a consecrated virgin, as did the Ever-Virgin Mary, in the service of God, devoting one's entire live in service to Him. For one who can, this is a most honorable and worthy state of life, honored by the Church throughout its entire history.

On the Sacrament of Anointing of the Sick:

Q. What is Anointing of the Sick?

A. Anointing of the Sick is a Sacrament in which, while the body is anointed with oil, God's grace is invoked on the sick person to heal him of spiritual and bodily illnesses.

Q. What is the origin in Scripture of this Sacrament?

A. From the Apostles, who having received power from Jesus Christ, *anointed with oil many that were sick, and healed them.* **Mark 6:13**

The Apostles left this Sacrament to the Priests of the Church, as is evident from the following words of the Apostle James: *Is any sick among you? Let him call for the Elders of the Church; and let them pray over him, anointing him with oil in the name of the Lord: and the prayer of faith shall save the sick, and the Lord shall raise him up: and if he have committed sins, they shall be forgiven him.* **James 5:14,15**

On the Eleventh Article:

Q. What is the *resurrection of the dead.* which, in the words of the Creed, we *look for* or expect?

A. An act of the almighty power of God, by which the bodies of dead men, being reunited to their souls, shall return to life, and shall be made glorious and immortal. *It is sown a natural body, it is raised a spiritual body.* **I Cor. 15:44**

For this corruptible must put on incorruption and mortal must put on immortality. **Ib. 53.**

Q. How shall the body rise again after it has decomposed in the ground?

A. Since God formed the body from the ground originally, He can equally restore it after it has perished in the ground. The Apostle Paul illustrates this by the analogy of a grain of seed, which decomposes in the earth, but from which there springs up afterwards a plant of tree. *That which thou sows in not quickened except it die.* **I Cor. 15:36**

Q. Shall all strictly speaking rise again?

A. All, without exception, that have died; but they, who at the time of the general resurrection shall still be alive, shall have their present mortal bodies changed in a moment, so as to become spiritual and immortal.

We shall not all sleep, but we shall all be changed, in a moment, in the twinkling of an eye, at the last trump; for the trumpet shall sound, and the dead shall be raised incorruptible, and we shall be changed. **I Cor. 15:36**

Q. When shall the resurrection of the dead be?

A. At the end of the visible world.

Q. Shall the world then too come to an end?

A. Yes; this corruptible world shall come to an end, and shall be transformed into an incorruptible one. *Because the creature itself also shall be delivered from the bondage of corruption into the glorious liberty of the children of God.* **Rom. 8:21**

Nevertheless we, according to His promise, look for new heavens and a new earth, wherein dwells righteousness. **II Pet. 3:13**

Q. How shall the world be transformed?

A. By fire. *The heavens and the earth, which are not, by the same,* that is by God's word, *are kept in store, reserved unto fire against the day of judgment and perdition of ungodly men.* **II Pet. 3:7**

Q. In what state are the souls of the dead until the general resurrection?

A. The souls of the righteous are in light and rest, with a foretaste of eternal happiness; but the souls of the wicked are in a state the reverse of this.

Q. Why may we not ascribe to the souls of the saved perfect happiness immediately after death?

A. Because it is ordained that the perfect retribution according to works shall be received by the perfect man, after the resurrection of the body and God's last judgment.

The Apostle Paul says: *Hence forth there is laid up for me a crown of righteousness, which the Lord, the righteous Judge, shall give me at that day: and not to me only, but unto all them also that love His appearing.* **II Tim. 4:8**

And again; *We must all appear before the Judgment-seat of Christ; that everyone may receive the things done in his body, according to what He has done, whether it be good or bad.* **II Cor. 5:10**

Q. Why do we speak of the souls of the saved as having a taste of bliss before the last judgment?

A. Jesus Christ Himself has said in a parable that Lazarus was immediately after death carried into Abraham's bosom. **Luke 16:22**

Q. Is this foretaste of bliss joined with a sight of Christ's own countenance?

A. It is so with the Saints, as we are given to understand by the Apostle Paul, who *had a desire to depart, and to be with Christ.* **Philipp. 1:23**

Q. What is to be said of such souls who have departed with faith, but without having had time to bring forth fruits worthy of repentance?

A. That they may be aided towards the attainment of a blessed resurrection by prayers offered in their behalf, especially such as are offered in union with the Bloodless Sacrifice of the Body and Blood of Christ, and by works of mercy done in faith for their memory.

Q. On what is this doctrine grounded?

A. On the constant tradition of the Catholic Church; the source of which may be seen even in the Church of the Old Testament. Judas Maccabeus offered sacrifice for his men who had died. **II Macc. 12:43** Prayer for the departed has ever formed a fixed part of the Liturgy of the Apostle James.

On the Twelfth Article:

Q. What is *the life of the world to come*?

A. The life that shall be after the resurrection of the dead and the general judgment of Christ.

Q. What kind of life shall this be?

A. For those who believe, who love God, and do what is good, it shall be a life of happiness. *It does not yet appear what we shall be.* **I John 3:2**

I knew a man in Christ, says the Apostle Paul, *who was caught up into Paradise, and heard unspeakable words, which it is not lawful for a man to utter.* **II Cor.12:2,4**

Q. What is the object of this great happiness?

A. The contemplation of God in light and glory, and union with Him. *For now we see through a glass darkly, but then face to face: now I know in part, but then shall I know, even as also I am known.* **I Cor. 13:12**

Then shall the righteous shine forth as the sun, in the kingdom of their Father. **Mat. 13:43**

God shall be all in all. **I Cor. 15:28**

Q. Shall the body also share in the happiness of the soul?

A. Yes; it, too, shall be glorified with the light of God, as Christ's body was at His Transfiguration on Mount Tabor. *It is sown in dishonor, it is raised in glory.* **I Cor. 15:43**

As we have borne the image of the earthy, that is of Adam, *we shall also bear the image of the heavenly.* **ib. 49**

Q. Will all be equally happy?

A. No. There will be different degrees of happiness, in proportion to the faith, love, and good works carried out in this life.

There is one glory of the sun, and another glory of the moon, and another glory of the stars: for one star differs from another star in glory. So also is the resurrection of the dead. **I Cor. 15:41,42**

Q. But what will be the lot of unbelievers and transgressors?

A. They will be given over to everlasting death, that is, to everlasting fire, to everlasting torment, with the devils. *Whosoever was not found written in the book of life, was cast into the lake of fire.* **Rev. 20:15**

That is the second death. **Rev. 20:14**

Depart from Me, ye cursed, into everlasting fire, prepared for the devil and his angels. **Mat. 25:41**

And these shall go away into everlasting punishment, but the righteous into life eternal. **ib. 46**

It is better for thee to enter into the kingdom of God with one eye, that having two eyes to be cast into hell fire; where their worm dies not, and the fire is not quenched. **Mark 9:47,48**

Q. Why will such severity be used with sinners?

A. Not because God willed them to perish, but they of their own will *perish, because they receive not the love of the truth, that they might be saved.* **II Thess. 2:10**

Q. Of what benefit will it be for us to meditate on death, on the resurrection, on the last judgment, on everlasting happiness, and on everlasting torment?

A. These meditations will assist us to abstain from sin, and to uplift our affections from earthly things; they will console us for the absence or loss of earthly goods, encourage us to keep our souls and bodies pure, to live for God, and for eternity.

THE SECOND PART: ON HOPE

Definition of Christian Hope:

Q. What is Christian Hope?

A. The resting of the heart on God, with full trust that He always cares for our salvation, and will give us the happiness He has promised.

Q. What is the Scriptural source of Christian Hope?

A. The Lord Jesus is our hope, or the source of our hope. **I Tim. 1:1** *Hope to the end for the grace that is to be brought unto you by the revelation of Jesus Christ.* **I Pet. 1:13**

Q. What are the means for attaining to a saving hope?

A. The means to this are: first, prayer: second, the Beatitudes, and their practice.

On Prayer:

Q. Is there any testimony of God's word, that prayer is a means for attaining a saving hope?

A. Jesus Christ Himself joins the hope of receiving our desire with prayer: *Whatsoever ye shall ask of the Father in My name, that will I do, that the Father may be glorified in the Son.* **John 14:13**

Q. What is prayer?

A. The lifting up of man's mind and heart and soul to God.

Our English word, "pray", means "to ask". Strictly speaking prayer is asking of God, both directly and also accompanied with the intercessory prayers of saints, both those in the Church Militant on earth and those in the Church Triumphant in Heaven, some divine blessing, forgiveness or the granting of some petition.

This is meant differently than prayer to saints, which is always understood, as asking them to pray *with* us and *for* us, with respect to our petition. It is *never* understood to mean that the saints in heaven are accorded any honor other than that accorded a creation glorified by our Creator as faithful servants (dulia). This, as well as the great honor given the Ever-Virgin Mary (hyper-dulia), is not the same as that unbridled praise, worship and superlative honor that is due to God, *and God alone* (latria).

Q. What should Christians do when we they lift up our minds and hearts and souls to God?

A. First, we should glorify Him for His divine perfection; second, give thanks to Him for his mercies; third, seek His forgiveness; and fourth, ask God for what we need, So there are four chief forms of prayer: Praise, Thanksgiving, Contrition, and Petition.

Q. Can a man pray without words?

A. He can; in mind and heart. An example of this may be seen in Moses before the passage through the Red Sea. **Exod. 15:15**

On the Lord's Prayer:

Q. Is there a prayer which may be termed the common Christian prayer, and pattern of all prayers?

A. Such is the Lord's Prayer.

Q. What is the Lord's Prayer?

A. A prayer which our Lord Jesus Christ taught the Apostles, and which they delivered to all believers:

Q. How may we divide the Lord's Prayer?

A. Into the invocation and seven petitions.

"Our Father, Who art in heaven;
1. Hallowed be Thy name;
2. Thy kingdom come;
3. Thy will be done, on earth as it is in heaven.

4. Give us this day our daily bread,

5. And for give us our trespasses, as we for give those who trespass against us.

6. And lead us not into temptation;

7. But deliver us from evil. Amen."

On the Invocation:

Q. How are we able to call God *Father*?

A. By faith in Jesus Christ, and by the grace of regeneration. *As many as received Him, to them gave He power to become sons of God, even to them that believe on His name; which were born, not of blood, nor of the will of the flesh, nor of the will of man, but God.* **John 1:12,13**

"Therefore be imitators of God, as beloved children. And walk in love, as Christ loved us and gave himself up for us, a fragrant offering and sacrifice to God." **Eph 5:1-2.**

"For all who are led by the Spirit of God are sons of God. For you did not receive the spirit of slavery to fall back into fear, but you have received the spirit of sonship. When we cry, 'Ab'ba! Father!' it is the Spirit himself bearing witness without spirit that we are children of God, and if children, then heirs, heirs of God and fellow heirs with Christ, provided we suffer with him in order that we may also be glorified with him." **Rom. 8:14-17.**

Salvation then, is nothing less than Divine Sonship, wherein we are adopted into the Household of God. We are, in salvation and justification, not merely declared justified, but at that same moment we become spiritually justified by God's grace. For that which God declares, in that selfsame act; He does, as He spoke the entire world into existence.

Q. Why do we say *Our Father* even when we pray alone?

A. Because Christian charity requires us to call upon God, and ask good things of Him, for all our brethren, no less than for ourselves.

Q. Why in the invocation do we say, *Who art in heaven*?

A. That entering into prayer we may leave everything earthly and corruptible and raise our minds and hearts to what is heavenly, everlasting, and Divine.

On the First Petition:

Q. Is God's Name holy?

A. *Holy is His Name.* Luke 1:49

Q. How then can it yet be made holy?

A. It may be made holy in men; that is, His eternal holiness may be made known in them. Mat. 5:16

On the Second Petition:

Q. What is the kingdom of God, spoken of in the second petition of the Lord's Prayer?

A. The kingdom of grace, which, as St. Paul says, is *righteousness, and peace, and joy in the Holy Spirit.* Rom. 14:17

Q. Has not this kingdom come already?

A. To some it has not come in its full sense; while to others it has not yet come at all, inasmuch as *sin still reigns in their mortal bodies, that they should obey it in the lusts thereof.* Rom. 7:12

Q. How does it come?

A. Secretly and inwardly. *The kingdom of God comes not with observation; for behold, the kingdom of God is within you.* Luke 17:20,21

Q. May not the Christian ask for something further under the name of God's kingdom?

A. He may ask for the kingdom of glory, that is, for the perfect bliss of the faithful. *Having a desire to depart, and be with Christ.* Philipp. 1:23

On the Third Petition:

Q. What does the petition. *Thy will be done* mean?

A. In this petition we ask God, that all we do, and all that happens to us may be not as we will, but as pleases Him.

Q. Why should we ask this favor?

A. Because we often err in our wishes; but God unerringly, and incomparably more than we ourselves, wishes for us all that is good, and is ever ready to bestow it, unless He be prevented by our willingness and stubbornness.

Unto Him that is able to do exceeding abundantly above all that we ask or think, according to the power that works in us, unto Him be glory in the Church. **Ephes. 3:20,21**

Q. Why do we ask that God's will be done in earth *as in heaven*?

A. Because in heaven the Holy Angels and Saints in bliss, all without exception, always, and in all things, do God's will.

On the Fourth Petition:

Q. What is *our daily bread*?

A. The bread which we need in order to subsist or live.

Q. With what thoughts should we ask God for this bread?

A. Agreeably with the instruction of Our Lord Jesus Christ, we should ask no more than bread for subsistence; that is, necessary food, and such clothing and shelter as is likewise necessary for life; but whatever is beyond this, and serves not so much for necessity as for gratification, we should leave to the will of God; and if it be given, return thanks to Him; if it be not given, we should be content without it.

Q. Why are we directed to ask for bread for subsistence only for this day?

A. That we may not be too anxious about the future, trusting God. *Take therefore no thought for the morrow, for the morrow shall take thought for the things of itself: sufficient unto the day is the evil thereof.* **Mat. 6:34**

For your heavenly Father knows that ye have need of all these things. **ib. 32**

Q. May we not ask for something further under the name of bread for subsistence?

A. Since man is made of both bodily and a spiritual substance, and the substance of the soul far excels that of the body, we may and should seek for the soul also that bread of subsistence, without which the inward man must perish of hunger.

Q. What is the bread of subsistence for the soul?

A. The Word of God, and the Body and Blood of Christ. *Man shall not live by bread alone, but by every word that proceeds out of the mouth of God.* **Matt 4:4**

My Flesh is meat indeed, and my Blood is drink indeed. **John 6:55**

On the Fifth Petition:

Q. What is meant in the Lord's Prayer by *our trespasses*?

A. Our sins.

Q. Why are our sins called trespasses?

A. Because we, having received all from God, ought to render all back to Him, that is subject all to His will and law.

Q. Who are *those who trespass against us*?

A. People who have not rendered us that which they owed us by the law of God; as, for instance, have not shown us love, but malice.

Q. If God is just, how can we be forgiven our trespasses?

A. Through the mediation of Jesus Christ. *For there is one God, and one Mediator between God and man, the man Jesus Christ, who gave himself ransom for all.* **I Tim. 2:5,6**

Q. What will be the consequence if we ask God to forgive us our sins without ourselves forgiving others?

A. In that case we shall not be forgiven.

For if ye forgive men their trespasses, your heavenly Father will also forgive you; but if you forgive not men their trespasses, neither will your Father forgive you your trespasses. **Mat. 6:14,15**

Q. Why will God not forgive us if we do not forgive others?

A. Because we show ourselves unrepentant, and so alienate from us God's goodness and mercy.

In becoming the adopted sons and daughters of God, we are expected to imitate our Heavenly Father in His ways of love and compassion.

Q. What disposition then must we have when we pray *we forgive those who trespass against us*.

A. These words absolutely require that when we pray we should bear no malice nor hatred, but be in peace and charity with all men.

Therefore if thou bring thy gift to the altar, and there remember that thy brother has aught against thee, leave there thy gift before the altar, and go thy way; first be reconciled to thy brother, and then come and offer thy gift. **Mat. 5:23,24**

If you have wronged someone, or are inclined to continue to wrong someone, you must ask forgiveness and you must release your malice against that person, so that your sacrifice be brought with a pure heart.

Q. But what am I to do if I cannot readily find him who holds malice toward me, or if he is unwilling to be reconciled?

A. In such a case it is enough to be reconciled with him in heart, before the eyes of the all-seeing God. *If it be possible, as much as lies in you, live peaceably with all men.* **Rom. 12:18**

On the Sixth Petition:

Q. What is meant in the Lord's Prayer by *temptation*?

A. Any circumstance in which there is imminent danger of losing the faith, or falling into great sin.

Q. What are the sources of temptation?

A. From our flesh, from the world, or other people, and from the devil.

Q. What do we ask in these words of the prayer, *Lead us not into temptation*?

A. That God guide us during times of temptation in the keeping of His laws.

On the Seventh Petition:

Q. What do we ask in these words of the prayer, *deliver us from evil?*

A. We ask for deliverance from all evil that can reach us in the world, which since the fall *lies in wickedness*; I John 5:19; but especially from the evil of sin, and from the evil temptations of the spirit of evil, which is the devil.

Q. What does the word *Amen* mean?

A. It means <u>so be it</u>.

Q. Why is this word added to the end of prayers?

A. To signify that we offer the prayer in faith, and with out doubting, as we are taught to do by the Apostle James in his Epistle, 1:6.

On the Doctrine of Blessedness:

Q. What must we join with prayer, in order to be grounded in the hope of salvation and blessedness?

A. Our own works for the attainment of blessedness. Of the point the Lord Himself says: *Why call ye Me Lord, Lord, and do not the things which I say?* **Luke 6:46**

Not every one that says unto Me Lord, Lord shall enter into the kingdom of heaven, but he that does the will of my Father, which is in heaven. **Mat. 7:21**

Q. What doctrine may we take as our guide in these works?

A. The doctrine of our Lord Jesus Christ, which is briefly set forth in His Beatitudes, or sentences on blessedness.

Q. How many such sentences are there?

A. The Following nine:

1. Blessed are the poor in spirit: for theirs is the kingdom of Heaven.
2. Blessed are they that mourn: for they shall be comforted.
3. Blessed are the meek: for they shall inherit the earth.
4. Blessed are they which hunger and thirst after righteousness: for they shall be filled.

5. Blessed are the merciful: for they shall obtain mercy.

6. Blessed are the pure in heart: for they shall see God.

7. Blessed are the peacemakers: for they shall be called the children of God.

8. Blessed are they that are persecuted for righteousness' sake: for theirs is the kingdom of heaven.

9. Blessed are ye, when men shall revile you, and persecute you, and shall say all manner of evil against you falsely, for My sake. Rejoice, and be exceedingly glad: for great is your reward in heaven. **Mat. 5:3-12**

Q. What is to be observed of all these Beatitudes?

A. That the Lord proposed in these sentences a doctrine for the attainment of blessedness, as is expressly said in the Gospel; *He opened His mouth, and taught*; but, being meek and lowly of heart, He proposed His doctrine not in the form of a commandment, but a blessing to those, who should of their own free will receive and fulfill it. Consequently in each sentence or Beatitude we must consider, first, the doctrine or precept, and second, the blessing or promise of reward.

On the First Beatitude:

Q. What is the Lord's first precept of blessedness?

A. They who would be blessed must be *poor in spirit.*

Q. What does it mean to be *poor in spirit*?

A. It is to have a spiritual conviction that we have nothing of our own, nothing but what God bestows upon us, and that we can do nothing good without God's help and grace, thus counting ourselves as nothing, and in all things, throwing ourselves upon the mercy of God: in brief, as St. John Chrysostom explains it, *spiritual poverty is humility.* **Hom. on Mat. 15**

Q. Can the rich too be poor in spirit?

A. Most certainly, if they live in a manner that shows that visible riches are corruptible and soon pass away, and can never compensate for the want of spiritual goods. *What is a man profited, if he gain the whole world, and lose his own soul? Or what shall a man give in exchange for his soul?* **Mat. 16:26**

Q. Can bodily poverty aid in spiritual perfection?

A. It can, if the Christian chooses it voluntarily for God's sake. Of this, Jesus Christ Himself said to the rich man: *If thou will be perfect, go, sell that thou has, and give to the poor, and thou shalt have treasure in heaven; and come follow Me.* Mat. 19:21

Q. What does our Lord promise to the poor in spirit?

A. The kingdom of heaven.

Q. How is the kingdom of heaven theirs?

A. In the present life, inwardly through faith and hope; but in the life to come perfectly, by their being made partakers of everlasting blessedness.

On the Second Beatitude:

Q. What is the Lord's second precept for blessedness?

A. They who would be blessed must mourn.

Q. What is meant in this precept by the word *mourn*?

A. Sorrow and change of heart for unworthy serving the Lord, or even rather for deserving His anger by our sins. *For godly sorrow works repentance unto salvation not to be repented of; but the sorrow of this world works death.* **II Cor. 7:10**

Q. What special promise does the Lord make to mourners?

A. They *shall be comforted.*

Q. What comfort is here to be understood?

A. That of grace, consisting in the pardon of sins and in peace of conscience.

Q. Why is this promise joined with a precept for mourning?

A. In order that sorrow for sin may not reach to despair.

On the Third Beatitude:

Q. What is the Lord's third precept of blessedness?

A. They who would be blessed must be meek.

Q. What is meekness?

A. A quiet attitude of spirit, joined with the care neither to offend any man, nor be offended at anything.

Q. What are the special effects of Christian meekness?

A. That we never speak against God, nor against men, nor give way to anger.

Q. What is promised by the Lord to the meek?

A. That *they shall inherit the earth.*

Q. How are we to understand this promise?

A As regards Christ's followers generally it is a prediction which is being literally fulfilled; for the ever-meek Christians instead of being destroyed by the anger of unbelievers, will inherit the universe. But the further sense of the promise, as regards Christians both generally and individually, is this that they shall receive an inheritance, as the Psalmist says, *in the land of the living:* that is, where men live and never die; in other words, that they shall receive everlasting blessedness. *See* Psalm 27:15.

On the Fourth Beatitude:

Q. What is the Lord's fourth precept for blessedness?

A. They who would be blessed must *hunger and thirst after righteousness.*

Q. What is meant here by the word *righteousness?*

A. Though this word may well stand for every virtue, which the Christian ought to desire, yet we should especially understand it to mean the justification of guilty man through grace and faith in Jesus Christ. **Dan. 9:24**

The Apostle Paul speaks thus: *The righteousness of God which is by faith of Jesus Christ unto all, and upon all them that believe: for there is no difference: for all have sinned, and come short of the glory of God; being justified freely by His grace through the redemption that is in Christ Jesus, whom God has set forth to be a propitiation through faith in His blood, to declare His righteousness for the remission of sins that are past.* **Rom. 3:22-25**

Q. Who are they that *hunger and thirst after righteousness?*

A. They who, while they love to do good, do not become proud, nor rest on their own good works, but admit that they are sinners and guilty before God; and who, through the prayer of faith, seek after justification of grace through Jesus Christ.

Q. What does the Lord promise to them who hunger and thirst after righteousness?

A. That they *shall be filled.*

Q. What is meant here by *filled?*

A. As the filling or satisfying of the body produces, first, an end to the sense of hunger and thirst, and second, the strengthening of the body by food; so the filling of the soul means, first, the inward peace of the pardoned sinner, and second, the ability to do good, given through justifying grace. The perfect filling, however, of the soul created for the enjoyment of eternal good, is to follow in the life eternal, according to the words of the Psalmist: *When I awake up after Thy likeness, I shall be satisfied with it.* **Ps. 17:15**

On the Fifth Beatitude:

Q. What is the Lord's fifth precept of blessedness?

A. They who would be blessed must be merciful.

Q. How are we to fulfill this precept?

A. By works of mercy, corporal and spiritual; for as St. John Chrysostom says, *the forms of mercy are manifold, and this commandment broad.* **Hom. on Mat. 15**

Q. Which are the corporal works of mercy?

A. 1. To feed the hungry.
    2. To give drink to the thirsty.
    3. To clothe the naked, or such as have not necessary and decent clothing.

4. To visit those who are in prison.

5. To visit the sick, minister to them, or aid them in Christian preparation for death.

6. To show hospitality to strangers.

7. To bury those who have died in poverty.

Q. Which are the spiritual works of mercy?

A. 1. By exhortation *to convert the sinner from the error of his way.* **James 5: 20**

2. To instruct the ignorant in truth and virtue.

3. To counsel our neighbor in times of difficulty.

4. To pray for others to God.

5. To comfort the afflicted.

6. Not to return the evil which others may have done to us.

7. To forgive injuries from our heart.

Q. Is it not contrary to the precept of mercy for civil justice to punish criminals?

A. Not in the least; if this be done as a duty, and with a good intent, that is, in order to correct them, or to preserve the innocent from their crimes.

Q. What does the Lord promise to the merciful?

A. That they *shall obtain mercy.*

Q. What specific kind of mercy is to be understood?

A. That of being delivered from everlasting condemnation for sin at God's Judgment.

On the Sixth Beatitude:

Q. What is the Lord's sixth precept for blessedness?

A. They who would be blessed must be *pure in heart.*

Q. Is not purity of heart the same thing as sincerity?

A. Sincerity which shows the really good disposition of the heart through good deeds is only the lowest degree of purity of heart. The greater form is attained by a constant and strict watchfulness over oneself, driving away from one's heart every unlawful wish and thought, and every attachment for earthly things, and ever preserving the remembrance of God and our Lord Jesus Christ with faith and charity.

Q. What does the Lord promise to the pure in heart?

A. That they *shall see God.*

Q. How are we to understand this promise?

A. The word of God compares the heart of man to the eye, and ascribed to perfect Christians *enlightened eyes of the heart.* **Ephes. 1:18** As the eye that is perceptive can see the light, so the heart that is pure can behold God. But since the sight of God's countenance is the very source of everlasting blessedness, the promise of seeing God is the promise of the highest degree of everlasting blessedness.

On the Seventh Beatitude:

Q. What is the Lord's seventh precept for blessedness?

A. They who would be blessed must be *peace-makers.*

Q. How are we to fulfill this commandment?

A. We must live peaceably with all men; if quarrels arise, we must try all possible ways to put a stop to it, even by yielding our own right, unless this be against duty, or hurtful to any other; if others are at odds, we must do all that we can to reconcile them, and if we fail, we must pray to God for their reconciliation.

Q. What does the Lord promise to the peace-makers?

A. That they *shall be called the Sons of God.*

Q. What is signified by this promise?

A. The sublimity both of their office and of their reward. Since in what they do they imitate the only-begotten Son of God, who came upon earth to reconcile fallen man with God's justice, they are for this act promised the gracious name of Sons of God, and without doubt a high degree of blessedness.

On the Eighth Beatitude:

Q. What is the Lord's eighth precept for blessedness?

A. They who would be blessed must be ready *to endure persecution for righteousness' sake,* without betraying it.

Q. What qualities are required by this precept?

A. Love of what is right, constancy and firmness in virtue, fortitude and patience when one is subjected to danger for refusing to betray truth and virtue.

Q. What does the Lord promise to those who are persecuted for righteousness' sake?

A. The *Kingdom of heaven.* In like manner the same is promised to the poor in spirit, to make up for the feeling of want and privation.

On the Ninth Beatitude:

Q. What is the Lord's ninth precept of blessedness?

A. They who would be blessed must be ready to take with joy reproach, persecution, suffering, and death itself, for the name of Christ, and for the true Christian faith.

Q. What is the name for the state required by this precept?

A. The state of Martyrdom.

Q. What does the Lord promise for this course?

A. *A great reward in heaven*; that is, a special and high degree of blessedness.

THE THIRD PART: ON CHARITY

On the Union between Faith and Charity:

Q. What should be the effect and fruit of true faith in the Christian?

A. Charity, or love, and good works. *In Jesus Christ,* says the Apostle Paul, *neither circumcision avails anything, nor uncircumcision, but faith which works by love.* **Gal. 5:6**

Q. Is not faith alone enough for a Christian, *without love and good works*?

A. No; for faith without love and good works is inactive and dead, and so cannot lead to eternal life. *He that loves not his brother, abides in death.* **I John 3:14**

A genuine faith is lived out in the life of the Christian. Scripture instructs us that Christian faith is concerned with the health and welfare of others; not only those we know and have brotherly affection for, but also and especially for those we do not. These good works are not to be confused with "works of the law" which St. Paul speaks against, which are the Mosaic laws that the Judiazers wanted the Gentile Christians compelled to observe, such as circumcision, the dietary kosher laws, the temple sacrifices and others. "Works of the law" is always a Jewish euphemism for Mosaic law, while the "works" identified by John and James are the corporal works of mercy, which should be in every Christian heart to do.

What does it profit, my brethren, though a man say he has faith, and have not works? Can faith save him? For as the body without the spirit is dead, so faith without works is dead also. James 2:14,26

Q. May not a man on the other hand be saved by love and good works, without faith?

A. It is impossible that a man who has not faith in God should really love Him: besides, man, being ruined by sin, cannot do truly good works, unless he receives through faith in Jesus Christ spiritual strength, or grace from God. **Heb. 11:6; Gal. 3:10; Ib. 5:5; Ephes. 2:8,9**

Q. What is to be thought of love that is not accompanied by good works?

A. Such love is not real: for true love naturally shows itself by good works. Jesus Christ says: *He that has my commandments, and keeps them, he it is that love me; if a man loves Me, he will keep My word.* **John 14:21,23**

The Apostle John writes: For this is the love of God, that we keep His commandments. **I John 5:3** Let us not love in word, neither in tongue, but in deed and in truth. **ib. 3:18**

On the Law of God and the Commandments:

Q. What means do we have to know good works form bad?

A. The inward law of God, or the witness of our conscience, and the outward law of God, or God's commandments.

Q. Does Holy Scripture speak of the inward law of God?

A. The Apostle Paul says of the heathen: *Which show the work of the law written in their hearts, their conscience also bearing witness, and their thoughts the meanwhile accusing or else excusing one another.* **Rom. 2:15**

Q. If there is in man's heart an inward law, why was the outward given?

A. It was given because men did not obey the inward law, but led carnal and sinful lives, and silenced within themselves the voice of the spiritual law, so that it was necessary to express this outwardly through the commandments. *Wherefore then serves the law? It was added because of transgressions.* **Gal. 3:19**

Q. When, and how, was God's outward law given to men?

A. When the Hebrew people, descended from Abraham, had been miraculously delivered from bondage in Egypt, on their way to the promised land, in the desert, on Mount Sinai, God manifested His presence in fire and clouds, and gave them the law, by the hand of Moses, their leader.

Q. Did Jesus Christ teach men to walk by the ten commandments?

A. He taught us that if we wished to attain everlasting life, to keep the commandments, and taught us to understand and fulfill them more perfectly, than had been done before He came. **Mat. 19:17, and 5**

On the Division of the Commandments into Two Tablets:

The division of the commandments is made in the Church, by example of the Hebrew text, made by St. Augustine in the fifth century. There is no numerical numbering of the commandments in the books of Moses, so the natural understanding of how they are divided must then come from how they were understood by the nation of Israel. This understanding is followed by the Church.

Q. What are the two divisions of the ten commandments?

A. Love of God, and love for our neighbor.

Q. Has not Jesus Christ taught the twofold commandments?

A. Jesus said: *Thou shalt love the Lord thy God with all thy heart, and with all thy soul, and with all thy mind. This is the first and greatest commandment. And the second is like unto it: "Thou shalt love thy neighbor as thyself." On these two com-mandments hang all the law and the prophets.* **Mat. 22:36-40**

Q. Are all men our neighbors?

A. Yes, all; because all are the creation of one God, and have come from one man: but our neighbors in faith are doubly neighbors to us, as being children of one heavenly Father by faith in Jesus Christ

Q. But why is there no commandment of love to ourselves?

A. Because normally we love ourselves naturally, and without any commandment. *No man ever yet hated his own flesh, but nourishes it and cherishes it.* **Ephes. 5:29**

Q. What order should there be in our love of God, our neighbor, and ourselves?

A. We should love ourselves not for our own but for God's sake, and partly also for the sake of our neighbors: we should love our neighbor for the sake of God: but we should love God for Himself, and above all. Love of self should be sacrificed to the love of our neighbor; but both should be sacrificed to the love of God. *Greater love has no man than this, that a man lay down his life for his friends.* **John 15:13**

He that loves father or mother more than Me, said Jesus Christ, *is not worthy of Me: and he that loves son or daughter more than Me, is not worthy of Me.* **Mat. 10:37**

Q. If the whole law is contained in two commandments, why are they divided into ten?

A. In order to more clearly set forth our duties towards God, and towards our neighbor.

Q. What are the Ten Commandments?

A. 1. I am the Lord thy God; thou shalt not have strange gods before Me.
2. Thou shalt not take the name of the Lord thy God in vain.
3. Remember thou keep holy the Sabbath Day.
4. Honor thy father and thy mother.
5. Thou shalt not kill.
6. Thou shalt not commit adultery.

7. Thou shalt not steal

8. Thou shalt not bear false witness against thy neighbor.

9. Thou shalt not covet thy neighbor's wife.

10. Thou shalt not covet thy neighbor's goods.

Q. Where do we find the Ten Commandments?

A. We find the Ten Commandments in the Book of Exodus, Chapter 20, verses 1-17.

Q. To whom did God give the Ten Commandments?

A. God gave the Ten Commandments to Moses, who in turn gave them to the Jewish people. **Ex. 31:18; Deut. 4:12-13; 5:22**

Q. Are we obliged to keep all the commandments?

A. Yes, we are obliged to keep the Ten Commandments, aided by the grace of God. **John 14:15, 24; James 2:10; Deut. 5:32-33**

Q. What is the first commandment?

A. The first commandment is: *I am the Lord thy God; thou shalt not have strange gods before me.* **Ex. 20:1-3; Deut. 5:6-7**

Q. What does the first commandment require of us?

A. By the first commandment we are required to worship God as Creator of heaven and earth, and Him alone. **Luke 10:25-28; Deut. 6:4-5**

Q. What is forbidden by this commandment?

A. 1. To worship false gods;

　　2. To give to anything or anyone the worship due God alone.

　　3. To worship Him with false worship.

　　Lev. 26:1; Is. 42:8; John 4:22

Q. In what ways would this commandment be broken?

A. This commandment can be broken in the following ways:

1. Idolatry, the worship of images and false gods.

2. By attributing to persons or things power that belongs to God alone, *i.e.* fortune tellers, spiritualists, Ouija boards, and the like;

3. By the participation in heretical worship.

Q. How do we show our adoration to God?

A. We show our adoration to God by keeping His commandments, by praying to Him, and especially by our participation in the holy Sacrifice of the Mass. **John 4:24; Rom. 12:1-2; I Cor. 2:17-27**

This extreme honor, and worship of God is called "latria", from the Latin, meaning "adoration." Accordingly the respect we pay to the Saints is not the same as this, and is called "dulia", from the Latin, meaning "veneration". The higher level of respect given to Mary is called "hyper-dulia", and is accorded her, as the "ark of the New Covenant" and Mother of God.

Q. Do Old Catholics break the first commandment by having crucifixes, statues, icons, pictures, or relics in their churches?

A. No, for crucifixes, statues, icons, pictures, and relics simply represent the persons symbolized as an aid to prayer. **Num. 21:8; Ex. 20:5**

The first commandment forbids idolatry and the worship of false gods; no member of the Church believes that a statue or icon is a god or any kind.

Q. What is the second commandment?

A. The second commandment is: *Thou shalt not take the name of the Lord thy God in vain.* **Ex. 20:7; Ez: 36:20-21; Rom. 2:24**

Q. When is God's name taken in vain?

A. God's Name is taken in vain whenever it is used improperly, especially when used in a lie or disrespectfully. **Lev. 5:4-5; II Chron. 32:16-17: Eccus. 23:9-12**

Q. What sins are forbidden by the second commandment?

A. The following sins are forbidden by the second commandment?

1. Blasphemy—daring words against God. **Ps 74:18**

2. Murmuring—complaining against God's Providence. **I Cor. 10:9-10**

3. Profanity—speaking lightly or irreverently about holy things. **Mal. 1:10-12**

4. Inattentiveness in prayer. **I Cor. 14:14-15**

5. Perjury—swearing a false oath. **Mat. 26:72**

6. Oath-breaking—breaking of promises. **Lev. 5:1,4**

Q. What is the third commandment?

A. The third commandment is; *Remember, thou keep holy the Sabbath Day.* **Ex. 20:8**

Q. Why did God command the Sabbath to be kept holy

A. God commanded the Sabbath to be kept holy because on this day God rested from His work of Creation. **Ex. 20:2** Also, by Church law, we are to give equal reverence to the Holy Days of Obligation.

Q. Why do we keep holy the first day of the week instead of the Sabbath or seventh day?

A. We keep holy the first day of the week faithful to the example of the Apostles in the early Church, who held the Eucharist on the first day of the week in remembrance of the facts that Christ rose from the dead and the Holy Spirit descended on the Apostles on a Sunday. **John 20:1; Acts 2:1-13; Acts 20:7**

Q. How are Old Catholics obliged to keep Sunday holy?

A. Old Catholics are obliged to keep Sunday holy by:

1. Assisting at Mass on all Sundays;

2. Refraining from all unnecessary servile work. **Acts 20:7; Deut. 5:13,14**

Q. What would excuse one from the obligation of attending Sunday Mass?

A. The following reasons would excuse one from the obligation of attending Sunday Mass:

1. Illness;

2. Great distance from a church;

3. Necessary occupation;

4. A necessary act of Charity.

Q. What kinds of labor are permitted on Sunday?

A. Any absolutely necessary work is permitted on Sunday. **Mat. 12:1-13; Mark 3:4, 5; Deut. 20:1**

Q. Besides attending Mass and abstaining from work, how are we recommended to spend Sundays?

A. We are encouraged to spend Sundays in a way befitting the Lord's Day. For example, attending services, spending time in prayer and spiritual reading, and wholesome relaxation with family and friends would be profitable ways of spending the Lord's Day.

Q. Are we permitted amusements on Sunday?

A. Yes, amusements and relaxation are permitted provided that they do not interfere with our religious obligations.

Q. What is the fourth commandment?

A. The fourth commandment is: *Honor thy father and thy mother.* **Deut. 5:16; Eph. 6:1,2; Mark 7:10**

Q. What does this commandment require of us?

A. This commandment requires that we:

1. Love and respect our parents, and obey them in all that is not sinful;
2. Respect and obey every lawful authority, both religious and civil;

Prov. 1:8; Eph. 6:1,2; Mark 7:10

Q. What is the fifth commandment?

A. The fifth commandment is: *Thou shalt not kill.* **Ex. 5:15; Rom. 13:9; Mat. 5:21**

Q. What is forbidden by this commandment?

A. The following are forbidden by this commandment:

1. The unjust taking of a human life, including that of the unborn, or one's own life.
2. Hatred, physical abuse, quarreling, or jealousy, because these may lead to killing or to the injury of ourselves or others. **I John 3:15; Mat. 5:21,22; Col. 3:8**

Q. What is the sixth commandment?

A. The sixth commandment is: *Thou shalt not commit adultery.* **Ex. 20: 4; I Cor. 6:18; Mat. 5:27**

Q. What is the sin of adultery?

A. Adultery is the act whereby married persons unlawfully give that love which they owe each other to someone else. Covered under this commandment is the obligation of the unmarried to remain chaste.

Q. What does the sixth commandment forbid?

A. The sixth commandment forbids, in addition to adultery, all impurity and immodesty in words, looks, and actions, whether alone or with others. **Gal. 5:19-21; Eph. 5:3,4; Mat. 5:28**

Q. What is the seventh commandment?

A. The seventh commandment is: *Thou shalt not steal.* **Deut. 5:19; Rom. 13:9; Jer. 22:13**

Q. What is forbidden by this commandment?

A. 1. It is forbidden to take anything that rightly belongs to someone else;
    2. It is forbidden to destroy or injure the property or possessions of another person.

   Lev. 19:15; Job 24:9; Ex. 23:8

Q. What does stealing include?

A. Stealing includes the following: robbery and burglary; graft and bribes; cheating and fraud; not paying bills, taxes, and debts; non-support of dependents; wasting time or materials on a job; and not paying a just wage to employees. **Lev. 19:11; Mat. 22:21; Luke 3:12-14**

Q. What in general are all people obliged to do by this commandment?

A. Everyone is obliged to respect and uphold the just rights of others. **Deut. 24:13-15; Tob. 4:15**

Q. If we have broken this commandment, what are we obliged to do?

A. We are obliged to give back anything that we have taken, and to repair any damage that we have caused, insofar, as it is possible to do so.

Q. If we have found some article of value, what are we obliged to do?

A. We are obliged to try to find the owner and return the article to him. Lev. 5:4; Prov. 29:24; Eccus. 5:10

Q. What is the eighth commandment?

A. The eighth commandment is: *Thou shalt not bear false witness against thy neighbor.* Ex. 20:16; Deut. 5:20; Lev. 19:11

Q. What is the meaning of this commandment?

A. By the eighth commandment we are commanded to speak the truth in all things, especially in what concerns the good name and honor of others. Lev. 19:15; I Pet. 2:1; James 4:11

Q. What is forbidden by this commandment?

A. The eighth commandment forbids lying, hurting someone's reputation, unjust criticism, gossip, insults, violating entrusted confidences, judging another's actions without evidence, publicizing the sins of another, and perjury. Eph. 4:25; I Pet 3:10; James 1:26

Q. Is it ever permissible to reveal the faults of another?

A. We are permitted to reveal the faults of another only to a person in authority, and only for the sake of fraternal correction and the avoidance of continued evil. Gal. 6:1

Q. What are we bound to do if we have injured the character of another unjustly?

A. We must do everything in our power to restore his good name by correcting the evil report we have spread against him. Mat. 5:23-25

Q. What is the ninth commandment?

A. The ninth commandment is: *Thou shalt not covet thy neighbor's wife.* Ex. 20:17; Mat. 5:28; Deut. 5:21

Q. What is forbidden by this commandment?

A. This commandment forbids all lustful thoughts or wishes, or inward adultery. Mat. 5:28; Mark 7:21; James 1:14-15

Q. Are involuntary, impure thoughts sinful?

A. No, but they become sinful when we knowingly and willingly entertain such thoughts.

Q. What is the tenth commandment?

A. The tenth commandment is *Thou shalt not covet thy neighbor's goods.* Ex. 27:28; Psalm 36:7; Eccus. 9:16

Q. What is forbidden by the tenth commandment?

A. It is forbidden to envy the fortune of another, and to seriously lust after what belongs to another. Luke 12:15

CHURCH CALANDAR AND SCHEDULE

The Holy Days of Obligation

1. January 1—Circumcision
2. January 6—Epiphany
3. March 25—Annunciation
4. 40 Days after Easter—Ascension
5. August 6—Transfiguration
6. August 15—Assumption
7. November 1—All Saints
8. December 25—Christmas

Church Calendar

Fasting Days
On which only one meal is allowed, and flesh meat is forbidden.

The forty days of Lent.
The Ember days, which are the Wednesday, Friday, and Saturday in the first week of Lent, in Whitsun—week, in the third week of September, and in the third week of Advent.
The Vigils or Eves of Whit Sunday, SS. Peter and Paul, the Assumption, All Saints, and Christmas. All Wednesdays and Fridays in Advent.

Abstinence Days
On which it is forbidden to eat flesh meat.

The Sundays in Lent, unless leave be given to the contrary, which is usually done in this country. Every Friday, unless it be Christmas Day.

A. Abbot
Arch. Archangel
Ap. Apostle
App. Apostles
B. Bishop
C. Confessor
D. Doctor of the Church
d. Double
d. 1 or 2 Double of the First or Second Class

gr. d. Greater Double
E. Evangelist
Emp. Emperor
K. King
M. Martyr
MM. Martyrs
P. Patriarch
Qu. Queen
s. Semidouble
V. Virgin
W. Widow

January, 31 Days

1. *Circumcision of Our Lord, d. 2*

2. Octave of St. Stephen, d.

3. Octave of St. John, d.

4. Octave of Holy Innocents, d.

5. Vigil of the Epiphany, d.

6. *Epiphany of Our Lord*, d. 1, with an octave

7. Of the Octave, s.

8. Of the Octave, s.

9. Of the Octave, s.

10. Of the Octave, s.

11. St. Hyginus, P. M.

12. Of the Octave, s.

13. Octave Day of the Epiphany, d.—Second Sunday after Epiphany, Feast of the Holy Name of Jesus, d. 2

14. St. Hilary, B.C. s.

15. St. Paul, the first Hermit, d.

16. St. Marcellus, P. M. s.

17. St. Anthony, A. d.

18. *St. Peter's Chair at Rome*, gr. d.

19. St. Wolstan, B. C. d.

20. SS. Fabian and Sebastian, MM. d.

21. St. Agnes, V. M. d.

22. SS. Vincent and Anastasius, MM. d.

23. *Desponsation of B. V. Mary*, gr. d.

24. St. Timothy, B. M. s.

25. *Conversion of St. Paul*, Ap. gr. d.

26. St. Polycarp, B. M.

27. St. John Chrysostom, B. C. D. d.

28. St. Raymond of Pennafort, C. s.

29. St. Francis of Sales, B. C. d.

30. St. Martina, V. M. d.

31. St. Peter Nolasco, C. d.

February, 28 Days; Leap Year, 29

1.   St. Ignatius, B. M. s.

2.   *Purification of the B. V. Mary*, d. 2

3.   St. Blase, B. M.

4.   St. Andrew Corsini, B. C. d.

5.   St. Agatha, V. M. d.

6.   St. Dorothy, V. M.

7.   St. Romuald, A. d.

8.   St. John of Matha, C. d.

9.   St. Appolonia, V. M.

10. St. Scholastica, V. d.

11.

12. Archbishop Paulo Pereira, Primate, Old Catholic Church of Brazil, B. M.

13.

14. St. Valentine, Priest, M.

15. St. Faustina and Jovita, MM.

16.

17.

18. St. Simeon, B. M.

19.

20.

21.

22.

23. *St. Peter's Chair at Antioch*, gr. d.

24.

25. *St. Matthias, Ap.* d. 2

26. (alternate for St. Matthias)

27.

28.

March, 31 Days

1. St. David, B. C. d.

2. St. Chad, B. C. d.

3.

4. St. Casimir, C. s.

5.

6.

7. St. Thomas of Aquin, C. D. d.

8. St. Felix, Apostle of the East Angles, B. C. d.

9. St. Frances, W. d.

10. The Forty Martyrs, s.

11. St. John of God, C. d.

12. St. Gregory the Great, P. C. D. d.

13.

14.

15.

16.

17. St. Patrick, Apostle of Ireland, B. C. s.

18. St. Gabriel, Arch. gr. d.

19. *St. Joseph, Spouse of the B. V. Mary,* d. 2

20. St Cuthbert, B. C. d.

21. St. Benedict, A. d.

22.

23.

24.

25. *Annunciation of the B. V. Mary,* d. 2

26.

27.

28.

29.

30.

31.

Note: *Monday after Passion Sunday*: transferred Feast of the Most Precious Blood of Our Lord Jesus Christ, gr. D

April, 30 Days

1.

2.   St. Francis of Paula, C. d.

3.   St. Richard, B. C. d.

4.   St. Isidore, B. C. D. d.

5.   St Vincent Ferrer, C. d.

6.

7.   Archbishop Carmelo Henry Carfora, (Consecration) Feast Day, B. D.

8.

9.

10.

11. St. Leo, P. C. D. d.

12.

13. St. Hermenegild, M. s.

14. SS. Tiburtius, Valerian, and Maximus, MM. d.

15.

16.

17. S. Anicetus, P. M.

18.

19.

20.

21. St. Anselm, B. C. D. d.; St. Benedict, A. d.

22. Archbishop Arnold Harris Mathew (Consecration) Feast Day, B. D.

23. *St. George, M. Patron of England*, d. 1, with Octave

24. St. Fidelis of Sigmaringa, M. d.

25. *St. Mark, E.* d. 2

26. SS. Cletus and Marcellinus, BB. and MM. s.

27. Within the Octave of St. George, s.

28. Within Octave of St. George, s.

29. St. Peter, M. d.

30. Octave of St. George, M. d.

May, 31 Days

1. *SS. Philip and James, App.* d. 2

2. St. Athanasius, B. C. D. d.

3. *Finding of the Holy Cross*, d. 2

4. St. Monica, W. d.

5. St. Catherine of Siena, W. d.

6. St. John before the Latin Gate, gr. d.

7. St. Stanislaus, B. M. d.

8. Apparition of St. Michael, Arch. gr. d.

9. St. Gregory Nazianzen, B. C. D. d.

10. St. Antoninus, B. C. d.

11.

12. SS. Nereus, Achilleus, et alii, MM. s.

13.

14. St. Boniface, M. d.

15.

16. St. John Nepomucen, M. d.

17. St. Paschal Baylon, C. d.

18. St. Venantius, M. d.

19. St. Dunstan, B. C. d.

20. St. Bernardin, C. s.

21. St. Peter Celestin, P. C. d.

22. St. Ubaldus, B. C. s

23.

24. B. V. M. the Help of Christians, gr. d.

25. St. Aldhelm, B. C. d.

26. St. Augustine, B. C., Apostle of England, d. 2

27. St. Philip Neri, C. d.

28.

29. Archbishop Joseph Rene Vilatte (Consecrated) Feast Day, B. D.

30. St. Felix, P. M.

31. St. Petronilla, V.

June, 30 Days

1.

2. Octave Day of St. Augustine, Ap. of England, d.

3.

4. St. Francis Caracciolo, C. d.

5.

6. St. Norbert, B. C. d.

7.

8. St. William, B. C. d.

9. SS. Primus and Felicianus, MM.

10. St. Margaret, Queen of Scotland, W. s.

11. St. Barnabus, Ap. gr. d.

12. St. John a Facundo, C. d.

13. St. Anthony of Padua, C. d.

14. St. Basil, B. C. D. d.

15. SS. Vitus, Modestus, and Crescentia, MM.

16.

17.

18. SS. Marcus and Marcellianus, MM.

19. St. Juliana Falconieri, V. d.

20. St. Silverius, P. M.

21.

22. St. Alban, Protomartyr of England, gr. d.

23.

24. *Nativity of St. John Baptist*, d. 1 with an Octave

25. St. William, A. d.

26. SS. John and Paul, MM. d.

27. Within the Octave of St. John Baptist, s.

28. St. Leo, P. C. s.

29. *SS. Peter and Paul, App.* d. 1, with an Octave

30. Commemoration of St. Paul, Ap. d.

July, 31 Days

1. Octave Day of St. John Baptist, d.

2. Visitation of the Blessed Virgin Mary, gr. d.

3. Within the Octave of SS. Peter and Paul, s.

4. Within the Octave of SS. Peter and Paul, s.

5. Within the Octave of SS. Peter and Paul, s.

6. Octave Day of SS. Peter and Paul, App. d.

7.

8. St. Elizabeth, Queen of Portugal, W. s.

9.

10. Seven Brothers, and SS. Rufina and Secunda, VV. MM. s.

11.

12. St. John Gualbert, A. d.

13. St. Anacletus, P. M. s.

14. St. Bonaventure, B. C. D. d.

15. Translation of St. Swithin, B. C. d.

16.

17. Translation of St. Osmund, B. C. d.

18. St. Camillus de Lellis, C. d.

19.

20. St. Jerome Emilian, C. d.

21. St. Henry, Emp., C. s.

22. St. Mary Magdalen, d.

23. St. Apollinaris, B. M. d.

24. St. Alexius, C. s.

25. *St. James the Greater, Ap.* d. 2

26. *St. Ann, Mother of B. V. Mary*, gr. d.

27. St. Pantaleon, M.

28. SS. Nazarius, et al., MM.

29. Mar Julius I, Archbishop—Met. of Ceylon, Goa and Whole of India (Consecration) B. D.

30. SS. Abdon and Sennen, MM.

August, 31 Days

1. St. Peter's Chains, gr. d.

2.

3. Finding of St. Stephen, Protomartyr, s.

4. St. Dominic, C. d.

5.

6. Transfiguration of Our Lord, gr. d.

7. St. Cajetan, C. d.

8. SS. Cyriacus, Largus, and Smaragdus, MM. s.

9.

10. *St. Laurence*, M. d. 2

11.

12. St. Clare, V. d.

13. Within the Octave of St. Laurence, s.

14.

15. *Assumption of the B. V. Mary*, d. 1, with an Octave; and the Sunday with the Octave of the Assumption, St. Joachim, Father of the B. V. Mary, C. gr. d.

16. St. Hyacinth, C. d.

17. Octave Day of St. Laurence, M. d.

18.

19.

20. St. Bernard, A. C. D. d.

21. St. Jane Frances, W. d.

22. Octave Day of the Assumption, d.

23. St. Philip Benitus, C. d.

24. St. Bartholomew, Ap. d. 2

25. St. Louis, K. C. s.

26. St. Zephyrinus, P. M.

27. St. Joseph Calasanctius, C. d.

28. St. Augustine, B. C. D. d. e.

29. *Beheading of St. John Baptist*, gr. d.

30. St. Rose, V. d.

31. St. Aidan, B. C. d.

September, 30 Days

1. St. Raymond, Nonnatus, C. d.

2. St. Stephen, K. C. s.

3.

4.

5. St. Laurence Justinian, B. C. s.

6.

7.

8. *Nativity of the Blessed Virgin Mary*, d. 2 with an Octave

9. Of the Octave, s.

10. St. Nicholas of Tolentino, C. d.

11. Of the Octave, s.

12. Of the Octave, s.

13. Of the Octave, s.

14. Exaltation of the Holy Cross, gr. d.

15. Octave of the Nativity of the B. V. Mary, s.

16. SS. Cornelius and Cyprian, s.

17.

18. St. Joseph of Cupertino, C. d.

19. SS. Januarius, B. and Companions, MM. d.

20. SS. Eustachius and Companions, MM. d.

21. *St. Matthew, Ap. and E.* d. 2

22. St. Thomas of Villanova, B. C. d.

23. St. Linus, P. M. s.

24. *The B. V. Mary of Mercy*, gr. d.

25.

26. SS. Cyprian and Justina, MM.

27. SS. Cosmas and Damian, MM. s.

28. St. Wenceslaus, Duke and Martyr, s.

29. *Dedication of St. Michael, Arch.* d. 2

30. St. Jerome, Priest, C. D. d.

October, 31 Days

1. St. Remigius, B. C. s. *ad lib.*

2. The Holy Angels Guardians, d.

3. St. Thomas of Hereford, B. C. d.

4. St. Francis of Assisi, C. d.

5. SS. Placid and Companions, MM.

6. St. Bruno, C. d.

7. St. Mark, P. C.

8. St. Bridget, W. d.

9. SS. Dionysius, Rusticus, and Eleutherius, MM. s.

10. St. Paulinus, Archbishop of York, C. d.

11.

12. St. Wilfrid, Archbishop of York, C. d.

13. Translation of St. Edward, K. C. d. 2 with an Octave

14. St. Callistus, P. M. d.

15. St. Teresa, V. d.

16. Within in the Octave of St. Edward, s.

17. St. Hedwige, W. d.

18. *St. Luke, E.* d. 2

19. St. Peter of Alcantara, C. d.

20. Octave of St. Edward, C. d.

21. SS. Ursula, et alii, VV. MM. gr.

22. St. John Cantius, C. d.

23. *Feast of our Most Holy Redeemer*, gr d.

24. St. Raphael, Arch. gr. d.

25. St. John of Beverly, Archbishop f York, C. d.

26. St. Evaristus, P. M.

27.

28. *SS. Simon and Jude, App.* d. 2

29. Venerable Bede, C. d.

30.

31. *Second Sunday—Maternity of B. V. M.* gr. d. *Third Sunday—Purity of B. V. M.* gr. d. *Fourth Sunday—Patronage of B. V. M.* gr. d.

November, 30 Days

1. *All Saints*, d. 1, with an Octave

2. All Souls, d.

3. St. Winefrid, V. M. d.

4. St. Charles Borromeo, B. C. d.

5. Within the Octave of All Saints

6. Within the Octave of All Saints

7. St. Willibrord, Ap. of the Netherlands

8. Octave of All Saints, d.

9.

10. St. Andrew Avellino, C. d.

11. St. Martin, B. C. d.

12. St. Martin, P. M. s.

13. St. Didacus, C. s.

14. St. Erconwald, B. C. d.

15. St. Gertrude, V. d.

16. St. Edmund, B. C. d.

17. St. Hugh, B. C. d.

18.

19. St. Elizabeth, W. d.

20. St. Edmund, K. M. gr. d.

21. *Presentation of the B. V. Mary*, gr. d.

22. St. Cecily, V. M. d.

23. St. Clement, P. M. d.

24.

25. St. Catherine, V. M. d.

26. St. Felix of Valois, C. d.

27. St. Gregory of Thaumaturgus, B. C. d.

28.

29. St. Saturninus, M.

30. *St. Andrew, Ap.* d. 2

December, 31 Days

1.

2. St. Bibiana, V. M. s.

3.

4. St. Peter Chrysologus, B. C. D. d.

5. St. Birinus, B. C. d.

6. St. Nicholas of Myra, B. C. d.

7. St. Ambrose, B. C. d.

8. *Conception of the B. V. Mary*, d. 2 with an Octave

9. Within the Octave, s.

10. Within the Octave, s.

11. St. Damasus, P. C. s.

12. Within the Octave, s.

13. St. Lucy, V. M. d.

14. Within the Octave, s.

15. Octave Day of the Conception of the B. V. Mary, d.

16. St. Eusebius, B. M. s.

17.

18. *Expectation of B. V. M.* gr. d.

19.

20.

21. *St. Thomas, Ap.* d. 2

22.

23.

24.

25. **Nativity of Our Lord**, d. 1, with an Octave

26. *St. Stephen, Protomartyr*, d. 2, with an Octave

27. *St. John, Ap. E.* d. 2, with an Octave

28. *Holy Innocents, MM.* d. 2, with an Octave

29. *St. Thomas, Archbishop of Canterbury*, M. d. 1

30. Sunday within the Octave of the Nativity.

31. St. Sylvester, P. C. d.

Days of Devotion

On which it is earnestly recommended to hear Mass.

Feb 2 Purification of the Blessed Virgin Mary, or Candlemas Day.
   24 (in leap year, Feb. 25) St. Matthias, Apostle.

March 17 St. Patrick, Apostle of Ireland.
   19 St. Joseph, Spouse of the B. V. Mary.

March 25 Annunciation of the B. V. Mary, or Lady Day.

April 23 St. George, Martyr, Patron of England.

May 1 SS. Philip and James, Apostles.
   3 Finding of the Holy Cross.
   14 St. Boniface, Apostle of the Teutons. Variable Whit Monday and Tuesday.

June 24 Nativity of St. John Baptist.

July 25 St. James the Greater, Apostle.
   26 St. Ann, Mother of the B. V. Mary.

August 10 St. Laurence, Martyr.
   24 St. Bartholomew, Apostle.

September 8 Nativity of the Blessed Virgin Mary.
   21 St. Matthew, Apostle and Evangelist.
   29 Dedication of St. Michael, or Michaelmas Day.

October 28 SS. Simon and Jude, Apostles.

November 7 St. Willibrord, Apostle of the Netherlands.
   30 St. Andrew, Apostle.

December 8 Conception of the B. V. Mary.
   21 St. Thomas, Apostle.
   26 St. Stephen, the First Martyr.
   27 St. John, Apostle and Evangelist.
   28. Holy Innocents.

An Examination of Conscience Before Confession

Before going to Confession the penitent should make a self-appraisal of personal shortcomings. For guidance, the following questions are suitable for self-examination of conscience:

Have you experienced doubts in your faith?

Have you despaired of God's mercies and spoken against the Lord in time of adversity?

Have you attended church regularly?

Have you prayed regularly, remembering other in your prayers?

Have you kept the Sabbath holy and refrained from doing any unnecessary work on Sundays or Holy Days?

Have you observed Lent and kept the fasts of the Church?

Have you attended dances or indulged in entertainments during Lent?

Have you put your belief into fortunetellers or consulted those who presume to predict the future?

Have you spoken lightly of religious matters or of sacred objects?

Have you taken the name of God in vain? Have you cursed yourself or others?

Have you become angry at others or caused others to anger?

Have you honored your parents, superiors, teachers and spiritual advisors?

Have you shown respect to the infirm and the aged?

Have you oppressed anyone, held hatred for others, envied others or desired revenge on anyone?

Have you injured anyone by word or deed?

Have you caused strife between others?

Have you desired or hastened the death of anyone?

Have you chosen your companions wisely?

Have you willfully entertained impure thoughts or desires?

Have you read obscene literature or been guilty of unchaste words or actions?

Have you taken any property belonging to others?

Have you deceived anyone in business transactions?

Have you coveted the possessions of others?

Have you witnessed falsely against anyone or passed unconfirmed judgment on anyone?

Have you partaken of confession and Holy Communion at least once a Year?

CHAPTER 3

The Ecumenical Councils &
The Early Church Fathers

The Ecumenical Councils

'Ecumenical' comes from the Greek word for house, *"oikos"*. The *"oikoumene"* was the household of the Roman emperor, which meant the whole world. Thus the emperor Constantine brought the Church official toleration and then favor and establishment. He also brought the Church throughout the empire together at Nicaea in 325 and presided over the Council.

Council of Nicea 325: Rejected the heresy of *Arianism*, which held that Christ is a creature, less than God the Father. The orthodox, led by St. Athanasius taught that Christ is "of one substance (homoousios) with the Father" and "God of God, light of light". There never was a was when the Son was not. The Son is co-eternal with the Father. He is not, as Arius and Bishop Eusebius of Nicomedia a sympathizer would state that Christ is a created being and that Christ is of like substance (homoiousios) with the Father. They said that Christ was the son by adoption and that the Logos/Christ was the first of God's creatures. They would agree that Christ was pre-existent to creation but the first to be created.

Council of Constantinople 381: Rejected the heresy of *Apollinarianism*, which held that Christ is not fully and perfectly human. For the Apollinarians, Christ was a kind of composite with a human body and mind, but without a human soul or spirit in Christ or even worse Christ also lacked a human mind. This view was rejected by the orthodox, led by the Cappodocian Fathers (Sts. Basil the Great, Gregory of Nyssa, and Gregory Nazianzus. St. Gregory Nazianzus: Doctor of the Church (329-389), and in 358 he joined St. Basil in the solitude of Pontus until he was appointed Bishop of Sasima in 372. In 379, he was made Bishop of Constantinople and remained there until 381. He preferred solitude. He was a great influence in restoring the Nicene Faith at the Council of Constantinople in 381. The orthodox position was that Christ redeems only what he assumed: That if Christ did not have a human mind or soul, then the human mind or soul remains unredeemed. This council reaffirmed the decisions of Nicea.

The Council also stated that the Holy Spirit is worshipped and glorified with the Father and the son. The Holy Spirit is not a creature. The Council extended to the Holy Spirit their teaching concerning the homoousios against the heresies of *Macedonianism* (The Macedonians objected to the divinity of the Holy Spirit) or of the *Pneumatomachi*, which held that the Holy Ghost is a creature or less than the Father. In summary the Council reasserted the homoousios, identical essence. The Father is the Source and the Son is begotten and the Holy Spirit proceeds from the Father. The Holy Spirit is not a creature created by the Father.

The Council of Ephesus 431: The Council, rejected the heresy of *Nestorianism*, which held that Christ is two persons united accidentally or "paper-clipped" together. Nestorius would state that the divine nature and human nature were in partnership. Nestorius considered himself a bastion of orthodoxy, he was called in by Cyril of Alexandria from Antioch to combat paganism and suppressing heresy. However Nestorius had trouble with the 'Mother of God' concept. "How can God be an infant?" To him the relationship between the divinity and the humanity is divided into a partnership. He "paper-clipped" the divine and the human nature of Christ into one person rather than stating the orthodox position that Christ's person was both God and Man at the same time. God adopted the manhood of Christ for his purpose. St. Cyril of Alexandria led the orthodox in teaching that Christ is in fact one person. Cyril taught that Christ's person had both a divine and human nature that were one and without confusion. The infant Jesus was divine and human just as he was divine and human as an adult. The orthodox slogan became that "Mary is the God-bearer" (Theotokos): that is because Christ is a single person, the being born of Mary is God; thus, although Mary is the Mother of Christ's human nature, she may fittingly be called also the Mother or Bearer of God the Son. The orthodox affirmed that Christ was perfect God and perfect man: union of two natures.

Pelagius gets condemned. *(Pelagianism)* wrongly teaches that we can achieve salvation on our own good acts and works.

Once the Church had defined that Christ is perfectly and fully divine (Nicea) and human (Constantinople), it naturally became necessary to define how these two natures are related. Ephesus provided the first part of the answer. The next Council provided the counterpoint.

The Council of Chalcedon 451: The Council rejected the heresy of *Monophysicism* (one nature-ism) a.k.a *Eutychianism,* which held that Christ is not only one divine person, but also one divine nature. Christ's humanity, on this view, was absorbed into the divinity and overwhelmed by the union. *Monophysicism* is a teaching that says the divine nature of Christ overcame the human nature where Christ was no longer with a human body nor a human mind but a one divine being. Chalcedon rejected this view and adopted the Tome of Leo the Great that taught that Christ is one person in whom a divine and human nature are united permanently, but without being mixed or confused or changed into some third entity. The Council concluded that the Son of God in his incarnation really and truly became man. On His two natures: The one and the same Son is made known in two natures: Real Godhead and Real Manhood. From Leo's Tome: "The Two natures meet in one person, lowliness is assumed by majesty, weakness by power, mortality by eternity, in order to pay for the debt of our condition." Apollinarius, Bishop of Laodicea stated that Christ is one person with one nature. The flesh has no independence and is moved by the Word itself. The **Monophysite** formula (one physis, one hypostasis after the union) states that there are two natures before the union and then after the union there is one nature. Ultimately the error is the denial of the human nature of Christ. Leo taught that Jesus had both a human and divine nature into one person that was without confusion. Jesus was truly God and truly man. If Jesus was only a divine person then he could not redeem the human nature that we are. (See St. Augustine) (The Greek Church is more concerned about the nature of Christ while the Roman Church is more concerned about the nature of man and how he is to be redeemed.)

The Council of Constantinople 553: Held under Emperor Justinian the Great. 165 Bishops were present.

The Council was called in hope of putting an end to the Nestorian and the *Eutychian (Monophysite)* controversies). The Council confirmed Church's teaching regarding the two natures of Christ (human and divine) and condemned certain writings with Nestorian leanings. Emperor Justinian himself confessed his Orthodox faith in a form of the famous Church hymn "Only begotten Son and Word of God" which is sung during the Divine Liturgy.

The Council of Constantinople 680: Held 680. Under Emperor Constantine IV. 170 Bishops were present. The council made the last attempt to compromise with the *Monophysites.* Although Christ did have two natures (divine and human), He nevertheless, acted as God only, In other words, His divine nature made all the decisions and His human nature only carried and acted them out. Hence, the name: *"Monothelitism" ("mono" one and "thelesis" will.)*

"Christ had two natures with two activities: as God working miracles, rising from the dead and ascending into heaven; as Man, performing the ordinary acts of daily life. Each nature exercises its own free will." Christ's divine nature had a specific task to perform and so did His human nature. Each nature performed those tasks set forth without being confused, subjected to any change or working against each other. The two distinct natures and related to them activities were mystically united in the one Divine Person of our Lord and Savior Jesus Christ."

The Council of Nicaea II 787: *The Iconaclastic controversy* was settled. Before this time, things were not going well for the Byzantine Empire. Its emperors felt that perhaps the attacks by Islamic groups were punishment by God for the Byzantine people's belief in graven images, an item clearly condemned in the Old Testament. Therefore, there was a rampage to destroy all Icons in the empire. It was the *Iconoclasts (anti-Iconists vs. the Iconodules (pro-Iconists).* The Nicaea II Council was called by Empress Irene and the Patriarch Tarasius to settle the matter. It was resolved that in the Old Testament, one could not see an image of God, therefore any rendering of God the Father would be in error. However, God the Son was seen by men and therefore men could make images of the Son. The Icon is the material representation for Christ who existed in a material world by His incarnation. This artistic representation on wood, includes the lives that Jesus touched, like Mary, The Apostles and Saints. Therefore icons are not prototypes but artistic representations. Icons are to be venerated, and worship belongs solely to God. The Nicea Council condemned the decrees of the Synod of Hieria (753) that supported *iconoclasm.* The Nicaea Council supported *Iconodulism* which states that the Son of God truly and really became man. The Nicaea Council also condemned the Synod of Hieria's pronouncement that, "pictures and images may not be used for devotions." This synod also denied the invocation of saints and encouraged the destruction of relics.

The Great Schism of 1054 (Between Rome and Constantinople)

Normans invaded the southern regions of Italy, which politically was governed by East but belonged, in fact, to the West. The Byzantine emperor needed aid from the West to conquer the Normans, but the pope was unwilling to help because he wished to claim back jurisdiction over southern Italy from the patriarch of Constantinople. Pope Leo IX sparked a clash with Byzantium by asserting his spiritual authority, holding a synod to reform the Sicilian church and appointing a new archbishop of Sicily. Furious opposition by the patriarch of Constantinople, Michael Cerularius, met him. Cerularius, in retaliation for Pope Leo's refusal to cooperate, ordered the closure of the Western churches in Constantinople, and expelled the clergy. The pope dispatched his legate Cardinal Humbert de Silva Candida who in turn excommunicated the patriarch of Constantinople in Hagia Sophia, July 16, 1054. The patriarch responded in kind. The stickler for the East is Papal authority intruding into the affairs of the Eastern Church. An inconvenient theological difference is the West's insistence on the "filioque", which states that the Holy Spirit proceeds from the Father and the Son. The East might be able to tolerate this doctrine if it was understood that the Holy Spirit proceeds from the Father through the Son. The West used unleavened bread for the Eucharist while the East used leavened bread. The East emphasized in devotional life the place of the glorious mystery of God and on the resurrection of Christ. The West emphasized Christ's sufferings whereby he atoned for human sin. Eventually the Mass became more of a means to salvation than as an act of worship.

In a period of 450 years Rome and Constantinople were out of communion with each other at least 200 years at different times.

1. The Eastern Church considered fasting on certain Saturdays, an insult to the Jewish Sabbath and the OT.

2. The East abhorred the West's eating of milk, cheese, and eggs during Lent. To the East, Lent is a period of abstinence from meat and animal products.

3. The East had married deacons and clergy. Eastern bishops had to be unmarried.

4. The East kept Baptism and Confirmation together. In the early church this could be possible because each church had its own bishop to perform the rites twice a year.

5. The East could not accept the "Filioque".

The Schism And Reconciliation Between Rome and Constantinople

The division between Roman Catholicism and Eastern Orthodoxy is one of the saddest pages in Church history. Both have valid holy orders and apostolic succession, both celebrate the same sacraments, and both proclaim the same faith in Christ. Both churches had been in and out of communion with each other before the 1054 incident between Cardinal Humbert and the Eastern Patriarch Michael Cerularius. Even though 1054 is admittedly the catalyst for the split between the two communions, neither the Cardinal nor the Patriarch intended to excommunicate the Churches. They only wanted to excommunicate each other. The two churches were in and out of communion voluntarily and involuntarily up until the invasion of the Turks in 1453.

Let us digress for a little and attempt to understand the history of Eastern Orthodoxy in order to understand events leading up to the break between Rome and Constantinople of 1054. The Eastern Patriarchs had been under the heavy influence of Byzantine emperors with their influential armies. The Patriarch of Constantinople had jurisdiction over the patriarchates of Alexandria, Antioch and Jerusalem while serving under the emperor. The emperors were extremely powerful and expected patriarchs to submit to their authority. Some emperors even appointed the patriarch for Constantinople. Many patriarchs of Constantinople were good and holy bishops who ruled well and resisted imperial encroachments on church affairs. However, when the patriarch resisted the emperor by elevating his positional authority he found himself in conflict with Rome.

Rome exercised pastoral care by supporting the Eastern Patriarch, against heresies and immoral secular powers. For example, Pope Julian who excommunicated the appointed Arian patriarch in 343. Constantinople remained in schism until Patriarch John Chrysostom took office in 398. Moving to the eighth century, it was the Pope who helped resolve the Iconoclastic heresy. The patriarch of Constantinople had sided with the heretical, iconoclastic emperors.

In the eleventh century, after the Norman conquest of southern Italy the Norman Catholics required the Byzantine-Rite Greek colonies to use unleavened bread for the Eucharist. Patriarch Cerularius aggravated by this insensitivity ordered Latin-rite Churches in his jurisdiction to use leavened bread. When the Latins, refused he closed their churches and sent a hostile letter to Pope Leo IX. The Pope had already been unsettled with the East over the lack of military support against the Normans. Thus, the action between the Pope's representative Cardinal Humbert and Patriarch Cerularius made the 1054 event a travesty for Christian love between the churches. There is some question about the validity of the Papal Bull of excommunication that Cardinal Humbert presented to the Eastern Patriarch because the Pope had already been dead.

After 1054 relations between the East and West continued, but were cautiously strained. The East was extremely aggravated with the 4th Crusade that sacked and pilfered Constantinople. Pope Innocent III denounced vigorously the diversion of the 4th Crusade of 1204, an attack on Zara and Constantinople for almost exclusive profit of Venice. However, church historians do agree in the last analysis that the final break between Rome and the East came in the 1453 Turkish invasion of Constantinople. Under pressure from Muslims most of the Eastern churches renounced their relation with Rome.

There were two variables that reduced the patriarchs' status to that of a figurehead. Although Islam protected the Eastern Church, the Muslim sultan frequently sold the office of patriarch to the highest bidder to keep money rolling in. From 1453 to 1923, the Turkish sultans deposed 105 out of the 159 patriarchs. Six were murdered, and only 21 died of natural causes while in office.

The other variable that weakened the patriarch's authority was from the Czar of Russia. Ivan the Great of Russia considered Moscow the "third Rome". Ivan tried to assume the role of protector for Eastern Christianity.

When the patriarchal system in Constantinople essentially collapsed, the Eastern Church fragmented along national lines. Russia claimed independence from the patriarch of Constantinople in 1589. Other ethnic and regional splintering followed. The Russian Orthodox Church represents about seven eights of the total Eastern Orthodox Churches.

There is some optimism that the two churches will eventually come into communion with one another again and fulfill Christ's desire "that they may be one" (John 17:11). In 1965, Pope Paul VI and Patriarch Athenagoras I of Constantinople lifted mutual excommunications dating from the eleventh century, and in 1995, Pope John Paul II and Patriarch Bartholomew I of Constantinople concelebrated the Eucharist together. John Paul II, the first Slavic pope, has made the reconciliation of Eastern and Western Christendom a special theme of his pontificate.

CHAPTER 4

An Exploratory Catechism

Overview

The faith of the Old Catholic Church is, indeed, a catholic faith. The very word "catholic" comes from the Greek and means "universal". The Catholic faith is the universal faith, held and agreed to by the entire church, East and West. The word "Catholic" is not a denominational name, as some would believe, but an adjective to describe the both the scope and calling of the Church of Christ. This universal faith is held and believed by the entire church, through all her branches that have maintained Apostolic Succession and faithful adherence to the Sacraments, the Magisterium of the Church, and the Faith in Holy Scripture and Sacred Tradition. As we combine these Statements of Faith into one *Symbolon* (Symbol), we also consider the Eastern expressions of faith and understanding, anchored to fundamental Catholic theology, as it existed prior to the Council of Trent, and Vatican Councils I & II. The Old Catholic Church does not accept the dogmatic claims of infallibility of the Pope, nor Papal claims to universal jurisdiction and authority over all of Christendom. The Church acknowledges Christ Jesus as the one, infallible Head of the Church of God. Members of the Church may personally belief doctrines espoused by particular ancient Eastern or Western Churches, insofar as they are not contrary to Old Catholic faith, but such pious beliefs may not be imposed upon the conscience of the entire Church. The faith we profess is ancient, as indicated by Archbishop Joseph Renee Vilatte in his letter, "We Maintain The Faith Once For All Given To The Saints", of 1910:

"We maintain that the only historical and consistent bond of church unity is that of 'the faith once for all delivered to the Saints' (Jude 3), as held by the United Church of Christendom, East and West, during the period of the Seven General Councils.

(We) join in faith, hope and love with all churches having the Apostolic ministry and accepting the teaching of the Holy Scriptures as understood by the Fathers,

Doctors and Confessors of the undivided Church. But valid ministry alone is not sufficient for Christian unity. Christians must also accept the Apostles and the Nicene Creed without addition or subtraction. We likewise acknowledge the dogmatic decrees of the seven Ecumenical Councils as the fundamental basis of unity, and the consentient definitions of the councils of Bethlehem and Trent concerning the seven sacraments, as being a clear and concise statement of the doctrine held by the Catholic Church throughout the world.

We reject and deny the supremacy or infallibility of any patriarch or prelate who demands sole jurisdiction over the Holy Catholic and Apostolic Church of Christ.

The Monastic life among Orthodox Catholics is a devout life of sacrifice and love towards God and man.

We do not adore the images of Jesus Christ, the Blessed Virgin Mary and the Saints but venerate them as sacred things representing sacred persons. We believe there is but '*One Mediator of Redemption between God and man.*' But that it is a good and useful thing to invoke the Saints who are our glorified brethren, even as we invoke the prayers of our brethren on earth.

We allow no dissent in matters of faith for no one has a right to add or take away from the faith of the Catholic Church.

The day is at end to meet the Lord, and the Spirit of God impels us to cry, *Come Lord Jesus. Come King of Kings.* For the prosperity of the Christian Church and for its union, let us pray constantly."

The Symbolon

1. We believe Sacred Scripture as interpreted by the Church, together with the Seven Undisputed General Councils of the Whole Church, together with doctrines believed by the Church as a whole prior to the Great Schism of 1054, as defining the belief of the Whole Church. The entire Church of God, when assembled together in an Oecumenical Council, in determining matters of faith, is infallible, being guided by the Holy Spirit. Every person wishing to become a member of this Church must affirm this Faith as contained in the articles below.

No one symbol, creed or statement of faith, can adequately or completely identify the essence of the Almighty God, convey His greatness or provide the ultimate definitive statement. Each creed or symbol then, is a guidepost that points us in the proper direction, as we seek to grow closer to Him, as the stars guided the captains of the ships of old towards their ultimate destination, these guides point the way towards the Light, which is the true Light that enlighteneth every man.

We accept the seven councils recognized by all Catholic Churches, namely:[1]

First Council of Nicaea	AD 325	against Arianism
Second Council of Constantinople	AD 381	against Appolinares/Macedonians
Third Council of Ephesus	AD 431	against Nestorianism
Fourth Council of Chalcedon	AD 451	against Monophysites
Fifth Council of Constantinople	AD 553	against Nestorianism/Monophysites
Sixth Council of Constantinople	AD 680	against Monothelites
Seventh Council of Nicaea	AD 787	against Iconoclastes

Within the Councils, we find a deeper understanding of who Christ is in relation to the Church, and us.

The confession proposed by Saint Cyril of Alexandria and ratified by the 4th Ecumenical Council Concerning the Mother of God:

"We confess, therefore, our Lord Jesus Christ, the Only Begotten Son of God, perfect God, and perfect Man of a reasonable soul and flesh consisting; begotten before the ages of the Father according to his Divinity, and in the last days, for us and for our salvation, of Mary the Virgin according to his humanity, of the same substance with his Father according to his Divinity, and of the same substance with us according to his humanity; for there became a union of two natures. Wherefore we confess one Christ, one Son, one Lord. According to this understanding of this unmixed union, we confess the holy Virgin to be Mother of God; because God the Word was incarnate and became Man, and from this conception he united the temple taken from her with himself."[1A]

The confession of the 5th Ecumenical Council Concerning the Consubstantial Nature of Christ:

"We all with one voice teach the confession of one and the same Son, our Lord Jesus Christ: the same perfect in divinity and perfect in humanity, the same truly God and truly man, of a rational soul and a body; consubstantial with the Father as regards his divinity, and the same consubstantial with us as regards his humanity; like us in all respects except for sin; begotten before the ages from the Father as regards his divinity, and in the last days the same for us and for our salvation from Mary, the virgin God-bearer as regards his humanity; one and the same Christ, Son, Lord, only-begotten, acknowledged in two natures which undergo no confusion, no change, no division, no separation; at no point was the difference between the natures taken away through the union, but rather the property of both natures is preserved and comes together into a single person and a single subsistent being; he is not parted or divided into two persons, but is one and the same only-begotten Son, God, Word, Lord Jesus Christ, just as the prophets taught from the beginning about him, and as the Lord Jesus Christ himself instructed us, and as the creed of the fathers handed it down to us."[1B]

The confession of the 6th Ecumenical Council Concerning the Will and Natural Operations of Christ:

"We also declare that concerning our Lord Christ Jesus are two natural wills and two natural operations indivisibly, inconvertibly, inseparably, inconfusedly, according to the teaching of the holy Fathers. And these two natural wills are not contrary the one to the other (God forbid!) as the impious heretics assert, but his human will follows and that not as resisting and reluctant, but rather as subject to his divine and omnipotent will. For it was right that the flesh should be moved but subject to the divine will, according to the wisest Athanasius. For as his flesh is called and is the flesh of God the Word, so also the natural will of his flesh is called and is the proper will of God the Word, as he himself says: "I came down from heaven, not that I might do mine own will but the will of the Father which sent me!" where he calls his own will the will of his flesh, inasmuch as his flesh was also his own. For as his most holy and immaculate animated flesh was not destroyed because it was deified but continued in its own state and nature, so also his human will, although deified, was not suppressed, but was rather preserved according to the saying of Gregory Theologus: "His will is not contrary to God but altogether deified."

We glorify two natural operations indivisibly, immutably, inconfusedly, inseparably in the same our Lord Jesus Christ our true God, that is to say a divine operation and a human operation, according to the divine preacher Leo, who most distinctly asserts as follows: "For each form does in communion with the other what pertains properly to it, the Word, namely, doing that which pertains to the Word, and the flesh that which pertains to the flesh."

For we will not admit one natural operation in God and in the creature, as we will not exalt into the divine essence what is created, nor will we bring down the glory of the divine nature to the place suited to the creature.

We recognize the miracles and the sufferings as of one and the same Person, but of one or of the other nature of which he is and in which he exists, as Cyril admirably says. Preserving therefore the inconfusedness and indivisibility, we make briefly this whole confession, believing our Lord Jesus Christ to be one of the Trinity and after the incarnation our true God, we say that his two natures shone forth in his one subsistence in which he both performed the miracles and endured the sufferings through the whole of his economic conversation, and that not in appearance only but in very deed, and this by reason of the difference of nature which must be recognized in the same Person, for although joined together yet each nature wills and does the things proper to it and that indivisibly and inconfusedly. Wherefore we confess two wills and two operations, concurring most fitly in him for the salvation of the human race."1C

The confession of the 7th Ecumenical Council Concerning Icons, Symbols, and other Christian Art Forms:

"We, therefore, following the royal pathway and the divinely inspired authority of our Holy Fathers and the traditions of the Catholic Church (for, as we all know, the Holy Spirit indwells her), define with all certitude and accuracy that just as the figure of the precious and life-giving Cross, so also the venerable and holy images, as well in painting and mosaic as of other fit materials, should be set forth in the holy churches of God, and on the sacred vessels and on the vestments and on hangings and in pictures both in houses and by the wayside, to wit, the figure of our Lord God and Savior Jesus Christ, of our spotless Lady, the Mother of God, of the honorable Angels, of all Saints and of all pious people. For by so much more frequently as they are seen in artistic representation, by so much more readily are men lifted up to the memory of their prototypes, and to a longing after them; and to these should be given due salutation and honorable reverence, not indeed that true worship of faith which pertains alone to the divine nature; but to these, as to the figure of the precious and life-giving Cross and to the Book of the Gospels and to the other holy objects, incense and lights may be offered according to ancient pious custom. For the honor that is paid to the image passes on to that which the image represents, and he who reveres the image reveres in it the subject represented. For thus the teaching of our holy Fathers, that is the tradition of the Catholic Church, which from one end of the earth to the other have received the Gospel, is strengthened. Thus we follow Paul, who spoke in Christ, and the whole divine Apostolic Company and the holy Fathers, holding fast the traditions that we have received. So we sing prophetically the triumphal hymns of the Church, "Rejoice greatly, O daughter of Zion; Shout, O daughter of Jerusalem. Rejoice and be glad with all your heart. The Lord has taken away from you the oppression of your adversaries; you are redeemed from the hand of your enemies. The Lord is a King in the midst of you; you shall not see evil any more, and peace be unto you forever."[1D]

2. We affirm the Holy Scriptures of the Old and New Testaments as interpreted by the Church, as containing everything that is necessary for salvation, and as being the rule and ultimate statement of the Faith of the Church.

Holy Scripture is to be taught and interpreted by the Church, under the instruction and guidance of the Bishops of the Church. Scripture itself affirms this: "First of all you must understand this, that no prophecy of scripture is a matter of one's own interpretation, because no prophesy ever came by the impulse of man, but men moved by the Holy Spirit spoke from God." (2 Pet. 1:20-21) The teaching authority of the Church is a living breathing entity, and the Sacred Tradition, which complements and not replaces Holy Scripture, provides the understanding of the Church throughout nearly two thousand years. Any interpretation or teaching as to the meaning of Sacred Scripture that is made separate from the Deposit of Faith, is then suspect.

Holy Scripture itself warns that interpretation must come from the teaching authority of the Church and that Scripture contains some things in them difficult to understand, that some misconstrue or misinterpret to their own detriment. A true understanding of Scripture is found within the Church and not without.

So then the interpretation of Holy Scripture by the Church must necessarily include Sacred Tradition as passed on from the Apostles, through their successors, down to us today. The two are inseparably linked, they are not two separate things, but two parts of learning, living, expressing and teaching the one Deposit of Faith.

3. We accept the Canon of Scripture as handed down from of Old.

The witness of the Church affirms the Greek Septuagint Canon of Old Testament Hebrew Scripture as complete and authoritative. Of the various texts and canon of Old Testament Scripture, this version bears witness as the canon and translation most quoted and cited by Christ Himself, and having His approval, the Church is obedient in her adherence to the use of this translation and canon as authoritative Old Testament Scripture for the faithful.

The canon of New Testament Scripture can only be those inspired letters and writings of the Apostolic age, whose veracity and apostolic pedigree have been attested to by the Universal Church. The Fathers, Teachers, and Martyrs have attested to the inspired truth they speak, attesting not only in word, but also in accepting martyrdom. The blood of the early Church bears witness to both the content and canon of our Scripture.

We obtain this certain knowledge of the authenticity of Scripture from the early Church, the Apostles themselves, and those who were instructed at the very foot of these blessed men, called forth for Holy Ordination by them, and ordained into the Sacred Diaconate, Priesthood and Episcopate by them. The early Church, having been instructed themselves by the Apostles, attest to their writings and those of their companions, because they know them to be so. The Church, having been imbued with the power of the Holy Spirit, was led and inspired to hear and know the truth of God's Holy Message in these writings, and not others, which lacked that supernatural message.

4. We affirm the Nicene Creed as the principal creed of the Faith of the Church. We also recognize the Western Baptismal Creed, commonly called the "Apostles

Creed," and the hymn commonly called the "Athanasian Creed" as representing statements of the Nicene Faith.

Nicene Creed

I believe in one God, the Father Almighty, maker of heaven and earth, and of all things visible and invisible. And in one Lord, Jesus Christ, the only begotten Son of God, and born of the Father before all ages; God of God, light of light; true God of true God; begotten, not made; consubstantial to the Father, by whom all things were made. Who for us men, and for our salvation, came down from heaven and became incarnate by the Holy Ghost, of the Virgin Mary; AND WAS MADE MAN. He was crucified also for us, suffered under Pontius Pilate, and was buried. And the third day he rose again according to the Scriptures; and ascended into heaven, sitteth at the right hand of the Father; and He is to come again with glory, to judge both the living and the dead; of whose kingdom there shall be no end. And in the Holy Ghost, the Lord and giver of life, who proceedeth from the Father; who together with the Father and the Son, is adored and glorified; who spoke by the Prophets. And in one holy Catholic and Apostolic Church. I confess one Baptism for the remission of sins. And I expect the resurrection of the dead, and the life of the world to come. Amen.

Jesus Christ did not merely *appear* to be human, nor did He simply *seem* to be human, He truly became human. He was like us "in all things, but sin". Christ possessed the full range of human feelings and emotions. He was truly God and truly man, of one nature, both human and supernatural. We reject any claim that Jesus merely appeared as though He was a man, as an attempt to undermine His great salvific actions on our behalf.

Jesus truly sacrificed Himself for us, to pay the price of our sin as a perfect sacrifice, as we ourselves never could. He truly suffered and died. He truly rose from the dead, body and soul, physically as well as spiritually.

The Apostles Creed

I believe in God the Father Almighty, Maker of heaven and earth.

And in Jesus Christ his only Son our Lord; who was conceived by the Holy Ghost, born of the Virgin Mary, suffered under Pontius Pilate, was crucified, dead, and buried; he descended into hell; the third day he rose again from the dead; he ascended into heaven, and sitteth on the right hand of God the Father Almighty; from thence he shall come to judge the quick and the dead.

I believe in the Holy Ghost; the holy catholic Church; the communion of saints; the forgiveness of sins; the resurrection of the body; and the life everlasting. AMEN.

Athanasian Creed
(Marquess of Bute's English translation)

Whosoever will be saved, before all things it is necessary that he hold the Catholic Faith. Which Faith except everyone do keep whole and undefiled, without doubt he shall perish everlastingly. And the Catholic Faith is this, that we worship one God in Trinity and Trinity in Unity. Neither confounding the Persons, nor dividing the Substance. For there is one Person of the Father, another of the Son, and another of the Holy Ghost. But the Godhead of the Father, of the Son and of the Holy Ghost is all One, the Glory Equal, the Majesty Co-Eternal. Such as the Father is, such is the Son, and such is the Holy Ghost. The Father Uncreate, the Son Uncreate, and the Holy Ghost Uncreate. The Father Incomprehensible, the Son Incomprehensible, and the Holy Ghost Incomprehensible. The Father Eternal, the Son Eternal, and the Holy Ghost Eternal and yet they are not Three Eternals but One Eternal. As also there are not Three Uncreated, nor Three Incomprehensibles, but One Uncreated, and One Uncomprehensible. So likewise the Father is Almighty, the Son Almighty, and the Holy Ghost Almighty. And yet they are not Three Almighties but One Almighty.

So the Father is God, the Son is God, and the Holy Ghost is God. And yet they are not Three Gods, but One God. So likewise the Father is Lord, the Son Lord, and the Holy Ghost Lord. And yet not Three Lords but One Lord. For, like as we are compelled by the Christian verity to acknowledge every Person by Himself to be God and Lord, so are we forbidden by the Catholic Religion to say, there be Three Gods or Three Lords. The Father is made of none, neither created, nor begotten. The Son is of the Father alone; not made, nor created, but begotten. The Holy Ghost is of the Father, and of the Son neither made, nor created, nor begotten, but proceeding.

So there is One Father, not Three Fathers; one Son, not Three Sons; One Holy Ghost, not Three Holy Ghosts. And in this Trinity none is afore or after Other, None is greater or less than Another, but the whole Three Persons are Co-eternal together, and Co-equal. So that in all things, as is aforesaid, the Unity is Trinity, and the Trinity is Unity is to be worshipped. He therefore that will be saved, must thus think of the Trinity.

Furthermore, it is necessary to everlasting Salvation, that he also believe rightly the Incarnation of our Lord Jesus Christ. For the right Faith is, that we believe and confess, that our Lord Jesus Christ, the Son of God, is God and Man.

God, of the substance of the Father, begotten before the worlds; and Man, of the substance of His mother, born into the world. Perfect God and Perfect Man, of a reasonable Soul and human Flesh subsisting. Equal to the Father as touching His Godhead, and inferior to the Father as touching His Manhood. Who, although He be God and Man, yet He is not two, but One Christ. One, not by conversion of the Godhead into Flesh, but by taking of the Manhood into God. One altogether, not by confusion of substance, but by Unity of Person. For as the reasonable soul and flesh is one Man, so God and Man is one Christ. Who suffered for our salvation, descended into Hell, rose again the third day from the dead. He ascended into Heaven, He sitteth on the right hand of the Father, God Almighty, from whence he shall come to judge the quick and the dead. At whose coming all men shall rise again with their bodies, and shall give account for their own works. And they that have done good shall go into life everlasting, and they that have done evil into everlasting fire. This is the Catholic Faith, which except a man believe faithfully and firmly, he cannot be saved.

5. We believe that the Nicene Creed is a literal statement of the belief of the Church and is not subject to interpretation, which dismisses as merely allegorical or merely mythological any portion thereof.

The Nicene Creed, as a tool of testimony against heresy, and also as a symbolon (symbol) of faith testifies to both natural and supernatural truths, brought about by the one true God. Alongside all of the creeds and symbols of faith of the Church, it testifies to the spiritual reality of

God, His salvific work in our lives, and the promise of a future with Him if we turn to Him and confess His Truth.

6. We affirm the Seven Sacraments Baptism, Holy Eucharist, Confirmation, Holy Order, Holy Matrimony, Penance and Holy Unction administered with the unfailing use of the traditional outward and visible signs, and the form, matter, ministers and intention received of old.

"Because Jesus is *The* Sacrament which makes all sacraments possible, every sacrament finds its unity in Him. No one sacrament, therefore, can be isolated from the others, nor is each sacrament administered to perform a different "job" (i.e. baptism to erase Original Sin, confirmation to impart the Spirit, the Eucharist to communicate Christ's atonement). Each sacrament manifests Christ in his wholeness, not "pieces" of His power; each brings union in and with the one Lord"[2]

"It is for this reason that the Early Christian saw the initiatory sacraments (Baptism, Confirmation, Eucharist) as a *collective whole,* each one *standing in symphony with the others* to manifest the redemptive mystery. Thus, baptism, Confirmation and the Eucharist are *inseparable,* each disclosing the reality of Christ's saving union with us. Baptism reveals God's *union* with us through Christ, Confirmation (in the East 'chrismation') manifests God's *union* with us through the Spirit's indwelling within and among us, and the Eucharist actualizes the reality of God's *union* with us as the Body of Christ. What Christ is to us in Baptism, He is to us in Confirmation and the Eucharist. Each sacrament reveals the one and same mystery, 'Christ, in you, the hope of glory' (Col. 1:27)."[3]

"Sacraments, therefore, are not empowered objects that give private blessings to solitary individuals. In no way do they fit into an individualistic frame of reference. The mysteries reveal the *bond* we share with Christ *and* the brethren (His body)."[4]

"If one sees grace as something distinct from God Himself, or as some substance He created to save us, he is bound to misunderstand sacraments and their purpose. Grace is not a mysterious force enabling man to come to God. Grace is not something God manufactured in heaven and then sent to earth to save us. Grace *is the direct and personal communion of God with His people,* and the sacraments manifest that communion. When someone is strengthened or saved by grace, he is not strengthened or saved by 'a thing' but by a *Person*."[5]

"If the sacraments reveal and manifest the presence of God and His union with men, they must be communal. God Himself is Three Persons in communion, and His union with men is through Christ in the Church Community. A Christian's reception of the sacraments, then, is to manifest his participation both in God's Communal Life and in the divine-human Community (the Church). Hence, the sacraments cannot be given to the lone, "unconnected" individual; no sacrament can exist apart from Christ Who dwells *within* His body."[6]

The mind of the Church has been expressed through her Apostles, Bishops, Teachers and Martyrs down throughout history, who, with one voice, confidently profess the spiritual truths of the sacraments, which flow from Christ Jesus Himself.

Baptism.

Baptism is the initiation of the new believer into life as a Christian. It is mandated and established by Christ Himself, and the Apostles strictly instructed every new convert that they must be baptized. Entire households were baptized, including servants, children and infants, without delay. Indeed, St. Paul answers the jailer who asks, "What must I do to be saved?" by responding that he must believe and be baptized, which he did, along with his entire household. (Acts 16:27-33)

Inherent in baptism is God's grace, His love, and a beginning for us to commune with Him through the sacramental covenant bond begun through baptism. For this reason, He commanded His Disciples to baptize, so as to initiate individuals into the Body of Christ.

(Matthew 28:18-20) "All authority in heaven and on earth has been given to me. Go therefore and make disciples of all nations, baptizing them in the name of the Father and of the Son and of the Holy Spirit, teaching them to observe all that I have commanded you; and lo, I am with you always, to the close of the age."

Baptism is not optional, nor is it a mere ceremony to demonstrate one's belief in God. (Ref. Acts 2:37, 1 Peter 3:21, Mark 16:15) Baptism is commanded by Christ Himself, a necessity for us to be able to "enter into the kingdom of God."

(John 3:4-5,22) "Jesus answered him, 'Truly, truly, I say to you, unless one is born anew, he cannot see the kingdom of God.' Nicodemus said to him, 'How can a man be born when he is old? Can he enter a second time into his mother's womb and be born?' Jesus answered, 'Truly, truly, I say to you, unless one is born of water and the Spirit, he cannot enter the kingdom of God. That which is born of the flesh is flesh, and that which is born of the Spirit is spirit...' After this Jesus and his disciples went into the land of Judea; there he remained with them *and baptized.*" [emphasis added]

Infants and children too, are to be baptized as soon as possible. (Matthew 19:13-15) "Then children were brought to him that he might lay his hands on them and pray. The disciples rebuked the people; but Jesus said, 'Let the children come to me, and do not hinder them; for to such belongs the kingdom of heaven.' And he laid his hands on them and went away."

"At dawn a prayer shall be offered over the water. Where there is no scarcity of water the stream shall flow through the baptismal font or pour into it from above; but if water is scarce, whether as constant condition or on occasion, then use whatever water is available. Let them remove their clothing. Baptize first the children; and if they can speak for themselves, let them do so. Otherwise, let the parents or other relatives speak for them." St. Hippolytus of Rome, *The Apostolic Tradition,* 215 AD[7]

"The Church received from the Apostles the tradition of giving Baptism even to infants. For the Apostles, to whom were committed the secrets of divine mysteries, knew that there is in everyone the innate stain of sin, which must be washed away through water and the Spirit." Origen, *Commentaries on Romans,* 244 AD[8]

"If, in the case of the worst sinners and of those who formerly sinned much against God, when afterwards they believe, the remission of their sins is granted and no one is held back from Baptism and grace, how much more, then, should an infant not be held back, who, having but recently been born, has done no sin, except that, born of flesh according to Adam, he has contracted the contagion of that old death from his first being born. For this very reason does he approach more easily to receive the remission of sins: because the sins forgiven him are not his own but those of another." St. Cyprian of Carthage, *Letter of Cyprian and his Colleagues in Council to the Number of Sixty-six: To Fidus,* 251/252 AD[9]

As circumcision was for the Jew, initiation into accountability under Mosaic Law and the Old Covenant, Baptism is the initiation into accountability as a Christian and the New Covenant. And like the requirement of circumcision of the Old Covenant, one who was born into the first-born nation of God was circumcised on the eight day (Luke 1:21) or if converting as an adult, would still undergo circumcision (Genesis 17:9-14). The law of God is absolute, and to violate it would bring God's judgment (Exodus 4:24-26). In the New Testament man receives instruction directly from God made man, in Christ Jesus, that, in order to be saved, it was necessary to repent and be baptized. Jesus instructed His disciples to "Go therefore, and make disciples of all nations, baptizing them in the name of the Father, and of the Son and of the Holy Spirit, teaching them to observe all that I have commanded you; and lo, I am with you always, to the close of the age." (Matthew 28:19-20)

Baptism is no mere symbol, it actually confers God's grace upon the new believer. This is not a new concept, but taught throughout the existence of the Church. Early Church Father, St. Justin the Martyr [A.D. 110-165], in his *First Apology,* in giving a defense of the beliefs of the Church, states:

"I will also relate the manner in which we dedicated ourselves to God when we had been made new through Christ; lest, if we omit this, we seem to be unfair in the explanation we are making. As many as are persuaded and believe that what we teach and say is true, and undertake to be able to live accordingly, are instructed to pray and to entreat God with fasting, for the remission of their sins that are past, we are praying and fasting with them. Then they are brought by us where there is water, and are regenerated in the same manner in which we were ourselves regenerated. For, in the name of God, the Father and Lord of the universe, and of our Savior Jesus Christ, and of the Holy Spirit, they then receive the washing with water. For Christ also said, 'Except ye be born again, ye shall not enter into the kingdom of heaven.' Now, that it is impossible for those who have once been born to enter into their mothers' wombs, is manifest to all. And how those who have sinned and repent shall escape their sins, is declared by Esaias the prophet, as I wrote above; he thus speaks: 'Wash you, make you clean; put away the evil of your doings from your souls; learn to do well; judge the fatherless, and plead for the widow: and come and let us reason together,' saith the Lord. And though your sins be as scarlet, I will make them white like wool; and though they be as crimson, I will make them white as snow. But if ye refuse and rebel, the sword shall devour you: for the mouth of the Lord hath spoken it." (Ch. LXI) CCEL.

And for this [rite] we have learned from the apostles this reason. Since at our birth we were born without our own knowledge or choice, by our parents coming together, and were brought up in bad habits and wicked training; in order that we may not remain the children of necessity and of ignorance, but may become the children of choice and knowledge, and may obtain in the water the remission of sins formerly committed, there is pronounced over him who chooses to be born again, and has repented of his sins, the name of God the Father and Lord of the universe; he who leads to the laver the person that is to be washed calling him by this name alone. For no one can utter the name of the ineffable God; and if any one dare to say that there is a name, he raves with a hopeless madness. And this washing is called illumination, because they who learn these things are illuminated in their understandings. And in the name of Jesus Christ, who was crucified under Pontius Pilate, and in the name of the Holy Ghost, who through the prophets foretold all things about Jesus, he who is illuminated is washed."

Holy Eucharist.

(John 1:28-30) "...The next day he saw Jesus coming towards him, and said, 'Behold, the Lamb of God, who takes away the sin of the world."

(1 Cor. 11:25) "This is my body which is for you. Do this in remembrance of me.' In the same way also the cup, after supper, saying 'This cup is the new covenant in my blood. Do this, as often as you drink it, in remembrance of me."

Throughout both the Old and the New Testament, we see God present to His people under the appearance of various created things. We turn to Scripture and see this in Exodus 3:2-6, Exodus 13:21-22, Matthew 3:16, Genesis 18:1-2 and Matthew 13:55.

(1 Cor. 10:16) "This cup of blessing which we bless, is it not a participation [koinonia—Greek (communion)] in the blood of Christ? The bread that we break, is it not a participation in the body of Christ? Because there is one bread, we who are many are one body."

Christ Himself taught us that He is truly present in the consecrated Bread and Wine, and repeated this teaching several times in His ministry. When He taught that we must eat His flesh and drink His blood, many of His followers departed. Did they misunderstand? Apparently not, a mere misunderstanding would not warrant leaving the company of the man they believed was the Messiah. All too clearly they understood that this was *not* a euphemism, but a testimony of a supernatural reality, one that they refused to accept, since their human intellect could not comprehend it. Nowhere does Jesus indicate that he meant that the bread and wine "represent" His Body and Blood, or that he was merely speaking metaphorically. The writers, teachers, bishops and leaders of the early church all speak unanimously about their belief of the Real Presence of Christ in the Eucharist. Thus, the Church, in union with this timeless witness, teaches the doctrine of the Real Presence of Jesus Christ in the Holy Eucharist, and also the spiritual efficacy of the Sacrifice of the Holy Mass.

"The most intimate link between the Eucharist and a meal is the Passover meal. This is particularly evident in the way the Old Testament Jew celebrated it as a means to remember his deliverance from Egypt.…'to remember' had a distinctively different meaning to the Jew and other Eastern peoples that merely 'to recount' or 'to recall.' This is a crucial point. When Jesus asked us to perform the Eucharistic rite in 'remembrance' of Him, He obviously had the Jewish understanding of 'remember' in mind…

The word 'remembrance' in the Gospel accounts of the Lord's Supper is translated from the Greek word anamnesis. This word is difficult to translate into just one English word. When we use 'remembrance' or 'memorial' to translate it, we are often led astray from its deeper significance. These usually connote something absent-something which is only mentally recollected. However, they do not capture the Biblical sense of 'remembrance' (anamnesis)."[10]

"According to the Scriptures, when an event from the past is being 're-presented' before God in such a way that what is being symbolized becomes operative in the present, one 'remembers' it. To remember in this sense, then is to defy the historical limitations of time. When the Jews 'remembered' the Passover, for instance, they re-lived and re-entered their exodus from Egypt once again. God's deliverance of them was again made real."[11] In no way, does Old Catholic belief say, that Christ is crucified again or sacrificed again—in this anamnesis, we participate in Christ's offering, which was "once, for all".

"This background ties directly into our understanding of the Eucharist. When the Lord asked us to 'do this in remembrance' of Him, He was asking us to remember—'to do anamnesis'—in the same sense as the Jews 'remembered' their deliverance in the Passover Feast. He was not asking us merely to mentally recall His death on our behalf. In the Eucharistic celebration, we are to 'remember' our salvation through Christ's offering of Himself. Through this 're-living' or 're-entering' connoted by anamnesis, each believer personally participates in the event of His once-for-all sacrifice."[12]

"In this Eucharistic remembrance—like the Jews in their Passover celebration—each is actively delivered afresh from slavery, sin and death. Anamnetically, each enters into God's salvation in the corporate celebration of the Eucharist, just as anamnetically each Jew entered into the experience of deliverance again and again at each Passover. And just as the Jews would not have said that the firstborn of Egypt were slain again and again because of this 'remembrance' of their deliverance, so neither did the Early Church say that Christ is crucified again and again through her "remembrance' of His sacrifice. The spirit-filled celebration of the Eucharist does not re-create history. It allows the Church to experience the saving effects Christ accomplished in History, effects that are now experienced and manifested in the gathered Assembly's 'remembrance."[13]

Anamnesis not only calls us to re-live (and thus to re-experience) what is being 'remembered,' it also invites us to taste the future. The Passover did this by foreshadowing the Eucharistic celebration not only in its rite, but also in the salvation which was yet to come. Passover night was the night on which the Jews had been redeemed in the past, and on which they would be redeemed in the future. 'When the Jews at the first Passover remembered their deliverance, they also 'remembered-anticipated' their ultimate deliverance in the One who was to come.'

The Eucharist is a celebration of the Pascal mystery now completed in Christ..."

"...Christ Jesus is truly present in the Eucharist, body, blood, soul and divinity. The accidents of bread and wine continue after the prayers of consecration [and the Epiclesis], and retain their physical reality after the change of the substance."[14]

"The Body and Blood of Christ together with His Soul and His Divinity and therefore the Whole Christ are truly present in the Eucharist."[15] We find testimony to this again and again in the Bible, as well as throughout nearly two thousand years of Christianity.

We see that Christ is both High Priest, and Perfect Sacrifice: "So also Christ did not exalt himself to be made a high priest, but was appointed by him who said to him, 'Thou are a priest for ever, after the order of Mel-chiz-e-dek." (Heb 5:5-6)

"I have no delight in corruptible food, nor in the pleasures of this life. I desire the bread of God, the heavenly bread, the bread of life, which is the flesh of Jesus Christ, the Son of God, who became afterwards of the seed of David and Abraham; and I desire the drink of God, namely His blood, which is incorruptible love and eternal life." St. Ignatius of Antioch, *Letter To The Romans* 110 A.D.[16]

"And this food is called among us [the Eucharist], of which no one is allowed to partake but the man who believes that the things which we teach are true, and who has been washed with the washing that is for the remission of sins, and unto regeneration, and who is so living as Christ has enjoined. For not as common bread and common drink do we receive these; but in like manner as Jesus Christ our Savior, having been made flesh by the Word of God, had both flesh and blood for our salvation, so likewise have we been taught that the food which is blessed by the prayer of His word, and from which our blood and flesh by transmutation are nourished, is the flesh and blood of that Jesus who was made flesh. For the apostles, in the memoirs composed by them, which are called Gospels, have thus delivered unto us what was enjoined upon them; that Jesus took bread, and when He had given thanks, said, "This do ye in remembrance of Me, this is My body;" and that, after the same manner, having taken the cup and given thanks, He said, "This is My blood; "and gave it to them alone." St. Justin the Martyr, *First Apology*, inter 148-155 A.D.[17]

"But vain in every respect are they who despise the entire dispensation of God, and disallow the salvation of the flesh, and treat with contempt its regeneration, maintaining that it is not capable of incorruption. But if this indeed does not attain salvation, then neither did the Lord redeem us with His blood, nor is the cup of the Eucharist the communion of His blood, nor the bread which we break the communion of His body. For blood can only come from veins and flesh, and whatsoever else makes up the substance of man, such as the Word of God was actually made. By His own blood he redeemed us, as also His apostle declares, "In whom we have redemption through His blood, even the remission of sins." And as we are His members, we are also nourished by means of the creation (and He Himself grants the creation to us, for He causes His sun to rise, and sends rain when He wills). He has acknowledged the cup (which is a part of the creation) as His own blood, from which He bedews our blood; and the bread (also a part of the creation) He has established as His own body, from which He gives increase to our bodies.

When, therefore, the mingled cup and the manufactured bread receives the Word of God, and the Eucharist of the blood and the body of Christ is made, from which things the substance of our flesh is increased and supported, how can they affirm that the flesh is incapable of receiving the gift of God, which is life eternal, which [flesh] is nourished from the body and blood of the Lord, and is a member of Him?—even as the blessed Paul declares in his Epistle to the Ephesians, that "we are members of His body, of His flesh, and of His bones." St. Irenaeus, *Against Heresies*, inter 180/199 A.D.[18]

"You know that you were ransomed from the futile ways inherited from your fathers, not with perishable things such as silver or gold, but with the precious blood of Christ, like that of a lamb without blemish or spot. He was destined before the foundation of the world but was made manifest at the end of times for your sake." (1 Pet. 1:18-20) Indeed, as Christ was being prepared for crucifixion, the sacrificial lambs of Passover were, at that very time, being prepared for slaughter as well. So He became our new Paschal sacrifice, and we were commanded to "remember" and spiritually re-enter the communal meal with Him during the Eucharist, partaking of a supernatural gift that human knowledge cannot explain and is a mystery of faith. Worthy is the Lamb that was slain!

Confirmation.

"We believe that the Bishop is the ordinary minister of Confirmation and that in this Sacrament, the Holy Ghost is given with the fullness of His gifts. 'For they had only been baptized in the Name of the Lord Jesus, then the Apostles laid their hands upon them and they received the Holy Ghost".[19]

"Confirmation, or Chrismation, is a Sacrament in which the baptized person, on being anointed with Sacred Chrism consecrated by the Bishops of the Church, with the imposition of hands, receives the sevenfold gifts of the Holy Ghost to strengthen him in the grace which he received at Baptism, making him a strong and perfect Christian and a good soldier of Christ."[20]

"Now when the apostles at Jerusalem heard that Samaria had received the word of God, they sent to them Peter and John, who came down and prayed for them that they might receive the Holy Spirit; for it had not fallen on any of them, but they had only been baptized in the name of the Lord Jesus. Then they laid their hands on them and they received the Holy Spirit." (Acts 8:14-17)

"And to you in like manner, after you had come up from the pool of the sacred streams, there was given chrism, the antitype of that with which Christ was anointed and this is the Holy Spirit. But beware of supposing that this is ordinary ointment. For just as the Bread of the Eucharist after the invocation of the Holy Spirit is simple bread no longer, but the Body of Christ, so also this holy ointment is no longer plain ointment, nor so to speak, common, after the invocation. Rather, it is the gracious gift of Christ; and it is made fit for the imparting of His Godhead by the coming of the Holy Spirit. This ointment is symbolically applied to your forehead and other senses; and while your body is anointed with the visible ointment, your soul is sanctified by the Holy and Lifecreating Spirit." St. Cyril of Jerusalem, *Catechetical Lectures,* 350 A.D.[21]

"While Apollos was at Corinth, Paul passed through the upper country and came to Ephesus. There he found some disciples. And he said to them, 'Did you receive the Holy Spirit when you believed?' And they said, 'No, we have never even heard that there is a Holy Spirit.' And he said, 'Into what then were you baptized?' They said, 'Into John's baptism.' And Paul said, 'John baptized with the baptism of repentance, telling the people to believe in the one who was to come after him, that is, Jesus.' On hearing this, they were baptized in the name of the Lord Jesus. And when Paul had laid his hands upon them, the Holy Spirit came on them; and they spoke in tongues and prophesied." (Acts 19:1-7)

"Therefore let us leave the elementary doctrine of Christ and go on to maturity, not laying again a foundation of repentance from dead works and of faith toward God, with instruction about ablutions, the laying on of hands, the resurrection of the dead, and eternal judgment." (Heb. 6:1-2)

Holy Orders.

"We believe that Orders is a Sacrament which confers upon those who validly receive it the power to exercise the several functions of the ministry. Bishops are the ministers of this Sacrament. The Old Catholic Church makes a distinction between the Minor Orders and the greater or Holy Orders; the latter being so called by reason of eminent dignity they confer and the grave obligations they impose."[22]

Although not necessary for ordination, the state of celibacy in the priesthood is an honorable, sacred and altogether wholesome thing, for those men who are truly called to it. Celibacy for the sake of the Kingdom of God is biblically supported, "For there are eunuchs who have been so from birth, and there are eunuchs who have been made eunuchs by men, and there are eunuchs who have made themselves eunuchs for the sake of the kingdom of heaven. He who is able to receive this, let him receive this." (Matthew 19:12)

The beginning of married men in the ordained ministry is through Christ Jesus. Jesus chose men, some of whom we know to have been married, as His apostles. The identified leader of the Twelve, Simon Peter, who had been given the "keys to the Kingdom" by Christ Jesus Himself, was married. The New Testament instructions on the selection of clergy indicate that there were married deacons, priests and bishops. During the first twelve centuries of the church's life, numerous popes were married, and many priests and bishops as well. In addition, three popes, Pope Anastasius I, St. Pope Hormidas, and Pope Sergius III, sired sons that later became popes themselves, two of whom were later declared saints [St. Innocent I, and St. Silverius].

Priests who are married and priests who are celibate, share the same supernatural sacerdotal priesthood, without differentiation. Each priest brings his unique witness of Christianity to bear, and both complement the nature of the sacramental priesthood. The celibate priesthood more closely represents the monastic life, which the celibate priest imitates, whereas, in the Eastern Orthodox Churches, as well as the Eastern Rite Roman Catholic Churches, clerical celibacy is uniquely linked to monks in monastic life, and the married priesthood is the norm. Priests faithfully living in either estate glorify God in their lives, and provide a balance to our Church.

The appointment and selection to Holy Orders is to a supernatural and sacred *office*, as a priest of the New Covenant, prefigured in the Levitical priesthood of the Old Covenant. That this is a sacred office, established by Christ, and understood as such by the Apostles is thus underscored, "For he was numbered among us, and allotted his share in this ministry. (Now this man bought a field with the reward of his wickedness; and falling headlong he burst open in the middle and all his bowels gushed out. And it became known to all the inhabitants of Jerusalem, so that the field was called in their language A-kel da-ma, that is, Field of Blood.) For it is written in the book of Psalms, 'Let his habitation become desolate, and let there be no one to live in it'; and 'His *office* let another take." (Acts 1:17-20) [emphasis added]

Likewise, St. Paul, too, understood Apostleship to be a sacred office, established by Christ in His appointment of the Twelve, and carried on by others appointed and selected by them, through the laying on of hands and prayer:

"This saying is sure: If any one aspires to the *office* of bishop, he desires a noble task. Now a bishop must be above reproach, the husband of one wife, temperate, sensible, dignified, hospitable an apt teacher, no drunkard, not violent but gentle, not quarrelsome, and no lover of money." (1 Tim 3:1-3) [emphasis added]

Sacramental ordination to Holy Orders takes place with the laying on of hands by a bishop and with the prayer of consecration. The importance of this act is seen throughout Scripture, and the understanding that, through the laying on of hands, a spiritual authority, originating with Christ and passed to the Disciples, is supernaturally conveyed.

"Do not be hasty in the laying on of hands, nor participate in another man's sins; keep yourself pure." (1 Tim 4:22)

Every deacon and priest is tied to the bishop spiritually, as the bishop possesses the fullness of the priesthood, given the Apostles by Christ Jesus Himself. Every bishop then, is spiritually bound to Christ who is the High Priest of the New Covenant. "So also Christ did not exalt himself to be made a high priest, but was appointed by him who said to him, 'Thou are a priest for ever, after the order of Mel-chiz-e-dek." (Heb 5:5-6)

Holy Matrimony.

Sacramental matrimony is only possible between a man and woman who are both of the single estate and Christian, as evidenced by Trinitarian baptism. While a "natural marriage" may be possible between a Christian and a non-Christian, the same bond is not created as the non-Christian is not a believer and does not agree and believe in the sacramental covenant. However, the Christian spouse may yet bring God's blessing to the unbelieving spouse through obedience to God, fidelity in all things to the spouse, prayer and supplication. For the Christian, no marriage outside of the Church, whether to a Christian or a non-believer, is valid. A marriage contract executed by the parties, through governmental authorities, is never valid in the eyes of the Church, although a civil contract of marriage may exist. Civil government can never provide the necessary essentials for a sacramental marriage. Sacramental marriage is to be effected among the brethren of the Church, officiated by the Bishop, priest, or deacon, and in the presence of the Church as a witness.

Matrimony is the bonding of two complete people into one union, in which each spouse freely and unselfishly gives completely of themselves to the other. It is this selfless and loving act of complete giving that creates new life, as the union results in children. In the first marital sexual bond is a loving sharing of each with the other, and this is renewed continually within the marriage covenant.

"Matrimony is a Sacrament in which the voluntary union of husband and wife is sanctified to become an image of the union of Christ and His Church; and grace is imparted to them to fulfill the duties of their estate and its great responsibilities, both to each other and to their children."[23]

Civil divorce does not terminate a sacramental marriage. A valid marriage is indissoluble unto death of one of the spouses, releasing the other. However, a marriage, presumed to be sacramentally conferred, may be found to have not been, due to some defect of the essential matter, form or intent of one or both of the intended parties. Should it be found that a defect did, in fact, exist, which prevented the sacramental marriage from being conferred, then the Church, upon due examination, would issue a Declaration of Nullity. Such a declaration would have no effect upon the legitimacy of any children conceived during the cohabitation. To eliminate most problems before they occur, the Church, through the parish priest, provides pre-nuptial instruction, to ensure, as much as is possible, that both parties understand the sacramental nature of marriage. This pre-nuptial instruction is invaluable and essential to a proper understanding of a sacramental marriage, and should be undertaken with all due serious study and thought. The Church has no authority to sever a valid, sacramental marriage.

Matrimony is the union of two lives, a man and a woman, into one. This union, for the Christian is holy and sacramental, for we invoke the holy name of God, and ask him to bless and ratify the union, entering the man and woman into a covenant agreement with God, asking His help. This covenant, then, is not only between the man and woman, but is between the man, the woman, and God. They ask for, in making a sacred oath (sacramentum—Latin), God's conditional blessings as a result of honoring and keeping inviolate this covenant; and His conditional punishment for violating it. When the bonds of Matrimony are violated, the covenant promises made to God are also violated, and the violating partner sins against both the spouse and God. Our heavenly Father, as perfect Judge, shall demand justice both for Himself, and the injured spouse.

(Matthew 19:4) "He answered, 'Have you not read that he who made them from the beginning made them male and female, and said, 'For this reason a man shall leave his father and mother and be joined to his wife, and the two shall become one'? So they are no longer two but one. What God has joined together, let no man put asunder.' They said to him, 'Why then did Moses command one to give a certificate of divorce, and to put her away?' He said to them, 'For your hardness of heart *Moses* allowed you to divorce your wives, but from the beginning it was not so. And I say to you: whoever divorces his wife, except for unchastity, and marries another, commits adultery; and he who marries a divorced woman, commits adultery."(emphasis added) Divorce had been a concession of *Moses*, and not of God, due to the uncharitable disposition of the people. Matrimony was, from the beginning, meant to be a permanent state. As a covenant made between a man, a woman and God, it was, and is, a sacred, holy estate, sealed with God's covenant blessing. To break the vows of Matrimony then, necessarily mean that one subjects themselves to God's punishment for breaking the covenant with the spouse and with Him.

"For I hate divorce, says the Lord the God of Israel, and covering one's garments with violence, says the Lord of Hosts. So take heed to yourselves and do not be faithless." (Mal. 2:16)

For anyone who thinks that the prohibition was abolished in the New Covenant with Christ, they would be woefully mistaken, for we read: "Everyone who divorces his wife and marries another commits adultery, and he who marries a woman divorced from her husband commit adultery." (Luke 16:18)

We also read: "Do you not know that the unrighteous will not inherit the Kingdom of God? Do not be deceived; neither the immoral, nor idolators, nor adulterers, nor homosexuals, nor thieves, nor the greedy, nor drunkards, nor revilers, nor robbers will inherit the Kingdom of God." (1 Cor. 6:9-11) Especially for Christians, the life we live on this earth affects the measure of reward or judgment we shall inherit in the life to come. One cannot become part of the Body of Christ, that is to say, the Church, and not strive to live the Christ-like life, but wallow rebelliously in sin, and expect reward.

Penance.

"Penance is a Sacrament in which the Holy Ghost bestows the forgiveness of sins, by the ministry of the Priest, upon those who, having sinned after Baptism, confess their sins with true repentance; and grace is given to amend their lives thereafter."[24]

Christ left us the gift of forgiveness of sins committed throughout our lives, entrusting the power to bind and loose, and to forgive or retain sins to His Disciples, who, in the sacrament of Holy Orders, passed this sacred authority on to the priests and bishops of the Church. Christ recognized our need to verbally confess, and our human need to hear Him, through the leaders of the Church, say, "In the name of Jesus Christ, your sins are forgiven you". The sacrament of penance is a hard one for many, who are too proud or embarrassed or concerned about what others will say. We must remember that "all have sinned, and fallen short of the glory of God" and so we must put our spiritual life first, and if humbled in doing so, all the better.

(Matthew 9:1-8) "And getting into a boat he crossed over and came to his own city. And behold, they brought to him a paralytic, lying on his bed; and when Jesus saw their faith he said to the paralytic, 'Take heart, my son; your sins are forgiven.' And behold, some of the scribes said to themselves, 'This man is blaspheming.' But Jesus, knowing their thoughts, said, 'Why do you think evil in your hearts? For which is easier; to say, "Your sins are forgiven," or to say, "Rise and walk"? But that you may know that the Son of man has authority on earth to forgive sins'—he said to the paralytic—'Rise, take up your bed and go home.' And he rose and went home. When the crowds saw it, they were afraid, and they glorified God, who had given such authority to men."

Scripture bears witness to Christ imparting His spiritual authority to the Disciples, to bind and loose, to forgive or retain sins. Christ Himself established the sacrament of Penance and gave His disciples the mandate to go forth and do it.

(Matthew 18:18-19) "Truly, I say to you, whatever you bind on earth shall be bound in heaven, and whatever you loose on earth shall be loosed in heaven. Again I say to you, if two of you agree on earth about anything they ask, it will be done for them by my Father in heaven."

(John 20:22) "And when he had said this, he breathed on them, and said to them, 'Received the Holy Spirit. If you forgive the sins of any, they are forgiven; if you retain the sins of any, they are retained."

Confessing our sins is necessary in our journey with Christ, and cleanses us so that we may better continue that journey, conforming our life to Him. Refusal to do penance is gravely sinful, whether out of obstinate refusal, guilt or embarrassment. It is far more important for us to obtain God's grace through the sacrament of penance than be concerned about what other people think. A confession must be voluntary, and must be genuine, not merely a process or procedure adhered to for rote's sake. Confession is to be sought after only when a person's soul is in need of it.

(1 John 1:8) "If we say we have no sin, we deceive ourselves, and the truth is not in us. If we confess our sins, He is faithful and just, and will forgive our sins, and cleans us from all unrighteousness."

"Therefore confess your sins to one another, and pray for one another, that you may be healed." (James 5:16) This can be seen in the general confession of the "Confiteor" during the Sacred Mass, where we say, "I confess to Almighty God......"

Holy (Extreme) Unction.

"We believe Extreme Unction to be a Sacrament of the New Dispensation, instituted for the spiritual and corporal solace of the sick. Its efficacy and mode of administration are plainly indicated in the Catholic Epistle of Saint James. "Is any sick among you, let him bring in the priests of the Church and let them pray over him, anointing him with oil in the Name of the Lord."[25]

"Unction is a Sacrament in which the Priests of the Church anoint the sick with oil, for the healing of the infirmities of their souls, and if it should please God those of their bodies also."[26]

Holy Unction is also called "Anointing of the Sick" and has been a sacrament of the Church from its inception. Scripture bears witness to the establishment of this sacrament and the proper minister of it.

"Is any among you sick? Let him call for the elders of the church, and let them pray over him, anointing him with oil in the name of the Lord; and the prayer of faith will save the sick man, and the Lord will raise him up; and if he has committed any sins, he will be forgiven." (James 5:14-15)

The elders (bishops and priests) of the Church were (and are) the proper ministers of this sacrament, and so it continues from the beginning of Christianity to our present age. They are the successors to the Apostles, to whom Christ gave the authority to anoint and pray for the healing of the sick. "And they cast many demons, and anointed with oil many that were sick and healed them." (Mark 6:13)

7. We affirm the Historic three-fold ministry of Bishops, Priests and Deacons, and the traditional rights and powers thereof, locally adapted in the methods of its administration according to the needs of the nations in which the Church resides, but historic in form, matter, ministers and intention.

The proper understanding of the three-fold ministry is that of a sacred and supernatural office. This priesthood was not established instead of, or opposed to, the common priesthood of the people of God, but to offer sacrifice on behalf of them, as established by Jesus Christ. The Twelve Apostles saw themselves as holders of Divine Offices, established by Christ Himself. This understanding is clearly seen in the Book of Acts, in deciding to replace Judas;

"In those days Peter stood up among the brethren (the company of persons was in all about a hundred and twenty), and said, 'Brethren, the scripture had to be fulfilled, which the Holy Spirit spoke beforehand by the mouth of David, concerning Judas who was guide to those who arrested Jesus. For he was numbered among us, and was allotted his share in this ministry. (Now this man bought a field with the reward of his wickedness; and falling headlong he burst open on the middle and all his bowels gushed out. And it became known to all the inhabitants of Jerusalem, so that the field was called in their language Akeldama, that is, Field of Blood.) For it is written in the book of Psalms,

'Let his habitation become desolate, and let there be no one to live in it'; and 'His office, let another take." (Acts 1:15-20)

"And they prayed and said, 'Lord, who knowest the hearts of all men, show which one of these two thou hast chosen to take the place in this ministry and apostleship from which Judas turned aside, to go to his own place.' And they cast lots for them, and the lot fell on Matthias; and he was enrolled with the eleven apostles." (Acts 1:24-26)

The Greek word for office is "episcopi", from which we get "Episcopal", and so name this succession of office, "Episcopal" or "Apostolic Succession".

Deacon.

The deacon has the ministry of service to others as an assistant to the bishop, but differently from the priest. The deacon ministers to the temporal need of the community, ensuring that all are cared for, especially the very young and very old or infirmed. Like the priest, he is ordained through the laying on of hands to his sacred office.

"Now in these days when the disciples were increasing in number, the Hellenists murmured against the Hebrews because their widows were neglected in the daily distribution. And the twelve summoned the body of the disciples and said, 'It is not right that we should give up preaching the word of God to serve tables. Therefore, brethren, pick out from among you seven men of good repute, full of the Spirit and of wisdom, whom we may appoint to this duty. But we will devote our-selves to prayer and to the ministry of the word.' And what they said pleased the whole multitude, and they chose Stephen, a man full of faith and of the Holy Spirit, and Philip, and Prochorus and Nicanor, and Timon and Parmenas, and Nicolaus, a proselyte of Antioch. These they set before the apostles, and they prayed and laid their hands upon them." (Acts 6:1-7)

"In like manner, let all reverence the deacons as an appointment of Jesus Christ, and the bishop as Jesus Christ, who is the Son of the Father, and the presbyters as the Sanhedrim of God, and assembly of the apostles. Apart from these, there is no Church. Concerning all this, I am persuaded that ye are of the same opinion. For I have received the manifestation of your love, and still have it with me, in your bishop, whose very appearance is highly instructive, and his meekness of itself a power; whom I imagine even the ungodly must reverence, seeing they are also pleased that I do not spare myself. But shall I, when permitted to write on this point, reach such a height of self-esteem, that though being a condemned man, I should issue commands to you as if I were an apostle?" *The Epistle of St. Ignatius to the Trallians* (short version)— Ch. 3. CCEL.

Priest.

The priest is the assistant of the bishop, at the sacrifice of the Mass, in administering the sacraments of Baptism, Holy Matrimony, and the Anointing of the Sick. To the priest is given the spiritual authority from the bishop to consecrate the bread and wine into the Body and Blood of our Lord, during the Mass.

Bishop.

The Church's bishops are the successors to the Apostles, and posses (and are possessed by) the fullness of the priesthood of the New Covenant. From the bishop, the deacon and priest is spiritually linked, for it is the bishop alone who ordains those called to the diaconate and the priesthood. To the bishop is charged the spiritual welfare of the local church, its instruction, guidance and process of spiritual maturity. The bishop is the spiritual Shepherd, the Father of the local church in their faith, and is configured to Christ. Every validly ordained (consecrated) bishop stands in a line of succession, through prayer and the laying on of hands when ordained, back in time to the Apostles themselves, *and ultimately to Christ Jesus.*

As Christ empowered the twelve disciples, we see a clear establishment of divine authority to them, as Christ likens to being ministers over the Divine Kingdom, in which He is King. We see this distinctively in Matthew 16:15–19; "He said to them, 'But who do you say that I am?' Simon Peter replied, 'You are the Christ, the Son of the living God.' And Jesus answered him, 'Blessed are you, Simon Bar-Jona! For flesh and blood has not revealed this to you, but my Father who is in heaven. And I tell you, you are Peter, and on this rock I will build my church, and the powers of death shall not prevail against it. I will give you the keys of the kingdom of heaven, and whatever you bind on earth shall be bound in heaven, and whatever you loose on earth shall be loosed in heaven."

Jesus, in this reference to the "keys of the kingdom", is understood to be establishing in Peter a successive office akin to that of a "Prime Minister" appointed by a Davidic King, as illustrated in Isaiah 22:15–22, which shows a successive dynastic office under the King, from which Shebna was removed and Eliakim succeeded him;

"I will thrust you from your office, and you will be cast down from your station. In that day I will call my servant Eliakim the son of Hilkiah, and I will clothe him with your robe, and will bind your girdle on him, and will commit your authority to his hand; and he shall be a father to the inhabitants of Jerusalem and to the house of Judah. And I will place on his shoulder the key of the house of David; he shall open, and none shall shut; and he shall shut, and none shall open."

In these verses, we see an almost identical establishment of a prime minister, in the person of Simon Peter, and in the apostles as fellow ministers holding a supernatural office only hinted at in the Old Covenant, prefigured in the earthly Davidic kingdom, perfected in the Heavenly kingdom, through Jesus Christ. Unlike Eliakim, what was opened or shut by Peter, as prime minister, and by the twelve collectively as fellow ministers, as we see in John 20:19–23, and elsewhere in Scripture, was not confined to the earthly, but included the spiritual as well.

Bishops then, as successors of the disciples, are partakers in holding a successive, dynastic Divine office, established by Jesus Christ himself, to be a father to the inhabitants of the local Church, as ministers of that heavenly Davidic Kingdom, in which Christ Himself is King. As illustrated, this is what Christ established, and this is how the disciples understood their office, and how it was to continue after their death.

Each bishop is responsible for the conduct and welfare of the local church under his care. "While the bond of concord remains and the indivisible sacrament of the Catholic Church continues, each bishop disposes and directs his own work as one who must give an account of his administration to the Lord." St. Cyprian of Carthage, *Letter of Cyprian to Antonias, A Bishop in Numidia* 251–252 A.D.[27]

Each member of the Church likewise, is responsible for their obedience to the bishop, for his care and welfare as their "Father in the faith". Although theologians and biblical scholars teach the Word and assist the Church in unfolding Scriptural meaning, they are not official teachers in the same unique sense and manner that bishops are. Unlike bishops, theologians and scholars have not received the sacramental empowerment to teach the Gospels, as those with this important apostolic commission. Thus a family relationship exists within the Church, with the local bishop as the father, the presbyters and deacons as elder brothers, in concert with the efforts of the religious men and women under vows. The laity live out this teaching as the members of the family, and teach others through both word and their lives, as defined and held by the Church—some of whom will succeed the offices of their elder family members, as God calls them:

"Now it becomes you also not to treat your bishop too familiarly on account of his youth, but to yield him all reverence, having respect to the power of God the Father, as I have known even holy presbyters do, not judging rashly, from the manifest youthful appearance [of their bishop], but as being themselves prudent in God, submitting to him, or rather not to him, but to the Father of Jesus Christ, the bishop of us all. It is therefore fitting that you should, after no hypocritical fashion, obey [your bishop], in honor of Him who has wired us [so to do], since he that does not so deceives not [by such conduct] the bishop that is visible, but seeks to mock Him that is invisible. And all such conduct has reference not to man, but to God, who knows all secrets.

Now it becomes you also not to despise the age of your bishop, but to yield him all reverence, according to the will of God the Father, as I have known even holy presbyters do, not having regard to the manifest youth [of their bishop], but to his knowledge in God; inasmuch as 'not the ancient are [necessarily] wise, nor do the aged understand prudence; but there is a spirit in men.' For Daniel the wise, at twelve years of age, became possessed of the divine Spirit, and convicted the elders, who in vain carried their grey hairs, of being false accusers, and of lusting after the beauty of another man's wife. Samuel also, when he was but a little child, reproved Eli, who was ninety years old, for giving honor to his sons rather than to God. In like manner, Jeremiah also received this message from God, 'Say not, I am a child.' Solomon too, and Josiah, [exemplified the same thing.] The former, being made king at twelve years of age, gave that terrible and difficult judgment in the case of the two women concerning their children. The latter, coming to the throne when eight years old cast down the altars and temples [of the idols], and burned down the groves, for they were dedicated to demons, and not to God. And he slew the false priests, as the corrupters and deceivers of men, and not the worshippers of the Deity. Wherefore youth is not to be despised when it is devoted to God. But he is to be despised who is of a wicked mind, although he be old, and full of wicked days. Timothy the Christ-bearer was young, but hear what his teacher writes to him: 'Let no man despise thy youth, but be thou an example of the believers in word and in conduct.' It is becoming, therefore, that ye also should be obedient to your bishop, and contradict him in nothing; for it is a fearful thing to contradict any such person. For no one does [by such conduct] deceive him that is visible, but does [in reality] seek to mock Him that is invisible, who, however, cannot be mocked by any one. And every such act has respect not to man, but to God. For God says to Samuel, 'They have not mocked thee, but Me.'

And Moses declares, 'For their murmuring is not against us, but against the Lord God.' No one of those has, [in fact,] remained unpunished, who rose up against their superiors. For Dathan and Abiram did not speak against the law, but against Moses, and were cast down alive into Hades. Korah also, and the two hundred and fifty who conspired with him against Aaron, were destroyed by fire. Absalom, again, who had slain his brother, became suspended on a tree, and had his evil-designing heart thrust through with darts. In like manner was Abeddadan beheaded for the same reason. Uzziah, when he presumed to oppose the priests and the priesthood, was smitten with leprosy. Saul also was dishonored, because he did not wait for Samuel the high priest. It behooves you, therefore, also to reverence your superiors.

It is fitting, then, not only to be called Christians, but to be so in reality: as some indeed give one the title of bishop, but do all things without him. Now such persons seem to me to be not possessed of a good conscience, seeing they are not steadfastly gathered together according to the commandment.

It is fitting, then, not only to be called Christians, but to be so in reality. For it is not the being called so, but the being really so, that renders a man blessed. To those who indeed talk of the bishop, but do all things without him, will He who is the true and first Bishop, and the only High Priest by nature, declare, 'Why call ye Me Lord, and do not the things which I say?' For such persons seem to me not possessed of a good conscience, but to be simply dissemblers and hypocrites." St. Ignatius. *The Epistle of St. Ignatius to the Magnesians* [Short & Long]— Ch. 3 & 4. CCEL.

8. We affirm that, in accordance with Sacred Scripture and ancient Tradition, only males may be ordained to the Diaconate, Priesthood, or Episcopate.

The selection of the twelve disciples is representative of the twelve tribes of Israel, being re-established, but this time in a manner that includes peoples of every nation, into this new kingdom, the Kingdom of God. As the Levitical priests offered tribute and sacrifice to God on behalf of the people, this natural symbol, which lacked supernatural grace, was perfected in the New Testament, with new priests who offer a supernatural Sacrifice which did not merely atone for sin, but cleansed us from sin, and purchased our freedom, as no Old Testament sacrifice could do. And so the supernatural reality of spiritual freedom from sin realized in the New Covenant, perfects what could not have been achieved through sacrifice in the Old Covenant. The selection of the twelve was prophetic, and emphasizes that Christ replaced the *natural symbols* of the Old Covenant with the *supernatural realities* of the New Covenant, and He selected the twelve to bring to fulfillment what was pre-figured in the old. His selection of the twelve was His choice, for His reasons, and not those of society. Likewise did the Apostles select men for ordination, and so it has been for the entire life of the Church.

Priesthood, in the New Covenant, is empowered by Christ Himself, to impart God's grace in a way that the Levitical priesthood could not. The Levitical priesthood of the Old Covenant, offered imperfect sacrifice, which could never completely and truly atone for the sin committed, and served to confront man with his sin, as he awaited the coming of the Messiah. In both the Old Covenant Levitical priesthood and the New Covenant sacramental priesthood, both priesthood and fatherhood are considered to be integral and complementary. Not physical bloodline fatherhood, but the concept that the priest is also a "Father in the faith", and that the priest *fathers* the people, according to God's law. In the book of Judges, we see this illustrated, in Judges 17:10, where a Levitical priest, in traveling to find a place to live, came upon Micah. Micah asked him, "Stay with me, and be to me a *father and a priest...*"[emphasis added] Later, in Judges 18:18, when soldiers entered the home of Micah and began to remove the items in it, this priest confronted them. Recognizing that he was a Levitical priest, they too, asked him to be to them, "a father and a priest" as well. Clearly, this was the true understanding of the Levitical priesthood.

The understanding of spiritual fatherhood did not, as some Protestant sects assert, cease with Jesus, who, speaking metaphorically, is misunderstood by them as to forbid the use of the words "father", "master" or "rabbi". The disciples identified themselves as the "fathers in the faith" of various individuals and communities in the early Church, as well as continue to refer to historic Jewish figures as "fathers", as in Romans 9:10, 2 Timothy 1:2, 2 Timothy 1:11, 1 Corinthians 4:17, Philippians 2:22, Tit 1:4, Philemon 10, and 1 Corinthians 4:14-15. In addition, nearly all Protestant seminary's have professors with Doctorate's degrees, calling them "Doctor" Smith or "Rev. Doctor", which would also violate this prohibition, if that is what it were, as "Doctor" comes from the Latin word for "Teacher", which is what a "rabbi" was, at *that* time in history, a teacher. Finally, addressing any individual today, as Mister, Mrs., Miss, or Ms., would also violate such a prohibition, as these are modern day derivatives of the word rendered in English as "Master". Clearly, there was no such understanding of a prohibition on the use of these words. Jesus was teaching against self-aggrandizing and seeking to be called by honorific titles, seeking after fame, and popularity. These things draw the faithful Christian away from Christ and his teaching. And so, we can, rightly and in agreement with the teachings of the Church from its earliest days, address our parish priest as "Father" with tenderness, love and respect.

Attempts to impute a sociopolitical concept into the faith for a perceived wrong are misguided, and demean the singular dignity of female and male alike, as each, being equal in human dignity, has certain uniqueness, given by God to each for a particular purpose. To attempt to negate or minimize these uniquenesses is to reject the gifts of God, in whatever form they take, and live in rebellion against His plan for our life.

9. We affirm the Real Presence of Our Lord in the Eucharist when the Eucharist is performed by a validly ordained Priest of the Holy Catholic Church, with the elements ordained by Christ, and a valid Canon of the Mass including Christ's Words of Institution and the Epiklesis.

Christ is truly present in the Eucharist; Body, Blood, Soul and Divinity. Jesus left no room for doubt in His words "This is My Body"…"This Is My Blood" and "do this in *remembrance* of me". Remembrance being understood in the Jewish context of supernaturally revisiting that event, and participating in it, through the spiritual power of God, in a way that we can only simply confess as a mystery of faith.

There can be no communion with an individual who claims to be Christian, yet rejects this mystery of faith, the Real Presence of Christ in the Eucharist. Indeed to partake of the consecrated bread and wine is to sin against the Body and Blood of Christ. "Whoever therefore, eats the bread or drinks the cup of the Lord in an unworthy manner will be guilty of profaning the Body and Blood of the Lord."(1 Cor. 11:27-30)

10. We affirm that those who receive the Sacraments unworthily do so to their detriment, but do so without effecting the nature or efficacy of the Sacrament itself.

> The Sacraments themselves are infused with the grace of God, empowered by Him, and not through us. The Sacraments are given to us to infuse us with His sanctifying grace to further enable us to conform our life to God's will. Anyone receiving the sacraments unworthily only serves to deceive himself or herself into believing that, not being properly disposed, they can receive the blessings of God dishonestly. One cannot steal grace, nor can we, as the creation, destroy or otherwise affect detrimentally the supernatural grace of an omnipotent God.

> One is to never partake of this most holy gift, knowing that they are not properly disposed to do so, merely for the sake of keeping up appearances, or out of concern for what other people would say, seeing that they did not partake. The church provides that the sacrament of Penance be available prior to Mass, so that the faithful may be properly disposed and in a state of grace in order to receive the Eucharist. Persons refusing to turn from an ongoing sinful state, are not properly disposed, as they refuse to reform their lives and turn from that sin, as admonished be the priest in the sacrament of Penance. And so the sacrament of Penance is of no effect to one who's heart has no intention to turn away from the sin that has so ensnared it, and reform their life. There exists no absolution for one who is not penitent, and has no intention of turning from sin.

> It is a sin against God to rebelliously partake of the sacraments, not being properly disposed to do so, and refusing to honor what God requires of us to be properly disposed to receive so profound and necessary a gift. We, as the adopted sons and daughters of God, knowing what we should do and our responsibility to our heavenly Father, heap wrathful judgment upon ourselves, being held to a much higher standard than those who do not know God, in disobeying Him who has made possible for us the gift of eternal life in His Kingdom.

11. We affirm that the unworthiness of a minister of a Sacrament does not invalidate the Sacrament, but, rather, that a Sacrament performed with the proper matter and form, and with the intention of the Church to make such action a

Sacrament, remains valid, whether or not the minister is worthy to administer that Sacrament.

> While we want to ensure that our ministers of the Sacraments are good men, properly instructed and strong in the faith, it is not the worthiness of the minister that makes the sacraments valid, for no man of his own accord is worthy, but through the power of God, as promised by Christ Himself, that all sacraments of the Church are valid, effective and confer God's supernatural and sanctifying grace. Christ protects the sacraments and the Church by infusing His supernatural grace into them, and the Holy Spirit lovingly guides and protects the Church, leading it into all Truth.

12. We affirm that marriage, conducted as a Sacrament, with the full understanding and intention of both parties to make a marriage, is indissoluble except by death. We believe that the Church may issue a "Declaration of Nullity" in the case of "marriages" which have taken place without proper form, full understanding and intention of the parties involved, or both individuals being able to enter into a valid marriage (matter); and counsel that error be made on the side of compassion for those seeking to make marriages after divorce.

> The mission of the Church is varied with respect to the Sacrament of Marriage, insofar as the Church is responsible for teaching her members, and especially those about to enter into the sacrament of matrimony, the holy and permanent nature of sacramental marriage, and what it means within the teaching of the Church.
>
> The Church is also responsible for the ongoing instruction, care and nurturing of the married estate within the Church, helping to ensure that the seed of matrimony in new couples is lovingly attended to, and enabled to fully grow and develop. This is done through a variety of special programs at the parish or diocesan level, such as special retreats for married couples, social events, and dedicated Masses, just to name a few. These precious unions will in their own time, assist those prospective persons who come after them in matrimony, to prepare them through their own experiences and knowledge.
>
> In addition, the Church is charged to lovingly care for those who are divorced, and work towards the healing of such persons emotionally and spiritually, as well as physically if need be. For those whose

marriage lacked the necessary form, matter or intent in the understanding and teaching of the Church as handed down to us, the Church may, after due examination, determine that such attempted marriage did not, in fact occur, due to a particular defect. Such a determination would render the individual parties free to marry, after proper and due instruction within the Church. Failing such a determination, individuals validly within sacramental marriage, separated from their spouse, are to live continent, chaste lives. Sacramentally married persons, living separate chaste lives, are free to marry again after their current spouse is deceased.

13. We affirm an openness to all of the gifts of the Holy Spirit, including the so-called "Charismata," but finding it unscriptural to require that anyone exercise any particular Charism to be considered a full, believing member of this body. (I Corinthians 12:21) Those who exercise the Charismata are welcome and encouraged to exercise their gifts to the edification of the Church in an orderly, Biblical manner, subject to the godly discipline of the Pastor of the Parish to which they have allegiance.

14. We believe in an intermediate state wherein all persons, after death and individual (particular) judgment, will have an opportunity to repent their sins, acknowledge Jesus as the only Way, Truth and Life, and grow "from strength to strength." We deny that this intermediate state is a place of torture and fear, but affirm that any pains endured in this state are gladly embraced, as they are the pains of releasing our earthly bondage and conforming to the Will of God in all things.

> For those who are members of the Household of God, yet die with the stain of sin still on their soul, is the state of existence in which they are cleansed of the last bit of disordered selfishness and self-love, so that they may enter into the heavenly Kingdom of God. They must be purged of this last bit of sin, for as Scripture states, nothing unclean may enter heaven.

> For those souls in this state of existence, we believe, as Scripture instructs us, that our prayers for them assist them, and through our pleas to God, lessen this process and hasten their entrance into heaven.

15. We believe that there is a possibility that some will reject grace, no matter how often it is offered, and these people freely choose to remain in a state of

separation from God. This state of spirit we call "Hell." It is a freely chosen state of the damned to be damned. It is not the will of the Father that any be lost.

> God gives us free will, to choose to follow Him, or to reject Him. No one is born into a life devoid of this ability to determine for one's self which direction their life will go. During our life, we are given guides and signs of God's love along the way, he calls us to Him, and we decide. God's love touches even and especially, those persons who may not be able to communicate, or communicate effectively or maturely with their fellow man, and provides for such a manner, in accordance with His perfect love and judgement, an opportunity to accept the gift of grace.

> Some people will choose to reject God, and in so doing, will be judged by Him, and be forever separated from God. Such individuals choose this, in spite of God's love for them, and despite His will that they be saved. God gives His grace freely to those who accept and love Him, and walk in His ways, but will not force His grace, nor the gift of salvation upon any who reject Him.

> It is our responsibility as Christians to bring the Good News of Jesus Christ to as many people as possible, and give each an opportunity to become part of our Christian family, the Bride of Christ. This is to be understood as a sacred duty, not to be entered into lightly. Special care is to be given to the proper introduction of the faith to those who do not know Christ. In addition, to those who are Christians, yet do not posses the fullness of the faith, we are to share the completeness of Christian faith with them, inviting them into the deep and rich communion of Christ's Church and His sacramental blessings.

16. We believe that humans are truly endowed with free-will and can freely choose life in Christ Jesus or death through the rejection of grace.

> Humans are free to choose and determine for themselves what they will do. No one is born disposed to reject God, as Man was created in the image and likeness of God. Although our intellect may fail us, our soul yearns for communion with God. By allowing ourselves to be distracted by the pursuit of earthly riches or pleasures, accepting the morality of this world over God's, our ability to come closer to Him is impaired. For too many people, by the time they understand how

much time has been wasted in trivial pursuits, it is too late. We as Christians are called to be vigilant against such distractions, focusing on the true riches of the Heavenly Kingdom, and we are called to draw others to Christ as well.

And so, it is vitally important, that our introduction of the faith to others is complete, informative and presented in love. We do not wish to be the instrument, which causes another to reject the faith.

17. We believe that the Holy Scriptures are inerrant on all matters of faith and morals.

Holy Scripture, being the written Word of God, teaches us what we need to know in order to live the Christ-like life. Scripture comes alive when joined with Sacred Tradition, the orally transmitted expression and understanding of our faith, and empowers us with God's grace, so that the Good News is expressed in a living Church.

It is imperative then, that Holy Scripture be properly interpreted, the words infused with a proper understanding, which comes through Sacred Tradition, as taught authoritatively by the Church; because the Bible was compiled under the inspiration of the Holy Spirit *by* the Church, *for* the Church, to be understood *within* the Church. The Scriptures themselves are not a catechism, that is, they are not, and never were assembled for the purpose of convincing a non-believer to become a Christian. The inspired writers of the Gospels and the Epistles were not writing to or for non-believers, but to full fledged members of the Church, who had a full and proper understanding of what the inspired writer way saying. These writings, which became the New Testament, were not shared with the public at large. Only the members of the Church could hear these writings, in addition to the singing of songs, readings from the Old Testament (Hebrew Scripture), and partake of the Eucharist. Thus, Scripture must be interpreted within the life and understanding of the Church. The most powerful and effective tool for conversion is not the Bible, but the Christian believer whose life lived in faith is a public witness and testimony of Christ alive in him or her.

The New Testament writings are all written to particular individuals or local Churches who are already Christian. Not a single Gospel nor Epistle is written to an unbeliever, but to people who have already been

properly baptized and instructed in the faith, and hold full membership in the Church. In every case, the presumption then, is that the
reader is already a Christian, which means that the sacred writer presumes that there are certain fundamental teachings and understanding
that the reader(s) already possesses. A non-Christian reading the
Gospels or an Epistle, would be unable to adequately understand them,
in the same way the Ethiopian eunuch, referred to in Scripture, was
unable to understand the passages of Hebrew Scripture he was reading.
Upon receiving proper instruction, he was soon baptized into the
family of faith, as scripture chronicles.

18. We believe that people are justified by faith, which is demonstrated in good
works and obedient practice. Both faith and works are necessary to the living of a
Christian life.

To truly believe in Christ is not only mental assent to the "concept" of
Christ: It is not a one-time acceptance of Christ, only to be followed by
a lifetime of sin and continued disordered self-love. True belief requires
a change in the life of the believer, turning away from sin and towards
a life filled with God's love and self-sacrifice for others. True faith elicits
action on the part of the believer, not in order *to* be saved, but because
he *is* saved and *can be* saved, if he remains steadfast in faith, working
through love.

19. We believe that there is a "cloud of witnesses," the Saints, whom we may ask
to pray for us as one would ask any other member of the Church. It is an idola-
trous practice, however, to ask Saints to give us any material or physical blessing
of their own. For, while the prayer of the righteous is very effective (James 5:16),
yet every good thing comes from the Father (James 1:17).

In the same way in which Christians on earth ask one another to pray
for them, and also with them, in their time of illness or great tribula-
tion, Christians may ask those Christians already before the throne of
God to pray for us and with us. From Scripture we know that the
prayers and petitions of the saints are brought before God's altar.

It is through God's benevolence that He makes known to the Saints
our petitions for assistance. The Saints, our older brothers and sisters in
the faith, pray with us, and for us, in union with the Church on earth.
Christian tombs, in the first centuries of the Church down throughout

the years, have been discovered, by archaeologists and others, with inscriptions that those Christians who were martyred for the faith, or abided in the bosom of the Church until death, would pray for those members of the Church still on earth.

We know that the prayers of the saints are presented in heaven upon the altar before the throne of the Lamb. (Revelation 8:3–5)

20. We believe that the "Sacrifice of the Mass" is a "making present" (anamnesis) of Jesus' One Sacrifice, once offered, forever. Jesus' sacrifice is made present on the altar, and, as such, the Mass may be spoken of as a Sacrifice. Therefore, it is appropriate that Masses be offered for the living and the dead, making present to the Church now the One Sacrifice once offered, and making very present the benefits of Christ's Holy Sacrifice to the benefit of those present at the offering.

21. We believe that Mary, the mother of Jesus, was truly the Theotokos, or bearer of the Incarnation of the Second Person of the Trinity. When Mary is called "Mother of God" we truly honor her who gave everything of herself to secure our Salvation. However, the Theotokos is called "Mother of God" in the sense that she bore Jesus, who was and is the Incarnation of the Son, not in the sense that she generated, in any way, the Godhead.

> As Jesus Christ is true God and true Man, like us in all things but sin, it is not possible to profess that the Ever-Virgin Mary gave birth to only the physical human nature of Jesus, as her very conception itself was an act of God's grace. Nor was the physical body of Jesus later infused with His divinity after his birth. Jesus in human form is true God and true Man from conception. This is not to say that the Second Person of the Triune Godhead did not exist prior to this, but that He had not taken corporeal human form up until that time.

22. We believe that the prayers of the Blessed Virgin are effective because of her great and unique faith. Mary is unique because of her great faith, and it is this, which gives particular effectualness to her prayers.

> The ever-Virgin Mary is honored very highly in the Church (hyper-dulia) due to her great faith and unswerving obedience to God. Most highly favored due to her great faith, and obedience in faith. Her faith in God made her His choice to be the virgin who would fulfill the prophecy, and bear the Messiah. From the day of His earthly birth, she

carried Jesus in her arms, to the day of His death. Now it is she who is carried in the majesty and splendor of God's special place for her, His beloved creation, who served faithfully and steadfastly. All generations do call her blessed.

23. We believe that all Bishops who have valid orders and remain in the orthodox faith, are successors of the Apostles, and, while we accord to the Bishop of Rome great respect, and primacy of position, we see him as first among equals, however completely reject the Papal Claims of Universal Jurisdiction and Infallibility.

There was no consensus in the early Church establishing universal jurisdiction of the Bishop of Rome. The Church at Rome, being one of the ancient sees of the Church and it having been established by Peter, as was the Church at Antioch, naturally had a place of honor, and the determinations of the Bishop of Roman carried great weight within the Church. Several noted Fathers of the early Church did not teach or espouse the concept of universal jurisdiction of the Bishop of Rome, but a collegial model of Church.

During the fifteenth century, the church at Utrecht, became known for its piety, through the efforts of a society there called "The Brothers of the Common Life", founded by Gerard the Great (Geert Groote), whose charge was to instruct people in the faith, support evangelization where priests were in short supply and promote regular reading of Scripture. This organization, not a monastic order but a voluntary organization, based at Deventer, had a profound impact on many theologians of the day, and are noted for such famous members as Desiderius Erasmus and Thomas a Kempis, regarded as the author of the *Imitation of Christ*. This piety would come to mark the differences between the church at Utrecht and the piety of the Jesuits. It is this piety that was infused into the church of Utrecht and survived there during the persecution of the Church caused by the Reformation, and continued within the Old Catholic Church later on.

The Brothers of the Common Life also instructed a young man who was to become the head of the Roman Catholic Church in 1522 AD, Pope Adrian VI. Born Adrian Florensz, of working class parents in 1459 AD in Utrecht, he became a professor at the University of Louvain. He became bishop of Tortosa, later a cardinal, and then teacher to Emperor Maximilian's son, Charles. Pope Adrian VI generated resentment because of his moral conservatism and commitment to eradicating corruption within the Church. Interestingly enough, and related to our understanding of Old Catholic theology, Pope Adrian VI is widely known as a result of his having given his private opinion that the Pope is not infallible.

24. We believe that faithful Christian Marriage between a male and a female, free of impediments, is the only legitimate state for sexual expression between individuals.

Christian marriage, being a sacrament established by God Himself, and not merely an institution of any civil secular government, is therefore validly defined only by God, and He has established the natural and supernatural nature of marriage. The covenant bonds of marriage are sealed with an oath (sacramentum) which creates family, supernaturally empowered by God, as He is the first party of the vows given. The sacred vows exchanged involve one man, one woman and God, and are professed in the presence of the family of God, the Church.

A part of marital responsibility concerns the regulation of procreation. For appropriate reason, spouses may wish to space the births of their children. But this should not be accomplished through immoral means. Artificial contraception demeans the meaning of the conjugal marital act. Artificial contraception is the using of mechanical, chemical, or medical procedures to prevent conception from taking place, as a natural result of the marital conjugal act. Artificial contraception is a sin against the openness to procreation required of marriage, the permanence of the covenant marital bond in fidelity to one another and what that covenant bond brings, and also the inner truth of conjugal love. The marital conjugal act is intended to be a profoundly meaningful act, due to the fact that the act could result in the blessings and gift of children. Children are a sign of the marital bond as a lifetime of commitment and love.

Natural Family Planning (NFP) are methods of responsibly regulating births, and are not forms of artificial contraception. Periodic abstinence, that is, the methods of birth regulation based on self-observation and the use of natural infertile periods, is in conformity with the objective criteria of morality. These methods foster respect of the spouses for their bodies, encourage tenderness between them, and favor the education of an authentic freedom. In each case, the decision to engage in the marital act during fertile periods or to abstain must be made in love and selflessness, and free of any self serving reasoning. These methods do not prevent conception, which would, as a result, close the conjugal act to the potential of the gift of life. Artificial contraception has resulted in the general decline in our society's morality, a marked decline in respect for women, and an increase in the objectification of human beings as tools for selfish acts of sexual self-gratification. Given these tools, it is the responsibility of each marital couple to use NFP responsibly and within the spirit of the Deposit of Faith.

Marriage was created, as a permanent sacrament by Almighty God, for the mutual help of husband and wife, for the increase of mankind through an expression of commitment and love in the conjugal marital act, and of the Church with a seed sanctified by God's blessing.

It is lawful for all people to marry, who are of the single estate and are able, with proper judgment, to give their consent. Yet it is the duty of Christians to marry only in the Lord. And so Christians are not to be unequally yoked, by marrying individuals who are not Christians, or are notoriously and unrepentantly sinful in their life, or maintain damnable heresies.

Marriage ought not to be within the degrees of consanguinity or affinity forbidden by the Sacred Scripture. Nor can such incestuous marriage ever be made valid by any law of man or consent of parties, so as to legitimize those persons living together as man and wife. Nor shall the faithful, in any way, tolerate, promote or facilitate such a purported union.

25. We believe that whatsoever is not repugnant to the Catholic Faith, but which aids in belief and devotion, may be believed as pious opinion, but may not be taught as doctrine of the Church.

Certain beliefs and devotions held by our brethren in the Eastern Orthodox, Oriental Orthodox and Roman Catholic Churches, some of which has even been dogmatized, that are not incompatible with the Old Catholic Faith, may be piously believed and privately practiced by the faithful, provided such pious belief is not imposed on other members of the Church. Any question of a potential conflict shall be settled by the College of Bishops under the guidance of the Archbishop-Metropolitan.

26. We affirm that the Eucharist is the principal service of the Church; that its celebration is commanded by the Lord, and that it shall be the regularly celebrated Sunday Worship whenever possible.

> The faithful have an inherent right to proper liturgical worship, and participation at Mass, if properly disposed, as members of the Church. The local Bishop shall, as Chief Shepherd of the local Church, ensure that the spiritual needs of the faithful are met, and that their temporal needs are ministered to, as the local Church is able.

> The Archbishop-Metropolitan and the College of Bishops are charged with ensuring that only authorized, approved liturgy is used. The normative liturgy is the Old Catholic Missal and Ritual of 1909. Also authorized is the Knott Missal, as is the Tridentine Mass in Latin. Eastern Rite Churches are authorized to use the ancient liturgies of St. John Chrysostom and Basil. Other ancient liturgical forms of the Mass may be used in certain and specific cases, approved in advance by the Archbishop-Metropolitan. The liturgy is, the "work of the people", their offering up of prayers and devotion to God, and participation in the communion of the entire Church through the Eucharist, and not the private property of any one individual or local church.

Apostolic Tradition

In explaining Apostolic Tradition, many Evangelical Protestants immediately begin to think of Christ's condemnation of "traditions of Men", and immediately assume that all tradition falls into this category; it does not. The term "Apostolic Tradition" does not refer to human customs, practices or ceremonies. Apostolic Tradition is the "Deposit of Faith", "The faith once and for all handed down to the saints." (Jude 3) The word selected by the sacred writer for "handed down" is *paradotheise*, the root form being *paradidomi*, from which we derive our English word "tradition".[28] As Tradition is understood in this verse, it refers to the "Deposit of Faith", the Holy Gospel or Good News of Jesus Christ.

Tradition, as referred to here, is not man-made, and it is not something apart from Scripture. Apostolic Tradition is God's Word, alive in the living experience and expression of faith of the Body of Christ, the Church. What is an example of Apostolic Tradition? The canon of the New Testament, that is, the recognized list of books that comprise the New Testament is Apostolic Tradition. Indeed, the entire canon of the Bible, of both Old and New Testament, is a matter of

Apostolic Tradition, and it is an Apostolic Tradition that must be followed or else you have no Bible.[29] Many books of the Bible do not, in their text, indicate their author, and yet, through Apostolic Tradition, we accept the authorship as given.

Is this to say that all traditions found in the Church are Apostolic Traditions? To say so, would be to confuse customs (tradition with a small t), with the Deposit of Faith, of which Apostolic teaching (Tradition with a capital T for our discussion) is part.

But let us not forget the Lord's condemnation of the "traditions of men", "Then the Pharisees and scribes came to Jesus and said, 'Why do your disciples transgress the traditions of the elders? For they do not wash their hands when they eat". (Matthew 15:1-2) The washing of the hands was a human restriction imposed by the elders, and not part of any deposit of Divine Revelation. Christ's condemnation too, was of the elders' creation of "loopholes" in Mosaic Law to allow the violation of commandments, such as the creation of the "Corban rule" found in Mark 7:9–13. In the "Corban Rule" a son was "lawfully" able to keep money that should have been given to support one's parents in their old age, by claiming that it had been given for use at the Temple, yet maintaining control over it.

Apostolic Tradition then, is not man-made customs or ceremony. In the early years of the Church, the teaching of the Gospel of Christ (which was and is termed the "Apostolic Tradition") was done orally, as for about the first three hundred years in the life of the Church, there was not a Bible as we know it today. There was the Hebrew Scripture (Old Testament) in the form of the Septuagint and, in time, the Apostolic Letters (New Testament) which at first, circulated to a few, but not all of the early churches. Most people could not read or write, but could listen, and learned the Good News in the same way the Oral Torah had been transmitted to their Hebrew forebearers, alongside and with the Written Torah, both as the Word of God.

An interpretation of the written Bible, absent the understanding of the Faith that is conveyed with it, as the Apostolic Tradition, opens the door to an individual, subjective and private approach to interpretation of Scripture that the Bible itself warns us to shun and avoid. Consider the points raised by the following:

> "To separate the Bible from the Church is to make it a 'free-floating' balloon, whereby an endless number of interpreters can blow it in any

direction their doctrinal biases please. However, the Spirit-led Church throughout time does not leave room for such a subjective approach. She, through the co-operation of her members, is able to discern God's Word because she is a body, a network of relationships which transcends 'private' interpretations or limited eras. This all-encompassing union is possible because of the unique spiritual bond, which exists between the Body of Christ and Jesus the Word.

God's Word is intended for *God's* people, not for unbelievers. *The Word of God is revealed and experienced as the Word of God only when it is received by a people of faith.* How, then, does the unbeliever hear God's Word? God's Word is spoken to unbelievers *through* believers (either via their testimony in the scriptures, or through those now living). But in either case, God's Word is not heard as God's Word unless the Spirit of the Word reveals it to those who listen. This is why Jerome (342-420) stated that even though the Gnostics had Biblical texts in their possession, they still did not posses the Gospel. For the same reason Tertullian (155-220 AD), a teacher and leader of the African Church, never discussed the Bible with Heretics. They had no right to use the Scriptures…they did not belong to them. Scriptures are the Church's possession."[30]

And even more succinctly;

"The Bible without the Spirit and Christ's Body is only potentially sufficient. *It is all sufficient only when read within the fellowship of all the saints of all time.* The ministry of Spirit in the Church (Tradition) lets us see the Biblical Message clearly. *Here,* within the Community of God, one can begin to comprehend the 'breadth, length, height and depth' of God's love in Christ. (Eph. 3:17-19) *Here,* the Scriptures become self-evident to the individual believer. *Here,* they can be understood for what they really are: the revelation of God among His people."[31]

"I hope to come to you soon, but I am writing these instructions to you so that, if I am delayed, you may know how one ought to behave in the household of God, which is the pillar and bulwark of the truth." (1 Tim. 3:14-15) And so, it is the Church that is the ultimate arbiter.

And so, Apostolic Tradition is not some foreign concept espoused only by the Roman Catholic Church, as many Protestants wrongly believe, it is the understanding of Scriptural understanding, teaching and interpretation, as espoused by all of Christendom, Eastern and Western.

"So then, brethren, stand firm and hold to the Traditions which you were taught by us, either by word of mouth or by letter." (2 Thess. 2:15) Here we see Apostolic Tradition conveyed verbally having the same weight and authority as that which was written down.

Paul instructs Timothy thus: "…you have heard from me before many witnesses entrust to faithful men who will be able to teach others also." (2 Tim 2:2)

"Now we command you, brethren, in the name of our Lord Jesus Christ, that you keep away from any brother who is living in idleness and not in accord with the Tradition that you have received from us." (2 Thess. 3:6)

"Follow the pattern of the sound words which you have heard from me, in the faith and love which are in Christ Jesus; guard the truth that has been entrusted to you by the Holy Spirit who dwells within us." (2 Tim. 1:13-14)

Jesus did not write the New Law on papyrus or skins, He wrote it in the hearts, minds and souls of the Apostles: "Then he opened their minds to understand the scriptures, and said to them, 'Thus it is written, that the Christ should suffer and on the third day rise from the dead, and that repentance and forgiveness of sins should be preached in his name to all nations, beginning in Jerusalem." (Luke 24:45-47) This Truth, which was taught to us by the Church, lives in each Christian, and is a part of us. To deviate from it is to deviate from the Deposit of Faith inherent in the Church of God.

On Apostolic Tradition:

"As I have already observed, the Church, having received this preaching and this faith, although scattered throughout the whole world, yet, as if occupying but one house, carefully preserves it. She also believes these points [of doctrine] just as if she had but one soul, and one and the same heart, and she proclaims them, and teaches them, and hands them down, with perfect harmony, as if she possessed only one mouth. For, although the languages of the world are dissimilar, yet the import of the Tradition is one and the same. For the Churches which have been planted in Germany do not believe or hand down anything different, nor do those in Spain, nor those in Gaul, nor those in the East, nor those in Egypt, nor those in Libya, nor those which have been established in the central regions of the world. But as the sun, that creature of God, is one and the same throughout the whole world, so also the preaching of the truth shineth everywhere, and enlightens all men that are willing to come to a knowledge of the truth. Nor will any one of the rulers in the Churches, however highly gifted he may be in point of eloquence, teach doctrines different from these (for no one is greater than the Master); nor, on the other hand, will he who is deficient in power of expression inflict injury on the Tradition. For the faith being ever one and the same, neither does one who is able at great length to discourse regarding it, make any addition to it, nor does one, who can say but little diminish it." Irenaeus, *Against Heresies* 1:10:2 189 A.D., CCEL.

"Since therefore we have such proofs, it is not necessary to seek the truth among others which it is easy to obtain from the Church; since the apostles, like a rich man [depositing his money] in a bank, lodged in her hands most copiously all things pertaining to the truth: so that every man, whosoever will, can draw from her the water of life. For she is the entrance to life; all others are thieves and robbers. On this account are we bound to avoid *them*, but to make choice of the thing pertaining to the Church with the utmost diligence, and to lay hold of the tradition of the truth. For how stands the case? Suppose there arise a dispute relative to some important question among us, should we not have recourse to the most ancient Churches with which the apostles held constant intercourse, and learn from them what is certain and clear in regard to the present question? For how should it be if the apostles themselves had not left us writings? Would it not be necessary, [in that case,] to follow the course of the tradition which they handed down to those to whom they did commit the Churches?" Irenaeus, *Against Heresies* 3:4:1 189 A.D., CCEL.

"Of the dogmas and kerygmas preserved in the Church, some we posses from written teaching and others we receive from the tradition of the Apostles, handed on to us in mystery. In respect to piety both are of the same force. No one will contradict any of these, no one, at any rate, who is even moderately versed in matters ecclesiastical. Indeed, were we to try to reject unwritten customs as having no great authority, we would unwittingly injure the Gospel in its vitals; or rather, we would reduce kerygma to a mere term. For instance, to take the first and most general example, who taught us in writing to sign with the sign of the cross those who have trusted in the name of our Lord Jesus Christ? What writing has taught us to turn to the East in prayer? Which of the saints left us in writing the words of the epiclesis at the consecration of the Bread of the Eucharist and the Cup of Benediction?…Where is it written that we are to bless the baptismal water, the oil of anointing, and even the one who is baptized? Is it not from silent and mystical tradition? Indeed, in what written word is even the anointing with oil taught? Where does it say that in baptizing there is to be a triple immersion?" St. Basil the Great, *The Holy Spirit,* 375 A.D.[32]

"Well, they preserving the tradition of the blessed doctrine derived directly from the holy apostles, Peter, James, John, and Paul, the sons receiving it from the father (but few were like the fathers), came by God's will to us also to deposit those ancestral and apostolic seeds. And well I know that they will exult; I do not mean delighted with this tribute, but solely on account of the preservation of the truth, according as they delivered it. For such a sketch as this, will, I think, be agreeable to a soul desirous of preserving from escape the blessed tradition." Clement of Alexandria, *Miscellanies,* 1:1 208 A.D. CCEL.

"At that time there flourished in the Church Hegesippus, whom we know from what has gone before, and Dionysius, bishop of Corinth, and another bishop, Pinytus of Crete, and besides these, Philip, and Apolinarius, and Melito, and Musanus, and Modestus, and finally, Irenaeus. From them has come down to us in writing, the sound and orthodox faith received from apostolic tradition." Eusebius, *Church History* 3:39, 312 A.D., CCEL.

"It is needful also to make use of Tradition; for not everything can be gotten from Sacred Scripture. The holy Apostles handed down some things in the Scriptures, other things in Tradition." St. Epiphanius of Salamis, *Against All Heresies,* inter 374–377 A.D.[33]

"Therefore, brethren, stand fast and hold the traditions which you have been taught, whether by word or by our letter.' From this it is clear that they did not hand down everything by letter, but there was much also that was not written. Like that which was written, the unwritten too is worthy of belief. So let us regard the tradition of the Church also as worthy of belief. Is it a tradition? Seek no further." St. John Chrysostom, *Homilies On The Second Epistle To The Thessalonians,* inter 398-404 A.D. CCEL.

On Abortion:

In Old Catholic concerns for quality of life issues today, there is and must rightly be, a hierarchy of truths. Any support or activism regarding social issues that is lacking in a definite and emphatic support of the right to life of the unborn child is fatally defective. Certainly the other life issues are important and must be strongly addressed. However, the Old Catholic position on abortion requires and demands of us assigning preeminence in according protection to the unborn child. The right to life is the foundation upon which all quality of life issues are laid. One can have no true Christian commitment to caring for the poor, feeding the hungry, housing the homeless, healthcare, medicine, "just war doctrines" or any other related issues, without an active commitment to the God-given right to life. Thus, among these life issues, the right to life tops the hierarchy of truth as it pertains to them.

It is also important to know and understand that Christians may inadvertently promote abortion through the use of contraceptive drugs and devices. Drugs such as Depo-Prevara, Norplant, and the contraceptive pill, ("The Pill") commonly used, is an abortifacient, and sometimes causes an early chemical abortion after a new life has been conceived, and not simply prevents conception from occurring. Thus, many Christians have unknowingly caused the deaths of many human beings, through the deception of others and unwillingness to thoroughly research such drugs before using them. Other so-called contraception devices actually mechanically cause the death of unborn children conceived. All potential and actual abortifacients are expressly forbidden and gravely sinful.

"You shall not procure abortion, nor destroy a new-born child." *The Didache*, 140 A.D.[34]

"A woman who has deliberately destroyed a fetus must pay the penalty for murder." St. Basil the Great, *Of Basil To Amphilochius, Bishop of Iconium; The First Canonical Letter*, 374 A.D.[30]

"And when we say that those women who use drugs to bring on abortion commit murder, and will have to give an account to God for the abortion, on what principle should we commit murder? For it does not belong to the same person to regard the very *foetus* in the womb as a created being, and therefore an object of God's care, and when it has passed into life, to kill it; and not to expose an infant, because those who expose them are chargeable with child-murder, and on the other hand, when it has been reared to destroy it. But we are in all things always alike and the same, submitting ourselves to reason, and not ruling over it." Athenagoras, *A Plea for the Christians,* 35, 177 A.D., CCEL.

"In our case, murder being once for all forbidden, we may not destroy even the foetus in the womb, while as yet the human being derives blood from other parts of the body for its sustenance. To hinder a birth is merely a speedier man-killing; nor does it matter whether you take away a life that is born, or destroy one that is coming to the birth. That is a man which is going to be one; you have the fruit already in its seed." Tertullian, *Apology* 9:8., 197 A.D., CCEL.

"Why sow where the ground makes it its care to destroy the fruit? Where there are many efforts at abortion? Where there is murder before the birth? For even the harlot thou dost not let continue a mere harlot, but makest her a murderess also. You see how drunkenness leads to whoredom, whoredom to adultery, adultery to murder; or rather to a something even worse than murder. For I have no name to give it, since it does not take off the thing born, but prevent its being born. Why then dost thou abuse the gift of God, and fight with His laws, and follow after what is a curse as if a blessing, and make the chamber of procreation a chamber for murder, and arm the woman that was given for childbearing unto slaughter? For with a view to drawing more money by being agreeable and an object of longing to her lovers, even this she is not backward to do, so heaping upon thy head a great pile of fire. For even if the daring deed be hers, yet the causing of it is thine." St. John Chrysostom, *Homilies on Romans* 24 391 A.D., CCEL.

On Communion Only To The Baptized:

"Let no one eat or drink of the Eucharist with you except those who have been baptized in the name of the Lord; for it was in reference to this that the Lord said: 'Do not give that which is holy to dogs." *The Didache,* 140 A.D.[35]

On Confession

"Confess your offenses in church, and do not go up to your prayers with an evil conscience. This is the way of life." *The Didache,* 140 A.D.[36]

"It is necessary to confess our sins to those to whom the dispensation of God's mysteries is entrusted. Those doing penance of old are found to have done it before the saints. It is written in the Gospel that they confessed their sins to John the Baptist; but in Acts they confessed to the Apostles, by whom also all were baptized." St. Basil the Great, *Rules Briefly Treated*, 370 A.D.[37]

"Let us therefore implore forgiveness for all those transgressions which through any [suggestion] of the adversary we have committed. And those who have been the leaders of sedition and disagreement ought to have respect to the common hope. For such as live in fear and love would rather that they themselves than their neighbors should be involved in suffering. And they prefer to bear blame themselves, rather than that the concord which has been well and piously handed down to us should suffer. For it is better that a man should acknowledge his transgressions than that he should harden his heart, as the hearts of those were hardened who stirred up sedition against Moses the servant of God, and whose condemnation was made manifest [unto all]. For they went down alive into Hades, and death swallowed them up." St. Clement, *Letter To The Corinthians*, 80 A.D.[38]

On Order Within The Church:

"See that ye all follow the bishop, even as Jesus Christ does the Father, and the presbytery as ye would the apostles; and reverence the deacons, as being the institution of God. Let no man do anything connected with the Church without the bishop. Let that be deemed a proper Eucharist, which is [administered] either by the bishop, or by one to whom he has entrusted it. Wherever the bishop shall appear, there let the multitude [of the people] also be; even as, wherever Jesus Christ is, there is the Catholic Church. It is not lawful without the bishop either to baptize or to celebrate a love-feast; but whatsoever he shall approve of, that is also pleasing to God, so that everything that is done may be secure and valid.

Moreover, it is in accordance with reason that we should return to soberness [of conduct], and, while yet we have opportunity, exercise repentance towards God. For "in Hades there is no one who can confess his sins." For "behold the man, and his work is before him." And [the Scripture saith], "My son, honor thou God and the king." And say I, Honor thou God indeed, as the Author and Lord of all things, but the bishop as the high-priest, who bears the image of God-of God. inasmuch as he is a ruler, and of Christ, in his capacity of a priest. After Him, we must also honor the king. For there is no one superior to God, or even like to Him, among all the beings that exist. Nor is there any one in the Church greater than the bishop, who ministers as a priest to God for the salvation of the whole world. Nor, again, is there any one among rulers to be compared with the king, who secures peace and good order to those over whom he rules. He who honors the bishop shall be honored by God, even as he that dishonors him shall be punished by God. For if he that rises up against kings is justly held worthy of punishment, inasmuch as he dissolves public order, of how much sorer punishment, suppose ye, shall he be thought worthy, who presumes to do anything without the bishop, thus both destroying the [Church's] unity, and throwing its order into confusion? For the priesthood is the very highest point of all good things among men, against which whosoever is mad enough to strive, dishonors not man, but God, and Christ Jesus, the First-born, and the only High Priest, by nature, of the Father. Let all things therefore be done by you with good order in Christ. Let the laity be subject to the deacons; the deacons to the presbyters; the presbyters to the bishop; the bishop to Christ, even as He is to the Father. As ye, brethren, have refreshed me, so will Jesus Christ refresh you. Ye have loved me when absent, as well as when present. God will recompense you, for whose sake ye have shown such kindness towards His prisoner. For even if I am not worthy of it, yet your zeal [to help me] is an admirable thing. For "he who honors a prophet in the name of a prophet, shall receive a prophet's reward." It is manifest also, that he who honors a prisoner of Jesus Christ shall receive the reward of the martyrs." St. Ignatius of Antioch, *Letter To The Smyrneans*, 110 A.D. CCEL.

On The Spiritual Realities Of The Sacraments:

"Also, the apostle testifies, and says, "Ye cannot drink the cup of the Lord and the cup of devils; ye cannot be partakers of the Lord's table and of the table of devils." He threatens, moreover, the stubborn and forward, and denounces them, saying, "Whosoever eateth the bread or drinketh the cup of the Lord unworthily, is guilty of the body and blood of the Lord." All these warnings being scorned and contemned,-before their sin is expiated, before confession has been made of their crime, before their conscience has been purged by sacrifice and by the hand of the priest, before the offence of an angry and threatening Lord has been appeased, violence is done to His body and blood; and they sin now against their Lord more with their hand and mouth than when they denied their Lord." St. Cyprian of Carthage, *The Lapsed*, 251 A.D. CCEL.

On Apostolic Succession:

"Since, however, it would be very tedious, in such a volume as this, to reckon up the successions of all the Churches, we do put to confusion all those who, in whatever manner, whether by an evil self-pleasing, by vainglory, or by blindness and perverse opinion, assemble in unauthorized meetings; [we do this, I say,] by indicating that tradition derived from the apostles, of the very great, the very ancient, and universally known Church founded and organized at Rome by the two most glorious apostles, Peter and Paul; as also [by pointing out] the faith preached to men, which comes down to our time by means of the successions of the bishops. For it is a matter of necessity that every Church should agree with this Church, on account of its pre-eminent authority, that is, the faithful everywhere, inasmuch as the apostolic tradition has been preserved continuously by those [faithful men] who exist everywhere.

The blessed apostles, then, having founded and built up the Church, committed into the hands of Linus the office of the episcopate. Of this Linus, Paul makes mention in the Epistles to Timothy. To him succeeded Anacletus; and after him, in the third place from the apostles, Clement was allotted the bishopric. This man, as he had seen the blessed apostles, and had been conversant with them, might be said to have the preaching of the apostles still echoing [in his ears], and their traditions before his eyes. Nor was he alone [in this], for there were many still remaining who had received instructions from the apostles. In the time of this Clement, no small dissension having occurred among the brethren at Corinth, the Church in Rome dispatched a most powerful letter to the Corinthians, exhorting them to peace, renewing their faith, and declaring the tradition which it had lately received from the apostles, proclaiming the one God, omnipotent, the Maker of heaven and earth, the Creator of man, who brought on the deluge, and called Abraham, who led the people from the land of Egypt, spoke with Moses, set forth the law, sent the prophets, and who has prepared fire for the devil and his angels. From this document, whosoever chooses to do so, may learn that He, the Father of our Lord Jesus Christ, was preached by the Churches, and may also understand the apostolic tradition of the Church, since this Epistle is of older date than these men who are now propagating falsehood, and who conjure into existence another god beyond the Creator and the Maker of all existing things. To this Clement there succeeded Evaristus. Alexander followed Evaristus; then, sixth from the apostles, Sixtus was appointed; after him, Telephorus, who was gloriously martyred; then Hyginus; after him, Pius; then after him, Anicetus. Sorer having succeeded Anicetus, Eleutherius does now, in the twelfth place from the apostles, hold the inheritance of the episcopate. In this order, and by this succession, the ecclesiastical tradition from the apostles, and the preaching of the truth, have come down to us. And this is most abundant proof that there is one and the same vivifying faith, which has been preserved in the Church from the apostles until now, and handed down in truth." St. Irenaeus, *Against Heresies,* 3: 2-3. A.D. 120-202.[39]

On The Essential Belief In The Trinity:

"But what is also to the point, let us note that the very tradition, teaching, and faith of the Catholic Church from the beginning, which the Lord gave, was preached by the Apostles, and was preserved by the Fathers. On this was the Church founded; and if anyone departs from this, he neither is nor any longer ought to be called a Christian: there is a Trinity, holy and perfect, acknowledged as God, in Father, Son and Holy Spirit, having nothing foreign or external mixed with It, not composed of a fashioner and an originated, but entirely creative and fashioning; It is consistent in Itself, indivisible in nature, and Its activity is one." St. Athanasius, *Four Letters To The Serapion of Thmius*, 359-360 A.D.[40]

Faith and Works

Faith in Christ is a faith that is operative in the life of the believing Christian. An individual who truly believes that Christ is the Messiah acts on that faith, not in order to be saved, but because he can, through Christ, be saved. A faith that is alive is not an intellectual assent to the "concept" of God and salvation, absent works of charity and love. Faith results in a conversion of the individual through this communion with God, and calls the Christian to transfigure his or her life into an expression and extension of Christ's sacrificial life among us. Faith works, and in so doing, directs our ongoing development and progression as Christians.

This does <u>not</u> mean, and the Church does <u>not</u> teach, any sort of "works-based salvation". She does not teach that we can do anything of our merit to earn salvation. This is the classic charge of some Protestant sects against Catholicism, and it is entirely false. But likewise, the Church does not teach, "We are saved by faith *alone*". The Bible doesn't teach it, the Early Church never believed it, and the only place in Scripture that we find "faith" alongside "alone" is where James said, "You see that a man is justified by works *and not by faith alone*." (James 2:24) [emphasis added]

To those who say that all that is required of an individual is to believe in the Lord, in order to be saved, in order to justify a minimal intrusiveness of God in the daily life of the Christian, the challenge is simply to look at: What does the word 'believe' mean? To answer that question, is to refer to the complete context of Scripture, and not isolate one sentence and take it out of context. In doing so, we see that this one word infers far more than intellectual assent.

St. Paul condemned the *"works of the law"* (literally translated as, "works of Torah"), that is, the Law of Moses, circumcision, kosher dietary rules, and the sacrifices for atonement for sin, because these requirements did not cleanse man of his sin. Rather, they served to bring man face-to-face with his sin, so that he would look forward to the coming of the Messiah, who had already come. This is not to be confused with St. James, speaking on faith without works being dead. He was speaking of the works of mercy and kindness to one another, that Christians, their lives configured to Christ, should be engaged it. Again, this indicates that a faith that is not operative in the life of the believer is not a mature faith.

"What does it profit, my brethren, if a man says he has faith but has not works? Can his faith save him? If a brother or sister is ill-clad and in lack of daily food, and one of you says to them 'Go in peace, be warmed and well filled,' without giving then the things needed for the body, what does it profit? So faith by itself, if it has no works, is dead." (James 2:14-17)

And again:

"You believe that God is one; you do well. Even the demons believe—and shudder. Do you want to be shown, you foolish fellow, that faith apart from works is barren? Was not Abraham our Father justified by works, when he offered his son Isaac upon the altar? You see that faith was active along with his works, and faith was completed by works, and the scripture was fulfilled which says, 'Abraham believed God, and it was reckoned to him as righteousness'; and he was called the friend of God. You see that a man is justified by works and not by faith alone." (James 2:19-24)

"When we hear, 'Your faith has saved you,' we do not understand [the Lord] to say simply that they will be saved who have believed in whatever manner, even if works have not followed. To begin with, it was to the Jews alone that He spoke this phrase, *who had lived in accord with the law and blamelessly*, and who had lacked only faith in the Lord." St. Clement of Alexandria, *Stromateis or Miscellanies*, post 202 A.D.[41] [emphasis added]

"By faith Noah, being warned by God concerning events as yet unseen, *took heed and constructed an ark* for the saving of his household; by this he condemned the world and became an heir of the righteousness which comes by faith." (Heb. 11:7) [emphasis added]

"Do not marvel at this; for the hour is coming when all who are in the tombs will hear his voice and come forth, those who have *done good*, to the resurrection of life, and those who have done evil, to the resurrection of judgment." (John 5:28-29) [emphasis added]

And so, having been given the eternal gift of Divine Sonship, through Christ's sacrifice, we are to take up our cross and follow Him. *We must work out our salvation, in fear and trembling* (Phil 2:12) and not be proud or arrogant in our adoption into the Divine Family, lest we fall (1 Cor. 9:27). We must walk in faith, and obey Christ not only in word, *but also in deed, lest we be cut off from Him.* (Rom. 11:21-22) [emphasis added]

On The Liturgy

The liturgy of the Church is the essential act of corporate worship of the Church. In the liturgy, the Church comes to the altar of God, to offer pray, worship and sacrifice to God and to enter mystically into the Eucharistic Meal. In a sense that is not merely metaphorical, but is real and supernatural (anamnesis), we enter the Upper Room and participate in the Last Supper.

The entire Church comes together as a united family each Sunday (the Lord's Day) and offer united and familial prayer, worship and sacrifice to God, in a way that is unknown among our non-Apostolic separated brethren. The specific prayers, and order of the Mass are not new, but rather point backward to that first Eucharistic Meal, and our fidelity to them indicates the superlative importance of this intimate, supernatural communion (koinonia). The significance of this fidelity is to be noted, as the Liturgy of the Mass is not a private prayer, it is not the possession of a local parish or even a diocese, but rather it is the prayer of the entire Catholic (universal) Church, and as such, is not to be subjected to local modification, innovation or alteration in any way. The faithful have a right to a proper, reverent and authentic Divine Liturgy, in the approved Rite for that Church. It is the responsibility of each member of this Church's clergy and laity to ensure that this right is proactively protected.

Modifications of the Liturgy

Ad hoc changes in prayer, readings, rubrics (posture and position of persons during worship) and types of music result in misunderstanding and indeed, misinterpretation of the proper nature and focus of worship during the Diving Liturgy. It is grave error to attempt to input Protestant worship types within

Catholic liturgical worship. Each member of the Church has a proper function in the Mass, which is not to be encroached upon, surrendered to another, nor arbitrarily assumed by others not formally trained and appointed or ordained to that particular office in the Church. The offices of the Church, both those appointed and those to which one is ordained, are to be revered as gifts from God, and respected, because we revere and respect He who established the Church.

Likewise the proper form, matter and intent are, in all things, to be correct and without defect. Substitution of ordinary bread for unleavened hosts is expressly prohibited; likewise using grape juice as a substitute for pure, unadulterated grape wine renders the consecration of such defective matter invalid. Likewise, substituting a personal prayer in place of the words of consecration on the part of the priest would render the consecratory act invalid. In addition, the scandal of the faithful and sacrilege against the most precious sacrifice of the altar that occurs with the usage of defective matter at Mass, severely damages the unity of the Church that is uniquely expressed in the Divine Liturgy and the Eucharistic Celebration.

The bishop, priest, deacon and the faithful are all to be properly disposed to receive the Sacrament of the Holy Eucharist, first having confessed grave sins in Auricular Confession and having received Absolution, and having asked for forgiveness in venial sins in the penitential rite of the liturgy. For the clergy, this preparation for Mass begins the night before with prayer and supplication, continues with fasting until after Mass, and precedes Mass with the vesting prayers in the sacristy. All is to be undertaken with the utmost reverence and piety, as one who is penitent. The Penitential Rite is *not* a substitute for Confession and Absolution for grave (mortal) sin, and individuals in a state of mortal sin may *not* receive the Precious Body and Blood. Likewise, any member of this Church who openly rejects any *de fide* article of faith is not to be attended to at altar, and shall in no way receive the Precious Body and Blood.

The homily is to be given by the deacon or priest (or bishop if presiding) at Mass. The homily is an integral part of the Mass, and the proper office of the priest as teacher is not to be substituted by individuals who are not ordained deacons or priests of this Church, or a fellow Church in communion with us, or a priest or bishop approved by the Archbishop-Metropolitan of this Church. Likewise, the homily is never to be invaded by the profane, such as political stumping, elections or other profane endeavors. It is, however, entirely fitting to re-read the readings and Gospel (if originally read in Latin), give prayers such as the "Our Father" and

"Hail Mary" for members or individuals in need of prayer, and pray Archbishop Mathew's "Prayer for Christian Unity", within the homily.

The position and posture of the faithful too, have very sacred and historically important meaning during the liturgy, and likewise are not to be modified or changed to reflect local preference, influence of non-apostolic faiths, or general misunderstanding of the nature of Catholic worship. For the approved Rites of this Church, in each and every case, the proper and normative form, matter and intent, as well as rubrics, vestments and understanding of piety proper to each, are to be strictly observed. Parts of rubrical forms of differing Rites may not be mixed or transplanted into another Rite. Each Rite has a piety and mode of worship that is unique to it, and to modify or mix rites muddles that sacred sacramental message of piety and faith, and confuses and befuddles the faithful in its innovation. Kneeling, sitting and standing at the appropriate times denote reverence and respect to God, and are to be strictly observed to prevent the sin of irreverence and the loss of the proper understanding of the Sacrifice of the Mass. Individuals who are physically unable to do so are excused from certain actions they cannot perform, yet must reverently and piously follow the Mass from a proper sacramental understanding.

Modification of Biblical Language

There is today, the so-called "inclusive language" which replaces "Father, Son and Holy Ghost" with "The Creator, Redeemer and Sanctifier" in an effort to remove the masculine references to God. We must remember that it was Jesus Christ himself that took human form born as a male. It was He who taught us to pray the "Our Father" and He who instructed the disciples to await the Holy Ghost. It is gravely sinful to interpolate secular feminism into the Word of God, in order to "fix it" so that it conforms to a politically correct understanding of the world. In addition, the "*Name* of God" is replaced *by what God has done for us*, and this diminishes the magnitude of God. God *is* Creator, but not *only* Creator, because before there was creation, God existed. God *is* Redeemer, but He existed far before there were sinners in a world in need of redemption. God *is* Sanctifier, but God is *more than* just Sanctifier. It is improper and incomplete to describe God *only* with respect to His creation, since He is uncreated and eternal. Jesus Himself gave us the Name of God, and we, His creation, should do nothing other than praise, laud and magnify His Holy Name. The Scriptures in our language must faithfully translate and interpret the Word of God as received by the divinely inspired writers as recorded in the original human languages. If the liturgy is the personal property of no individual group to change, then most certainly this is true also of Scripture. According, the so-called "inclusive language" translation is not to be used, nor authorized for teaching in the Church. The true "inclusive language" purpose of re-interpreting Scripture, in "forcing" the inspired writer write something that was not originally written, is not to grow closer to God, but is rather an effort to "remake" God into the "proper" and preferred image, one that is ethereal and unreal, inoffensive and not operative in our daily lives, by individuals who, at every step reject His salvation and deny His miracles and wonders. It is the duty of every Old Catholic to reject and speak against this heresy, which seeks to undermine the very salvific work of Christ. To minimize or disregard the danger of this type of theological revisionism is extremely dangerous.

Likewise, "liturgical dance", a liturgical abuse born of improper interpretation of Vatican II among some Roman Catholics, is also expressly prohibited. "Liturgical dance" is defined as the practice of introducing expressive dance into the Divine Liturgy. As dance in the Western world has not been historically seen in religious worship, and is rather viewed as amoral and sexually suggestive, coupled with the prohibition against unauthorized modification of the ancient Rites, preclude its use. In our secular Western society, dance has not been seen as related to sacred ritual or worship, and many of both the faithful and unchurched, are inundated with images which "train" western society to see dance only (or mainly) as part of the amoral sexual mating ritual, which ends not in loving, sacramental matrimony, but self-serving fornication and self-gratification at the expense of the depersonified sexual partner, who is later discarded in favor of the next.

On the Timelessness of the Mass

Rather than seek to modify the ancient liturgy, let us immerse ourselves in this great gift of Christ Jesus, and add our prayers and sacrifices to those of the Saints and Martyrs of the Church, who along with the Apostles and Fathers, have gone before us. Let us enjoy the great spiritual graces bestowed upon up by Christ Jesus during the Sacrifice of the Mass, and not be distracted from our true purpose for being there or from being attentive to the Real Presence of Christ in the Eucharist, on the altar. Only through prayer and careful study of Scripture, proper instruction and learning the Divine Liturgy, can we all work together to ensure a valid, proper, reverent and licit Sacrifice of the Mass. This great Sacrament, given us by our Lord Jesus Christ Himself, is a mystery of faith to be approached and received only with the most pious of intentions by the household of God. The Holy Eucharist is not for the curious, nor the causal observer who wishes to merely satisfy their intellectual inquiry, but for the believing members of the Church, who believe and profess the real presence of Christ in the Precious Body and Blood.

"Beware of curious and vain examination of this most profound Sacrament, if you do not wish to be plunged into the depths of doubt. He who scrutinizes its majesty too closely will be overwhelmed by its glory.

God can do more than man can understand. A pious and humble search for truth He will allow, a search that is ever ready to learn and that seeks to walk in the reasonable doctrines of the fathers. Blest is the simplicity that leaves the difficult way of dispute and goes forward on the level, firm path of God's commandments. Many have lost devotion because they wished to search into things beyond them.

Faith is required of you, and a sincere life, not a lofty intellect nor a delving into the mysteries of God. If you neither know nor understand things beneath you, how can you comprehend what is above you? Submit yourself to God and humble reason to faith, and the light of understanding will be given you so far as it is good and necessary for you. Some are gravely tempted concerning faith and the Sacrament but this disturbance is not laid to them but to the enemy.

Be not disturbed, dispute not in your mind, answer not the doubts sent by the devil, but believe the words of God, believe His saints and prophets, and the enemy will flee from you. It is often very profitable for the servant of God to suffer such things. For Satan does not tempt unbelievers and sinners whom he already holds securely, but in many ways he does tempt and trouble the faithful servant.

Go forward, then with sincere and unflinching faith, and with humble reverence approach this Sacrament. Whatever you cannot understand commit to the security of the all-powerful God, who does not deceive you. The man, however, who trusts in himself is deceived. God walks with sincere men, reveals Himself to humble men, enlightens the understanding of pure minds, and hides His grace from the curious and proud.

Human reason is weak and can be deceived. True faith, however, cannot be deceived. All reason and natural science ought to come after faith, not go before it, nor oppose it. For in this most holy and supremely excellent Sacrament, faith and love take precedence and work in a hidden manner. God, eternal, incomprehensible, and infinitely powerful, does great and inscrutable things in heaven and on earth, and there is no searching into His marvelous works. If all the works of God were such that human reason could easily grasp them, they would not be called wonderful or beyond the power of words to tell."[42]

Religious Orders are instructed to strictly and reverently pass on to novices and the professed, as well as new deacons and priests, the rubrics and proper way to pray the Divine Liturgy in the appropriate approved Rite. A proper, pious and reverent praying of the Mass is to be offered to God, in addition to the Sacrifice of the Mass itself, and no one should take for granted so great a spiritual privilege.

Many of the prayers of the Mass come to us from earlier liturgical forms and of course from Holy Scripture. It is our precious gift from Christ in that we receive Him in the Eucharist, that we hear Him instructing us in the Gospel, in that we see His eternal nature and continuity from the Old Testament, and we see the praise and worship of Him in Holy places, all in the culmination of the Mass, when Heaven and Earth meet supernaturally, and we join the Heavenly Host at His altar praising His Holy Name. Our incense joins the heavenly incense, our altar joins the heavenly altar, our voices join the never ceasing voices singing, "Holy, holy, holy, is He who was, and is, and is to come".

The Church Understood Itself As "Catholic" From The Beginning

We know that the term "catholic" is not a denominational description, but the nature of the Church of Christ, meaning that the Church is "universal", and that in it is the fullness of God's grace given the faithful at this time. The Church sees itself as such and always have, although some persons, wishing to be Christian yet distance themselves from liturgical worship and the sacraments, seek to identify the term in terms of a denomination, but this is error, as Church history very clearly indicates:

"See that ye all follow the bishop, even as Jesus Christ does the Father, and the presbytery as ye would the apostles; and reverence the deacons, as being the institution of God. Let no man do anything connected with the Church without the bishop. Let that be deemed a proper Eucharist, which is [administered] either by the bishop, or by one to whom he has entrusted it. Wherever the bishop shall appear, there let the multitude [of the people] also be; even as, wherever Jesus Christ is, there is the Catholic Church. It is not lawful without the bishop either to baptize or to celebrate a love-feast; but whatsoever he shall approve of, that is also pleasing to God, so that everything that is done may be secure and valid." St. Ignatius, Letter to the *Smyrneans* 8:2.110 A.D., CCEL.

That the church founded by Christ through His Apostles is the Universal Church, which identifies itself and its faith as "Catholic", is most profoundly illustrated in the willingness of the faithful laity and clergy of the Church who refused to reject Christ and the Catholic Church, and gave their lives for their faith;

"...this most admirable Polycarp was one, having in our own times been an apostolic and prophetic teacher, and bishop of the Catholic Church which is in Smyrna. For every word that went out of his mouth either has been or shall yet be accomplished." The Martyrdom of Polycarp, 16:2 155 A.D., CCEL.

The Church Understands Itself As "Catholic" Today, And For All Time

The Church continues to understand that the essential components must be present to be Catholic, and that the Church must continue to maintain its Catholicity. The early American Old Catholic Church expressed this understanding this way:

"Seven times the whole church was represented in council to uphold the purity of faith, spread over the world, taught alike in East and West. There was only One Church ruling the world. It was the time of Undivided Christendom. At that time nobody in search of the true Catholic Church could be perplexed or doubtful. The Church was like a city on the top of a mountain, visible everywhere. You could not mistake her, you had no choice, there was no rival...This state of things continued till the great schism between East and West...

What was Catholic once must be forever. The Catholicity of the East was recognized by the West before the latter separated. But the East did not change since, consequently, its Catholicity is unassailable, as it represents the faith of Undivided Christendom, to which every Christian is bound to return, if he does not already belong to it...This is our Christian (Old) Catholic standpoint, our platform. (Our) orthodox Old Catholic Church is the true Church (instituted by Christ) in the West...

There is only One Church which teaches all things whatsoever Christ has commanded (and) to this church He commands to convert mankind. 'Go ye therefore, and teach all nations', and His command is of the most pressing nature, as He himself shows in the parable of the great supper. The master not only invites his friends and acquaintances, but sends his servant 'into the highways and hedges' and tells him 'compel them to come in' (Luke 14,23). Apparently He means to continue its endeavors to bring safely home the poor wandered lost in the wilderness of unbelief, doubt, heresy and schism. The true shepherd 'goeth into the mountains, and seeketh the sheep which is gone astray.' He does not stand with folded arms, unconcerned about its fate, coolly waiting for its return, and ready not to shut the gate in its face. The true shepherd in search of the lost sheep does not ask whether he would perhaps 'would the sensibilities' of the stray sheep. He knows that the sheep is not on the right way, and consequently he thinks it his duty to call back the poor wanderer, however unwilling the latter may be.

Jesus Christ, our true Shepherd (…), went on preaching in spite of all resistance, persecution and scorn till they nailed Him to the cross…He will protect His church and ward off the dangers threatening her within and without…The gates of hell shall not prevail against (her).

While this is our belief, we desire to force no man's assent. Let every human being follow the light of his own conscience. For it is our absolute conviction it is only by so doing he can please the Great Giver of reason. We want freedom to worship God, but we demand equal freedom for our fellow men to worship or abstain from worship, to believe or to disbelieve. In other words, not mere tolerance but perfect liberty for one and all—the believer, the unbeliever, the Catholic, the agnostic, Jew, Turk and Hindu, Parsee and Buddhist, persuaded that if not in this life, then in a life to come, at some time, the TRUTH shall be so presented to the intellect that every rational soul 'shall receive the truth, and the truth shall set him free' (John 8,21)."[43]

ENDNOTES FOR CHAPTER FOUR

1. The Most Reverend Joseph Rene Vilatte, *A Sketch of the Belief of Old Catholics*, 1890.

1A–1D. The American Catholic Union, *Traditional Old Catholic Dogma,* Daniel Wells, Used by Permission, 2004.

2. Jordan Bajis, *Common Ground, An Introduction to Eastern Christianity For The American Christian*, Second Edition (Light and Life Publishing, 1989) Used by permission, 2004.

3. Ibid, p.171.

4. Ibid, p.172.

5. Ibid, p.172-173.

6. Ibid, p. 173-174.

7. William A. Jurgens, *The Faith of the Early Fathers Volume 1*, (The Liturgical Press Collegeville, MN, 1970), p. 169.

8. Ibid, p. 209 vol. 1.

9. Ibid, p. 233 vol. 1.

10. Jordan Bajis, *Common Ground, An Introduction to Eastern Christianity For The American Christian*, Second Edition (Light and Life Publishing, 1989), p.218. Used by permission, 2004.

11. Ibid, p.218.

12. Ibid, p.218.

13. Ibid, p.218.

14. Ludwig Ott, *Fundamentals of Catholic Dogma*, (Tan Books and Publishers 1974)

15. Ibid.

16. St. Ignatius of Antioch, *Letter To The Romans* 110 A.D., Christian Classics Ethereal Library, Public Domain.

17. St. Justin the Martyr. *First Apology, Ch. LXVI.*—Of the Eucharist. Christian Classics Ethereal Library, Public Domain.

18. St. Irenaeus, *Against Heresies*, inter 180/199 A.D. Christian Classics Ethereal Library, Public Domain.

19. Joseph Renee Vilatte, *A Sketch of the Belief of Old Catholics*, 1890.

20. Arnold Mathew, *Bishop Mathew's Act of Union*, (1911)

21. William A. Jurgens, *The Faith of the Early Fathers Volume 1*, (The Liturgical Press Collegeville, MN, 1970) p. 360 vol. 1.

22. Joseph Renee Vilatte, *A Sketch of the Belief of Old Catholics*, 1890.

23. Arnold Mathew, *Bishop Mathew's Act of Union*, (1911)

24. Ibid.

25. Joseph Renee Vilatte, A Sketch of the Belief of Old Catholics, 1890.

26. Arnold Mathew, *Bishop Mathew's Act of Union*, (1911)

27. William A. Jurgens, *The Faith of the Early Fathers Volume 1*, (The Liturgical Press Collegeville, MN, 1970) p.231, vol. 1.

28. Patrick Madrid, *Why Is That In Tradition?* (Our Sunday Visitor Publishing Division, 2002)

29. Ibid.

30. Jordan Bajis, *Common Ground, An Introduction to Eastern Christianity For The American Christian*, Second Edition (Light and Life Publishing, 1989) Used by permission, 2004.

31. Ibid.

32. William A. Jurgens, *The Faith of the Early Fathers*, (The Liturgical Press Collegeville, MN, 1970) p.19, vol. 2.

33. Ibid. p.73, vol. 2.

34. Ibid. p.2, vol. 1.

35. Ibid. p.6, vol. 2.

36. Ibid. p.3, vol. 1.

37. Ibid. p.26, vol. 2.

38. St. Clement, *Letter To The Corinthians*, 80 A.D. Christian Classics Ethereal Library, Public Domain.

39. St. Irenaeus, *Against Heresies*, 3: 2-3. A.D. 120-202. Christian Classics Ethereal Library, Public Domain.

40. William A. Jurgens, *The Faith of the Early Fathers*, (The Liturgical Press Collegeville, MN, 1970) p.336, vol. 1.

41. Ibid. p.181

42. Thomas, a Kempis, *The Imitation of Christ*, 1400. P. 122-123. A.D., Christian Classics Ethereal Library, Public Domain.

43. Archbishop Joseph Renee Vilatte, *What Was Catholic Once Must Be Forever*, 1914.

CHAPTER 5

Eastern and Western Expressions In American Old Catholicism

Old Catholic Churches, not being a part of the Roman Catholic Communion, function in separate autocephalous hierarchal organizations. As such is the case, the administration of Old Catholic parishes and dioceses are more collegial and less authoritarian in nature. While bishops maintain their traditional position as Elders and Shepherds of the local Church, determinations binding on the entire Church body are arrived at by the entire College of Bishops and not solely through one individual. Parish priests, while maintaining their traditional and scriptural role in the Church, empower the laity to be more operative in the missions and ministries of the Church, taking on roles as directing the efforts of the parish outreach programs, rather than relying on the pastor or assistant pastor to make the ministry successful.

The phenomenon of multiple Old Catholic jurisdictions within the Americas, required a method of establishing dialogue and inter-jurisdictional concordats drawn heavily on the model of relationships between the autocephalous Orthodox Churches of the East, which recognize the legitimacy of each other, and do not seek to usurp the existence of the other, but recognizes each as a sister Church in Christ. Since however, there exist organizations and churches possessing a theology that is markedly different from the faith described herein, strict examination to ensure a unity of theological belief is first required. Today there exists a confederacy of Old Catholic Churches, the International Synod of Old Catholic Churches (ISOCC), which aid and support one another as members of one communion.

In addition, with the merging of faithful and of clergy, and as the result of working together towards common goals, American Old Catholics have been exposed to Eastern Orthodox theological expressions of faith, through the early Russian

Orthodox efforts in the Americas. In many cases Russian and Greek Orthodox origins of Apostolic Succession have found their way alongside the Old Catholic lines of Archbishop Mathew and the Oriental lines of Archbishop Vilatte, as autocephalous Orthodox bishops assisted in the consecrations of Old Catholic bishops in the Americas. Throughout the years, some Old Catholic Churches of American origin have been received into various Eastern Orthodox Churches.[1]

Like the Eastern Orthodox Churches, the Old Catholics respect the Roman Pontiff and accord to him the respect due also as "First among equals" as the Bishop of Rome. But also like the Eastern Orthodox, the Old Catholics reject the concept of the "universal jurisdiction" of the Pope over all of Christendom. Old Catholics affirm the Seven Oecumenical Councils of the entire Church, and the Nicene Creed without the *filioque*. Old Catholics adopted a "polyvalent hermeneutic" approach to understanding the foundational teachings of the Church so that, instead of Eastern or Western, in many cases, it is Eastern—and *also* Western expressions of Christian truth that are taught. It is this understanding of theology, before the Council of Trent, before Vatican Councils I & II that permeate Old Catholic teaching.

Like the Eastern Orthodox, the Oriental Orthodox, and the Roman Catholic, the Old Catholic understands that proper interpretation of Holy Scripture takes place in the community of the Church and not apart from it, as an individual. Consider the following:

"In order to 'read the Bible in the Church', one must recognize that the Spirit of God had indeed inspired Christians in the past to unfold the Scripture's meanings. By 'the past' I do not mean only those who lived in Reformation times, but those who studied the Scriptures for the previous fifteen centuries as well. These men are popularly called 'Fathers.' They are called Fathers because many of their interpretations have valiantly preserved and defended the messages of the Scriptures, often in the face of great persecution, and for this we respect them. If we want to be in touch with the Spirit's lessons to the *whole* Church, we cannot confine ourselves to the teachers of our own time.

Some of these Church Fathers were immediate disciples and successors of the Apostles. Clement (30-100), an early bishop of Rome, was an acquaintance of both Peter and Paul, and Ignatius of Antioch (30-107) and Polycarp of Smyrna (69-155) were disciples of the Apostle John. Noted Church historians recognize these men, and others such as Papias (70-155), Barnabas (a letter of his dating

117/132), Hermas (140/155), and the unknown authors of the Epistle to Diogneus (150) and the Didache (100 AD–150), as 'The first church teachers after the apostles, who enjoyed in part personal [relationships]…with them…' Imagine the insight these men had! They learned from those who literally heard the very words of Christ with their own ears. Try to fathom the perspective they brought to the Scriptures! Is it really possible to consider ourselves serious students of the Scriptures if we choose to ignore what those earliest believers and martyrs had to say?"[2]

In addition, Eastern Orthodox, Roman Catholics and Old Catholics understand the Word of God to exist as more than merely words in print. The Word of God is also the living, breathing faith expressed by the believer, and it is revealed in communal membership with the Body of Christ, that is, His Church.

"God's Word is not bound by ink or held captive by bookbinding. His Word existed before the invention of books and would continue to exist even if every Bible were destroyed. God's Word is the 'Living Voice' which those who have united themselves to Christ can bear witness to as being of God. Thus, God's Word is understood in *relationship*, not in reading. The early Church was in deep communion with God's Word not because they had a Bible, but *because they had a New Covenant relationship with the living Word, Jesus Christ.*

The Truth of God's Word has been revealed not only *to* God's People but *in* God's people (1 Cor. 2:9-13). This gives the members of the Church alone the ability to understand the Scripture *as* Scripture. This divinely orchestrated marriage of Spirit and humanity makes the Bible truly sufficient in the Church. Unlike the heretics, the Church's members recognize its true message, for the 'anointing of truth' which rests upon them lets them know the teaching (1 John 3:27). The Bible is *their* book and they are of 'like Spirit' with it. Their Christian life and experience, which includes the experiences of their brethren before them, attests to the Bible's true teaching."[3]

This expression naturally leads to this unanimous conclusion, agreed upon by all:

"Without question, the Scriptures are an invaluable and essential expression of Divine Tradition. But when they are set apart from the Holy Spirit's ministry in the Church, they are no longer 'a sure foundation.' Outside the Church, the Bible's stabilizing legs are cut off by contradictory interpretations of 'individuals.' Our call to understand the Scriptures in concert with the Church prevents such an abuse. But this attentiveness to the Church is no an exhortation to sleepily submit to an ecclesiastical court. It is a call to take responsibility; to evaluate the reasons behind our present beliefs instead of accepting them without question, to take the initiative to seek the mind of those who have gone before us, and to pursue personal interaction with their perspectives. Only then will we, in union with the brethren of all ages, be able to demonstrate the Bible Truth entrusted to us."[4] It is the Divine Revelation, properly understood and operating within the Church, that gives meaning and life to what is written. No written book can cry out that it has been poorly understood or interpreted by the reader, and many deliberately twist Scripture in their interpretation, to lead others astray, yet without the Church, the individual with Bible in hand is buffeted about in a sea of misunderstandings and misinterpretation.

"To say that the Bible *alone* is sufficient as the guide of Christian doctrine is at best inadequate. For although both the heretic and the Christian can be sincere and agree on the Bible's 'infallibility' and authority, these shared perspectives do not erase their differences. They must ask themselves: *How* and *why* do I interpret the Scriptures the way I do? These questions free one to trace the rationale and development of his system of Bible interpretation and to judge its value."[5]

Particularly in the United States today, we see an almost fanatical adherence to ensuring that the individual's personal and private judgment reigns supreme—in fact, in many ways society today reviles the individual who submits himself or herself to the understanding or authoritative insight of another, be it in the secular sense or in the sacred. So much has this refusal to admit ignorance, or to at least acknowledge a deposit of knowledge deeper than our own individual selves, even the obviously and blatantly incorrect determinations are more highly valued than proven knowledge and understanding that has stood the test of time. With respect to the Bible, this has resulted in disunity, discord and confusion—something the Protestant Reformers were absolutely sure that the concept of "*sola Scriptura*" would permanently eliminate. "The right of 'private judgment'—wedded together with the Bible as 'ultimate and absolute authority'—results in Scripture *losing* authority. The individual's right to defend his or her interpretation over a legion of other understandings is of greatest importance. The contradictory opinions which result from such a premise are each given the right to be called "Scriptural." The consequence: The Bible's message is weakened by a democracy of conflicting ideas.

Paradoxically, those who support *"sola Scriptura"*, the right of each person to their own private interpretation of Scripture, have no defensive argument against the Old Catholic who claims the Church's nearly two thousand year old interpretation of Scripture as his own private interpretation. If every man's private interpretation is no more or less valid than anyone else's, then only through a disingenuous rebuttal, could the Old Catholic position, supported by nearly two thousand years of Christianity, be rejected.

Oddly enough, such a plurality gives permission to the religious tyrant. Now, in the name of fidelity to 'the Word,' he is able to impose his inaccurate interpretations and be respected as 'a Bible teacher.' In many cases, this means that the one who speaks the strongest, loudest and with the most influence, can get a "Christian" following—that is, as long as his ideas are footnoted with Biblical references. Mark A. Knolls, in Evangelicalism and Modern America, explains the problem of private interpretation in this respect:

> The naïve…American intellectual heritage leads not to depth but to superficiality. Ironically, it leads to a perverse kind of authoritarianism, in which a leader claiming to have no guide but the Bible rigidly imposes his form of Scriptural interpretation on followers who likewise profess to be heeding no guide but the Bible.[12]

A philosophy which advocates the Bible's 'independent authority' ironically ends up giving ultimate authority to 'the independent.' For instance, when someone says, 'I believe *ONLY* in what the Bible says', isn't he really saying, 'I only believe in the *way I interpret* the Bible?' Isn't he in effect stating that his understanding of the Scriptures *is as divinely inspired as the Scriptures themselves? In the final analysis, then, it is not Scripture that possesses final authority, but private interpretations.* Though an exaggeration, there is some truth to the saying, 'Before the Reformation there was only one Pope, but after the Reformation every man with Bible in hand is his own Pope."[6] *In effect, the Protestant Reformers rejected "papal infallibility" in favor of "individual infallibility", which raises each person's personal interpretation of the Bible to a level equal to the Bible itself.* In this way, no one's interpretation of the Bible is wrong, and the same "sola Scriptura" concept used to support the early Protestant Reformers and their Churches, is continuously being used to justify divisions and splits among them. Without a divinely authorized Church, guided by the Holy Spirit, to determine proper interpretation, it is perpetual confusion without end.

Biblical interpretation, indeed, salvation itself, is found, not in individual isolation, but within the Church, the Body of Christ. "Among the oldest and most consistent teachings of the Fathers of the Church is the notion that we are saved not alone, but as members of a community. By faith and through baptism God calls us into the community of the Church, and it is here, within the fellowship of the saved, that we find our salvation. It is true that God calls us each by name, that God reaches into our personal histories and, through faith, summons us to salvation in the Church. However, God does not save us independently and separately from others. God does not so individualize salvation that the only thing that should concern me is to know for certain that I am saved, disregarding what happens to anyone else. Moreover, God does not save me on the basis of my confidence in the providence of the Father and Jesus as my own personal savior, but on the basis of the faith of Jesus, which remains present in the community of his followers and extends to me as a member of that community. Jesus is not *my* savior, he is *our* savior, and we are not saved alone, we are saved in community."7 [emphasis added]

Once we come to understand the awe-inspiring purpose and nature of the Church, our entire attitude towards the community of believers must change. We must look to see Christ in the members of the Church, because He is there, among us, guiding, teaching and most of all, loving us. So then, to fail to be involved in the life of the Church is to keep the Church, and Christ, at arm's length, rejecting the grace that is bestowed through membership and participation in the communion (*koinonia*) of the Church. "Unfortunately, most Christians see the Church only as a place where they can get their private spiritual needs met. The Church, however, is foremost to be an environment of love where brethren care about each other. It is a family in communion, not a forum. Individualism and self centered independence are not characteristics of God's Church, they are characteristics of the world outside of Christ.16 It is love, for God and the people of God, which make the Church community.17"8

"The cup of thanksgiving which we bless, is it not a participation [koinonia] in the blood of Christ? The bread which we break, is it not a participation [koinonia] in the body of Christ?" (1 Cor. 10:16)

"*Koinonia* is the Greek word translated by our English New Testaments as *communion, association, fellowship, sharing, common, contribution*, and *partnership*. Not one of these spoken words, however, adequately captures what the early Christians meant when they spoke of the koinonia they had with one another and Christ. Koinonia expressed a relationship of great intimacy and depth, one so rich in fact that it even became the 'favorites expression for the marital relationship...the most intimate between human beings.'[1] The implications of this word when used to express the nature of our bond with Christ and the brethren are especially profound.

> ...*koinonia* implies a closeness of union approaching identity. Hence the significance of its use to express the believer's union with the 'Son of God, Jesus Christ our Lord' (1 Cor. 1:9), and with the Holy Ghost (2 Cor. 13:14 and Phil. 2:1)...With St. John indeed it is the predominant and determining note of Christianity. For the Fellowship as defined by him is only another word for that brotherhood or brotherly love which make the difference between darkness and light (1 John 2:9f), and is therefore the essential characteristic of one who calls himself a Christian...'[2]

For one to have fellowship with another Christian in the early Church meant much more to him than what it means today to many contemporary Christians. (i.e. Christians having donuts and coffee together in the 'fellowship' [social] hall after the Sunday service). Genuine fellowship demonstrates 'that bond which binds Christians to each other, to Christ and to God.'[3] Fellowship is all inclusive, deep, personal and intimate. The 'meaning of 'fellowship' or 'communion' in the New Testament relates to sharing one common life within the body of Christ at all levels of existence and experience—spiritual, social, intellectual, economic. No area of life can be excluded.'[4]

The Church is not simply a society; it is fellowship *in* God and *with* God. Every description of the Church is simply another way of expressing the depth of this fellowship: the Body of Christ, Ekklesia, Temple of the Spirit, covenant, Eucharist, catholicity, brotherhood, the life of God, etc.[5] This is why one can say salvation is of the Church.

> Christianity from the very beginning existed as a corporate reality, as a community. To be Christian meant just to belong to the community. Nobody could be Christian by himself, as an isolated individual, but only together with 'the brethren' in a 'togetherness' with them... Christianity means a 'common life,' in common.[6"9]

This understanding of Christianity is common and foundational to the essential understanding of Church, in both East and the West. It is the consistent teaching of the Church from the very beginning down to our present day. It is in the Church that God imparts the graces of the Sacraments, in the Church that we are first taught to see Christ in others, and it is in the Church that our faith is formed and we are taught the true meaning of what is written in Scripture, and what is lived in Apostolic Tradition, the two complementary sides of the same one Divine Revelation. One does not come to experience God's saving grace through scholastic endeavor, but through the Church, which is guided by the Holy Spirit, and is enlivened by the very essence of God's love for us. It is imperative to understand this, because, as a result of the fall of Adam, we cannot do anything out of super-natural love unless God gives us the special grace to do so.

ENDNOTES FOR CHAPTER FIVE

1. Karl Pruter, *A History of the Old Catholic Church*, (St. Willibrord's Press, 1973) Used by permission, 2004.

2. Jordan Bajis, *Common Ground, An Introduction to Eastern Christianity For The American Christian*, Second Edition (Light and Life Publishing, 1989) p. 86-87. Used by permission, 2004.

3. Ibid. p. 91.

4. Ibid. p. 92.

5. Ibid. p. 50.

6. Ibid. p. 49.

7. Edward Wm. Clark, *Five Great Catholic Ideas*, Crossroad Publishing Company, 1998.

8. Jordan Bajis, *Common Ground, An Introduction to Eastern Christianity For The American Christian*, Second Edition (Light and Life Publishing, 1989) p. 154. Used by permission, 2004.

9. Ibid. p. 151.

CHAPTER 6

Learning Through Explaining and Defending The Faith

The Old Catholic Church has much in common with our Eastern Orthodox, Oriental Orthodox, and Roman Catholic brethren, including Scripture, Apostolic Tradition, the Eucharist, as well as the common lines of Apostolic Succession flowing from each into our own Church. These three ancient families of Christ trace their spiritual heritage back to their founding by the Apostles, in various places around the world, and ultimately through them to Christ Himself.

We profess and give witness to the very same faith that these ancient families of faith all profess, in a common core of Christian beliefs that are held by all. Our faith and belief is that same faith and belief professed from the Apostles, in the Early Church, down to our own day. It is important to learn the faith well, in order to be able to explain it to those who are uninformed, misinformed, or unchurched, as well as to defend the faith against those persons who seek to attack the Church, her sacraments, priesthood, Apostolic Traditions, and teaching authority. To do this, you must be well instructed in the faith and well-versed in Holy Scripture. You must live out the faith in your life and engage in great prayer and devotion. The single best explanation of Old Catholics is found in the faithful child of God who lives out his or her faith every day in their life, so that the Light of Men can be seen operating in them. A faith that is alive is lived out in the life of the believing man—it is not found only on his lips, but also in his heart, and so glorifies his Father in Heaven.

In explaining the faith to others, it is of the utmost importance that it be done with respect, humility and charity. One does not convince another of a spiritual truth through belligerence or arrogant disposition. Patience is required, and a well-annotated Bible will assist you in illustrating the issue being discussed.

Rather than presume to know another individual's faith or theology, it is better to concentrate on being able to accurately explain and defend the teachings of the Church from mistake misunderstanding, misinformation or those simply seeking to make a name for themselves by attacking the Church. Through faithful study and prayer, your ability to understand more and explain to others, what we believe will increase. In explaining the faith to others, it is important also to understand that when we use words, such as prayer, worship, salvation, and justification, we are using them with the meaning that we normally attribute to them within our community of faith. This may <u>not</u> be the same meaning attributed to these words by other faiths, and you must always explain exactly what we mean when we use these terms (and others), and where this meaning comes from. In this way, some misunderstanding can be avoided at the onset, and perhaps eliminated, if past misunderstandings exist.

Ultimately, the knowledge and understanding of the faith obtained is nothing, if we do not live it in love in our daily lives. In this way, we become a living explanation of our faith. Others see and learn what we believe in the manner in which we live. We are saved by the grace of God, justified by faith, working in love in our lives.

Authority

In most cases, particularly when speaking with many Protestant groups, the primary issue is one of authority. Most Protestant Christians will quote several verses of Scripture to make their point, usually that the "Bible alone" is the only rule and guide for Christians, and that a Church although helpful, is not necessary.

The problem with this reformation-based concept is that Christ did not teach it, and the Bible itself does not say it. Usually the response is to show, from Scripture, that Scripture is "useful" for teaching and instructing (2 Tim. 3:16-17). But this does not equate to being all-sufficient. In fact, this particular passage of Scripture only refers to Hebrew Scripture (the Old Testament), the "Scriptures" that the intended audience would recognize and accept as such, and certainly not what we now consider to be the New Testament. At the time of this letter having been written, the Bible, as we know it, did not exist as a compiled, approved and divinely inspired group of texts, recognized as such as we do now. Even so, with respect to being "useful", one could say that a "Bible Tract" is "useful", if it causes a reader to convert to Christianity, even if it only paraphrases the Bible, and uses no direct Scripture quotes. So there is a true problem for the

"Bible Christian", since <u>the Bible itself does not teach that the "Bible alone" (sola</u> <u>scriptura) is the sole rule and guide of faith for Christians</u>. In order to make this concept fit into a faith that never heard of it until the Protestant Reformation, the "Bible Christian" must refer to extrabiblical sources to explain this position, which, in and of itself, negates the "Bible alone" position. One cannot use, as an infallible authority, something (or someone) other than the Bible, in order to prove that the "Bible alone" is the sole rule and guide of faith.

As Old Catholics we know that it was the Church, with the guidance of the Holy Spirit, that determined which books would be included in the canon of Scripture (i.e. the official list of sacred Christian texts), and which ones would not. It Is important to recognize the role of the Church in the process of determining the canon of Scripture, as the Church is the pillar and foundation of Truth, empowered by the Holy Spirit, and protected by Christ's promise that the gates of Hell would not prevail against her. *For the first three hundred years of the Church's existence, the Bible, as we now know it, did not exist.* Even after the canon of Scripture had been set and agreed upon, the vast majority of people could not read or write, and learned Scripture the same way the Apostles themselves were taught, at the foot of the teacher through oral teaching. The assembled individual books of the Bible did not all have titles (and of those that did, some are called by *different* titles now), nor did all identify their authors. The authenticity, accuracy and author-ship of many of the books of the Bible had to be determined by the Church, as well as which books would be considered as inspired and sacred and which would not; the Church, under the inspiration of the Holy Spirit, made this determina-tion. As the Church grew throughout the centuries, the vast majority of people continued to learn the Good News through oral teaching and preaching, and as the Church built the large edifices with mosaics, statuaries and stain glass windows, these visual depictions of important aspects of Christianity were their teachers, along with the readings of the Old Testament, the Psalms and the New Testament during the Divine Liturgy, as we still continue to do today.

In addition, Bibles were very hard to come by. Bibles were also very expensive, the inks and pages were costly, and each individual Bible was meticulously made by hand. Each page of the Bible was laboriously copied and reproduced, along with illustrations of various historical scenes, and took years to complete. An entire village would pool its financial resources so that the materials could be purchased and the labor done. Often decorated with precious jewels, these Bibles were avail-able publicly in the parish Churches, but due to theft (as the pages were many times gold-leafed, and the covers jeweled) had to be chained to the lectern. Many people, unable to read or write, would learn the Good News through the many illustrations in the Bible, as well as the paintings and statues in the Church, depicting various scenes in the Bible.

It would not be until after 1450 A.D., when German inventor Johannes Gutenberg invented the printing press, could large amounts of Bibles be printed inexpensively and quickly. The original texts of the various books of the Bible did not have chapter and verse numbers, as those were added arbitrarily by book printers after the invention of the printing press in 1450 A.D. Even then, most people could not read or write. There were no comprehensive public school systems to provide free education for everyone, as there is today (people often forget this). It was with the new printing press, that the individual books of the Bible then came to be printed with titles, for some of the books had none, along with chapter and verse numbering, for the original texts certainly had none of these.

Unfortunately, many individuals eventually produced their own Bibles, many with numerous typographical errors, sometimes purposefully omitting entire books of Scripture, or changing or adding words to Scripture that were never there, but the individual felt were inferred, such as Martin Luther. Martin Luther produced his own version of the Bible (the "September Bible"), inserting the German word for "alone" into St. Paul's writings, to make Scripture say that a man is justified "by faith *alone*" (Sola Fide). He also deleted the Books of James, Revelation and others, because he "could not find Christ in any of them". This shocking act harkens back to the Early Church's battle again the Marcionite heresy, in which Marcion in the second century, of his own determination, place all of the Old Testament and most of the New Testament on a lesser, lower level of spiritual authority than the ten Epistles of St Paul. This Gnostic heretic taught that under the Old Testament, the people lived under a different type of spiritual economy than people living in the time of the New Testament and the New Covenant. In addition, claims that Martin Luther produced for the German speaking people, the first bible in the German language are false, as nearly twenty previous German translations were in circulation prior to his translation.

The Church gathered many defective Bibles, some missing books of the Bible, some with modified wording, some with words added, and some simply with horrific typographical errors, and disposed of them in the reverent manner that the Church disposes of certain holy things, by fire. Unfortunately, the Church could not purge men's hearts of attempting to re-write the Bible, and to this day, there are sects that have re-worded the Bible to suit their particular theology, such as the Jehovah's Witness, and their "New World Bible". Others, such as the Mormons, seek to reinterpret Scripture by adding other "inspired texts" to "clarify" certain aspects of their own unique faith. Left without an infallible authority to determine which books are inspired and should be regarded as Scripture, and which are not, as well as which translations are authentic, and which are not, every individual is left to determine these things for his or herself, and becomes an "infallible authority" unto themselves, because they reject the authority of the Church, whose members wrote the New Testament books, determined which books were scriptural, and how the Bible should be understood and interpreted.

Absent this authority, improper interpretations of Scripture appear, such as the so-called "Roman Road", a Protestant "Bible-tract", which use the writings of St. Paul as a lens through which to view the Gospels, conspicuously absent any direct quotes of Jesus Christ Himself. Others focus on a single passage of Scripture as a means to dispute components of Christian faith taught elsewhere, such as the "Oneness Movement" which denies the Triune Godhead. Others still change a word in Scripture here and there, to "plainly show what a particular passage *really* means". This has been done, in certain instances, even to create "bibles" which deny the divinity of Christ. Without a divinely inspired authority, who has the right to say which is right and which is wrong, with the impact being more than mere personal opinion? These are clear examples of Scripture being twisted and abridged to obfuscate that which has been believed for nearly two thousand years.

In regards to the necessity of the Church, Jesus Himself teaches us that the individual Christian lives abundantly, joyfully thrives, profoundly learns and spiritually grows *within* the Family of God, which is the Church. Jesus teaches us, in His imagery and description of the kingdom of God as a household, a family, and His Father's house. To be part of a family is not to be a sole individual existing separately from the rest of the household, but rather an integral part of that family's life. We are not initiated into the household of God by a book, but by a people. As children, the lessons of Scripture come alive, taught to us not by a book, but by our parents, who explain the meaning of specific passages as understood by the Family of God, the Church. Adult converts receive what they are taught by the Church through her members, which give the proper understanding and meaning of sacred Scripture, as taught and passed down throughout nearly two thousand years. It is not enough that Scripture be read and studied, it must be *properly* read and *clearly* understood *within the context of the inspired writers who wrote it*. Considering the historical perspective of the inspired writer is essential for proper interpretation of Scripture. To merely read the words out of time and out of the proper historical context is to lose the true meaning of Scripture, possibly replacing it with a twenty-first century concept that would have been totally foreign to the ancient inspired writer. All Scripture is inspired by God, and it is communicated to humans through other humans, in human forms of communication. Human communication is easily misunderstood and misinterpreted, absent the original context and intent of the writer. This is true for both ordinary human communication, and divinely inspired human communication. Scripture itself teaches us, that it contains things within itself that are difficult to understand, and that men attempt to twist the Scriptures for their own means. Thus, the Church is charged with the faithful stewardship of that understanding of Scripture and the Apostolic Tradition, and is divinely charged with faithfully protecting and teaching this Deposit of Faith through her Magisterial Office.

As Old Catholics, we accept the teaching authority of the Church. We accept the Church's authority and inspired determination of the canon of Scripture and its interpretation and understanding. We have, through the guidance of the Holy Spirit, a Church that was able to infallibly determine which texts were inspired and scriptural and which were not. Without this authority, who would verify that a particular book of Scripture is authentic? Who would determine which books belong in the Bible, and which do not? To whom would you go to definitively know, that the translation you have of a particular book is accurate?

Scripture and Tradition

The authority of the oral teaching Tradition and its parity with written scripture is first proved in the Old Testament. We all read and accept the first five books of Hebrew (Old Testament) Scripture as inspired and valid. These books, written by Moses, we must consider how he came to know this information, in order to write it. Prior to him placing it in written format, he had to have received the teaching through oral tradition, and must have accepted it. When God encounters Moses, to send him back to Egypt, how does He identify Himself? "I am the God of your father, the God of Abraham, the God of Isaac, and the God of Jacob.' And Moses hid his face, for he was afraid to look at God" (Ex. 3:6). Obviously Moses immediately knew the significance of this, he knew about these individuals and about how God had called them to His service. Moses did not read this in any book, he received this through an oral tradition that had been supernaturally preserved for hundreds and hundreds of years.

This was not unusual, but a natural way for us to communicate and teach the next generation all that was (and is) important. The teachings about God, and what He had done and the covenants He made with their forbearers being passed on from parent to child, and from tribal elder to tribe members had been in force for centuries. Even today, in our own homes, parents, in teaching children, teenagers and young adults, communicate far more in verbal communication than they ever do in written form. And then, the written form usually refers to some oral teaching that the child is expected to already know and be familiar with. No parent composes a book of rules for the children to follow, and a book of family history for the children to refer to, and a written moral code for the children to abide by, yet each child in each home can clearly tell you their parent's expectations of them, the responsibilities that they have within the household, and the family list of do's and don't 's, all without referring to a volume of written text.

Imagine asking that same child, as she grown to adulthood, to write down every teaching, every piece of advice, "notable quotable", and "words of wisdom" of her parents. If she was able to record this great wisdom into a massive book; would she be able to give that book of great wisdom to *her* child, and achieve the same exemplary results, by merely having the child read the book? Would this book, absent the wisdom of a parent guide to explain and amplify its meaning, completely convey the wisdom it contains? Of course not. Some things are learned by reading, others by oral teaching, and others by guided "hands on" learning. This is why Scripture, Tradition and a Living Faith, operative in the life of the believer, guided by the Church, are all needed. These key components act in concert with (and not against) one another, to teach us what it truly means to be a "Child of God".

Some of the most important acts within the Hebrew faith had not been detailed in written form. Sacrifices for the atonement of sin, and offerings to God at the Temple were infinitely important, yet nowhere in the Old Testament do we find the particular and detailed instructions of exactly what had to be done in each particular case, yet the observant knew what to do and how to do it, and *that* extremely information was handed down by oral tradition. The most central act of worship, done in a specific way in order to be pleasing to God, was passed on from generation to generation through oral tradition, supplemented by Hebrew Scripture that provided only an overview of *what* was to be sacrificed and for what offense.

In our New Testament period, we observe that Jesus Himself did not write any of His teachings down, nor was His a ministry of written words, but of parables and teachings orally transmitted. No one thought to travel behind Jesus and transcribe everything He said or did onto papyrus. The people learned the Hebrew Scriptures from hearing them read and taught aloud at the temple and in synagogues. Committing all of His teachings to writing was not of primary concern, and so only a portion was ever actually written: "But there are also many other things which Jesus did; were every one of them to be written, I suppose that the world itself could not contain the books that would be written" (John 21:25).

His followers taught in the same fashion, preferring to speak and teach in person, rather than by written word, which could be easily misunderstood. "'Though I have much to write to you, I would rather not use paper and ink, but I hope to come to see you and talk with you face to face, so that our joy may be complete" (2 John 12). "I commend you because you remember me in everything and maintain the traditions even as I have delivered them to you" (1 Cor. 11:2).

Even today, many people either forget or totally ignore the teachings of the Apostles warning against personal interpretation of Scripture, instead preferring to state, on their own authority as Christians, what *they* believe Scripture is saying—much to their detriment and that of others. "First of all you must understand this, that no prophecy of Scripture is a matter of one's own interpretation, because no prophecy ever came by the impulse of man, but men moved by the Holy Spirit spoke from God" (2 Peter 1:20-21). Truth is objective, and Divine Truth is supernaturally so. There is no interpretation of Scripture that is "true" for one person, and a different interpretation of that same passage of Scripture that is "true" for someone else, yet diametrically opposed to the first. Such personal interpretation of Scripture is often used to justify sinful and rebellious refusal to live in accordance with God's plan for us.

"Follow the pattern of the sound words which you have heard from me, in the faith and love which are in Christ Jesus; guard the truth that has been entrusted to you by the Holy Spirit who dwells within us" (2 Tim. 1:13-14).

In our day, we follow this wise counsel:

"The validity of Sacred Tradition, written not on papyrus, but in the hearts of His people, professed in the daily life of the Church, is of co-equal dignity and sanctity with Holy Writ. Scripture and Tradition both expressions of the one true faith, having come to the Church from God, both inspired by the Holy Spirit, complement and not compete against, one another. Where would we be without Sacred Tradition? For If we lack Sacred Tradition, we lack the teaching of the

Holy Trinity, the order and Rite of the ancient Liturgy, an understanding of our own Apostolic Succession, and much that lives and gives life to the fullness of Catholic faith.

Both Scripture and Tradition, having been shown of equal validity and sacred inspired character, form our Catholic faith. Our faith, having thus been firmly established by Holy Scripture and Sacred Tradition, what proper basis can there be, for adopting other teachings which are contrary to it?" Bishop Andre' Queen, Apostolic Letter, *Ut Unum Sint*, 2003.

Our "Statement of Faith" reflects this truth regarding Scripture and Apostolic Tradition: "We affirm the Holy Scriptures of the Old and New Testaments *as interpreted by the Church*, as containing everything that is necessary for salvation, and as being the rule and ultimate statement of the Faith of the Church." Scripture must have proper interpretation, which come from Apostolic Tradition, taught through the teaching authority of the Church. We believe Sacred Scripture as interpreted by the Church, together with the Seven Undisputed General Councils of the Whole Church, together with doctrines believed by the Church as a whole prior to the Great Schism of 1054, as defining the belief of the Whole Church.

In our own meager way, we ourselves provide a fine example to use to explain the role of Scripture and Tradition in both providing the Deposit of Faith. In the United States, we have the Constitution of the United States, which lists the organization of government, the powers and authorities of each branch, the rights of individuals and more. However, for all of the detail and forethought of this document, when an issue of whether a particular law is constitutional or not surfaces, what do we do? What if we told each individual citizen to interpret the Constitution as they saw fit? Nonsense, you say? We have a Supreme Court, which determines whether a law is unconstitutional, we have a President who is our head and signs new bills into law, we have a bi-cameral legislature, which updates how the laws apply to our lives. Certainly, if every person were to interpret the Constitution for himself or herself, there would be pandemonium!

Yet, this is what you have in any Church where each individual member determines for his or herself what the proper interpretation of Scripture is. Even Churches which claim to "agree on the essentials" come up short, as there is no consensus on what the "essentials" are, or that everyone accepts them as such. Does it seem logical that an Almighty, Powerful and Loving God would give us a Bible, with no way of authoritatively authenticating and interpreting it?

nt to understand that the Good News of Jesus Christ is transmitted
..... oral Apostolic Tradition and in writing in Holy Scripture. Once we
understand that Tradition and Scripture amplify and complement one another,
and not compete with each other, we begin a deeper walk in faith. "So then,
brethren, stand firm and hold to the traditions which you were taught by us,
either by word of mouth or by letter" (2 Thess. 2:15).

Jesus Christ Himself, as well as His Apostles, acknowledged and believed the oral
traditions to have the same spiritual authority as the written, which was, at that
time, Hebrew scripture (the Old Testament). St. Matthew tells us that the Holy
Family fulfilled the prophesy that "He shall be called a Nazarene" (Matt. 2:23),
yet nowhere in the Old Testament do we find this prophesy. It comes to Him,
and us, by oral Tradition.

In Matthew, we read Jesus instructing the people "*The scribes and Pharisees sit on
Moses' seat, so practice and observe whatever they tell you*, but not what they do; for
they preach but do not practice" (Matt. 23:2). [emphasis added] There is no
reference anywhere in the Old Testament to the "seat of Moses", but it was commonly understood in ancient Israel, that there existed an authoritative office, to
teach and instruct, passed on by Moses. So valid was the authority of this office,
that Jesus instructed the people to obey what they taught, although the Pharisees
did not obey their own teachings themselves.

St. Paul draws from oral rabbinical tradition, when he names "Jannes and
Jambres" as the actual names of the magicians of Pharaoh who opposed Moses (2
Tim. 3:8). In the Old Testament (Ex. 7:8) these individuals are not named. These
names come to us from an extrabiblical source, which is quoted authoritatively by
St. Paul, included by the Church as inspired, and accepted as such by both Old
Catholic (as well as Eastern Orthodox, Oriental Orthodox, Roman Catholic) and
Protestant alike.

St. James teaches us that because of Elijah's prayer, there was no rain in all of Israel
for three years, yet the Old Testament's rendering of Elijah's conflict with King
Ahab does not mention Elijah praying (Jas. 5:17, 1 Kings 17:1). Clearly, St.
James was drawing on an authoritative source not found in Hebrew Scripture,
quoting it as the same authority of the written Scripture.

St. Jude quotes oral tradition in relating the struggle between the Archangel
Michael and the devil over the body of Moses, "When the archangel Michael,

contending with the devil, disputed about the body of Moses, he did not presume to pronounce a reviling judgment upon him, but said, 'The Lord rebuke you'" (Jude 9). This incident is not found anywhere in the Old Testament, but is pure oral tradition, which he quotes authoritatively as divinely inspired truth, and we, in accepting this book as inspired, thus also accept this oral teaching and tradition.

Rabbinical oral tradition is infused again into the New Testament teachings, in 1 Corinthians 10:4: "All drank from the same supernatural drink, for they drank from the supernatural Rock which followed them, and the Rock was Christ." In Exodus 17: 1-7 and Numbers 20:2-13, we read nowhere that after Moses struck the rock, that it followed the Israelites on their journey.

"You, then, my son, be strong in the grace that is in Christ Jesus, and what you have heard from me before many witnesses entrust to faithful men who will be able to teach others also" (2 Tim. 2:1-2). When we separate Holy Scripture from the environment of the Church, which is authoritatively empowered to interpret it, you begin to have various anomalies of faith, where segments of individuals develop some "new" interpretation of Scripture independent of the nearly two thousand years of Christian teaching which explains it. After the resurrection, when Christ appeared to the Apostles, He "opened their eyes to the Scriptures" so that they could authoritatively interpret and teach about it. Surely, if the Apostles needed to have Christ "open their eyes" so that *they* could understand Scripture, do *we* not need their spiritual successors to "open our eyes" as well? Do we know more about Christ than they who walked with Him, and learned at His feet?

Let us consider the importance of what is found in Scripture, and that is God's Truth. It is this, and not answers to preconceived notions that we must seek.

"Truth, not eloquence, is to be sought in reading the Holy Scriptures; and *every part must be read in the spirit in which it was written.* For in the Scriptures we ought to seek profit rather than polished diction." Thomas, à Kempis, *The Imitation of Christ*, A.D. 1400. CCEL. [emphasis added]

Sacramental Marriage

Marriage is the blessed joining of a man and a woman into a permanent and life-long bond of self-sacrificing love and commitment to one another. Because, in the Christian faith, it is ratifies by vows made to one another, and to Almighty

God, it is a Sacrament. The very word "sacrament" comes from the Latin and means an "oath". Originally meant to refer to the oath taken by Roman soldiers upon entering the Roman Army, the early Church adopted the word to refer to spiritual bonds and commitments made with respect to God and the Church.

So then, the marital bond, as all sacraments, is sealed with the spiritual, supernatural bonding of the man and woman to each other, by each other, and to God, within the community of the Church. Imitations of the marital bond, such as so-called "same-sex unions" are contrary to the understanding of marriage established by God Himself, and serve to promote what is an objectively immoral lifestyle, and obscure God's truth from individuals spiritually imprisoned in this sin.

Because sacramental marriage is permanent, as we have been taught by Jesus Christ Himself, the consideration of a future spouse is a gravely important action, not to be taken lightly. Marriage entered into lightly, or without proper forethought, can result in pain for all involved, most notably any children who are the product of such a union.

Marriage is to be considered thoroughly, and slow, deliberate steps taken, to ensure that both individuals have a concept of marriage that is both complementary to one another, and is in line with the teaching of the Church. Both parties must be free to marry, have no impediments that would prevent marriage, such as a previous, valid, sacramental marriage, degree of relation to one another, not of the age of assent, etc. Both must be open to the gift of children, as the natural result of their union, and raise their children in the faith.

Marriage requires each to vow to give of themselves for the sake of the other, thinking of their beloved before themselves, and making decisions and determination that take into account the feelings, and welfare of their spouse at all times. In order to be successful, marriage requires strong faith in God, and a faith that is active within the bonds of the marriage itself. Both parties are to be involved in ensuring that the Word of God is alive in their lives, both as individuals and as a married couple, as well as ensuring that any children the result of their matrimony are raised steeped in the faith. Love being the bond of any successful marriage, must be properly understood. Love is not merely an emotion or feeling. Love is an act, it is what one does for another, as a result of true caring and affection. Love then, is the self-sacrificing act of caring for another. Long after emotional exuberance has leveled off, true love is still there, expressed in selfless acts of care for one's spouse. This selfless love at work in the spouse is nothing less than Christ at work in that person. In fact, the bond between the Church and Christ is expressed in terms of marriage, whereas the Church is the Bride of Christ, and Jesus is the Bridegroom.

Marriage also requires communication between the two spouses. Decisions are to be made in concert with one another, and not apart from one another, under the loving guidance of God, as taught by the Church. When communication breaks down, communion within the marriage also breaks down, and that which was in unity, begins to be as two halves of one whole, which are together but not joined. Communication is essential to the marital relationship.

The Old Catholic Church teaches that a sacramental marriage, once entered into, is indissoluble by any human institution Even the Church herself, of divine origin, has not the authority to sunder that which God has joined. The reason is that marriage, as a sacrament, is a covenant bond entered into by a man, a woman and God. God is called upon to ratify and bless the union, thus imparting His grace upon it. Because marriage is a bond made by God, it is indissoluble by any institution of mankind.

Some individuals may wrongly believe that an Old Catholic Declaration of Nullity, determined by a duly constituted marriage tribunal, is the Old Catholic version of divorce. This illustrates a fundamental misunderstanding of the Church's authority and exactly what an annulment actually is.

In a marriage tribunal investigating a petition for a Declaration of Nullity, the Church is asked to investigate a particular marriage by one or both of the spouses, who may, for instance, claim that the spouse did not fully understand the nature of sacramental marriage at the time of the nuptial mass, or one of several issues regarding proper matter, form or intent. A declaration annulling the marriage is only constituted if the marriage tribunal determines that no valid marriage actually occurred, due to some profound defect. This does not affect the legitimacy of any children who are the product of the marriage, but does indicate that the two spouses, although engaged civilly in a civil marriage contract, were never sacramentally married. If no defect in matter, form or intent is found, then the marriage tribunal has no authority to declare null a marriage that is sacramentally valid. The Church may not issue a Declaration of Nullity to provide for the ease of conscience or comfort of a member (or members) of the Church. Persons in a sacramentally valid marriage are married, regardless of a secular determination of divorce by civil courts, which have no authority to sever a sacramental marriage. In such cases where a sacramentally married person obtains a civil divorce, they are instructed to live modestly. One cannot sacramentally marry a second time, if a Declaration of Nullity of a prior sacramental marriage was not first obtained. The permanence of sacramental marriage causes pause, and forces potential spouses to strictly consider what they do and whom they choose, far more than our secular society, which advocates changing spouses as often as one changes clothes, destroying long-term family permanence and stability, which benefits husband, wife and children.

The prohibition against divorce permeates Judeo-Christian teaching, beginning with God declaring that Adam and Eve constitute, "one flesh". That which God declares, He does, just as He declared the world into existence. In declaring this man and woman as "one flesh", *they became*, through the God's declaratory power, *one flesh*. It continues with His warning against the sins that cause divorce, such as adultery, and coveting thy neighbor's wife, as admonished in the Ten Commandments. In Malachi 2:16 we read, "For I hate divorce, says the Lord the God of Israel, and covering one's garment with violence, says the Lord of hosts. So take heed of yourself and do not be faithless." Hate is an extremely strong word, and here God equates divorce with faithlessness.

The Mosaic allowances for divorce at the time of Christ were given by the Hebrew Church alone, and not by decree of the Roman authorities. Although a wrong concept, it was rightly understood to have been an authority that, if actually possessed, would be effected *only through the Church* and not secular government. It is clear, by Jesus' denunciation of divorce as allowed by Mosaic law, that not even the Church has the authority to break a validly effected covenant bond and oath (sacramentum) entered into by, with, and through God.

Some believe they see valid exceptions by re-interpreting Matthew 5:31-32, "But I say to you that every one who divorces his wife, except on the ground of unchastity, makes her an adulteress; and whoever marries a divorced woman commits adultery." Some claim unchastity means adultery, but the word used is "porneia" and actually refers to illicit or incestuous marriages, of which Christians are not to be a part of. We know this to be the case, as St. Paul, in his admonishment to the Corinthians, uses the same word (porneia) to refer to an incestuous relationship, "It is actually reported that there is immorality (porneia) among you, and of a kind that is not found even among pagans: for a man is living with his father's wife."

Against the claims of those looking for exceptions that would justify the modern day's reasons for divorce, is the fact that none of the four Gospels provide any. "Everyone who divorces his wife and marries another commits adultery, and he who marries a woman divorced from her husband commit adultery" (Luke 16:18).

The Pharisees asked Jesus if it was unlawful for a man to divorce his wife, and He stated that, "Moses allowed a man to write a certificate of divorce, and to put her away.' But Jesus said to them, 'For your hardness of heart he wrote you this commandment But from the beginning of creation, "God made them male and female.' 'For this reason a man shall leave his father and mother and be joined to his wife, and the two shall become one.' So they are no longer two but one. What therefore God has joined together, let no man put asunder.' And in the house the disciples asked him again about this matter. And he said to them, 'Whoever divorces his wife and marries another, commits adultery against her; and if she divorces her husband and marries another, she commits adultery" (Mark 10:2-12). Jesus effectively reminds them that it was *Moses* and not God that had allowed them to provide a certificate of divorce. He then reaffirms God's plan and the permanence of marriage. It is this permanence of marriage, *spoken by Christ Himself,* that many Churches claiming to be Christian do not observe, rather holding civil authority equal to God's authority, in that they consider a marriage solemnized in the Church, with the blessing of God, to be *subordinate* to civil authority, the same civil authority that now advocates same sex unions and other abominations. There is no confusion, *divorce is alien to the Christian faith, and always has been.* One cannot have the permanence of sacramental marriage, as taught by Christ Himself, and at the selfsame time, have divorce of that same sacramental marriage by an anti-Christian civil authority.

Anyone believing that divorce and remarriage under these circumstances, which Scripture teaches is adultery, is a minor issue, would do well to consider the following, "Do you not know that the unrighteous will not inherit the Kingdom of God? Do not be deceived; neither the immoral, nor idolators, *nor adulterers,* nor homosexuals, nor thieves, nor the greedy, nor drunkards, nor revilers, nor robbers will inherit the kingdom of God" (1 Cor. 6:9-11). [emphasis added]

Those individuals involved in such relationships in open defiance to the incontrovertible teachings of Almighty God, risk everything. Open defiance and adultery, sins which cause an inability to appreciate the nature and gravity of further sinful acts compounded upon one another, cause a haughty arrogance that carries some to receive the sacraments in such a state. We are warned against such serious error, in the gravest terms, "Whoever therefore, eats the bread or drinks the cup of the Lord in an unworthy manner will be guilty of profaning the body and blood of the Lord" (1 Cor. 11:27-30).

The Shepherd of Hermas

"What then, sir, is the husband to do, if his wife continue in her vicious practices [adultery]?' And he said, 'The husband should put her away, and remain by himself. But if he put his wife away and marry another, he also commits adultery.'" (*The Shepherd* 4:1:6 [A.D. 80]).[1]

St. Justin Martyr

"Concerning chastity, He uttered such sentiments as these: 'Whosoever looketh upon a woman to lust after her, hath committed adultery with her already in his heart before God." And, "If thy right eye offend thee, cut it out; for it is better for thee to enter into the kingdom of heaven with one eye, than, having two eyes, to be cast into everlasting fire.' And, 'Whosoever shall marry her that is divorced from another husband, committeth adultery.' And, 'There are some who have been made eunuchs of men, and some who were born eunuchs, and some who have made themselves eunuchs for the kingdom of heaven's sake; but all cannot receive this saying.' So that all who, by human law, are twice married, are in the eye of our Master sinners, and those who look upon a woman to lust after her. For not only he who in act commits adultery is rejected by Him, but also he who desires to commit adultery: since not only our works, but also our thoughts, are open before God." (*First Apology* 15 [A.D. 151]).[2]

St. Basil the Great

"A man who marries after another man's wife has been taken away from him will be charged with adultery in the case of the first woman; but in the case of the second he will be guiltless" (*Second Canonical Letter to Amphilochius* 199:37 [A.D. 375]).[3]

St. Ambrose of Milan

"No one is permitted to know a woman other than his wife. The marital right is given you for this reason: lest you fall into the snare and sin with a strange woman. 'If you are bound to a wife do not seek a divorce'; for you are not permitted, while your wife lives, to marry another" (*Abraham* 1:7:59 [A.D. 387]).[4]

"You dismiss your wife, therefore, as if by right and without being charged with wrongdoing; and you suppose it is proper for you to do so because no human law forbids it; but divine law forbids it. Anyone who obeys men ought to stand in awe of God. Hear the law of the Lord, which even they who propose our laws must obey: 'What God has joined together let no man put asunder'" (*Commentary on Luke* 8:5 [A.D. 389]).[5]

St. Jerome

"Do not tell me about the violence of the ravisher, about the persuasiveness of a mother, about the authority of a father, about the influence of relatives, about the intrigues and insolence of servants, or about household losses. So long as a husband lives, be he adulterer, be he sodomite, be he addicted to every kind of vice, if she left him on account of his crimes, he is her husband still and she may not take another." (*Letters* 55:3 [A.D. 396])[6]

A spouse is not required to remain in the same home as an abusive spouse, nor subject minor children to the abuses of such spouse. In such a situation, a spouse may obtain a civil divorce in order to divide the marital assets, and ensure the financial well being of the victim spouse and children. This does not, however, terminate sacramental marriage, and both parties are to live chaste lives while the other lives, and only afterwards is the other free to marry again. In many such cases, due to the lack of maturity on the part of the offending spouse at the time marriage was entered into, which manifested itself as the marriage progressed, no sacramental marriage ever existed. Without a proper and mature intent, no valid marriage exists, and the Church should be consulted as to an annulment. However, if a valid, sacramental marriage exists, the Church cannot declare it null.

"Wherever there is fornication and a suspicion of fornication, a wife is freely dismissed. And because it is always possible that someone may calumniate the innocent and, for the sake of a second joining in marriage, act in criminal fashion against the first, it is commanded that when the first wife is dismissed, a second may not be taken while the first still lives." (*Commentaries on Matthew* 3:19:9 [A.D. 398])[7]

St. Augustine

"Neither can it rightly be held that a husband who dismisses his wife because of fornication and marries another does not commit adultery. For there is also adultery on the part of those who, after the repudiation of their former wives because of fornication, marry others. This adultery, nevertheless, is certainly less serious than that of men who dismiss their wives for reasons other than fornication and take other wives. Therefore, when we say: 'Whoever marries a woman dismissed by her husband for reason other than fornication commits adultery,' undoubtedly we speak the truth. But we do not thereby acquit of this crime the man who marries a woman who was dismissed because of fornication. We do not doubt in the least that both are adulterers. We do indeed pronounce him an adulterer who dismissed his wife for cause other than fornication and marries another, nor do we thereby defend from the taint of this sin the man who dismissed his wife because of fornication and marries another. We recognize that both are adulterers, though the sin of one is more grave than that of the other. No one is so unreasonable to say that a man who marries a woman whose husband has dismissed her because of fornication is not an adulterer, while maintaining that a man who marries a woman dismissed without the ground of fornication is an adulterer. Both of these men are guilty of adultery" (*Adulterous Marriages* 1:9:9 [A.D. 419]).[8]

"A woman begins to be the wife of no later husband unless she has ceased to be the wife of a former one. She will cease to be the wife of a former one, however, if that husband should die, not if he commit fornication. A spouse, therefore, is lawfully dismissed for cause of fornication; but the bond of chastity remains. That is why a man is guilty of adultery if he marries a woman who has been dismissed even for this very reason of fornication." (ibid, 2:4:4)[9]

"Undoubtedly the substance of the sacrament is of this bond, so that when man and woman have been joined in marriage they must continue inseparably as long as they live, nor is it allowed for one spouse to be separated from the other except for cause of fornication. For this is preserved in the case of Christ and the Church, so that, as a living one with a living one, there is no divorce, no separation forever." (*Marriage and Concupiscence* 1:10:11 [A.D. 419])[10]

"In marriage, however, let the blessings of marriage be loved: offspring, fidelity, and the sacramental bond. Offspring, not so much because it may be born, but because it can be reborn; for it is born to punishment unless it be reborn to life. Fidelity, but not such as even the unbelievers have among themselves, ardent as they are for the flesh.... The sacramental bond, which they lose neither through separation nor through adultery, this the spouses should guard chastely and harmoniously." (ibid, 1:17:19)[11]

In today's society, which promotes the individual's selfish needs and hunger for self gratification, this teaching is surely the twenty-first century's "this is a hard saying, who can even hear it" for many. Unfortunately, so many Christian Churches have acquiesced and chose to pander to these base emotions, abandoning the Commandment of God, for the "Counterproposal of man", passively accepting the steady erosion of Christian values, as the basic unit of Christian faith is attacked, which is the family. What husband or wife can rest and trust in the permanence of a marriage, when Churches accept civil government's declarations that sacramental marriages have ceased to exist, turning a blind eye in order to create a comfortable place to be, believe one is still living in accord with the teaching of Jesus and fill the Church coffers with empty faithless offerings? The teaching of the Old Catholic Church is in accord with that of Christ Jesus.

Even so, we must love and care for those members of the Church who have divorced and remarried outside of the Church, and make the sacraments available to them to assist them in their emotional and spiritual healing. Our clergy care for such members of their local parish in a caring and pastoral manner. The Church shall not abandon her position, but shall endeavor to love and care for her members who have erred in this part of their life.

In addition, the Church requires all couples intending to marry to undergo proper instruction and preparation. Marriage, as a sacrament, is no less important that any of the other sacraments, and we should expect that the Church would spend considerable time preparing her children for this great gift, as she spends considerable time preparing men preparing for the diaconate or priesthood, or men and women entering into religious orders, who are given a period of time to discern and prepare. Unfortunately, today many couples spend more time planning the actual wedding, than they do in planning the life that they will share after it is done and over. The permanence of sacramental marriage should also serve to cause those contemplating marriage to consider carefully the individual to whom they wish to be bound, ensuring that all of the necessary questions are answered, that a solid basis of trust has been established, and that the relationship is built on honesty, mutual love, respect for each other and a commitment to permanence in marriage.

Marriages entered into in the mindset of the secular world we live in, offer nothing of the nature that Catholic Marriage offers, instead causing a relationship to exist that is built on superficial infatuation, lust and a love of spouse second to one's own whims and motivations. Once a spouse becomes inconvenient due to illness, boredom, pregnancy, poverty or the emotional immaturity of the other, that spouse is summarily discarded in favor of some new diversion.

The Divinity of Jesus Christ

Some quasi-Christian sects today deny the divinity of Christ, contrary to the witness of the Church for nearly two thousand years. The divinity of Christ is unequivocally taught in Scripture and in Tradition, from before the birth of Christ, going back to the proto-evangelium in Genesis 3:15. The divinity of Christ is affirmed consistently:

"For to us a child is born, to us a son is given; and the government will be upon his shoulder, and his name will be called 'Wonderful Counselor, Mighty God, Everlasting Father, Prince of Peace'" (Is. 9:6).

"Simon Peter replied, 'You are the Christ, the Son of the living God.' And Jesus answered him, 'Blessed are you, Simon Bar-Jona! For flesh and blood has not revealed this to you, but my Father who is in heaven.'" (Matt. 16:16-17)

"In the beginning was the Word, and the Word was with God, and the Word was God." (John 1:1)

"Jesus said to them, "Truly, truly, I say to you, before Abraham was, I am" (John 8:58). In a very clear way here, Jesus is identifying Himself as God, by referring to the name that God identified himself to Moses, "I Am Who I Am", which the Jews would immediately recognize as an affirmation of Jesus' divine nature.

"I and the Father are one." (John 10:30)

"For in him the whole fullness of deity dwells bodily." (Col. 2:9) In the physical body of Jesus lives not part of God, but God in His fullness in ways both wonderful and mysterious.

"In many and various ways God spoke of old to our fathers by the prophets; but in these last days he has spoken to us by a Son, whom he appointed the heir of all things, through whom also he created the world. He reflects the glory of God and bears the very stamp of his nature, upholding the universe by his word of power…" (Heb. 1:1-3)

"But of the Son he says," Thy throne, O God, is for ever and ever, the righteous scepter is the scepter of thy kingdom…. And, "Thou, Lord, didst found the earth in the beginning, and the heavens are the work of thy hands." (Heb. 1:8, 10)

The Old Catholic Usage of Statues and Icons

Many Protestant sects speak against the Church's use of statues and images of the saints, angels and depictions of biblical events. But the Old Catholic Church teaches that God permits the use of religious statues and images, so long as we avoid idolatry, the worship of them as gods. Certainly, any Protestant who would ask an Old Catholic, as he sees him kneeling in prayer in front of a statue of some saint, as to if he believed that the statue was a god to be worshiped, the response from the Old Catholic would be, that the statue is nothing more than plaster (or wood, bronze, etc.), and that it is an aid to prayer. Reverence seen given to statues is actually given to show respect for the individual the statue *represents*, and certainly not the statue itself. The Church encourages these aids to prayer, which reminds us, upon arriving in the edifice of the Church, that we are in the House of God, that we stand before His altar, and our thoughts are to be only of the sacred and not the profane.

Examples of God commanding man to make images, and of God using images to convey His graces and blessing, are:

Exodus 25:18-20. "And you shall make two cherubim of gold; of hammered work you shall make them, on the two ends of the mercy seat."

Exodus 26:1. "Moreover you shall make the tabernacle with ten curtains of fine twined linen and blue and purple and scarlet stuff; with cherubim skillfully worked shall you make them."

Numbers 21:8-9. "And the Lord said to Moses, 'Make a fiery serpent, and set it on a pole; and everyone who is bitten, when he sees it, shall live."

1 Kings 7:23-29. "Then he made the molten sea."…"It stood upon twelve oxen"…"like the flower of a lily"…"were lions, oxen and cherubim…"…"and below the lions and oxen, there were wreaths of beveled work."

1 Kings 6:23-28. "In the inner sanctuary he made two Cherubim of olivewood." "He carved all the house round about with carved figures of cherubim and palm trees and open flowers."

God does not contradict Himself, and so if God does not mean to prohibit all carved images, statues, and such, what does He mean? We need to read the commandment in the proper continuity of though, not separating it prematurely; "...you shall not bow down to them or serve them; for I the Lord your God am a jealous God, visiting the iniquities of the Fathers upon the children to the third and fourth generations of those who hate me." Unfortunately, when the children of Israel were led from Egypt by Moses, many still had Egyptian ways, beliefs and religion in their hearts, which was centered around the worship of idols of the Egyptian gods, who often took the form of animals, such as the golden calf. God expressly forbids giving to any idol that worship, respect and reverence that is due to God and God alone. That an Old Catholic is seen kneeling in prayer *before a statute*, does not mean that he or she is praying *to the statute*. This does not mean that we cannot honor the saints of the Church who have gone before us; it simply means that we honor them as creations, but we honor God, and Him alone, as He Who Is Uncreated.

Brethren of the Lord

Many Protestants state that Mary had other children, and so Jesus had brothers. As proof, they offer Matthew 12:46, "his mother and his brethren were standing about." Also, "Is not his the carpenter, the son of Mary, the brother of James and Joseph and Judas and Simon, and are not his sisters here with us?" (Mark 6:3) In addition is provided: "For even his brethren did not believe in him." (John 7:5)

To this, we respond that the use of the term "brother" or "brethren" referred to more than just blood brother, in the sense we are used to seeing it. Neither Hebrew nor Aramaic, the languages spoken by Christ and the Apostles, had at that time, a special word meaning "cousin" as we do in English. Speakers of those languages used either the word for "brother" or a circumlocution, such as, "the son of the brother of my father". Translating the Hebrew or Aramaic into Greek, the word for "brother" is rendered as "adelphos" (meaning sons of the same parent), and so one must carefully understand and consider the wording within the proper context.

The word "brother" can refer to a kinsman, as in Deut.3:7, or Jer. 34:9. It could also refer to a friend, such as in 2 Sam. 1:26, or an ally as in Amos 1:9.

As opposed to seeing multiple sons mentioned, in Mark 6:3, we read "the son of Mary". In Matthew 1:25 we read, "And he knew her not till she brought fourth her first-born son." The term "till she" does not, as some believe, mean that immediately after that time, Joseph did "know" Mary. To illustrate this point, we turn to Deuteronomy 34:6 where scripture states, with regards to the burial of Moses and the location of his grave, that no man knows the place of his burial "until this present day." In fact, no one has ever known since that time where it is. Elsewhere in scripture, we read in Genesis 8:7 that Noah "sent forth a raven; and it went to and fro until the waters were dried up from the earth." We know that the raven did not come back at all. In this, we are taught by the early Church, as is explained below by St. Jerome:

> "Our reply is briefly this,—the words *knew* and *till* in the language of Holy Scripture are capable of a double meaning. As to the former, he himself gave us a dissertation to show that it must be referred to sexual intercourse, and no one doubts that it is often used of the knowledge of the understanding, as, for instance, 'the boy Jesus tarried behind in Jerusalem, and his parents knew it not.' Now we have to prove that just as in the one case he has followed the usage of Scripture, so with regard to the word *till* he is utterly refuted by the authority of the same Scripture, which often denotes by its use a fixed time (he himself told us so), frequently time without limitation, as when God by the mouth of the prophet says to certain persons, 'Even to old age I am he.' Will He cease to be God when they have grown old? And the Savior in the Gospel tells the Apostles, 'Lo, I am with you always, even unto the end of the world.' Will the Lord then after the end of the world has come forsake His disciples, and at the very time when seated on twelve thrones they are to judge the twelve tribes of Israel will they be bereft of the company of their Lord? Again Paul the Apostle writing to the Corinthians says, 'Christ the first-fruits, afterward they that are Christ's, at his coming. Then cometh the end, when he shall have delivered up the kingdom to God, even the Father, when he shall have put down all rule, and all authority and power. For he must reign, till he hath put all enemies under his feet.' Granted that the passage relates to our Lord's human nature, we do not deny that the words are spoken of Him who endured the cross and is commanded to sit afterwards on

the right hand. What does he mean then by saying, 'for he must reign, till he hath put all enemies under his feet'? Is the Lord to reign only until His enemies begin to be under His feet, and once they are under His feet will He cease to reign? Of course His reign will then commence in its fullness when His enemies begin to be under His feet. David also in the fourth Song of Ascents speaks thus, 'Behold, as the eyes of servants look unto the hand of their master, as the eyes of a maiden unto the hand of her mistress, so our eyes look unto the Lord our God, until he have mercy upon us.' Will the prophet, then, look unto the Lord until he obtain mercy, and when mercy is obtained will he turn his eyes down to the ground? Although elsewhere he says, 'Mine eyes fail for thy salvation, and for the word of thy righteousness.' I could accumulate countless instances of this usage, and cover the verbosity of our assailant with a cloud of proofs; I shall, however, add only a few, and leave the reader to discover like ones for himself." St. Jerome. A.D. 383 *The Perpetual Virginity of Blessed Mary—Against Helvidius*. CCEL.

The term "first-born" refers to Mosaic Law, and does not state a fact, that additional children were in fact born (Ex. 13:2, Num. 3:12). Under Mosaic Law, the first-born son was significant and special, and inherited the birthright from the father, and the headship of the family (Ex. 34:20). The first male child of a marriage was termed the "first-born", even if there were never any additional children born. In Exodus 13:1-2, we read, "The Lord said to Moses, 'Consecrate to me all the first-born; whatever is the first to open the womb among the people of Israel, both of man and of beast, is mine."

In Genesis 14:14 Lot, Abraham's nephew (Gen. 11:26-28) is described as Abraham's brother. In Genesis 29:15, Laban, Jacob's uncle, calls Jacob his "brother".

Mary, the wife of Cleophas, and "sister" of the Virgin Mary (John 19:25) is the mother of James and Joseph (Mark 15:47, Mat. 27:56) who are called the "brothers" of Jesus (Mk 6:3). In Acts 1:12-15, we read about the apostles, Mary, "some women" and Jesus "brethren" which number about 120. Certainly we are not to believe that Jesus had about 120 blood brothers. In John 19:26-27, we read that Jesus gives the care of his mother to John. Had Jesus blood brothers, *it would have been horrifically and sinfully negligent of them to not care for their mother*, particularly in Jewish culture and faith. She was placed in John's care because there were no other sons to care for her, as she had no other children. This is what the Church teaches, in agreement with both Scripture and Tradition:

"Let me point out then what John says, 'But there were standing by the cross of Jesus his mother, and his mother's sister, Mary the wife of Cleophas, and Mary Magdalene.' No one doubts that there were two apostles called by the name James, James the son of Zebedee, and James the son of Alphaeus. Do you intend the comparatively unknown James the less, who is called in Scripture the son of Mary, not however of Mary the mother of our Lord, to be an apostle, or not? If he is an apostle, he must be the son of Alphaeus and a believer in Jesus, 'For neither did his brethren believe in him.' If he is not an apostle, but a third James (who he can be I cannot tell), how can he be regarded as the Lord's brother, and how, being a third, can he be called *less* to distinguish him from *greater*, when *greater* and *less* are used to denote the relations existing, not between three, but between two? Notice, moreover, that the Lord's brother is an apostle, since Paul says, 'Then after three years I went up to Jerusalem to visit Cephas, and tarried with him fifteen days. But other of the Apostles saw I none, save James the Lord's brother.' And in the same Epistle, 'And when they perceived the grace that was given unto me, James and Cephas and John, who were reputed to be pillars,' etc. And that you may not suppose this James to be the son of Zebedee, you have only to read the Acts of the Apostles, and you will find that the latter had already been slain by Herod.

The only conclusion is that the Mary who is described as the mother of James the less was the wife of Alphaeus and sister of Mary the Lord's mother, the one who is called by John the Evangelist 'Mary of Cleophas,' whether after her father, or kindred, or for some other reason. But if you think they are two persons because elsewhere we read, 'Mary the mother of James the less,' and here, 'Mary of Cleophas,' you have still to learn that it is customary in Scripture for the same individual to bear different names. Raguel, Moses' father-in-law, is also called 'Jethro'. Gedeon, without any apparent reason for the change, all at once becomes 'Jerubbaal'. Ozias, king of Judah, has an alternative, 'Azarias'. Mount Tabor is called 'Itabyrium'. Again Hermon is called by the Phenicians 'Sanior', and by the Amorites 'Sanir'. The same tract of country is known by three names, Negebh, Teman, and Darom in Ezekiel. Peter is also called 'Simon' and 'Cephas'. Judas the zealot in another Gospel is called 'Thaddaeus'. And there are numerous other examples, which the reader will be able to collect for himself from every part of Scripture.

Now here we have the explanation of what I am endeavoring to show, how it is that the sons of Mary, the sister of our Lord's mother, who though not formerly believers afterwards did believe, can be called brethren of the Lord. Possibly the case might be that one of the brethren believed immediately while the others did not believe until long after, and that one Mary was the mother of James and Joses, namely, 'Mary of Cleophas,' who is the same as the wife of Alphaeus, the other, the mother of James the less. In any case, if she (the latter) had been the Lord's mother S. John would have allowed her the title, as everywhere else, and would not by calling her the mother of other sons have given a wrong impression. But at this stage I do not wish to argue for or against the supposition that Mary the wife of Cleophas and Mary the mother of James and Joses were different women, provided it is clearly understood that Mary the mother of James and Joses was not the same person as the Lord's mother. How then, says Helvidius, do you make out that they were called the Lord's brethren who were not his brethren? I will show how that is. In Holy Scripture there are four kinds of brethren-by nature, race, kindred, love. Instances of brethren by nature are Esau and Jacob, the twelve patriarchs, Andrew and Peter, James and John. As to race, all Jews are called brethren of one another, as in Deuteronomy, 'If thy brother, an Hebrew man, or an Hebrew woman, be sold unto thee, and serve thee six years; then in the seventh year thou shalt let him go free from thee.' And in the same book, 'Thou shalt in anywise set him king over thee, whom the Lord thy God shall choose: one from among thy brethren shalt thou set king over thee; thou mayest not put a foreigner over thee, which is not thy brother.' And again, 'Thou shalt not see thy brother's ox or his sheep go astray, and hide thyself from them: thou shalt surely bring them again unto thy brother. And if thy brother be not nigh unto thee, or if thou know him not, then thou shalt bring it home to thine house, and it shall be with thee until thy brother seek after it, and thou shalt restore it to him again.' And the Apostle Paul says, 'I could wish that I myself were anathema from Christ for my brethren's sake, my kinsmen according to the flesh: who are Israelites.' Moreover they are called brethren by kindred who are of one family, that is patria, which corresponds to the Latin *paternitas*, because from a single root a numerous progeny proceeds. In Genesis we read, 'And Abram said unto Lot, Let there be no strife, I pray thee, between me and thee, and between my herdmen and thy herdmen; for we are brethren.' And again, 'So Lot chose him all the plain of Jordan, and Lot journeyed east: and they separated each from his brother.' Certainly Lot was not Abraham's brother, but the son of Abraham's brother, Aram. For Terah begat Abraham and Nahor and Aram: and Aram begat Lot. Again we read, "And Abram was seventy and five years old when he departed out of Haran. And Abram took Sarai his wife. and Lot his brother's son." But if you still doubt whether a nephew can be called a son, let me give you an instance. 'And when Abram heard that his brother was taken captive, he led forth his trained men, born in his house, three hundred and eighteen.' And after describing the night attack and the slaughter, he adds, 'And he brought back all the goods, and also brought again his brother Lot.'

Let this suffice by way of proof of my assertion. But for fear you may make some cavilling objection, and wriggle out of your difficulty like a snake, I must bind you fast with the bonds of proof to stop your hissing and complaining, for I know you would like to say you have been overcome not so much by Scripture truth as by intricate arguments. Jacob, the son of Isaac and Rebecca, when in fear of his brother's treachery he had gone to Mesopotamia, drew nigh and rolled away the stone from the mouth of the well, and watered the flocks of Laban, his mother's brother. 'And Jacob kissed Rachel, and lifted up his voice, and wept. And Jacob told Rachel that he was her father's brother, and that he was Rebekah's son.' Here is an example of the rule already referred to, by which a nephew is called a brother. And again, 'Laban said unto Jacob. Because thou art my brother, shouldest thou therefore serve me for nought? Tell me what shall thy wages be.' And so, when, at the end of twenty years, without the knowledge of his father-in-law and accompanied by his wives and sons he was returning to his country, on Laban overtaking him in the mountain of Gilead and failing to find the idols which Rachel hid among the baggage, Jacob answered and said to Laban, 'What is my trespass? What is my sin, that thou hast so hotly pursued after me? Whereas thou hast felt all about my stuff, what hast thou found of all thy household stuff? Set it here before my brethren and thy brethren, that they may judge betwixt us two.' Tell me who are those brothers of Jacob and Laban who were present there? Esau, Jacob's brother, was certainly not there, and Laban, the son of Bethuel, had no brothers although he had a sister Rebecca." St. Jerome. *The Perpetual Virginity of Blessed Mary—Against Helvidius.* A.D. 383. CCEL

Faith and Works

Is faith in Christ a mere mental assent or agreement to the fact that He is the Son of God only, or is true faith operative in the life of the believer? Must true faith result in some response, generated by God's grace operative in our life, compelling us to live the Christ-like life? We believe this to be so. Furthermore, we believe that this is the proper understanding of faith and works. The Old Catholic Church does not now, nor has it ever, taught a "works-righteousness" type of salvation; that is, we do not teach that one can earn their way into heaven by doing good works. We do believe, that we are compelled as Christians to do good works—because Christ Himself taught us to do so. One's faith then, must work. We are saved by the grace of God, justified by faith. *working through love.*

"'Not everyone who says to me, "Lord, Lord," shall enter the kingdom of heaven, but he who does the will of my Father who is in heaven.'" (Matt. 7:21) This contradicts affirmations that all that is required is to "ask Jesus to be your personal Lord and Savior", in order to be saved. We are exhorted, not only be the prophets, and Apostles, but by Jesus Himself, not merely to profess Christ as Lord, but to go the next step and walk in faith, and do the will of His Father. This particular message is not isolated. It is not merely "nice to do" but absolutely essential to follow one's profession of believe with the actions that are manifest as a result of true faith, such as feeding the hungry, caring for the sick, and loving one another as Christ loves us. Our failure to obey Christ's instructions to us will not go unnoticed. He will hold us accountable for our failure to live out our faith in accordance with His teaching. "'Why do you call me "Lord, Lord," and not do what I tell you?'" (Luke 6:46)

"For he will render every man according to his works..." (Rom. 2:6-8)

"For it is not the hearers of the law who are righteous before God, but the doers of the law who will be justified." (Rom. 2:13)

"For if we sin deliberately after receiving the knowledge of the truth, there no longer remains a sacrifice for sins, but a fearful prospect of judgments..." (Heb. 10:26-27).

"What does it profit, my brethren, if a man says he has faith but has not works? Can his faith save him?" (Jas. 2:14) A profession of faith and believe not genuinely followed by acts of mercy and virtue, the corporal works of mercy, and acts of love for our fellow man, not just those whom we know and care about, but the stranger in our midst as well, profits us absolutely nothing. Ours is a faith of action, and not mere mental assent—one is to walk forward in faith, trusting in God.

"So faith by itself, if it has no works, is dead." (Jas. 2:17) Genuine faith operative in the life of the faithful is God's grace at work in us.

"But some one will say, 'You have faith and I have works.' Show me your faith apart from your works, and I by my works will show you my faith…. Do you want to be shown, you foolish fellow, that faith apart from works is barren?" (Jas. 2:18-20)

"You see that a man is justified by works and not by faith alone." (Jas. 2:24)

We see that faith is joined to works of charity and love to our fellow man. This agrees with Christ's exhortation to love God, and to love our neighbor as ourselves. When St. Paul, in Romans, speaks of "works of the law", he is referring to the obligations of the Mosaic law upon the observant Jew, such as circumcision, temple obligations, animal sacrifices for atonement for sins, the kosher laws, and the like. This understanding is evident in the context of the passage, as St. Paul is arguing with the Judiazers, who wanted the Gentile converts to be circumcised, which would initiate them into the Old Covenant and obligate them to obey Mosaic law. The phrase in Greek is "*erga nomou*" and usually is transferred as "works of the law", where the word "*nomou*" is the word used in the Septuagint, the Greek language book of Hebrew Scripture to translate the Hebrew word "Torah", the Law of Moses. This understanding of what St. Paul was saying is further supported by archeological proof, as the same phrase appears, in Hebrew, in the Dead Sea Scrolls of the first century. So then what St. Paul is talking about in referring to "works of the law" is the Law of Moses, and what St. James is talking about in referring to "works" are the acts of love and mercy, that we are enabled to do through God's grace. Jesus Christ never taught "faith alone".

The Trinity

The Church's teaching on the Trinity is not explicitly identified as such in the Bible. You will not find the Greek, Aramaic nor Hebrew word for "Trinity" anywhere in Scripture, yet it is a key teaching of Christianity. You will find guideposts in Scripture that teach about the nature of the Trinity. In addition, the Early Church Fathers, the teachers, deacons, priests and bishops of the Church in its infancy, wrote extensively on the Trinity as well.

Each person of the Trinity is a distinct person, yet each is part of the other two and each is God. We are taught, in a profound way, that the Holy Spirit is God. "But Peter said, 'Ananias, why has Satan filled your heart to lie to the Holy Spirit and to keep back part of the proceeds of the land? While it remained unsold, did it not remain your own? And after it was sold, was it not at your disposal? How is it that you have contrived this deed in your heart? You have not lied to men but to God.'" (Acts 5:3-4) Each person of the Trinity, we are taught, eternal. "In the beginning was the Word, and the Word was with God, and the Word was God." (John 1:1)

As having been made in the image and likeness of God, we possess, in a much-limited sense, in some way, characteristics of all three. "Then God said, 'Let us make man in our image, after our likeness...'" (Gen. 1:26)

"Go therefore and make disciples of all nations, baptizing them in the name of the Father and of the Son and of the Holy Spirit." (Matt. 28:19)

"The grace of the Lord Jesus Christ and the love of God and the fellowship of the Holy Spirit be with you all." (2 Cor. 13:14)

The Real Presence of Jesus Christ in the Eucharist

For many, the Christian belief in the Real Presence is baffling. But Christ's teaching in this area is without compromise. Christ did not say, nor did he infer that He was speaking symbolically, yet many Protestant sects claim just that, refusing to accept the literal statement as a supernatural Truth.

"'Truly, truly, I say to you, he who believes has eternal life. I am the bread of life. Your fathers ate the manna in the wilderness, and they died. This is bread which comes down from heaven, that a man may eat of it and not die. I am the living bread which came down from heaven; if any one eats of this bread, he will live for ever; and the bread which I shall give for the life of the world is my flesh.' The Jews then disputed among themselves, saying, 'How can this man give us his flesh to eat?' So Jesus said to them, 'Truly truly, I say to you, unless you eat the flesh of the Son of man and drink his blood, you have no life in you; he who eats my flesh and drinks my blood has eternal life, and I will raise him up at the last day. For my flesh is food indeed, and my blood is drink indeed'" (John 6:47-55). Why would many of the followers of Jesus go away, if He was only speaking *metaphorically*? It is clear that they understood all too well, that He was speaking literally, and not figuratively. Certainly if Jesus was speaking metaphorically, and the people misunderstood him, He would have re-phrased His teaching and explain it in a way that they would understand, as He had done in many instances before, as we read in the Gospels. But He did not back away from this teaching.

Christ reiterated this central focus more than once, repeating it again and again. It was a hard teaching for many of His followers to accept. Many ceased to follow Him because of it, and how it offended their sensibilities, and that was contrary to the Law of Moses, and was not presented in a way to signify that Jesus was only speaking figuratively. Jesus' followers understood Him to mean that they must eat His flesh, and drink His blood in a way that is genuine and real. If there was any confusion, or thought that He only meant this in a way that was only a symbol and nothing more, that would have disappeared when He reiterated Himself: "For my flesh is food *indeed*, and my blood is drink *indeed*." [emphasis added]

The Body of Christ, in all her varied splendors, Old Catholic, Eastern Orthodox, Roman Catholic, Oriental Orthodox, and others, have unwaveringly and steadfastly proclaimed and believed this Mystery of Faith, from the time of the Apostles down to the present day. This is the unified belief and proclamation of over 98% of all people who claim the name Christian.

"For I received from the Lord what I also delivered to you, that the Lord Jesus on the night when he was betrayed took bread, and when he had given thanks, he broke it, and said, 'This is my body which is for you. Do this in remembrance of me.' In the same way also the cup, after supper, saying, 'This cup is the new covenant of my blood. Do this, as often as you drink it, in remembrance of me.' For as often as you eat this bread and drink the cup, you proclaim the Lord's death until he comes." (1 Cor. 11:23-26)

"Whoever, therefore, eats the bread or drinks the cup of the Lord in an unworthy manner will be guilty of profaning the body and blood of the Lord." (1 Cor. 11:27) No mere symbol could elicit this type of response. No mere symbol could mean so much. Believing the Eucharist to be only a symbol, betrays the understanding of Christ replacing the physical symbols of the Old Covenant, with the supernatural Spiritual Realities of the New Covenant.

To those who say that Christ could not/would not appear to His people as created things, or be present for them, as in the Eucharist, we point to such examples in Scripture as: Exodus 3:2-6, Exodus 13:21-22, Matthew 3:16, Genesis 18:1-2 and Matthew 13:55. Furthermore, in the writings of the Fathers of the Early Church, they speak unanimously and with one voice, as to their unshakeable belief in the Real Presence of Christ in the Eucharist.

Who May Receive Communion?

The Holy Eucharist is the most important of the seven sacraments because, in this sacrament, we receive Christ Jesus, body, blood, soul and divinity. Countless precious graces come to us through the reception of Holy Communion.

Communion is an intimate encounter with Christ, in which we sacramentally receive Christ into our bodies, that we may be more completely assimilated into his.

The Eucharist also strengthens the individual because in it Jesus himself, the Word made flesh, forgives our venial sins and gives us the strength to resist mortal sin. It is also the very channel of eternal life: Jesus himself.

In John's gospel, Jesus summarized the reasons for receiving Communion when he said, "Truly, truly, I say to you, unless you eat the flesh of the Son of man and drink his blood, you have no life in you; he who eats my flesh and drinks my blood has eternal life, and I will raise him up at the last day. For my flesh is real food, and my blood is real drink. He who eats my flesh and drinks my blood abides in me, and I in him. As the living Father sent me, and I live because of the Father, so he who eats me will live because of me. This is the bread which came down from heaven, not such as the fathers ate and died; he who eats this bread will live forever" (John 6:53–58).

Because of the gravity of Jesus' teaching on the Eucharist, the Church encourages Old Catholics to receive frequent Communion, even daily Communion if possible, and mandates reception of the Eucharist at least once a year during the Easter season. Before going to Communion, however, there are several things one needs to know.

Old Catholics and Communion

The Church sets out particular guidelines regarding how we should prepare ourselves to receive the Lord's body and blood in Communion. To receive Communion worthily, you must be in a state of grace, have made a good confession since your last mortal sin, believe in transubstantiation, observe the Eucharistic fast, and, finally, not be under an ecclesiastical punishment such as excommunication or inhibition.

First, you must be in a state of grace. "Whoever, therefore, eats the bread or drinks the cup of the Lord in an unworthy manner will be guilty of profaning the body and blood of the Lord. Let a man examine himself, and so eat of the bread and drink of the cup." (1 Cor. 11:27–28) This is an absolute requirement, which can never be dispensed. To receive the Eucharist without sanctifying grace in your soul profanes the Eucharist in the most grievous manner.

A mortal sin is *any* sin whose matter is grave and which has been committed willfully and with knowledge of its seriousness. Grave matter includes, but is not limited to, murder, receiving or being complicit in an abortion, homosexual acts, fornication, adultery, and deliberately engaging in impure thoughts (Matt. 5:28–29). Scripture contains lists of mortal sins (1 Cor. 6:9–10 and Gal. 5:19–21).

Old Catholics are warned against, out of habit and out of fear of what those around them will think, while in a state of mortal sin, choosing to go forward and offend God, rather than stay in the pew while others receive the Eucharist. The Church's ancient teaching on this particular matter is expressed in the *Didache*, an early Christian document written around A.D. 70, which states: "Whosoever is holy let him approach. Whosoever is not, let him repent" (*Didache* 10).

Second, you must have been to confession since your last mortal sin. The *Didache* witnesses to this practice of the early Church. "But first make confession of your faults, so that your sacrifice may be a pure one" (*Didache* 14).

A person who is conscious of a grave sin is never to receive the body of the Lord without prior sacramental confession unless an extremely grave reason is present and there is no opportunity of confessing; in this case the person is to be mindful of the obligation to make an act of perfect contrition, including the intention of confessing as soon as possible.

The requirement for sacramental confession can be dispensed if four conditions are fulfilled: (1) there must be a grave reason to receive Communion (for example, danger of death), (2) it must be physically or morally impossible to go to confession first, (3) the person must already be in a state of grace through perfect contrition, and (4) he must resolve to go to confession as soon as possible.

Third, you must believe in transubstantiation. "For anyone who eats and drinks without discerning the body eats and drinks judgment upon himself" (1 Cor. 11:29). Transubstantiation means more than the Real Presence. According to transubstantiation, the bread and wine are actually transformed into the actual body, blood, soul, and divinity of Christ, with only the appearances of bread and wine remaining. This is why, at the Last Supper, Jesus held what *appeared* to be bread and wine, yet said: "This *is* my body.... This *is* my blood" (Mark 14:22-24, cf. Luke 22:14-20). If Christ were merely present along side bread and wine (consubstantiation), he would have said "This *contains* my body.... This *contains* my blood," which he did not say. Likewise, He did not say, "This represents my body...This represents my blood".

Fourth, you must strictly observe the Eucharistic fast. One who is to receive the most Holy Eucharist is to abstain from any food or drink, with the exception only of water and medicine, for at least the period of one hour before Holy Communion." Elderly people, those who are ill, and their caretakers are excused from the Eucharistic fast.

Lastly, one must not be under an ecclesiastical censure. Those who are excommunicated or inhibited, and others who obstinately persist in grave sin are not to be admitted to Holy Communion.

Provided you are in a state of grace and have met the above requirements, you should receive the Eucharist frequently.

Other Christians and Communion

We welcome our fellow Christians to this celebration of the Eucharist as our brothers and sisters. We pray that our common baptism and the action of the Holy Spirit in this Eucharist will draw us closer to one another and begin to dispel the sad divisions that separate us. We pray that these will lessen and finally disappear, in keeping with Christ's prayer for us 'that they may all be one' (John 17:21).

Because Old Catholics believe that the celebration of the Eucharist is a sign of the reality of the oneness of faith, life, and worship, members of those churches with whom we are not fully united are ordinarily not admitted to Communion. Eucharistic sharing in exceptional circumstances by other Christians requires permission according to the guidance of the local Ordinary and the provisions of the Church.

Scripture is clear that the partaking of the Eucharist is among the highest signs of Christian unity. "Because there is one bread, we who are many are one body, for we all partake of the one bread" (1 Cor. 10:17). For this reason, it is normally impossible for non-Old Catholic Christians to receive Holy Communion, for to do so would be to proclaim that a unity exists, which in reality, does not.

As many non-Old Catholic Christians reject the doctrine of the Real Presence of Christ in the Eucharist, another very important reason that many non-Old Catholic Christians may not ordinarily receive Communion is for their own spiritual protection. Scripture warns that it is very dangerous for one not believing in the Real Presence to receive Communion: "For any one who eats and drinks without discerning the body eats and drinks judgment upon himself. That is why many of you are weak and ill, and some have died" (1 Cor. 11:29–30). Every effort must be made to educate non-Old Catholics to this very real danger, lest some unknowingly partake of the precious Body and Blood to their detriment, and missalettes used in local parishes should, in the front pages, include these or similar acceptable instructions and directions regarding the reception of the Eucharist. In Masses where a large number of non-Old Catholic Christians may be present, appropriate instruction should be given prior to the commencement of the Divine Liturgy.

Possible exceptions

However, there are circumstances when non-Old Catholics may receive Communion from an Old Catholic priest. This is especially the case when it comes to Roman Catholic Christians, Oriental Orthodox Christians, and Eastern Orthodox Christians, who share the same faith concerning the nature of the sacraments:

Old Catholic ministers may licitly administer the sacraments of Penance, Eucharist and Anointing of the Sick to members of these churches, which do not have full Communion with the Old Catholic Church, if they ask on their own for the sacraments and are properly disposed. This holds also for members of other churches, which in the judgment of the Archbishop-Metropolitan are in the same condition as these churches as far as these sacraments are concerned.

Christians in these churches should, of course, respect their own church's guidelines regarding when it would be permissible for them to receive Communion in an Old Catholic Church.

The circumstances in which Protestants are permitted to receive Communion are more limited, though it is still possible for them to do so under certain specifically defined circumstances.

If the danger of death is present or other grave necessity, in the judgment of the diocesan bishop, Old Catholic ministers may licitly administer these sacraments to other Christians who do not have full Communion with the Old Catholic Church, who cannot approach a minister of their own community and on their own ask for it, provided they manifest catholic faith and understanding in these sacraments and are properly disposed.

It is important to remember that, under the possible exceptions specified, even in those rare circumstances when non-Old Catholics are able to receive Communion, the same requirements apply to them as to Old Catholics.

Non-Christians and Communion

We also welcome to this celebration those who do not share our faith in Jesus Christ. While we cannot admit them to Communion, we ask them to offer their prayers for the peace and the unity of the human family. A blessing may be received from the priest, by presenting themselves, at the time of communion, with both arms crossed across their chest. The priest will give a blessing to that individual in the spirit of Christian love.

Because they have not received baptism, and do not profess the Real Presence of Christ in the Eucharist, non-Christians cannot receive Communion. However, in emergency situations, they can be received into the Church via baptism, even if no priest is present, and an extraordinary minister of Holy Communion may bring them Communion as Viaticum.

How to receive Communion

Communicants may receive Communion either standing or kneeling. With regard to the manner of going to Communion the faithful can receive it either kneeling or standing, in accordance with the norms of the liturgy being used. When the faithful communicate kneeling, no other sign of reverence towards the Blessed Sacrament is required, since kneeling is itself a sign of adoration. When they receive Communion standing, it is strongly recommended that, coming up in procession, they should make a sign of reverence before receiving the Sacrament.

Communion is received on the tongue, (or spoon in the case of Byzantine liturgies used in Byzantine Rite Old Catholic Churches), as is appropriate to the liturgical rite used and the common practice of the parish, under the guidance of the local Ordinary.

After receiving Communion, it is appropriate to stay after Mass and thank Jesus for coming to you in the Holy Eucharist. The faithful are to be reminded not to omit to make a proper thanksgiving after Communion. They may do this during the celebration with a period of silence, with a hymn, psalm or other song of praise, or also after the celebration, if possible by staying behind to pray for a suitable time.

Purgatory

Purgatory has been described as a place, or process, in which our souls are purged of the sinful nature we have at the time of our death. It has been envisioned as a prison, in which we pay the spiritual price for our sins prior to entering in Heaven. The Old Testament and New Testament teach us to pray for one another, and that the "prayers of a righteous man availeth much". The ancient Jews prayed for the death and for their souls, and so we do as well, praying for those souls in purgatory so that their period of purgation will be shortened. How do we know that we are praying for souls in purgatory? If the person is in Heaven, he does not require our prayers, if he is in Hell, prayer won't help him. With this in mind, consider the following passage in Scripture. "For if he were not expecting that those who had fallen would rise again, it would have been superfluous and foolish to pray for the dead. But if he was looking to the splendid reward that is laid up for those who fall asleep in godliness, it was a holy and pious thought. Therefore he made atonement for the dead, that they might be delivered from their sin." (2 Macc. 12:44-45) This passage of Scripture refers to the Jewish practice of prayers for the dead, which is still observed by them to this day. First and second Maccabees were removed from the Protestant Canon of Old Testament Scripture (Bible), along with several other books of the Old Testament, during the Protestant Reformation, preferring a canon of Hebrew Scripture that was compiled by the Jewish community well after the death and resurrection of Christ, and with certain omissions of Scripture used by the Early Church to show that Jesus is the Messiah. Even so, there are many other passages of scripture to guide us.

"Make friends quickly with your accuser, while you are going with him to court, lest your accuser hand you over to the judge, and the judge to the guard, and you be put in prison; truly, I say to you, you will never get out till you have paid the last penny." (Matt. 5:25-26)

"Each man's work will become manifest; for the Day will disclose it, because it will be revealed with fire, and the fire will test what sort of work each one has done. If the work which any man has built on the foundation survives, he will receive a reward. If any man's work is burned up, he will suffer loss, though he himself will be saved, but only as through fire." (1 Cor. 3:13-15)

The citation of the above passage of Scripture as consistent with the continuous understanding of it to refer to a period or process of purgation, is illustrated here:

"Now, this fire, of which the apostle speaks, should be understood as one through which both kinds of men must pass: that is, the man who builds with gold, silver, and precious stones on this foundation and also the man who builds with wood, hay, and stubble. For, when he had spoken of this, he added: 'The fire shall try every man's work, of what sort it is. If any man's work abides which he has built thereupon, he shall receive a reward. If any man's work burns up, he shall suffer loss; but he himself shall be saved, yet so as by fire.' Therefore the fire will test the work, not only of the one, but of both.

The fire is a sort of trial of affliction, concerning which it is clearly written elsewhere: 'The furnace tries the potter's vessels and the trial of affliction tests righteous men.' This kind of fire works in the span of this life, just as the apostle said, as it affects the two different kinds of faithful men. There is, for example, the man who 'thinks of the things of God, how he may please God.' Such a man builds on Christ the foundation, with gold, silver, and precious stones. The other man 'thinks about the things of the world, how he may please his wife'; that is, he builds upon the same foundation with wood, hay, and stubble. The work of the former is not burned up, since he has not loved those things whose loss brings anguish. But the work of the latter is burned up, since things are not lost without anguish when they have been loved with a possessive love. But because, in this second situation, he prefers to suffer the loss of these things rather than losing Christ, and does not desert Christ from fear of losing such things—even though he may grieve over his loss—'he is saved,' indeed, "yet so as by fire.' He 'burns" with grief, for the things he has loved and lost, but this does not subvert nor consume him, secured as he is by the stability and the indestructibility of his foundation.

It is not incredible that something like this should occur after this life, whether or not it is a matter for fruitful inquiry. It may be discovered or remain hidden whether some of the faithful are sooner or later to be saved by a sort of purgatorial fire, in proportion as they have loved the goods that perish, and in proportion to their attachment to them. However, this does not apply to those of whom it was said, 'They shall not possess the Kingdom of God,' unless their crimes are remitted through due repentance. I say 'due repentance' to signify that they must not be barren of almsgiving, on which divine Scripture lays so much stress that our Lord tells us in advance that, on the bare basis of fruitfulness in alms, he will impute merit to those on his right hand; and, on the same basis of unfruitfulness, demerit to those on his left—when he shall say to the former, 'Come, blessed of my Father, receive the Kingdom,' but to the latter, 'Depart into everlasting fire.'" St. Augustine. *The Enchiridion, Handbook on Faith, Hope and Love.* CCEL

"For Christ also died for sins once for all, the righteous for the unrighteous, that he might bring us to God, being put to death in the flesh but made alive in the spirit; in which he went and preached to the spirits in prison, who formerly did not obey…" (1 Peter 3:18-20) If the spirits in prison had no chance for release, preaching to them would certainly be useless. The passage infers that they yet had an opportunity to be redeemed and saved.

"But nothing unclean shall enter it [heaven]..." (Rev. 21:27) This would certainly seem to indicate that we, who through sin are unclean, must have our spirits cleansed and purged of what is left of our sinful nature in order to enter into Heaven. Certainly, that would suggest some process for that occurring.

Praying To The Saints

Objections are sometimes raised to the Old Catholic Church's teaching on prayer to the saints. This objection is often based upon a misunderstanding between what Protestants and Old Catholics (in unison with Roman Catholics, Eastern Orthodox and Oriental Orthodox) understand prayer to be. Prayer, for most Protestant Churches, is worship and adoration due to God and God alone. This understanding of the word prayer is newer than the traditional meaning of the word, in which Old Catholics understand it to mean. In traditional usage of the word "prayer" in English, it simply means "to ask" or to make a request of someone. In the traditional usage of the word "pray" throughout history, we see, in old English usage "Pray thee" used in normal conversation. In legal documents, even in use in courts today in the U.S., lawyers still use the form term, "wherefore we *pray* this honorable court to rule in favor of..." For Old Catholics, having this more ancient and traditionally proper understanding of the word, prayer does not only mean praise and adoration due to God and God alone. Prayer can also be simple communication, and so we can communicate, speak and ask the saints in heaven to pray *for* us and *with* us, to God for our petition. Some objectors would say that this undermines the sole mediation of Christ, but does not, and is no different than asking a fellow Christian, who is here on earth with you, to pray *for you* when you are ill or in need, or *with you to God* for some great need. As Old Catholics, we believe that the Church here on earth, the Church undergoing purgation and the Church in Heaven are spiritually connected through Christ Jesus. Because we are one body in Christ, as Scripture teaches us, the members of the Church are connected supernaturally through the power of God. The Book of Revelation teaches us that the prayers and petitions of the saints are brought before the altar of God, so we know that their prayers are heard. What would the saints in heaven pray for? They are in Heaven, in the presence of God, and have need for nothing. It must be our prayers and petitions that they, in unison with us, ask God for, and so their prayers are brought before His holy altar. For if "the prayers of a righteous man availeth much", how much more then, do the prayers of the saints in Heaven availeth us, when they pray *with us* and *for us,* asking God to grant our petitions?

For persons who are fond of Protestant "altar calls", how much greater of an altar call can one have, when the very saints in Heaven are praying with you and for you to God for your petition? This is no different than asking a fellow parishioner or the priest to pray with you and for you to God to answer your petition with regard to some hardship or illness you or a loved one may be going through. And because we know, through Scripture, that the angels and the saints are aware of us and our actions here on earth, and that their prayers and petitions are brought before God, how much more will God hear our prayers when joined by those of the saints already in heaven. This is not a substitution of the divine mediatorship of Christ the Creator, with the mediatorship of the saints. Such a notion would indicate a profound lack of understanding of the "communion of saints" we profess in the Nicene Creed, believed by the vast majority of Christians, and all of the ancient Churches established by the Apostles themselves.

"'And as for the dead being raised, have you not read in the book of Moses, in the passage about the bush, how God said to him, "I am the God of Abraham, and the God of Isaac, and the God of Jacob"? He is not God of the dead, but of the living…'" (Mark 12:26-27)

"Pray at all times in the Spirit with all prayer and supplication. To that end keep alert with all perseverance, making supplication for all the saints, and also for me…" (Eph. 6:18)

"Therefore, since we are surrounded by so great a cloud of witnesses, let us also lay aside every weight, and sin which clings so closely…" (Heb. 12:1)

"And when he had taken the scroll, the four living creatures and the twenty-four elders fell down before the Lamb, each holding a harp, and with golden bowls full of incense, which are the prayers of the saints…" (Rev. 5:8)

We even see, in scripture, examples of prayers making their way to God assisted by angels. In Genesis we read of Jacob, on his deathbed, praying that the angel who had protected him, bless his grandchildren. In the book of Tobias, we read that the angel Raphael, upon revealing himself to Tobias, informed him that when Tobias prayed in his times of sorrow, that he offered Tobias' prayers to God.

How do we know that those saints and angels in Heaven even are aware of what happens on earth? In the book of Luke we see that the angels rejoice when a sinner repents. (Luke 15:10) In 1 Corinthians 4:9, we are taught by St. Paul, "For I think that God has exhibited us apostles as last of all, like men sentenced to death; because we have become a spectacle to the world, to angels and to men." So scripture teaches that the angels and saints in Heaven see what we know and in seeing what is in the heart of a penitent sinner, sees the condition of our soul. This is the teaching from Scripture and is witnessed and testified to by the Early Church.

"[An] angel came and stood at the altar [in heaven] with a golden censer; and he was given much incense to mingle with the prayers of all the saints upon the golden altar before the throne; and the smoke of the incense rose with the prayers of the saints from the hand of the angel before God." (Rev. 8:3–4)

"See that you do not despise one of these little ones; for I tell you that in heaven their angels always see the face of my Father who is in heaven." (Matt. 18:10)

The Shepherd of Hermas

"But those who are weak and slothful in prayer, hesitate to ask anything from the Lord; but the Lord is full of compassion, and gives without fail to all who ask him. But you, [Hermas,] having been strengthened by the holy angel, and having obtained from him such intercession, and not being slothful, why do not you ask of the Lord understanding, and receive it from him?'" (*The Shepherd* 3:5:4 [A.D. 80])[12]

St. Clement of Alexandria

"So is he always pure for prayer. He also prays in the society of angels, as being already of angelic rank, and he is never out of their holy keeping; and though he pray alone, he has the choir of the saints standing with him." (*Miscellanies* 7:12 [A.D. 208])[13]

In praying to the saints and angels for assistance, we do not ask them to provide for our petitions based on their own merit or authority, but rather we ask them to pray for us, and with us, through the merits of Christ Jesus—as we also ask Christ to assist us through His own gracious mercy, pardon and merits.

In the Early Church we find multiple examples that this was common Christian practice, and not something alien to the faith, nor something added in later years. Through their examples we see the true practice of the Church, from the time of the Apostles down to present days. Their historical witness cannot be ignored, nor nullified.

St. Cyprian of Carthage

"Let us remember one another in concord and unanimity. Let us on both sides always pray for one another. Let us relieve burdens and afflictions by mutual love, that if any one of us, by the swiftness of divine condescension, shall go hence the first, our love may continue in the presence of the Lord, and our prayers for our brethren and sisters not cease in the presence of the Father's mercy." (*Letters* 56[60]:5 [A.D. 253])[14]

St. Methodius

"Hail to you for ever, Virgin Mother of God, our unceasing joy, for to you do I turn again. You are the beginning of our feast; you are its middle and end; the pearl of great price that belongs to the kingdom; the fat of every victim, the living altar of the Bread of Life [Christ]. Hail, you treasure of the love of God. Hail, you fount of the Son's love for man…. You gleamed, sweet gift-bestowing Mother, with the light of the sun; you gleamed with the insupportable fires of a most fervent charity, bringing forth in the end that which was conceived of you…making manifest the mystery hidden and unspeakable, the invisible Son of the Father—the Prince of Peace, who in a marvelous manner showed himself as less than all littleness." (*Oration on Simeon and Anna* 14 [A.D. 305])[15]

"Therefore, we pray you [i.e., we ask of you], the most excellent among women, who glories in the confidence of your maternal honors, that you would unceasingly keep us in remembrance. O holy Mother of God, remember us, I say, who make our boast in you, and who in august hymns celebrate the memory, which will ever live, and never fade away." (ibid)

"And you also, O honored and venerable Simeon, you earliest host of our holy religion, and teacher of the resurrection of the faithful, do be our patron and advocate with that Savior God, whom you were deemed worthy to receive into your arms. We, together with you, sing our praises to Christ, who has the power of life and death, saying, 'You are the true Light, proceeding from the true Light; the true God, begotten of the true God.'" (ibid)

St. Cyril of Jerusalem

"Then we commemorate also those who have fallen asleep before us, first Patriarchs, Prophets, Apostles, Martyrs, that at their prayers and intercessions God would receive our petition. Then on behalf also of the Holy Fathers and Bishops who have fallen asleep before us, and in a word of all who in past years have fallen asleep among us, believing that it will be a very great benefit to the souls, for whom the supplication is put up, while that holy and most awful sacrifice is set forth." (*Catechetical Lectures* 23:9 [A.D. 350])[16]

St. Ephraim the Syrian

"You victorious martyrs who endured torments gladly for the sake of the God and Savior, you who have boldness of speech toward the Lord himself, you saints, intercede for us who are timid and sinful men, full of sloth, that the grace of Christ may come upon us, and enlighten the hearts of all of us so that we may love him." (*Commentary on Mark* [A.D. 370])[17]

"Remember me, you heirs of God, you brethren of Christ; supplicate the Savior earnestly for me, that I may be freed through Christ from him that fights against me day by day." (*The Fear at the End of Life* [A.D. 370])[18]

The Liturgy of St. Basil

"By the command of your only-begotten Son we communicate with the memory of your saints…by whose prayers and supplications have mercy upon us all, and deliver us for the sake of your holy name." (*Liturgy of St. Basil* [A.D. 373])[19]

Pectorius

"Aschandius, my father, dearly beloved of my heart, with my sweet mother and my brethren, remember your Pectorius in the peace of the Fish [Jesus]." (*Epitaph of Pectorius* [A.D. 375])[20]

St. Gregory of Nazianz

"May you [referring to the deceased St. Cyprian] look down from above propitiously upon us, and guide our word and life; and shepherd this sacred flock…gladden the Holy Trinity, before which you stand." (*Orations* 17[24] [A.D. 380])[21]

"Yes, I am well assured that [my father's] intercession is of more avail now than was his instruction in former days, since he is closer to God, now that he has shaken off his bodily fetters, and freed his mind from the clay that obscured it, and holds conversation naked with the nakedness of the prime and purest mind..." (ibid., 18:4)

St. Gregory of Nyssa

"[referring to the deceased St. Ephraim], you who are standing at the divine altar [in heaven]...bear us all in remembrance, petitioning for us the remission of sins, and the fruition of an everlasting kingdom." (*Sermon on Ephraim the Syrian* [A.D. 380])[22]

St. John Chrysostom

"For he that wears the purple himself goes to embrace those tombs, and, laying aside his pride, stands begging the saints to be his advocates with God, and he that hath the diadem implores the tent-maker and the fisherman, though dead, to be his patrons." (*Homilies on Second Corinthians* 26 [A.D. 392])[23]

"When you perceive that God is chastening you, fly not to his enemies...but to his friends, the martyrs, the saints, and those who were pleasing to him, and who have great power [in God]." (*Orations* 8:6 [A.D. 396])[24]

St. Ambrose of Milan

"May Peter, who wept so efficaciously for himself, weep for us and turn towards us Christ's benign countenance." (*The Six Days Work* 5:25:90 [A.D. 393])[25]

St. Jerome

"You say in your book that while we live we are able to pray for each other, but afterwards when we have died, the prayer of no person for another can be heard.... But if the apostles and martyrs while still in the body can pray for others, at a time when they ought still be solicitous about themselves, how much more will they do so after their crowns, victories, and triumphs?" (*Against Vigilantius* 6 [A.D. 406])[26]

St. Augustine

"A Christian people celebrates together in religious solemnity the memorials of the martyrs, both to encourage their being imitated and so that it can share in their merits and be aided by their prayers." (*Against Faustus the Manichean* [A.D. 400])[27]

"There is an ecclesiastical discipline, as the faithful know, when the names of the martyrs are read aloud in that place at the altar of God, where prayer is not offered for them. Prayer, however, is offered for the dead who are remembered. For it is wrong to pray for a martyr, to whose prayers we ought ourselves be commended." (*Sermons* 159:1 [A.D. 411])[28]

"For on these very grounds we do not commemorate them at that table in the same way, as we do others who now rest in peace, as that we should also pray for them, but rather that they should do so for us, that we may cleave to their footsteps; because they have actually attained that fullness of love, than which, our Lord hath told us, there cannot be a greater." (*Homilies on John* 84 [A.D. 416])[29]

"For the souls of the pious dead are not separated from the Church, which even now is the kingdom of Christ; otherwise there would be no remembrance made of them at the altar of God in the partaking of the body of Christ, nor would it do any good in danger to run to His baptism, that we might not pass from this life without it; nor to reconciliation, if by penitence or a bad conscience any one may be severed from His body." (*The City of God* 20:9:2 [A.D. 419])[30]

Venerating the Saints

Other people contend that we detract from the honor and majesty due to God alone, by holding His creations in such high esteem. Others maintain that showing any honor at all to the saints somehow infers that they are deity, in some way. Others still, maintain that honor should only be shown to Jesus alone, in concert with God the Father and the Holy Spirit. All of these objectors believe that we act contrary to scripture; certainly quite the opposite is true.

Is it right to presume that the saints in Heaven are due any honor or veneration over and above the average individual? If so, how would we justify it?

We look to Jesus for the answers, and in Him we do find them. In Matthew 19:27, Peter asks Jesus what the twelve apostles would gain for following Him, and Jesus replied, "Truly, I say to you, in the new world, when the Son of Man shall sit on His glorious throne, you who have followed me will also sit on twelve thrones, judging the twelve tribes of Israel." Does this mean that Jesus had only twelve followers? Absolutely not, as scripture teaches, we know of "the seventy" and others who are identified as followers of Jesus, but not disciples. To these twelve disciples only He gives this unique place in His Kingdom, not inherited by all Christians. Jesus, as our perfect example, bestows some of His honor upon His creations.

We are absolutely sure that this honor is given only to the Twelve as heavenly princes of the heavenly King of kings, as is illustrated, "And in the Spirit he carried me away to a great, high mountain, and showed me the holy city Jerusalem coming down out of heaven from God, having the glory of God, its radiance like a most rare jewel, like a jasper, clear as crystal. It had a great, high wall, with twelve gates, and at the gates twelve angels, and on the gates the names of the twelve tribes of the sons of Israel were inscribed; on the east three gates, on the north three gates, on the south three gates and on the west three gates. And the wall of the city had twelve foundations, and on them the twelve names of the twelve apostles of the Lamb."

We read of Christ's honor bestowed by Him on his creations elsewhere in scripture as well. In Revelation 4:4, we read, "Round the throne were twenty-four thrones and seated on the thrones were twenty-four elders, clad in white garments, with golden crowns upon their heads."

Also, in Revelation 12:1-6, we see the ever-Virgin Mary, the Ark of the New Covenant, depicted in honor as well, "And a great portent opened in heaven, a woman clothed with the sun, with the moon under her feet, and on her head a crown of twelve stars; she was with child and she cried out in her pangs of birth, in anguish for delivery." This created being, this woman, was clothed with the sun, crowned with twelve stars, certainly by the heavenly King Himself.

We know that this is the ever-Virgin Mary, through her Son, Christ Jesus, "she brought forth a male child, one who is to rule all nations with a rod of iron, but her child was caught up to God and to his throne…" In this, we see a reference to Psalms 2:7–9, in which is told a declaration of God the Father, "I will tell of the decree of the Lord: He said to me, 'You are my son, today I have begotten you.

Ask of me, and I will make the nations your heritage, and the ends of the earth your possession. You shall break them with a rod of iron, and dash them in pieces like a potter's vessel.'"

Is this truly a reference to Jesus? Christ Himself affirms such, in Luke 24:44, "Then he spoke to them, 'These are my words, which I spoke to you, while I was still with you, that everything written about me in the law of Moses and the prophets and the psalms must be fulfilled.'" He deemed these individuals, created by God, worthy of places of honor in His kingdom, and because they have been so honored by God Himself, we should certainly regard them as worthy of our respect. Clearly they are not honored in the same manner and magnitude as God, but because they have been placed in places of honor by God, failure to respect and honor them is failure to respect He who has placed them in these heavenly positions. Without God's special grace, it is impossible for us to do anything to please Him. In the martyrs and saints, we see God's grace at work in them. In His honoring of the saints and martyrs, God also crowns His work in them, in the efficacious grace He imparted to them, in addition to the sufficient grace He imparts to all. In our honoring the saints in heaven, we simply follow His example, as God bestows honors and authority to them.

The saints and martyrs of worthy of honor, for their great faith in the face of adversity, lest we forget horrific tortures and deaths they willingly endured. Having had every opportunity to simply repudiate Christ and be set free, they refused and steadfastly walked, head held high, into derision and death. The most moving of these being the Martyrdom of St. Polycarp:

> "The Church of God which sojourns at Smyrna, to the Church of God sojourning in Philomelium, and to all the congregations of the Holy and Catholic Church in every place: Mercy, peace, and love from God the Father, and our Lord Jesus Christ, be multiplied.
>
> Chapter I.—Subject of Which We Write.
>
> We have written to you, brethren, as to what relates to the martyrs, and especially to the blessed Polycarp, who put an end to the persecution, having, as it were, set a seal upon it by his martyrdom. For almost all the events that happened previously [to this one], took place that the Lord might show us from above a martyrdom becoming the Gospel. For he waited to be delivered up, even as the Lord had done, that we also might become his followers, while we look not merely at what

concerns ourselves but have regard also to our neighbors. For it is the part of a true and well-founded love, not only to wish one's self to be saved, but also all the brethren.

Chapter II.—The Wonderful Constancy of the Martyrs.

All the martyrdoms, then, were blessed and noble which took place according to the will of God. For it becomes us who profess greater piety than others, to ascribe the authority over all things to God. And truly, who can fail to admire their nobleness of mind, and their patience, with that love towards their Lord which they displayed?— who, when they were so torn with scourges, that the frame of their bodies, even to the very inward veins and arteries, was laid open, still patiently endured, while even those that stood by pitied and bewailed them. But they reached such a pitch of magnanimity, that not one of them let a sigh or a groan escape them; thus proving to us all that those holy martyrs of Christ, at the very time when they suffered such torments, were absent from the body, or rather, that the Lord then stood by them, and communed with them. And, looking to the grace of Christ, they despised all the torments of this world, redeeming themselves from eternal punishment by [the suffering of] a single hour. For this reason the fire of their savage executioners appeared cool to them. For they kept before their view escape from that fire which is eternal and never shall be quenched, and looked forward with the eyes of their heart to those good things which are laid up for such as endure; things "which ear hath not heard, nor eye seen, neither have entered into the heart of man," but were revealed by the Lord to them, inasmuch as they were no longer men, but had already become angels. And, in like manner, those who were condemned to the wild beasts endured dreadful tortures, being stretched out upon beds full of spikes, and subjected to various other kinds of torments, in order that, if it were possible, the tyrant might, by their lingering tortures, lead them to a denial [of Christ].

Chapter III—The Constancy of Germanicus. The Death of Polycarp is Demanded.

For the devil did indeed invent many things against them; but thanks be to God, he could not prevail over all. For the most noble Germanicus strengthened the timidity of others by his own patience, and fought heroically with the wild beasts. For, when the proconsul sought to persuade him, and urged him to take pity upon his age, he attracted the wild beast towards himself, and provoked it, being desirous to escape all the more quickly from an unrighteous and impious world. But upon this the whole multitude, marveling at the nobility of mind displayed by the devout and godly race of Christians, cried out, "Away with the Atheists; let Polycarp be sought out!"

Chapter IV—Quintus the Apostate.

Now one named Quintus, a Phrygian, who was but lately come from Phrygia, when he saw the wild beasts, became afraid. This was the man who forced himself and some others to come forward voluntarily [for trial]. Him the proconsul, after many entreaties, persuaded to swear and to offer sacrifice. Wherefore, brethren, we do not commend those who give themselves up [to suffering], seeing the Gospel does not teach so to do.

Chapter V—The Departure and Vision of Polycarp.

But the most admirable Polycarp, when he first heard [that he was sought for], was in no measure disturbed, but resolved to continue in the city. However, in deference to the wish of many, he was persuaded to leave it. He departed, therefore, to a country house not far distant from the city. There he stayed with a few [friends], engaged in nothing else night and day than praying for all men, and for the Churches throughout the world, according to his usual custom. And while he was praying, a vision presented itself to him three days before he was taken; and, behold, the pillow under his head seemed to him on fire. Upon this, turning to those that were with him, he said to them prophetically, "I must be burnt alive."

Chapter VI.—Polycarp is Betrayed by a Servant.

And when those who sought for him were at hand, he departed to another dwelling, whither his pursuers immediately came after him. And when they found him not, they seized upon two youths [that were there], one of whom, being subjected to torture, confessed. It was thus impossible that he should continue hid, since those that betrayed him were of his own household. The Irenarch then (whose office is the same as that of the Cleronomus), by name Herod, hastened to bring him into the stadium. [This all happened] that he might fulfill his special lot, being made a partaker of Christ, and that they who betrayed him might undergo the punishment of Judas himself.

Chapter VII.—Polycarp is Found by His Pursuers.

His pursuers then, along with horsemen, and taking the youth with them, went forth at supper-time on the day of the preparation with their usual weapons, as if going out against a robber. And being come about evening [to the place where he was], they found him lying down in the upper room of a certain little house, from which he might have escaped into another place; but he refused, saying, "The will of God be done." So when he heard that they were come, he went down and spoke with them. And as those that were present marveled at his age and constancy, some of them said. "Was so much effort made to capture such a venerable man? Immediately then, in that very hour, he ordered that something to eat and drink should be set before them, as much indeed as they cared for, while he besought them to allow him an hour to pray without disturbance. And on their giving him leave, he stood and prayed, being full of the grace of God, so that he could not cease for two full hours, to the astonishment of them that heard him, insomuch that many began to repent that they had come forth against so godly and venerable an old man.

Chapter VIII.—Polycarp is Brought into the City.

Now, as soon as he had ceased praying, having made mention of all that had at any time come in contact with him, both small and great, illustrious and obscure, as well as the whole Catholic Church throughout the world, the time of his departure having arrived, they set him upon an ass, and conducted him into the city, the day being that of the great Sabbath. And the Irenarch Herod, accompanied by his father Nicetes (both riding in a chariot), met him, and taking him up into the chariot, they seated themselves beside him, and endeavored to persuade him, saying, "What harm is there in saying, Lord Caesar, and in sacrificing, with the other ceremonies observed on such occasions, and so make sure of safety?" But he at first gave them no answer; and when they continued to urge him, he said, "I shall not do as you advise me." So they, having no hope of persuading him, began to speak bitter words unto him, and cast him with violence out of the chariot, insomuch that, in getting down from the carriage, he dislocated his leg [by the fall]. But without being disturbed, and as if suffering nothing, he went eagerly forward with all haste, and was conducted to the stadium, where the tumult was so great, that there was no possibility of being heard.

Chapter IX.—Polycarp Refuses to Revile Christ.

Now, as Polycarp was entering into the stadium, there came to him a voice from heaven, saying, "Be strong, and show thyself a man, O Polycarp!" No one saw who it was that spoke to him; but those of our brethren who were present heard the voice. And as he was brought forward, the tumult became great when they heard that Polycarp was taken. And when he came near, the proconsul asked him whether he was Polycarp. On his confessing that he was, [the proconsul] sought to persuade him to deny [Christ], saying, "Have respect to thy old age," and other similar things, according to their custom, [such as], "Swear by the fortune of Caesar; repent, and say, Away with the Atheists." But Polycarp, gazing with a stern countenance on all the multitude of the wicked heathen then in the stadium, and waving his hand towards them, while with groans he looked up to heaven, said, "Away with the Atheists." Then, the proconsul urging him, and saying, "Swear, and I will set thee at liberty, reproach Christ;" Polycarp declared, "Eighty and six years have I served Him, and He never did me any injury: how then can I blaspheme my King and my Savior?"

Chapter X—Polycarp Confesses Himself a Christian.

And when the proconsul yet again pressed him, and said, "Swear by the fortune of Caesar," he answered, "Since thou art vainly urgent that, as thou sayest, I should swear by the fortune of Caesar, and pretend not to know who and what I am, hear me declare with boldness, I am a Christian. And if you wish to learn what the doctrines of Christianity are, appoint me a day, and thou shalt hear them." The proconsul replied, "Persuade the people." But Polycarp said, "To thee I have thought it right to offer an account [of my faith]; for we are taught to give all due honor (which entails no injury upon ourselves) to the powers and authorities which are ordained of God. But as for these, I do not deem them worthy of receiving any account from me."

Chapter XI.—No Threats Have Any Effect on Polycarp.

The proconsul then said to him, "I have wild beasts at hand; to these will I cast thee, except thou repent." But he answered, "Call them then, for we are not accustomed to repent of what is good in order to adopt that which is evil; and it is well for me to be changed from what is evil to what is righteous." But again the proconsul said to him, "I will cause thee to be consumed by fire, seeing thou despisest the wild beasts, if thou wilt not repent." But Polycarp said, "Thou threatenest me with fire which burneth for an hour, and after a little is extinguished, but art ignorant of the fire of the coming judgment and of eternal punishment, reserved for the ungodly. But why tarriest thou? Bring forth what thou wilt."

Chapter XII.—Polycarp is Sentenced to Be Burned.

While he spoke these and many other like things, he was filled with confidence and joy, and his countenance was full of grace, so that not merely did it not fall as if troubled by the things said to him, but, on the contrary, the proconsul was astonished, and sent his herald to proclaim in the midst of the stadium thrice, "Polycarp has confessed that he is a Christian." This proclamation having been made by the herald, the whole multitude both of the heathen and Jews, who dwelt at Smyrna, cried out with uncontrollable fury, and in a loud voice, "This is the teacher of Asia, the father of the Christians, and the overthrower of our gods, he who has been teaching many not to sacrifice, or to worship the gods." Speaking thus, they cried out, and besought Philip the Asiarch to let loose a lion upon Polycarp. But Philip answered that it was not lawful for him to do so, seeing the shows of wild beasts were already finished. Then it seemed good to them to cry out with one consent, that Polycarp should be burnt alive. For thus it behooved the vision which was revealed to him in regard to his pillow to be fulfilled, when, seeing it on fire as he was praying, he turned about and said prophetically to the faithful that were with him, "I must be burnt alive."

Chapter XIII.—The Funeral Pile is Erected.

This, then, was carried into effect with greater speed than it was spoken, the multitudes immediately gathering together wood and fagots out of the shops and baths; the Jews especially, according to custom, eagerly assisting them in it. And when the funeral pile was ready, Polycarp, laying aside all his garments, and loosing his girdle, sought also to take off his sandals,—a thing he was not accustomed to do, inasmuch as every one of the faithful was always eager who should first touch his skin. For, on account of his holy life, he was, even before his martyrdom, adorned with every kind of good. Immediately then they surrounded him with those substances which had been prepared for the funeral pile. But when they were about also to fix him with nails, he said, "Leave me as I am; for He that giveth me strength to endure the fire, will also enable me, without your securing me by nails, to remain without moving in the pile."

Chapter XIV—The Prayer of Polycarp.

They did not nail him then, but simply bound him. And he, placing his hands behind him, and being bound like a distinguished ram [taken] out of a great flock for sacrifice, and prepared to be an acceptable burnt-offering unto God, looked up to heaven, and said, "O Lord God Almighty, the Father of thy beloved and blessed Son Jesus Christ, by whom we have received the knowledge of Thee, the God of angels and powers, and of every creature, and of the whole race of the righteous who live before thee, I give Thee thanks that Thou hast counted me, worthy of this day and this hour, that I should have a part in the number of Thy martyrs, in the cup of thy Christ, to the resurrection of eternal life, both of soul and body, through the incorruption [imparted] by the Holy Ghost. Among whom may I be accepted this day before Thee as a fat and acceptable sacrifice, according as Thou, the ever-truthful God, hast fore-ordained, hast revealed beforehand to me, and now hast fulfilled. Wherefore also I praise Thee for all things, I bless Thee, I glorify Thee, along with the everlasting and heavenly Jesus Christ, Thy beloved Son, with whom, to Thee, and the Holy Ghost, be glory both now and to all coming ages. Amen."

Chapter XV—Polycarp is Not Injured by the Fire.

When he had pronounced this amen, and so finished his prayer, those who were appointed for the purpose kindled the fire. And as the flame blazed forth in great fury, we, to whom it was given to witness it, beheld a great miracle, and have been preserved that we might report to others what then took place. For the fire, shaping itself into the form of an arch, like the sail of a ship when filled with the wind, encompassed as by a circle the body of the martyr. And he appeared within not like flesh which is burnt, but as bread that is baked, or as gold and silver glowing in a furnace. Moreover, we perceived such a sweet odor [coming from the pile], as if frankincense or some such precious spices had been smoking there.

Chapter XVI.—Polycarp is Pierced by a Dagger.

At length, when those wicked men perceived that his body could not be consumed by the fire, they commanded an executioner to go near and pierce him through with a dagger. And on his doing this, there came forth a dove, and a great quantity of blood, so that the fire was extinguished; and all the people wondered that there should be such a difference between the unbelievers and the elect, of whom this most admirable Polycarp was one, having in our own times been an apostolic and prophetic teacher, and bishop of the Catholic Church which is in Smyrna. For every word that went out of his mouth either has been or shall yet be accomplished.

Chapter XVII.—The Christians are Refused Polycarp's Body.

But when the adversary of the race of the righteous, the envious, malicious, and wicked one, perceived the impressive nature of his martyrdom, and [considered] the blameless life he had led from the beginning, and how he was now crowned with the wreath of immortality, having beyond dispute received his reward, he did his utmost that not the least memorial of him should be taken away by us, although many desired to do this, and to become possessors of his holy flesh. For this end he suggested it to Nicetes, the father of Herod and brother of Alce, to go and entreat the governor not to give up his body to be buried, "lest," said he, "forsaking Him that was crucified, they begin to worship this one." This he said at the suggestion and urgent persuasion of the Jews, who also watched us, as we sought to take him out of the fire, being ignorant of this, that it is neither possible for us ever to forsake Christ, who suffered for the salvation of such as shall be saved throughout the whole world (the blameless one for sinners), nor to worship any other. For Him indeed, as being the Son of God, we adore; but the martyrs, as disciples and followers of the Lord, we worthily love on account of their extraordinary affection towards their own King and Master, of whom may we also be made companions and fellow-disciples!

Chapter XVIII.—The Body of Polycarp is Burned.

The centurion then, seeing the strife excited by the Jews, placed the body in the midst of the fire, and consumed it. Accordingly, we afterwards took up his bones, as being more precious than the most exquisite jewels, and more purified than gold, and deposited them in a fitting place, whither, being gathered together, as opportunity is allowed us, with joy and rejoicing, the Lord shall grant us to celebrate the anniversary of his martyrdom, both in memory of those who have already finished their course, and for the exercising and preparation of those yet to walk in their steps.

Chapter XIX.—Praise of the Martyr Polycarp.

This, then, is the account of the blessed Polycarp, who, being the twelfth that was martyred in Smyrna (reckoning those also of Philadelphia), yet occupies a place of his own in the memory of all men, insomuch that he is everywhere spoken of by the heathen themselves. He was not merely an illustrious teacher, but also a pre-eminent martyr, whose martyrdom all desire to imitate, as having been altogether consistent with the Gospel of Christ. For, having through patience overcome the unjust governor, and thus acquired the crown of immortality, he now, with the apostles and all the righteous [in heaven], rejoicingly glorifies God, even the Father, and blesses our Lord Jesus Christ, the Savior of our souls, the Governor of our bodies, and the Shepherd of the Catholic Church throughout the world.

Chapter XX.—This Epistle is to Be Transmitted to the Brethren.

Since, then, ye requested that we would at large make you acquainted with what really took place, we have for the present sent you this summary account through our brother Marcus. When, therefore, ye have yourselves read this Epistle, be pleased to send it to the brethren at a greater distance, that they also may glorify the Lord, who makes such choice of His own servants. To Him who is able to bring us all by His grace and goodness into his everlasting kingdom, through His only-begotten Son Jesus Christ, to Him be glory, and honor, and power, and majesty, for ever. Amen. Salute all the saints. They that are with us salute you, and Evarestus, who wrote this Epistle, with all his house.

Chapter XXI.—The Date of the Martyrdom.

Now, the blessed Polycarp suffered martyrdom on the second day of the month Xanthicus just begun, the seventh day before the Kalends of May, on the great Sabbath, at the eighth hour. He was taken by Herod, Philip the Trallian being high priest, Statius Quadratus being proconsul, but Jesus Christ being King for ever, to whom be glory, honor, majesty, and an everlasting throne, from generation to generation. Amen.

Chapter XXII.—Salutation.

We wish you, brethren, all happiness, while you walk according to the doctrine of the Gospel of Jesus Christ; with whom be glory to God the Father and the Holy Spirit, for the salvation of His holy elect, after whose example the blessed Polycarp suffered, following in whose steins may we too be found in the kingdom of Jesus Christ!

These things Caius transcribed from the copy of Irenaeus (who was a disciple of Polycarp), having himself been intimate with Irenaeus. And I Socrates transcribed them at Corinth from the copy of Caius. Grace be with you all.

And I again, Pionius, wrote them from the previously written copy, having carefully searched into them, and the blessed Polycarp having manifested them to me through a revelation, even as I shall show in what follows. I have collected these things, when they had almost faded away through the lapse of time, that the Lord Jesus Christ may also gather me along with His elect into His heavenly kingdom, to whom, with the Father and the Holy Spirit, be glory for ever and ever. Amen." *Martyrdom of Polycarp* 16:2. 155 A.D., CCEL.

We sometimes forget the persecutions of Christians from the very beginning of the Church, down throughout the ages, in many countries around the world. We must not forget the greatest profession of faith that can be given, and that is the profession given under pain of death, and imminent threat of martyrdom for the sake of the Kingdom of God. These men and women were faithful to the end, honored by Christ as illustrated in the Book of Revelation, and are worthy of our honor and special remembrance.

The Queenship of Mary, As Mother Of Jesus

As Old Catholics, we say, "Hail Holy Queen Enthroned Above" in unison with the ancient apostolic Churches. We say this in recognition of Queenship of Mary, by virtue of the Kingship of Jesus. Her Queenship is rightly understood, in the context of the ancient nations and kingdoms of the Middle East. Many people today object strenuously to this term, "Mary, Queen of Heaven" because they wrongly believe the ever-Virgin Mary is regarded by Catholics, Orientals and Orthodox as the spouse of Christ. This shows a misunderstanding of the term and its application.

In the ancient nations of the Near East and Middle East, the King had many wives, and indeed we see this in scripture when the King of the Nation of Israel began to behave as the kings of lesser nations, and took many wives. Each wife was not a queen, as has been the practice in western monarchy, as this would create serious problems. The queen was the mother of the king, a visible sign of the continuity of the bloodline and the king's royal heritage. The "Queen Mother" (the ancient Hebrew term was "Gebirah", literally; "great lady") was named in respect to the reigning king, as a public declaration of the proof of his royal lineage.

"Now in the eighteenth year of King Jeroboam the son of Nebat, Abijam began to reign over Judah. He reigned for three years in Jerusalem. His mother's name was Maacah the daughter of Abishalom." (1 Kings 15:1-2)

Thus, the "Queen Mother" was an important individual, symbolically tying the heritage together, as well as having the ear and influence over the King. It would be natural for individuals to petition the "Queen Mother" on their behalf, to make some request for them of the King, in hopes that her influence would ensure a favorable response.

"So Bathsheba went to King Solomon, to speak to him on behalf of Adonijah. And the king rose to meet her, and bowed down to her; then he sat on his throne, and had a seat brought for the king's mother; and she sat on his right. Then she said, 'I have one small request to make of you; do not refuse me.' And the king said to her, 'Make your request, my mother; for I will not refuse you.'" (1 Kings 2:19–20) The significance of the "Queen Mother" is seen clearly, as she sits at the right hand of the king. This position is reserved for the individual who is second only to the king in authority, in the entire kingdom.

In the angel's declaration, we hear Mary's impending installation as "Queen Mother" in the pronouncement that her son would be given the throne of David; "And behold, you will conceive in your womb and bear a son, and you shall call his name Jesus. He will be great, and will be called the Son of the Most High; and the Lord God will give to him the throne of his father David, and he will reign over the house of Jacob forever for ever; and of his kingdom there will be no end." (Luke 1:31-33) This understanding is immediately understood in the early Church, knowing well the position, role and influence the Gebirah has had in the previous Davidic dynasties. Unfortunately, nearly two thousand years later, today many have forgotten or were not provided in-depth instruction in Scripture, but rather left to interpret it themselves, completely missing this powerful piece of the Davidic kingdom hierarchy.

If we understand and believe Jesus to be the heavenly King of Kings, and ruler of the New Jerusalem in the line of ancient Davidic Kings, then we must accept Mary as the "Queen Mother". In Isaiah 7:14, we see Jesus' royal lineage and kingship described, "a virgin shall conceive and bear a son, and shall call his name 'Immanu-el'", and this child is to sit "upon the throne of David, and over his kingdom, to establish it, and to uphold it with justice and with righteousness from this time forth and for evermore." (Is. 9:7) Jesus is the Son of David, in the dynastic bloodline, and as a Davidic King, the ever-Virgin Mary is the Gebirah, or "Queen Mother".

Certainly, in this context, we see a greater depth in Elizabeth's exclamation, "Why is this granted to me, that the mother of my Lord should come to me?" (Luke 1:43) Scripture informs us that Elizabeth was filled with the Holy Spirit when she said this. (Luke 1:41)

In heaven, in the book of Revelation 12:1-6, we see the ever-Virgin Mary, depicted in a royal, majestic manner, "And a great portent opened in heaven, a woman clothed with the sun, with the moon under her feet, and on her head a crown of twelve stars". She is crowned and honored by her son, the King of Kings. Dare we do any less, than follow the example set by our heavenly King? If we truly love Jesus, shouldn't we love whom He loves, and honor whom He honors. If we wish to be more like Christ, should we not follow His example?

Calling Priests "Father"

Some people contend that the Church should not address its priests as "Father", stating (incorrectly) that Jesus expressly forbade us to call any man "father". This is a misinterpretation of Scripture, based upon a misunderstanding of Jesus' instructive method, using hyperbole. Certainly, if Jesus had meant to expressly forbid calling any man "father", we would expect that His own Apostles and Church would strictly follow this admonition. But this is not what Scripture teaches us, and certainly not our faith, through Apostolic Tradition, is lived out in the life of the Church.

It begins in the Old Testament. In Genesis 45:8, we see the identification with fatherhood, "So it was not you who sent me here, but God; and he has made me a father to Pharaoh, an lord of all his house and ruler over all the land of Egypt." In Job 29:16, we read, "I was a father to the poor, and I searched out the cause of him when I did not know."

Even more strongly, we see the identification of an individual as "Father", in Isaiah 22:20; "In that day I will call my servant Eliakim, the son of Hilkiah…and I will clothe him with (a) robe, and will bind a girdle on him and will commit… authority to his hand; *and he shall be a father to the inhabitants of Jerusalem and to the house of Judah.*" [emphasis added]

And it continues, as in 2 Kings 2:12 when Elisha cries, "*My father, my father*", as Elijah is carried up to Heaven. And later, in 2 Kings 6:21, when Elisha himself is called a "father" by the King of Israel. [emphasis added]

In the New Testament, after the death and resurrection of Jesus Christ, His Apostles are regarded and regard themselves as "fathers", as we see here:

Acts 7:2 St. Stephen begins his address to the Sanhedrin as "*brothers and fathers.*" Scripture indicates that these words were spoken by St. Stephen, while he was under the inspiration of the Holy Spirit. [emphasis added]

1 Cor. 4:17. "Therefore I sent you Timothy, *my beloved and faithful child in the Lord*, to remind you of my ways in Christ." [emphasis added]

1 Cor. 4:14-15. "I do not write this to make you ashamed, but to admonish you as my beloved children. For though you have countless guides in Christ, you do not have many fathers. *For I became your father in Christ Jesus through the Gospel.*" [emphasis added] Not only does St. Paul see himself as their spiritual father, but claims that authority by way of the Gospel. So too, do our priests and bishops claim their authority as spiritual fathers of the faithful under their care, and claim it by way of the Gospel.

Again we see the same: "To Titus, *my true child in a common faith*: grace and peace from God the Father and Christ Jesus our Savior." (Titus 1:4) [emphasis added]

2 Tim. 1:2. "You then, *my son*, be strong in the grace that is in Christ Jesus our Lord." [emphasis added]

Philemon 10. "I appeal to you for my child, Onesimus, *whose father I have become in my imprisonment…*" [emphasis added]

1 John 2:1. "*My little children*, I am writing this to you so that you may not sin; but if anyone does sin, we have an advocate with the Father, Jesus Christ the righteous." [emphasis added]

1 Tim. 1:2. "To Timothy, *my true child in the faith*; grace, mercy, and peace from God the Father and Christ Jesus our Lord." [emphasis added]

1 Peter 5:13. "She who is at Babylon, who is likewise chosen, sends you greetings; *and so does my son Mark.*"

1 John 2:13-15. "I am writing to you, *fathers*, because you know him who is from the beginning." [emphasis added]

So we see then, that certainly Christ never meant us to literally understand that we could never call any man "father", or "master" or "teacher" for that matter, but rather do not seek to be regarded as great and important before men, do not become puffed up with pride and arrogance at being regarded as more important than your fellow man. If this were not the meaning of His teaching, as some protest, then they should not (but do) call men, "Doctor" which means, "teacher" or actually "teacher", or even allow oneself to be called, "Mister, Miss, Mrs. or Ms." as these are all derivations of the word, "Master". What would we call our biological fathers? However, Scripture and Tradition both teach and attest that the Old Catholic Church understands this teaching of Christ in the proper context and understanding.

Repetitious Prayer

Certain sects argue that our use of repetition in prayer is contrary to Scripture, identifying it as "vain repetition", which Jesus identified as useless. The proper understanding is this; Jesus condemned the lack of true faith of those heaping up empty prayers for the sake of being seen and thought of by others as holy. Prayer, any prayer, regardless of short prayer or long prayer, is useless and in vain, if it is without faith, if it is done to give others an outward appearance of piety on the part of the individual praying. All prayer in faith is effective and useful. We see examples of repetitive prayer in Holy Scripture itself:

"For his steadfast mercy endures forever". (Psalm 136) This phrase is repeated many times.

In Daniel 3:57-88, we read, "Bless the Lord" at the end of each individual verse.

In Revelation 4:8-11, we see a heavenly example of perfect prayer; "And the four living creatures, each of them with six wings, are full of eyes all round and within, and day and night they never cease to sing, 'Holy, holy, holy is the Lord God Almighty, who was and is and is to come.'" There can be no better example of prayer that is pleasing to Almighty God, than that perfect prayer and adoration given Him in Heaven itself.

Jesus Himself engaged in repetitive prayer: "And going a little farther he fell on his face and prayed 'My Father, if it is possible, let this cup pass from me; nevertheless, not as I will, but as thou wilt'...Again, for the second time, he went away and prayed, 'My Father, if this cannot pass unless I drink it, thy will be done.'" "So, leaving them again, he went away and prayed for the third time, saying the same words." (Matthew 26:39, 42, 44)

Apostolic Succession

Pope Clement I

"Our apostles also knew, through our Lord Jesus Christ, and there would be strife on account of the office of the episcopate. For this reason, therefore, inasmuch as they had obtained a perfect fore-knowledge of this, they appointed those [ministers] already mentioned, and afterwards gave instructions, that when these should fall asleep, other approved men should succeed them in their ministry." (*Letter to the Corinthians* 42:4–5, 44:1–3 [A.D. 80])[31]

Hegesippus

"When I had come to Rome, I [visited] Anicetus, whose deacon was Eleutherus. And after Anicetus [died], Soter succeeded, and after him Eleutherus. In each succession and in each city there is a continuance of that which is proclaimed by the law, the prophets, and the Lord." (*Memoirs*, cited in Eusebius, *Ecclesiastical History* 4:22 [A.D. 180])[32]

St. Irenaeus

"It is possible, then, for everyone in every church, who may wish to know the truth, to contemplate the tradition of the apostles which has been made known to us throughout the whole world. And we are in a position to enumerate those who were instituted bishops by the apostles and their successors down to our own times, men who neither knew nor taught anything like what these heretics rave about." (*Against Heresies* 3:3:1 [A.D. 189])[33]

"But since it would be too long to enumerate in such a volume as this the successions of all the churches, we shall confound all those who, in whatever manner, whether through self-satisfaction or vainglory, or through blindness and wicked opinion, assemble other than where it is proper, by pointing out here the successions of the bishops of the greatest and most ancient church known to all, founded and organized at Rome by the two most glorious apostles, Peter and Paul—that church which has the tradition and the faith with which comes down to us after having been announced to men by the apostles. For with this Church, because of its superior origin, all churches must agree, that is, all the faithful in the whole world. And it is in her that the faithful everywhere have maintained the apostolic tradition." (ibid, 3:3:2)

"Polycarp also was not only instructed by apostles, and conversed with many who had seen Christ, but was also, by apostles in Asia, appointed bishop of the church in Smyrna, whom I also saw in my early youth, for he tarried [on earth] a very long time, and, when a very old man, gloriously and most nobly suffering martyrdom, departed this life, having always taught the things which he had learned from the apostles, and which the Church has handed down, and which alone are true. To these things all the Asiatic churches testify, as do also those men who have succeeded Polycarp down to the present time." (ibid, 3:3:4)

"Since therefore we have such proofs, it is not necessary to seek the truth among others which it is easy to obtain from the Church; since the apostles, like a rich man [depositing his money] in a bank, lodged in her hands most copiously all things pertaining to the truth, so that every man, whosoever will, can draw from her the water of life.... For how stands the case? Suppose there arise a dispute relative to some important question among us, should we not have recourse to the most ancient churches with which the apostles held constant conversation, and learn from them what is certain and clear in regard to the present question?" (ibid, 3:4:1)

"[I]t is incumbent to obey the presbyters who are in the Church—those who, as I have shown, possess the succession from the apostles; those who, together with the succession of the episcopate, have received the infallible charism of truth, according to the good pleasure of the Father. But [it is also incumbent] to hold in suspicion others who depart from the primitive succession, and assemble themselves together in any place whatsoever, either as heretics of perverse minds, or as schismatics puffed up and self-pleasing, or again as hypocrites, acting thus for the sake of lucre and vainglory. For all these have fallen from the truth." (ibid, 4:26:2)

"The true knowledge is the doctrine of the apostles, and the ancient organization of the Church throughout the whole world, and the manifestation of the body of Christ according to the succession of bishops, by which succession the bishops have handed down the Church which is found everywhere." (ibid, 4:33:8)

Tertullian

"They then in like manner rounded churches in every city, from which all the other churches, one after another, derived the tradition of the faith, and the seeds of doctrine, and are every day deriving them, that they may become churches. Indeed, it is on this account only that they will be able to deem themselves apostolic, as being the offspring of apostolic churches. Every sort of thing must necessarily revert to its original for its classification. Therefore the churches, although they are so many and so great, comprise but the one primitive church, (rounded) by the apostles, from which they all (spring). In this way all are primitive, and all are apostolic, whilst they are all proved to be one, in (unbroken) unity, by their peaceful communion, and title of brotherhood, and bond of hospitality,—privileges which no other rule directs than the one tradition of the selfsame mystery." (*Demurrer Against the Heretics* 20 [A.D. 200])[34]

"Now, what that was which they preached-in other words, what it was which Christ revealed to them-can, as I must here likewise prescribe, properly be proved in no other way than by those very churches which the apostles rounded in person, by declaring the gospel to them directly themselves...If, then, these things are so, it is in the same degree manifest that all doctrine which agrees with the apostolic churches-those moulds and original sources of the faith must be reckoned for truth, as undoubtedly containing that which the (said) churches received from the apostles, the apostles from Christ, Christ from God. Whereas all doctrine must be prejudged as false which savors of contrariety to the truth of the churches and apostles of Christ and God. It remains, then, that we demonstrate whether this doctrine of ours, of which we have now given the rule, has its origin in the tradition of the apostles, and whether all other *doctrines* do not *ipso facto* proceed from falsehood. We hold communion with the apostolic churches because our doctrine is in no respect different *from theirs*. This is our witness of truth." (ibid, 21)

"But if there be any (heresies) which are bold enough to plant themselves in the midst Of the apostolic age, that they may thereby seem to have been handed down by the apostles, because they existed in the time of the apostles, we can say: Let them produce the original records of their churches; let them unfold the roll of their bishops, running down in due succession from the beginning in such a manner that [that first bishop of theirs] bishop shall be able to show for his ordainer and predecessor some one of the apostles or of apostolic men,-a man, moreover, who continued steadfast with the apostles. For this is the manner in which the apostolic churches transmit their registers: as the church of Smyrna, which records that Polycarp was placed therein by John; as also the church of Rome, which makes Clement to have been ordained in like manner by Peter." (ibid 32)

"But should they even effect the contrivance [of composing a succession list for themselves], they will not advance a step. For their very doctrine, after comparison with that of the apostles [as contained in other churches], will declare, by its own diversity and contrariety, that it had for its author neither an apostle nor an apostolic man; because, as the apostles would never have taught things which were self-contradictory." (ibid)

"Then let all the heresies, when challenged to these two tests by our apostolic Church, offer their proof of how they deem themselves to be apostolic. But in truth they neither are so, nor are they able to prove themselves to be what they are not. Nor are they admitted to peaceful relations and communion by such churches as are in any way connected with apostles, inasmuch as they are in no sense themselves apostolic because of their diversity as to the mysteries of the faith." (ibid)

St. Cyprian of Carthage

"Wherefore, since the Church alone has the living water, and the power of baptizing and cleansing man, he who says that any one can be baptized and sanctified by Novatian must first show and teach that Novatian is in the Church or presides over the Church. For the Church is one, and as she is one, cannot be both within and without. For if she is with Novatian, she was not with Cornelius. But if she was with Cornelius, who succeeded the bishop Fabian by lawful ordination, and whom, beside the honor of the priesthood, the Lord glorified also with martyrdom, Novatian is not in the Church; nor can he be reckoned as a bishop, who, succeeding to no one, and despising the evangelical and apostolic tradition, sprang from himself. For he who has not been ordained in the Church can neither have nor hold to the Church in any way." (*Letters* 69[75]:3 [A.D. 253])[35]

St. Jerome

"Far be it from me to speak adversely of any of these clergy who, in succession from the apostles, confect by their sacred word the Body of Christ and through whose efforts also it is that we are Christians." (*Letters* 14:8 [A.D. 396])[36]

St. Augustine

"The consent of peoples and nations keeps me in the Church; so does her authority, inaugurated by miracles, nourished by hope, enlarged by love, established by age. The succession of priests keeps me, beginning from the very seat of the Apostle Peter, to whom the Lord, after His resurrection, gave it in charge to feed His sheep, down to the present episcopate. And so, lastly, does the name itself of Catholic, which, not without reason, amid so many heresies, the Church has thus retained; so that, though all heretics wish to be called Catholics, yet when a stranger asks where the Catholic Church meets, no heretic will venture to point to his own chapel or house." (*Against the Letter of Mani Called "The Foundation"* 4:5 [A.D. 397])[37]

Assurance of Salvation

Sometimes you will hear an objection to the Old Catholic teaching on salvation, coupled with a fervent declaration by the professor that they are assured of salvation. Further, they state that, once saved (that is, once they confess Jesus Christ as their personal Lord and Savior, and ask Him to come into their life, from that point on their salvation is assured, and there is nothing that they can do to lose their salvation) they are assured of going to heaven, regardless of how they live there life. Many times, cryptic quotation of certain passages of Scripture, followed by inaccurate or misleading interpretation is used to bolster this position. However, no one in the Early Church believed this recent doctrine, born out of the Reformation. The teaching of the Old Catholic Church, of the Eastern Orthodox Churches, of the Oriental Orthodox Churches and the Roman Catholic Church is that we believe and know that God will fulfill His promise to us, and that we can have a moral certitude that God will do what He promises. God will be faithful to us, but will we be faithful to Him? If we profess our belief in Him today, and promise to live our life in accordance with the teachings of Christ today, will we still be doing so five, ten or fifteen years from now, or will we have forsaken Him? Scripture does not teach us that "once saved" we can live a life of sin and rebellion, but be assured of entering into Heaven. We know from Scripture that there is that sin which is unforgivable, and if this is so, then we cannot presume that a one-time profession of faith will mitigate a lifetime afterwards of disobedience and sin. Scripture teaches, and we can expect, however, to be judged by Him even more severely, because we knew Him and rejected Him.

Philippians 2:12 says, "Therefore, my beloved, as you have always obeyed, so now, not only as in my presence but much more in my absence, *work out your own salvation* with fear and trembling." This is not an affirmation of an assurance of salvation, in which how one lives one's live is irrelevant, with respect to one's salvation. This is not to say that we can do anything of our own accord to merit salvation—we cannot obtain salvation for ourselves, it is a gift which is freely given and which we freely accept. However, salvation being a gift, can be rejected, either at the onset of its being offered or at a later time. God does not force His will upon our own; no one goes to heaven against their own will, rejecting God's love and living in rebellion against Him, and so if salvation cannot be lost, then we must then assume that there are those persons who are in heaven against their own will. But this supposition is contrary to Scripture, as nothing unclean exists in heaven. Clearly a soul and will which are contrary to God (which is sinful) cannot be found in heaven. We must then, have a clear choice to be obedience and accept the loving gift of salvation, or disobedience and reject God, and the salvation He has to offer, or else Scripture cannot be reconciled, for it teaches that we reap the benefits of God's promise of salvation to us only after we, as good and faithful servants, finish the race in fidelity to Him.

"I have fought the good fight, I have finished the race, I have kept the faith. Henceforth there is laid up for me the crown of righteousness, which the Lord, the righteous judge, will award to me on that Day." (2 Tim. 4:7-8) What must we as Christians do in order to obtain the crown of righteousness, awarded by Christ? It is clear; we must keep our faith, from beginning to end, enduring until our time is complete. We must approach this with the utmost of humility, humbleness and caution. No one can state for themselves that they are in perfect accord with the will of the Father, regardless of how obedient they see themselves, for God knows the hearts of man, and He cannot be deceived, as we can, by our own human pride, hubris or ignorance. "I am not aware of anything against myself, but I am not thereby justified. It is the Lord who judges me." (1 Cor. 4:4)

"I pummel my body and subdue it, lest after preaching to others I myself should be disqualified." (1 Cor. 9:27) Even the Leaders of the Church did not regard themselves as assured of their own salvation, in respect to their own faithfulness to God. They saw themselves and indeed the entire Church, as being made up of individuals who must actively strive to remain faithful to God, lest they lose their place as being of the elect, that is, those who will end up with God in heaven. There are people who experience initial salvation, but do not continue onward to final salvation. Scripture warns of the consequences of those who "believe for a while and in time of temptation fall away." (Luke 8:13) Such are individuals clearly identified as separate from the current body of believers being addressed. These are not individuals who never really did believe, but rather people who let their love for God run cold, and let the fire of the Holy Spirit within them be extinguished. The emphasis is on endurance, maintaining one's faith and not losing the gifts given to them. We must pray to God to ask Him to give to us that grace which empowers us to persevere in the faith, to the end of our days.

If any one says, 'I love God,' and hates his brother, he is a liar; for he who does not love his brother whom he has seen, cannot love God whom he has not seen," (1 John 4:20) "For this is the love of God, that we keep his commandments. And his commandments are not burdensome." (1 John 5:3) Jesus taught us to love God, but also to love our brother. This familial love is not a warm feeling for our fellow man but the actual act of caring for our brethren, feeding the hungry, clothing the naked, visiting the sick and caring for those unable to care for themselves. This calls for far more than merely sitting in a Church building every Sunday attending Mass. This requires us to actively love one another, as we have been taught both by word and example by Jesus Christ Himself. To be Christian is to be bound in family bonds, and to be a member of a family requires us to be responsible for others. To be a part of the Family of God, is to accept responsibility for others in that family, not only those you know and love but also those you do not. To fail to love your brother, is to fail to love God.

"Not everyone who says to me, 'Lord, Lord' shall enter the kingdom of heaven." (Matt. 7:21) It is not enough to simply make a one-time verbal profession of faith, we must, in our faith, continually do the will of the Father, professing our faith in thought, word and deed, until our earthly time is finished.

"He who endures to the end will be saved." (Matt. 24:13; cf. 25:31–46) Endurance is shown as immensely important: the ability to continue to do, over a long period of time, and not get tired and simply give up. This clearly illustrates the necessity for continued faithfulness and fidelity to God, in the manner taught us by Jesus Himself. Those who do not endure, who fail to continue on God's path, lose their share in the inheritance of the kingdom of God. "See then the kindness and the severity of God: severity toward those who have fallen, but God's kindness to you, provided you continue in his kindness; *otherwise you too will be cut off.*" (Rom. 11:22) Keep in mind that the inspired writer is not writing to a group of people interested in becoming Christians, *he is writing to baptized full members of the Early Christian Church.* He is instructing them that they, even baptized members of the Household of God, could lose their honored place within its doors, and be completely cut off from it. We see the same message else in Scripture as well. (Heb. 10:26–29, 2 Pet. 2:20–21)

The Validity of Old Catholic Sacraments and Orders

On various occasions, members of the Roman Catholic Church coming for the first time into contact with the Old Catholic Church, have inquired of their pastors or other clergy and supposedly "informed" laity as to the position of the Roman Catholic Church on the validity of Sacraments which are administered by the Old Catholic Church. Frequently the inquirers are told that our Sacraments are not recognized by Rome. This is written to clear up any confusion that there might be on this point. The opinions of uninformed persons cannot substitute for the official opinion of the communion of which they are a member, *unless they wish to reject the teachings of their own Church.* The statements presented here are from *official* authorities, theologians and publications of the Roman Catholic Church in the affirmation of the validity of Old Catholic Holy Orders and Sacraments. The sources referred to herein were printed with the imprimatur of various Roman Catholic Bishops.

In reading these resources quoted, consider also, that, in addition to the Apostolic Succession received from the Old Catholic Church of Utrecht through Archbishop Arnold Mathew, the Church also has valid lines of succession from the Oriental Orthodox Churches through Archbishop Joseph Renee Vilatte, from the Russian Orthodox Church through Archbishop Aftimos Ofiesh, and from the Roman Catholic lines through Archbishop Carlos Duarte Costa, Roman Catholic Diocesan Bishop of Botucatu, Brazil.

Bishop Salomao Ferraz was a former Roman Catholic Priest, who married and was later consecrated a bishop by Archbishop Carlos Duarte Costa, for the Brazilian National Catholic Church in 1945. He later left the Brazilian National Catholic Church and was eventually reconciled to the Roman Catholic Church in 1958, during the pontificate of Pope Pius XII. Bishop Ferraz was named by the Holy See to be Titular Bishop of Eleuterna on May 12, 1963. Although he was a married bishop, Bishop Ferraz was later appointed Auxiliary Bishop of Rio de Janeiro by Pope John XXIII. Bishop Ferraz was later called by Pope Paul VI to serve on a working commission of the Second Vatican Council and addressed the Council Fathers in session. No only does this affirm the validity of his Holy Orders, but the legitimacy of a married episcopate.

It is notable that Bishop Ferraz, from whom we have received the valid lines of the Roman Catholic Church through Archbishop Duarte Costa, *was never re-consecrated by the Roman Catholic Church, even conditionally,* and later was buried with the full honors accorded Bishops of the Roman Catholic Church. The Roman Catholic Church, by accepting Bishop Ferraz in this manner, without any re-consecration, acknowledged the sacramental validity of the Duarte Costa Apostolic Succession, which was no longer a part of the Roman Catholic Communion. Bishop Ferraz's lines of Apostolic Succession are part of the apostolic lines of succession of the Old Catholic Church of the United States.

On June 1, 1925, Archbishop Joseph Renee Vilatte, from whom we have received the valid lines of the Oriental Orthodox Churches, reconciled himself to the Roman Catholic Church, and made his formal declaration before Bishop Ceretti, Apostolic Nuncio at Paris. A week later *La Croix* and other newspapers announced that Vilatte, was staying at the Cistercian Abbey of Port-Colbert. He was there at the request of Pope Pius XI. The Holy See granted him a pension of 22,000 francs annually in recognition of his episcopal status. On June 23, 1925, the *Bayerischer Kurieg* published at statement, at the orders of the Swiss Christian [Old] Catholic Church, to the effect that Vilatte had never been a priest of this body nor any other genuine Old Catholic Church. Bishop Ceretti defended and upheld Vilatte's Episcopal status by responding to the newspaper as follows:

> "Archbishop Vilatte received Minor Orders and the Order of Subdeacon on June 5, 1885, The Order of Deacon of June 6 of the same year, and on the following day, June 7, 1885, the Ordination to the Priesthood. All these orders were conferred upon him by Bishop Herzog (Old Catholic Bishop) in the Old Catholic Church in Berne.

This proved by documents, seals and signatures of Bishop Herzog. Concerning his Episcopal Consecration, it took place on May 29, 1892. Archbishop Vilatte was consecrated by three Jacobite Bishops in the Cathedral of Archbishop Alvarez in Colombo (Ceylon). Archbishop Vilatte is likewise in the possession of the consecration deed in question bearing the signatures of the three above mentioned bishops and of the American Consul, who was present at the ceremony."

That having been illustrated, it is of interest to note that the various lines of Apostolic Succession held by the Church come from the earliest Christian communities set up by the Apostles, such as St. Andrew (Scythia), St. Thomas (India), Sts. Peter & Paul (Rome), and others. The Old Catholic Church has become, not through human design but through Divine Providence, a point of convergence of the spiritual gifts given these early communities through their apostolically appointed Bishops. The Old Catholic Church draws her valid sacraments and lines of succession from these ancient Churches, founded by the Apostles and empowered by Christ Himself.

The Old Catholic Church believes and professes the same Creeds, administers and believes in the Sacraments in the same manner, and teaches the same fundamental meaning and substance of them in unison with the Oriental Orthodox Churches, the Eastern Orthodox Churches, and the Roman Catholic Church. She does not stand opposed to, but rather in solidarity with, these ancient Apostolic Communions.

The Roman Catholic Church teaches an understanding of a type of a communion among the apostolic, sacramental churches in it's official document "DOMINUS IESUS," issued during the reign of Pope John Paul II, June 16, 2000, and signed by Joseph Cardinal Ratzinger, Prefect of the Congregation for the Doctrine of the Faith, August 6, 2000. We refer to Section IV: Article 17:

> "Therefore, there exists a single **Church of Christ***, which subsists in the [Roman] Catholic Church, governed by the Successor of Peter and by the Bishops in communion with him. The Churches which, while not existing in perfect communion with the [Roman] Catholic Church, remain united to her by means of the closest bonds, that is, by apostolic succession and a valid Eucharist, are true particular Churches. Therefore, *the Church of Christ is present and operative also in these*

Churches*, even though they lack full communion with the [Roman] Catholic Church, since they do not accept the [Roman] Catholic doctrine of the Primacy, which, according to the will of God, the Bishop of Rome objectively has and exercises over the entire Church." [*emphasized for clarity]

That the Old Catholic Church is seen by our sister church, the Roman Catholic Church, as one of these churches united by apostolic succession and a valid Eucharist, is seen in her continued affirmation of Old Catholic orders and sacraments.

1] "When a [Roman] Catholic sacred minister is unavailable and there is urgent spiritual necessity, [Roman] Catholics may receive the Eucharist, penance, or anointing from sacred ministers of non-[Roman] Catholic denomination whose holy orders are considered valid by the [Roman] Catholic Church. This includes all Eastern Orthodox priests, as well as priests of the Old Catholic or Polish National Church." Rights and Responsibilities, A Catholics' Guide to the New Code of Canon Law, Thomas P. Doyle, O.P., page 44.

2] "A validly consecrated bishop can validly confer all orders from the minor orders to the episcopate inclusively…For this reason the ordinations performed by the bishops of the Old Catholics are consider valid." A Practical Commentary on the Code of Canon Law, revised and enlarged edition, by Rev. Stanislaw Woywod, OFM, LLB. Vol. 1, Sec. 881, P. 558.

3] "They [Old Catholics] have received valid orders." Roman Catholic Dictionary, by Addison Arnold.

4] "The Old Catholic Church has received valid episcopal consecration", Christian Denominations, by Rev. Konrad Algemissen.

"The validity of episcopal consecration in the Church of Utrecht cannot be doubted, nor I this regard can that of the Old Catholic Church, which depend upon the former. The Utrecht Union came into existence in 1889, through a consolidation of the Church of Utrecht and the Old Catholic Church." P. 349.

"Since the episcopal consecration in the Church of Utrecht is valid, the validity of the prescribed consecration performed in the Old Catholic Church cannot be doubted." P. 357.

"In America, for instance, The American Catholic Church, The Old Catholic Church in America, the North American [Old Roman] Catholic Church, have all received valid episcopal consecration from the Old Catholic Church." P. 363.

5] "Their [Old Catholic] Orders and Sacraments are valid." A Catholic Dictionary, by Donald Attwater.

6] "The Far East Magazine of June, 1928, published by the Saint Columban Fathers of St. Columbans, Nebraska, in reply to any inquiry about the Old Catholic Church, published the reply that: "These [Old Catholics] Orders are valid."

7] "The Roman Church recognizes the validity of Old Catholic Orders and other Sacraments." 1974 Catholic Almanac, by Felician A. Roy, OFM, page 368. "Our Sunday Visitor."

8] "We have no reason to doubt that the Old Catholic Orders are valid. The Apostolic Succession does not depend on obedience to the See of Peter but rather on the objective line of succession from Apostolic sources, the proper matter and form, and the proper intention…likewise Old Catholic bishops are bishops in Apostolic Succession…The Old Catholics, like the Orthodox, posses a valid priesthood." Separated Brethren, William J. Whalen, pp. 204, 248.

9] (Apostolicae Curae) "…Whenever there is no appearance of simulation on the part of the minister, the validity of the sacrament is sufficiently certain…"

10] "Every validly consecrated bishop, including heretical, schismatic, simonistic or excommunicated bishops, can validly dispense the Sacrament of Order, provided that he has the requisite intention, and follows the essential external rite (set. Certa). Cf. D 855, 860; CIC 2372." 1952 *Fundamentals of Catholic Dogma*, by Dr. Ludwig Ott, pp. 456.

The Old Catholic Church of Utrecht and Jansenism

This is an old charge against the Church of Utrecht, and through Utrecht to all Old Catholic Churches. This is a case of "guilt by association". In 1592, the Jesuits first entered the Kingdom of the Netherlands, and began to centralize the authority previously held by the local diocesan organizations into the office of the papacy, administered by the Congregation for the Propagation of the Faith. The Dutch Church held ancient canonical rights and privileges which had g\been given to the Church permanently. The Jesuits contended that rather than have locally selected diocesan bishops chosen by the Chapters, and having their own canonical rights which would interfere with the Jesuit's plans to consolidate authority, that the bishops needed should be vicar-apostolics, appointed by the Pope, who could be removed by the Pope. This power struggle began forty years prior to the printing of *Augustinus*, but served to lay the foundation for further acrimony between the Dutch Church and the Jesuits in years to come.

When Jansenism was prevalent in the Roman Catholic Church, many Jansenists fled other European countries to the Kingdom of the Netherlands in order to gain sanctuary. The Church of Utrecht provided sanctuary, and certainly some of the Church there sympathized with the pursued Jansenists. The Jesuits, in emulation of their founder, St. Ignatius Loyola, strongly espoused and practiced blind obedience to the Pope, and strenuously taught other Catholics to believe the same. The Jansenists were free-thinkers, espousing independent thought and reasoning, and no less loyal to the Pope, but not proponents of blind obedience. Because the Church in the Netherlands provided sanctuary, in addition to previous negative dealings with the Jesuits, the Church of Utrecht was branded "Jansenist". In reality, Jansenism had a much lasting and profound effect upon the Roman Catholic Church in Europe, than it did within the Old Catholic Church of Utrecht, and certainly none on the Old Catholic Churches formed in the 1870's in response to the Vatican Council which opened December 8, 1869.

Well before the 1870's, the bishops of the Church of Utrecht had indicated to representatives of the Pope, on more than one occasion, that they "reject[ed] and condemn[ed] the "Five Propositions" condemned by the Holy See, which are stated to be found in the book of Jansenius called '*Augustinus*'". (*History of the Church of Holland*, J.M. Neale, p. 351.) This however, was not good enough, and the specific Formulary was required to be signed. The problem was that the Formulary was factually incorrect, insofar as the Formulary stated that the "Five Propositions" that it objected to, were all contained in the written work of Cornelius Jansen, entitled *Augustinus*, when in fact, all of them were not. Pope VIII had condemned *Augustinus* in his Bull 'In Emineti' I 1642, and it was forbidden to read the book. Many people blindly signed the Formulary, not first having read it to determine whether it really espoused the "Five Propositions" in question or not. For those who had read the book and knew that all five propositions were not in the written work, or refused to sign the Formulary until first having read the written work in question, the matter was forced into an issue of papal obedience. The issue then was the coercion of clergy and religious alike to sign a statement that was factually false, being ordered to accept it as true as a matter of faith, in obedience to the Pope.

The Church of Utrecht was not then, and is not now, "Jansenist", nor is the Old Catholic Church today. This label is used now, as it was then, in a vain attempt to discredit the Church of Utrecht and those Churches descended from her, to prevent large amounts of people from flocking to their doors. To those individuals who, to this day, hate the fact of the existence of the Old Catholic Church and her having valid Sacraments and Apostolic Succession, this label is still used. But a simple reading of what the Church believes clearly indicates that the charges are utterly false.

ENDNOTES FOR CHAPTER SIX

1. *The Shepard of Hermas*, 4:1:6 [A.D. 80]. Christian Classics Ethereal Library, Public Domain.

2. St. Justin the Martyr, *First Apology 15*. Christian Classics Ethereal Library, Public Domain.

3. William A. Jurgens, *The Faith of the Early Fathers Volume 2*, (The Liturgical Press Collegeville, MN, 1970), vol. II, p. 8.

4. Ibid, vol. II, p. 169.

5. Ibid, vol. II, p. 162.

6. Ibid, vol. II, p. 185.

7. Ibid, vol. II, p. 202.

8. Ibid, vol. III, p. 132.

9. Ibid, vol. III, p. 133.

10. Ibid, vol. III, p. 135.

11. Ibid, vol. III, p. 135.

12. William A. Jurgens, *The Faith of the Early Fathers Volume 1*, (The Liturgical Press Collegeville, MN, 1970), vol. I, p. 34.

13. St. Clement of Alexandria, *Miscellanies* 7:12 [A.D. 208]. Christian Classics Ethereal Library, Public Domain.

14. St. Cyprian of Carthage, *Letters* 56[60]:5 [A.D. 253]. Christian Classics Ethereal Library, Public Domain.

15. William A. Jurgens, *The Faith of the Early Fathers Volume 1*, (The Liturgical Press Collegeville, MN, 1970).

16. St. Cyril of Jerusalem, *Catechetical Lectures* 23:9 [A.D. 350]), Christian Classics Ethereal Library, Public Domain.

17. William A. Jurgens, *The Faith of the Early Fathers Volume 1*, (The Liturgical Press Collegeville, MN, 1970),

18. Ibid,

19. Ibid,

20. Ibid,

21. Ibid,

22. Ibid.

23. St. John Chrysostom, *Homilies on Second Corinthians* 26 [A.D. 392]. Christian Classics Ethereal Library, Public Domain.

24. William A. Jurgens, *The Faith of the Early Fathers Volume 1*, (The Liturgical Press Collegeville, MN, 1970),

25. Ibid.

26. William A. Jurgens, *The Faith of the Early Fathers Volume 2*, (The Liturgical Press Collegeville, MN, 1970), vol. II, p. 206.

27. St. Augustine. *Against Faustus the Manichean* [A.D. 400]. Christian Classics Ethereal Library, Public Domain.

28. William A. Jurgens, *The Faith of the Early Fathers Volume 2*, (The Liturgical Press Collegeville, MN, 1970), vol. III, p. 29.

29. St. Augustine. *Homilies on John* 84 [A.D. 416]. Christian Classics Ethereal Library, Public Domain.

30. St. Augustine. *The City of God* 20:9:2 [A.D. 419]. Christian Classics Ethereal Library, Public Domain.

31. Pope Clement I. *Letter to the Corinthians* 42:4–5, 44:1–3 [A.D. 80]. Christian Classics Ethereal Library, Public Domain.

32. William A. Jurgens, *The Faith of the Early Fathers Volume 1*, (The Liturgical Press Collegeville, MN, 1970), vol. I, p. 80.

33. Ibid, vol. I p. 89

34. Tertullian *Demurrer Against the Heretics* 20 [A.D. 200]. Christian Classics Ethereal Library, Public Domain.

35. St. Cyprian of Carthage, *Letters* 69 [75]:3 [A.D. 253]. Christian Classics Ethereal Library, Public Domain.

36. St. Augustine, *Against the Letter of Mani Called "The Foundation"* 4:5 [A.D. 397]. Christian Classics Ethereal Library, Public Domain.

37. William A. Jurgens, *The Faith of the Early Fathers Volume 3*, (The Liturgical Press Collegeville, MN, 1970), vol. III, p. 51.

CHAPTER 7

A Treasury of Prayers

Archbishop Arnold Mathew's Prayer on Catholic Unity

Almighty and everlasting God, Whose only begotten Son, Jesus Christ the Good Shepherd, has said, 'Other sheep I have that are not of this fold: them also I must bring, and they shall hear My voice, and there shall be one fold and one shepherd. Let Thy rich and abundant blessing rest upon the Old Roman Catholic Church, to the end that it may serve Thy purpose by gathering in the lost and straying sheep. Enlighten, sanctify, and quicken it by the indwelling of the Holy Ghost, that suspicions and prejudices may be disarmed, and the other sheep being brought to hear and to know the voice of their true Shepherd thereby, all may be brought into full and perfect unity in the one fold of Thy Holy Catholic Church, under the wise and loving keeping of Thy Vicar, through the same Jesus Christ, Thy Son, who with Thee and the Holy Ghost, liveth and reigneth God, world without end. Amen.

Prayer of Thanksgiving—I

O Lord my Savior and my Master, I, Thine unprofitable servant, with fear and trembling give thanks unto Thy loving goodness for all Thy benefits which Thou hast poured so abundantly upon me, Thy servant. I fall down in adoration before Thee and offer Thee, O God, my praises; with fervor I cry to Thee: O God, deliver me henceforth from all adversities and mercifully fulfill in me such of my desires as may be expedient for me. Hear me, I entreat Thee, and have mercy, for Thou art the Hope of all the ends of the earth, and unto Thee, with the Father, and the Holy Spirit, be ascribed glory, now and ever, and unto ages of ages. Amen.

Prayer of Thanksgiving—II

I praise Thee, O God of our Fathers, I sing hymns of praise to Thee, I bless Thee, I give thanks unto thee for Thy great and tender mercy. To Thee I flee, O merciful

God. Shine into my heart with the True Sun of Thy righteousness. my mind and keep all my senses, that henceforth I may walk uprightly and keep Thy commandments, and may finally attain unto eternal life, even to Thee, Who art the source of life, and be admitted to the glorious fruition of Thy inaccessible Light. For Thou art my God, and unto Thee, O Father, Son and Holy Spirit, be ascribed glory, now and ever and unto ages of ages. Amen.

The Benedictus [Luke 1:68-79]

Blessed be the Lord God of Israel,
for He has visited and redeemed His people,

He has raised up a horn of salvation for us
in the house of His servant David,
as He spoke by the mouth of His holy prophets from of old,

That we should be saved from our enemies,
and from the hand of all who hate us;
to perform the mercy promised to our fathers,
and to remember His holy covenant,

The oath which He swore to our father Abraham,
to grant us that we, being delivered from the hand of our enemies,
might serve Him without fear, in holiness and righteousness
before Him all the days of our life.

And you, child,
will be called the prophet of the Most High;
for you will go before the Lord to prepare His ways,

To give knowledge of salvation to His people
in the forgiveness of their sins,
through the tender mercy of our God,
when the day shall dawn upon us from on high

To give light to those who sit in darkness
and in the shadow of death,
to guide our feet into the way of peace.

Prayer of Basil the Great

O God and Lord of the Powers, and Maker of all creation, Who, because of Thy clemency and incomparable mercy, didst send Thine Only-Begotten Son and our Lord Jesus Christ for the salvation of mankind, and with His venerable Cross didst tear asunder the record of our sins, and thereby didst conquer the rulers and powers of darkness; receive from us sinful people, O merciful Master, these prayers of gratitude and supplication, and deliver us from every destructive and gloomy transgression, and from all visible and invisible enemies who seek to injure us. Nail down our flesh with fear of Thee, and let not our hearts be inclined to words or thoughts of evil, but pierce our souls with Thy love, that ever contemplating Thee, being enlightened by Thee, and discerning Thee, the unapproachable and ever-lasting Light, we may unceasingly render confession and gratitude to Thee: The eternal Father, with Thine Only-Begotten Son, and with Thine All-Holy, Gracious, and Life-Giving Spirit, now and ever, and unto ages of ages. Amen.

Psalm 22
[A contemplative devotion on Good Friday, at the hour of death of our Lord, or in times of distress]

My God, my God, why hast thou forsaken me?
Why art thou so far from helping me, from the words of my groaning?
O my God, I cry by day, but thou dost not answer;
And by night, but find no rest.

Yet thou art holy, enthroned on the praises of Israel.
In thee our fathers trusted; they trusted, and thou didst deliver them.
To thee they cried, and were saved:
In thee they trusted, and were not disappointed.

But I am a worm, and no man;
Scorned by men, and despised by the people.
All who see me mock at me,
They make mouths at me, they wag their heads;
He committed his cause to the Lord; Let him deliver him, let him,
Let him rescue him, for he delights in him!

Yet thou are he who took me from the womb;
Thou didst keep me safe upon my mother's breasts.
Upon thee was I cast from my birth,
And since my mother bore me thou hast been my God.

Be not far from me, for trouble is near
And there is none to help.

Many bulls encompass me,
Strong bulls of Ba'shan surround me;
They open wide their mouths at me,
Like a ravening and roaring lion.

I am poured out like water,
And all my bones are out of joint;
My heart is lie wax,
It is melted within my breast;
My strength is dried up like potsherd,
And my tongue cleaves to my jaws;
Thou dost lay me in the dust of death.

Yea, dogs are round about me;
A company of evildoers encircle me;
They have pierced my hands and feet—
I can count all my bones—
They stare and gloat over me;
They divide my garments among them,
And for my raiment they cast lots.

But thou, O Lord, be not far off!
Thou my help, hasted to my aid!
Deliver my soul from the sword,
My life from the power of the dog!
Save me from the mouth of the lion,
My afflicted soul from the horns of the wild oxen!

I will tell of thy name to my brethren;
In the midst of the congregation I will praise thee:
You, who fear the Lord, praise him!
All you sons of Jacob, glorify him,
And stand in awe of him, all you sons of Israel!
For he has not despised or abhorred the affliction of the afflicted;
And he has not hid his face from him,
But has heard, when he cried to him.

From thee comes my praise in the great congregation;
My vows I will pay before those who fear him.
The afflicted shall eat and be satisfied;
Those who seek him shall praise the Lord!
May your hearts live forever!

All the end of the earth shall remember and turn to the Lord;
And all the families of the nations shall worship before him.
For dominion belongs to the Lord, and he rules over the nations.

Yea, to him shall all the proud of the earth bow down;
Before him shall bow all who go down to the dust, and he who cannot keep himself alive.
Posterity shall serve him; men shall tell of the Lord to the coming generation,
And proclaim his deliverance to a people yet unborn,
That he has wrought it.

Prayer of St. John Chrysostom—According to the hours of the day and night

1. O Lord, deprive me not of Thy heavenly blessings;

2. O Lord, deliver me from eternal torment;

3. O Lord, if I have sinned in my mind or thought, in word deed, forgive me.

4. O Lord, deliver me from every ignorance and heedlessness, from pettiness of the soul and stony hardness of heart;

5. O Lord, deliver me from every temptation;

6. O Lord, enlighten my heart darkened by evil desires;

7. O Lord, I, being a human being, have sinned; do Thou, being God, forgive me in Thy loving kindness, for Thou knowest the weakness of my soul.

8. O Lord, send down Thy grace to help me, that I may glorify Thy holy Name;

9. O Lord Jesus Christ, inscribe me, Thy servant, in the Book of Life, and grant me a blessed end;

10. O Lord my God, even if I have done nothing good in Thy sight, yet grant me, according to Thy grace, that I may make a start in doing good.

11. O Lord, sprinkle on my heart the dew of Thy grace;

12. O Lord of heaven and earth, remember me, Thy sinful servant, cold of heart and impure, in Thy Kingdom.

13. O Lord, receive me in repentance;

14. O Lord, leave me not;

15. O Lord, save me from temptation;

16. O Lord, grant me pure thoughts;

17. O Lord, grant me tears of repentance, remembrance of death, and the sense of peace;

18. O Lord, grant me mindfulness to confess my sins;

19. O Lord, grant me humility, charity, and obedience;

20. O Lord, grant me tolerance, magnanimity, and gentleness;

21. O Lord, implant in me the root of all blessings: the fear of Thee in my heart;

22. O Lord, vouchsafe that I may love Thee with all my heart and soul, and that I may obey in all things Thy will;

23. O Lord, shield me from evil persons and devils and passions and all other lawless matters;

24. O Lord, Who knowest Thy creation and that which Thou hast willed for it; may Thy will also be fulfilled in me, a sinner, for Thou art blessed forever-more. Amen.

Anima Christi

Soul of Christ, sanctify me,
Body of Christ, save me,
Blood of Christ, refresh me,
Water from the side of Christ, wash me,
Passion of Christ, strengthen me,
O Good Jesu, hear me,
Within your wounds hide me,
Suffer me not to be separated from thee,
From the malicious enemy defend me,
In the hour of my death call me,
And bid me come to thee,
That with your Saints I may praise thee
For all eternity. Amen.

O Saving Victim (O Salutaris Hostia.)

O Saving Victim, opening wide
The gate of heaven to man below,
Our foes press on from every side,
Thine aid supply, your strength bestow.
All praise and thanks to you ascend
For evermore, blest One in Three;
O grant us life that shall not end
In our true native land with thee. Amen.

Prayer to One's Patron Saint

O saint of God, *(the name of the saint)*, pray to God for me, for my home and my family. Amen. Pray to God for me, O saint *(the name of the saint)*, well-pleasing to God, for I readily recommend myself to you, who are the speedy helper and intercessor for my soul. Amen.

A Prayer for the Priesthood

O Jesus Christ, Lord of Lords and King of Kings, lay within the hearts of all thy Priests, the fire of zealous love for thee. Give them wisdom to see and combat the attacks of the enemy. Give them patience, to continue in the face of adversity. Give them strength that they may labor unceasingly in thine earthly vineyard for the salvation of all souls, and the glory of thine all-honorable and majestic Name: of the Father, and of the Son, and of the Holy Spirit, now and forever, unto ages of ages. Amen.

The Breastplate of St. Patrick

I arise today through a mighty strength, the invocation of the Trinity, through belief in the Threeness, through confession of the Oneness of the Creator of creation.

I arise today through the strength of Christ with his Baptism, through the strength of His Crucifixion with His Burial through the strength of His Resurrection with His Ascension, through the strength of His descent for the Judgment of Doom.

I arise today through the strength of the love of Cherubim in obedience of Angels, in the service of the Archangels, in hope of resurrection to meet with reward, in prayers of Patriarchs, in predictions of Prophets, in preachings of Apostles, in faiths of Confessors, in innocence of Holy Virgins, in deeds of righteous men.

I arise today, through the strength of Heaven; light of Sun, brilliance of Moon, splendor of Fire, speed of Lightning, swiftness of Wind, depth of Sea, stability of Earth, firmness of Rock.

I arise today, through God's strength to pilot me: God's might to uphold me, God's wisdom to guide me, God's eye to look before me, God's ear to hear me, God's word to speak for me, God's hand to guard me, God's way to lie before me, God's shield to protect me, God's host to secure me: against snares of devils, against temptations of vices, against inclinations of nature, against everyone who shall wish me ill, afar and anear, alone and in a crowd.

I summon today all these powers between me (and these evils): against every cruel and merciless power that may oppose my body and my soul, against incantations of false prophets, against black laws of heathenry, against false laws of heretics, against craft of idolatry, against spells of witches, smiths and wizards, against every knowledge that endangers man's body and soul. Christ to protect me today against poisoning, against burning, against drowning, against wounding, so that there may come abundance in reward.

Christ with me, Christ before me, Christ behind me, Christ in me, Christ beneath me, Christ above me, Christ on my right, Christ on my left, Christ in breadth, Christ in length, Christ in height, Christ in the heart of every man who thinks of me, Christ in the mouth of every man who speaks of me, Christ in every eye that sees me, Christ in every ear that hears me.

I arise today through a mighty strength, the invocation of the Trinity, through belief in the Threeness, through confession of the Oneness of the Creator of creation. Salvation is of the Lord. Salvation is of the Lord. Salvation is of Christ. May Thy Salvation, O Lord, be ever with us. Amen.

MORNING PRAYERS

<u>Morning Offering—I</u>

O my God, I offer to You all my thoughts, works, joys, and sufferings of this day. And I ask You to grant me your grace that I may not offend you this day; but may faithfully serve you and do your holy will in all things. Amen.

Glory be to the Father and to the Son and to the Holy Spirit.
As it was in the beginning, is now and ever shall be, world without end. Amen.

May the Lord bless us, and keep us from evil, and bring us unto everlasting life. Amen.

<u>Morning Offering—II</u>

O Jesus, I offer You all my prayers, works, joys and sufferings of this day, in union with the Most Holy Sacrifice of the Mass throughout the world, in reparation for my sins, for the intentions of all for whom we pray, and in particular for the intentions of our Archbishop. Amen.

<u>Morning Prayer</u>

Thou hast raised me from bed and sleep, O Lord; enlighten my mind and heart, and open my lips, that I may praise Thee, O Holy Trinity: Holy, Holy, Holy art Thou, O God. For the sake of the Mother of God, have mercy upon us.

O Christ, the True Light, Who illumines and sanctifies every human being coming into the world: let the light of Thy countenance be turned upon us, that in it we may behold the unapproachable Light. guide our footsteps toward working according to Thy commandments, through the intercessions of Thy most pure Mother, and of all the saints. Amen.

To Thee, O Master Who loves mankind, I hasten on rising from sleep; by Thy mercy I go forth to do Thy works, and I pray unto Thee: help me at all times, and in all things; deliver me from every evil thing of this world and from the pursuit of the devil; save me and lead me into Thine eternal Kingdom. For Thou art my Creator, Provider and Bestower of every good; wherefore all my hope is in Thee, and to Thee I ascribe glory, now and ever, and unto ages of ages. Amen.

We bless Thee, O God in the highest and Lord of mercies, Who ever works great and mysterious deeds for us, glorious, wonderful and countless, Who provides us with sleep as a rest from our infirmities, and as a repose for our bodies tired by labor. We thank Thee that Thou hast not destroyed us in our transgressions, but in Thy love toward mankind, Thou hast raised us up that we might glorify Thy Majesty. We entreat Thine infinite goodness, enlighten the eyes of our understanding and raise up our minds from the heavy sleep of indolence; open our mouths and fill them with Thy praise, that we may unceasingly sing and confess Thee, Who art God glorified in all and by all, the eternal Father, the Only-Begotten Son, and the All-Holy and Good and Life-Giving Spirit, now and ever, and unto ages of ages. Amen.

Grant unto me, my Lord, that with peace in mind I may face all that this new day is to bring. Grant unto me grace to surrender myself completely to Thy holy will. Instruct and prepare me in all things for every hour of this day. Whatsoever tidings I may receive during the day, do Thou teach me to accept them calmly, in the firm conviction that all eventualities fulfill Thy holy will. Govern Thou my thoughts and feelings in all I do and say. When things unforeseen occur, let me not forget that all cometh down from Thee. Teach me to behave sincerely and reasonable toward every member of my family and all other human beings, that I may not cause confusion and sorrow to anyone. Bestow upon me, my Lord, strength to endure the fatigue of the day and to bear my share in all its passing events. Guide Thou my will and teach me to pray, to believe, to hope, to suffer, to forgive, and to love. Amen.

Morning Prayer to the Holy Spirit

O Holy Spirit, Divine Spirit of light and love, I consecrate to You my mind, heart and will, my whole being for time and for eternity. May my mind be ever attendant to Thy divine inspirations and to the teachings of the Old Catholic Church whose infallible guide Thou art; my heart ever inflamed with the love of God and of my neighbor; my will ever conformable to the divine will; and my whole life a faithful imitation of the life and virtues of our Lord and Savior Jesus Christ, to whom with the Father and You be honor and glory forever. Amen.

Eternal Spirit, increase within my soul, faith, hope and charity, that I may embrace ever more firmly the truths which You have revealed, hope ever confidently in Your divine promises, and love sincerely You, my God, and all my fellow men who were created in Your image and likeness. Amen.

EVENING PRAYERS

<u>Evening Prayer—I</u>

And now as we lay down to sleep, O Master, grant us repose both of body and of soul, and keep us from the dark passions of the night. Subdue Thou the assaults of passions. Quench the fiery darts of the Wicked One which are thrown insidiously at us; calm the commotions of our flesh and put away all thoughts about worldly and material things as we go to sleep. Grant us, O God, a watchful mind, chaste thoughts, a sober heart, and a gentle sleep, free from all the fantasies of Satan. And raise us up again at the hour of prayer, established in Thy commandments and holding steadfast within ourselves the remembrance of Thy judgments. Give us the words of Thy glorification all night long, that we may praise, bless, and glorify Thy most honorable and magnificent name, O Father, Son and Holy Spirit, now and ever, and unto ages of ages. Amen.

<u>Evening Prayer—II</u>

O eternal God! Ruler of all creation! Who hast vouchsafed that I should live even down to the present hour, forgive the sins I have committed this day by deed, word or thought. Cleanse, O Lord, my humble soul of all corporal and spiritual stain. And grant, O Lord, that I may during this night have a peaceful sleep, so that on rising from my humble bed, I should continue to praise Thy holy Name throughout all the days of my life, and that I be victorious over all the physical and spiritual enemies battling against me. Deliver me, O Lord, from all vain thoughts that defile me, and from evil desires. For Thine is the Kingdom, and the Power, and the Glory of the Father, and of the Son, and of the Holy Spirit, now and ever, and unto ages of ages. Amen.

<u>Evening Prayer—III</u>

O Lord our God, however I have sinned this day in word, deed or thought, forgive me, for Thou art gracious and loves mankind. Grant me peaceful and undisturbed sleep. Send me Thy guardian angel to shield me and protect me from every evil; for Thou art the Guardian of our souls and bodies, and unto Thee we ascribe glory, to the Father and to the Son and to the Holy Spirit, now and ever, and unto ages of ages. Amen.

Evening Prayer—IV

Into Thy hands, O Lord, Jesus Christ, my God, I commend my spirit. Bless me, save me and grant unto me everlasting life. Amen.

Short Evening Devotional

V: In the Name of the Father, and of the Son and of the Holy Spirit.
R: Amen.

V: I will go unto the Altar of God,
R: Even unto the God of my joy and gladness.

Psalm XLIII

V: Give sentence with me, O God, and defend my cause against the ungodly people: O deliver me from the deceitful and wicked man.
R: For thou art the God of my strength; why hast thou put me from thee: and why go I so heavily, while the enemy oppresses me?

V: O send out thy light and thy truth that they may lead me: and bring me unto thy holy hill, and to thy dwelling.
R: And that I may go unto the altar of God, even unto the God of my joy and gladness, and upon the harp I will give thanks unto you, O God, my God.

V: Why art thou so heavy, O my soul: and why art thou so disquieted within me?
R: O put thy trust in God; for I will yet give him thanks: who is the help of my countenance, and my God.

R: Glory be to the Father, and to the Son, and the Holy Spirit.
V: As it was in the beginning, is now, and ever shall be, world without end. Amen.

V: Our help is in the Name of the Lord
R: Who hath made heaven and earth

The Hymn of Saint Ephrem the Syrian

[Verses are alternated if more than one person is praying]

V: Lord have mercy upon us
Kindly accept our prayers
Grant us mercy, redemption
From Thy treasury above.

R: Let me Lord, before Thee stand,
Wakeful my watch I'd keep,
Should I fall to slumber's hand,
Guard me from my sinful sleep.

V: If I do wrong while awake
Mercifully absolve me;
If I err in my sleep
In mercy, grant redemption.

R: By Thy cross ✠ of submission
Grant me, Lord, a restful sleep,
Forbid vain and evil dreams
O my Lord, from Thy servant.

V: Through the night conduct me, Lord,
Peaceful sleep give Thou to me,
Wroth and foul thoughts O Lord
May not govern me at all.

R: O Lord, Thy servant I am
Guard my body while I sleep
Keep Thy bright angel's guard
O my Lord, by my side.

V: Christ Thy life-abiding
Holy body that I ate
Keep away from my heart
Evil desires that destroy.

R: While I sleep in this night
May Thy holy blood guard me
Be Thou always redeemer
For I am Thine image.

V: Thy hand shaped me, O Lord
Shadow me with Thy right hand,
Let Thy mercy be a fortress
Shielding me-all around.

R: While my body silent lies,
May Thy power keep vigil;
Let my sleep in Thy presence
Be like the rising incense.

V: Thy mother who did bear Thee
By her prayers for me Lord
Let not evil touch my bed,
While I slumber in this night.

R: By Thy pleasing sacrifice
That absolved me from my distress
Forbid from me the wicked one
That keeps troubling me.

V: By Thy kindness O my Lord
Thy promise in me fulfilled
By Thy Holy Cross ✠ O Lord
Protect my life perfect.

R: Thou who pleased in me
Feeble and sinful servant I am
May I praise Thy mercy,
When I wake up from my sleep.

V: May Thy servant know Thy will
In Thy true loving kindness
Grant me O Lord Thy mercy
So that I may walk with Thee.

R: Jesus Christ, O my Lord
Grant to us Thy servants
An evening filled with peace
And a night of graceful sleep.

V: True light Thou art O Lord
Praise we Thy bright glory
We children of Thy light
Praise Thee for ever more.

R: O savior of mankind
Thy servants praise Thy mercy
As we do in this world
May it be in heaven above.

V: Praise to Thee, O my Lord
Praise to Thee, O my savior
Praise a thousand thousand fold
Praise we Thou O Jesus Christ.

R: Thou who does receive our prayers
Thou who grants supplications
Heed Thy servants' prayers
Kindly grant our petitions.

Let us pray:
O Lord! Instruct us all in all thy Commandments. By thine grace help us to live according to them. Almighty God, send forth thine angels to open the doors of our senses that the treasury of thy grace may not be withheld from us.

O holy God, Thy Holiness is adored by all the Saints. O Lord, cleanse our thoughts and make us worthy to glorify thy Holy Name as the seraphim, who proclaim and glorify Thy Holiness.
R: Amen.

BLESSING OVER MEALS

<u>Blessing Before Meals</u>

Bless us, O Lord, and these thy gifts, which we are about to receive from thy bounty, through Christ, our Lord, Amen.

<u>Blessing After Meals</u>

We give thee thanks, Almighty God, Heavenly Father for all Thy benefits, who lives and reigns, world without end, and time eternal. Amen.

May the Lord grant us His abiding peace, And life everlasting. Amen

BLESSING AT MEALS

<u>Before the Noonday Meal</u>

[The priest, or the father of the family, who is to bless the table says:]
V: Bless the Lord.
R: Bless the Lord.
V: The eyes of all hope in you, Lord.
R: You give them food in due time. You open your hand and fill all creatures with your blessing. Glory be to the Father, etc.
V: Lord, have mercy.
R: Christ, have mercy. Lord, have mercy.

Our Father…
[The rest inaudibly until:]
V: And lead us not into temptation.
R: But deliver us from evil.

V: Let us pray. Bless us, ✠ O Lord, and these your gifts which we are about to receive from your bounty; through Christ our Lord.
R: Amen.

[One of the family:]
Please, Father, give us a blessing.

V: May the King of everlasting glory give us a place at His heavenly table.
R: Amen.

After the Noonday Meal

[If there has been reading at table the reader concludes:]
But you, O Lord, have mercy on us.
R: Thanks be to God.
[Then all rise.]

V: Let all your works praise you, O Lord.
R: Let all your saints glorify you. Glory be to the Father, etc.
V: We give you thanks, almighty God, for all your benefits; you who live and reign forever and ever.
R: Amen.
V: Praise the Lord, all you nations; * glorify Him, all you peoples.
R: His love for us is enduring; * He is faithful forever.
V: Glory be to the Father.
R: As it was in the beginning.

V: Lord, have mercy.
R: Christ, have mercy. Lord, have mercy.

Our Father…
[The rest inaudibly until:]
V: And lead us not into temptation.
R: But deliver us from evil.
V: He has been generous to the poor.
R: His goodness is everlasting.
V: I will bless the Lord at all times.
R: His praises are ever on my lips.
V: My soul will exult in the Lord.
R: The meek will hear it with gladness.
V: Praise the Lord with me.
R: Let us heighten our praise of His name.
V: Blessed be the name of the Lord.
R: Both now and forevermore.
V: Lord, be pleased to award everlasting life to all who do good to us in your name.
R: Amen.

V: Let us bless the Lord.
R: Thanks be to God.

V: May the souls of the faithful departed through the mercy of God rest in peace.
R: Amen.

[Then an Our Father may be said silently, after which this conclusion is added:]
V: May the Lord grant us His peace.
R: Amen.

<u>Before the Evening Meal</u>

V: Bless the Lord.
R: Bless the Lord.
V: The poor will eat and receive their fill.
R: Those who seek the Lord will praise Him and will live forever. Glory be to the Father, etc.
V: Lord, have mercy.
R: Christ, have mercy. Lord, have mercy.

Our Father…
[The rest inaudibly until:]
V: And lead us not into temptation.
R: But deliver us from evil.

V: Let us pray. Bless us, ✠ O Lord, and these your gifts which we are about to receive from your bounty; through Christ our Lord.
R: Amen.

[One of the family:]
Please, Father, give us a blessing.

V: May the King of everlasting glory bring us to His heavenly banquet.
R: Amen.

[A reading from Scripture is commenced here, At the end of the reading, the priest says:]
But thou, O Lord have mercy upon us.
R: Thanks be to God.

After the Evening Meal

V: The kind and compassionate Lord has left us a memorial of His wondrous deeds.
R: He has given food to all who live in holy fear.
V: Glory be to the Father, and to the Son, and to the Holy Spirit.
R: As it was in the beginning, is now, and ever shall be, world without end. Amen.

[Then the Priest says:]
V: Blessed is God in His gifts and holy in all His works; ✠ He who lives and reigns forever and ever.
R: Amen.

[Then they alternate in saying Ps. 116 "Praise the Lord, all you nations" and the rest as given above after the noonday meal.]
V: O praise the Lord, all ye nations: praise him, all ye people.
R: For his mercy is confirmed upon us: and the truth of the Lord remains forever.

[If only one meal is taken the prayers are those of the evening meal. The preceding manner of blessing and giving thanks at meals is used at all times of the year, except on the days noted below, when there are some variations.]

On the Feast of Christmas—until supper on the eve of Epiphany exclusive

V: The Word was made flesh, alleluia.
R: And dwelt among us, alleluia. Glory be to the Father, etc., and the rest as above.

[At the end of the meal:]
V: The Lord has manifested Himself to us, alleluia.
R: The Savior has appeared to us, alleluia.
V: Glory be to the Father, etc.,
[and the rest as above.]

On Epiphany—and throughout the following week

[Before and after meals:]
V: The kings of Tarsis and the islands pay tribute, alleluia.
R: The kings of Arabia and Saba bring gifts, alleluia.
[And the rest as above.]

On Maundy Thursday

[Before meals:]
V: For our sake Christ was obedient unto death.

[Then the Our Father is said silently by all; after which the priest makes the sign of the cross over the table without saying anything.]
V: For our sake Christ was obedient unto death.

V: Have mercy on me, O God, according to thy great mercy. And according to the multitude of thy tender mercies blot out my iniquity.
R: Wash me yet more from my iniquity, and cleanse me from my sin.
V: For I know my iniquity, and my sin is always before me.
R: To thee only have I sinned, and have done evil before thee: that thou may be justified in thy words and may overcome when thou art judged.
V: For behold I was conceived in iniquities; and in sins did my mother conceive me.
R: For behold thou hast loved truth: the uncertain and hidden things of thy wisdom thou hast made manifest to me.
V: Thou shall sprinkle me with hyssop, and I shall be cleansed: thou shall wash me, and I shall be made whiter than snow.
R: To my hearing thou shall give joy and gladness: and the bones that have been humbled shall rejoice.
V: Turn away thy face from my sins, and blot out all my iniquities.
R: Create a clean heart in me, O God: and renew a right spirit within my bowels.
V: Cast me not away from thy face; and take not thy holy spirit from me.
R: Restore unto me the joy of thy salvation, and strengthen me with a perfect spirit.
V: I will teach the unjust thy ways: and the wicked shall be converted to thee.
R: Deliver me from blood, O God, thou God of my salvation: and my tongue shall extol thy justice.
V: O Lord, thou wilt open my lips: and my mouth shall declare thy praise.
R: For if thou had desired sacrifice, I would indeed have given it: with burnt offerings thou wilt not be delighted.
V: A sacrifice to God is an afflicted spirit: a contrite and humbled heart, O God, thou wilt not despise.
R: Deal favorably, O Lord, in thy good will with Zion; that the walls of Jerusalem may be built up. Then shall thou accept the sacrifice of justice, oblations and whole burnt offerings: then shall they lay calves upon thy altar.

[The doxology is:]
V: Lord, we beg you to look with favor on this family of yours, for which our Lord Jesus Christ did not hesitate to be handed over to wicked men and to submit to death on the cross.

[Then all say the Our Father silently; the rest is omitted.]

On Good Friday

[At both meals all is said as on Maundy Thursday, except that the versicle is:]
V: For our sake Christ was obedient unto death, even to death on the cross.

On Holy Saturday

[Before the noonday meal:]
V: For our sake Christ was obedient unto death, even to death on the cross.
R: This is why God has exalted Him, and given Him the name above all names.

[The rest as on Maundy Thursday.]

[After the noonday meal: the same versicle and response is said as before the meal:]
V: For our sake Christ was obedient unto death, even to death on the cross.

[Then follow the verses of psalm 50 as above on Maundy Thursday.]
V: Have mercy on me, O God, according to thy great mercy. And according to the multitude of thy tender mercies blot out my iniquity.
R: Wash me yet more from my iniquity, and cleanse me from my sin.
V: For I know my iniquity, and my sin is always before me.
R: To thee only have I sinned, and have done evil before thee: that thou may be justified in thy words and may overcome when thou art judged.
V: For behold I was conceived in iniquities; and in sins did my mother conceive me.
R: For behold thou hast loved truth: the uncertain and hidden things of thy wisdom thou hast made manifest to me.
V: Thou shall sprinkle me with hyssop, and I shall be cleansed: thou shall wash me, and I shall be made whiter than snow.
R: To my hearing thou shall give joy and gladness: and the bones that have been humbled shall rejoice.
V: Turn away thy face from my sins, and blot out all my iniquities.
R: Create a clean heart in me, O God: and renew a right spirit within my bowels.

V: Cast me not away from thy face; and take not thy holy spirit from me.

R: Restore unto me the joy of thy salvation, and strengthen me with a perfect spirit.

V: I will teach the unjust thy ways: and the wicked shall be converted to thee.

R: Deliver me from blood, O God, thou God of my salvation: and my tongue shall extol thy justice.

V: O Lord, thou wilt open my lips: and my mouth shall declare thy praise.

R: For if thou had desired sacrifice, I would indeed have given it: with burnt offerings thou wilt not be delighted.

V: A sacrifice to God is an afflicted spirit: a contrite and humbled heart, O God, thou wilt not despise.

R: Deal favorably, O Lord, in thy good will with Zion; that the walls of Jerusalem may be built up. Then shall thou accept the sacrifice of justice, oblations and whole burnt offerings: then shall they lay calves upon thy altar.

[Lastly the priest says:]
Grant, we beg you, almighty God, that we who devoutly anticipate the resurrection of your Son may partake of the glory of His resurrection.

[Then all say the Our Father silently; the rest is omitted.]

[Before the evening meal:]
V: The chief priests and the Pharisees went and secured the grave.

R: By sealing the slab and setting the guard.

[The rest as on Maundy Thursday.]

[After the evening meal the same versicle and response is said as before the meal; then follow the verses of psalm 116:]
V: Praise the Lord, all you nations; * glorify Him, all you peoples.

R: His love for us is enduring; * He is faithful forever.

[After this the Our Father is said silently; and then the prayer]
"Grant, we beseech thee, Almighty God" as after the noonday meal.

On Easter—and throughout the octave

[Before meals:]
V: This day was made by the Lord, alleluia.

R: We rejoice and are glad, alleluia. Glory be to the Father, etc.,

[and the rest as under Blessing at Meals.]

[After meals:]
[The same versicle and response are said as before the meal, and the rest is the same as Blessing at Meals.]

[On Ascension and throughout the following week]

[Before meals:]
V: God mounts His throne amid shouts of joy, alleluia.
R: The Lord rises on high amid trumpet blast, alleluia. Glory be to the Father, etc.,
[and the rest as Blessing at Meals.]

[After meals:]
V: Christ rises on high, alleluia.
R: He leads the onetime captives to freedom, alleluia. Glory be to the Father, etc.,

[and the rest as Blessing at Meals.]

On Pentecost—starting on the eve and throughout the octave

[Before meals:]
V: The Spirit of the Lord has filled the whole world, alleluia.
R: He sustains all things and knows man's words, alleluia.
V: Glory be to the Father, etc.,
R: As it was in the beginning, etc.,
[and the rest as Blessing at Meals.]

[After meals:]
V: They were all filled with the Holy Spirit, alleluia.
R: They spoke in foreign tongues, alleluia. Glory be to the Father, etc., and the rest as Blessing at Meals.

[On entering the home the priest sprinkles holy water in the living room and on the members of the family, saying:]
Cleanse me with hyssop, Lord, and I shall be clean of sin. Wash me, and I shall be whiter than snow. Have mercy on me, God in your great kindness. Glory be to the Father, and to the Son, and to the Holy Spirit,

R: As it was in the beginning, etc.
V: Our help is in the name of the Lord.
R: Who hath made heaven and earth.
V: O Lord, hear my prayer.
R: And let my cry come unto you.
V: The Lord be with you.
R: And with thy spirit.

Let us pray:
Hear us, holy Lord and Father, almighty everlasting God, and in your goodness send your holy angel from heaven to watch over and protect all who live in this home, to be with them and give them comfort and encouragement; pouring forth your divine blessings and grace, that they may abound in they who live herein, through Christ our Lord.
R: Amen.

Let us pray.
Lord Jesus Christ, as I, in all humility, enter this home, let there enter with me abiding happiness and God's choicest blessings. Let serene joy pervade this home and charity abound here and health never fail. Let no evil spirits approach this place but drive them far away. Let your angels of peace take over and put down all wicked strife, and set a holy watch round about this home. Teach us, O Lord, to recognize the majesty of your holy name. Sanctify our humble visit and bless ✠ what we are about to do; you who are holy, you who are kind, you who abide with the Father and the Holy Spirit forever and ever.
R: Amen.

MARIAN PRAYERS

<u>The Angelus</u>

V: The Angel of the Lord declared unto Mary
R: And she conceived by the Holy Ghost.

V: Hail Mary, full of grace: The Lord is with thee. Blessed art thou among women and blessed is the fruit of thy womb, Jesus.
R: Holy Mary, Mother of God: Pray for us sinners now and at the hour of our death. Amen.

V: Behold, the handmaid of the Lord
R: Be it done unto me according to thy word.

V: Hail Mary…
R: Holy Mary…

V: And the Word was made flesh
R: And dwelt among us.

V: Hail Mary…
R: Holy Mary…

V: Pray for us, O holy Mother of God,
R: That we may be made worthy of the promises of Christ.

V: Let us pray.
All: Pour forth, we beseech the, O Lord, thy grace unto our hearts, that we, to whom the Incarnation of Christ, thy Son, was made known by the message of an Angel, may by His Passion and Cross be brought to the glory of His Resurrection, through the same Christ, our Lord, Amen.

Ave Maria

Ave Maria, gratia plena, Dominus tecum.
Benedicta tu in mulieribus, et benedictus fructus ventris tui, Jesus.
Sancta Maria, Mater Dei, ora pro nobis peccatoribus,
nunc et in hora mortis nostrae. Amen.

Hail Mary

Hail Mary, full of grace, the Lord is with thee!
Blessed art thou among women, and blessed is the fruit of thy womb, Jesus.
Holy Mary, Mother of God, pray for us sinners, now and at the hour of our death. Amen.

The Memorare

Remember, O most gracious Virgin Mary,
that never was it known that anyone who fled to your protection,

implored your help or sought your intercession, was left unaided.
Inspired by this confidence, I fly unto you, O Virgin of virgins, my Mother.
To you I come, before you I stand, sinful and sorrowful.
O Mother of the Word incarnate, despise not my petitions,
but, in your mercy, hear and answer me. Amen.

The Magnificat

My soul magnifies the Lord,
And my spirit rejoices in God my Savior.
For He has regarded the low estate of His handmaiden,
For behold, henceforth all generations shall call me blessed.
For He who is mighty has done great things for me, and holy is His name.
And His mercy is on those who fear Him from generation to generation.
He has shown strength with His arm:
He has scattered the proud in the imagination of their hearts.
He has put down the mighty from their thrones,
and exalted those of low degree.
He has filled the hungry with good things;
and the rich He has sent empty away.
He has helped His servant Israel, in remembrance of His mercy;
As He spoke to our fathers, to Abraham and to His posterity forever.

Glory be to the Father and to the Son and to the Holy Spirit,
As it was in the beginning, is now and ever shall be, world without end. Amen

Regina Caeli (Queen of Heaven, Rejoice!)

Queen of Heaven, rejoice! Alleluia!
For the Son thou wast privileged to bear, Alleluia!
Is risen as He said. Alleluia!
Pray for us to God. Alleluia!
Rejoice and be glad, O Virgin Mary, Alleluia!
For the Lord is truly risen. Alleluia.

Let us pray:
O God, who gave joy to the world through the resurrection of Thy Son our Lord
Jesus Christ, grant, we beseech thee, that through the intercession of the Virgin
Mary, his Mother, we may obtain the joys of everlasting life: Through the same
Christ our Lord. Amen. ✠

Salve Regina (Hail, Holy Queen)

Hail, Holy Queen, mother of mercy, our life, our sweetness and our hope.
To thee do we cry, poor banished children of Eve.
To thee do we send up our sighs, mourning and weeping in this valley of tears.
Turn then, most gracious advocate, thine eyes of mercy toward us,
and after this, our exile, show unto us the blessed fruit of thy womb, Jesus.
O clement, O loving, O sweet Virgin Mary.

V. Pray for us, O holy mother of God:
R. That we may be made worthy of the promises of Christ.

Let us pray:
Almighty and everlasting God, by the cooperation of the Holy Spirit thou hast prepared the body and soul of Mary, glorious Virgin and Mother, to become the worthy habitation of Thy Son; Grant that by her gracious intercession, in whose commemoration we rejoice, we may be delivered from present evils and from everlasting death. Through the same Christ our Lord. Amen.

V. May divine assistance remain with us always.
R. Amen.

Prayer to Mary, the Theotokos

Rejoice Mary, Mother of God, Virgin, full of grace, the Lord is with thee: blessed art thou among women and blessed is the Fruit of thy womb, for thou hast borne the Savior of our souls. Meet it is in truth, to glorify thee, O Birth-giver of God, ever blessed, and all undefiled, the Mother of our God. More honorable than the Cherubim, and beyond compare more glorious than the Seraphim, thou who without stain didst bear God the word, true Birth-giver of God, we magnify thee.

O gracious Mother of the gracious God, O most pure and blessed Mary, the Mother of God, pour the mercy of thy Son and our God upon my impassionate soul, and with thine intercessions set me unto good deeds, that I may pass the rest of my life without blemish and, with thine aid, attain heaven. O Virgin mother of God, the only one who art pure and blessed. O Queen of the Heavenly Host, Defender of our souls: being delivered from evil, as thy servants, O Mother of God, we offer unto thee the hymns of thanks and victory; but as thou hast power invincible, deliver us from all calamity, that we may cry unto thee: Rejoice, O ever-Virgin Bride!

O virgin, spotless, undefiled, unstained, all-chaste and Pure Lady, Bride of God, who by the glorious birth-giving hast united God the Word with Man and linked our fallen nature with Heavenly Things; who art the hope of the hopeless, the helper of the oppressed, the ready protection of those who haste unto thee, and the refuge of Christians; despise me not, who am defiled and sinful, who by my wicked thoughts, words and deeds, have become an unworthy servant, and by my slothfulness have turned into a slave to evil affections. O Mother of the God of Love, have mercy and compassion upon me, a sinner and a prodigal. Accept this prayer which is offered to thee from my impure lips; and putting forward thy maternal influence with thy Son, my Lord and Master, beseech Him to open unto me the loving kindness of His grace; beseech Him to overlook my countless transgressions, to give me true repentance and to make me to be a zealous doer of His commandments. And thou, being gracious and compassionate and tender-hearted, be thou ever present with me in this life as my defender and helper, so that I may turn aside the assault of my enemies, and guide me into salvation; help my poor soul at the hour of my death, and drive far from it all the dark forms of the evil ones. And in the dreadful Judgment Day, deliver me from everlasting punishment, and present me as an inheritor of the ineffable glory of the son, our God.

O may I obtain this, most-holy Lady and Birth-giver of God, through thine intercessions and mediations, by the grace and exceeding great love of thine Only-Begotten son, my Lord and God and Savior, Jesus Christ, to Whom is due, with the eternal Father and the All-Holy, Good and Life-Giving Spirit, all honor and glory and worship, now and ever, and unto ages of ages. Amen.

O most glorious Ever-Virgin Mary, Mother of Christ our God, accept our prayers and present them to thy son and our God, that He may, for thy sake, enlighten and save our souls.

CREEDAL STATEMENTS OF THE CHURCH

The Nicene Creed

We believe in one God,
the Father, the Almighty,
maker of heaven and earth,
of all that is, seen and unseen.

We believe in one Lord, Jesus Christ,
the only Son of God
eternally begotten of the Father,
God from God, Light from Light,
true God from true God,
begotten, not made, one in Being with the Father.
Through Him all things were made.
For us men and for our salvation
He came down from heaven:
by the power of the Holy Spirit
He was born of the Virgin Mary, and became man. *[all bow during these words.]*
For our sake He was crucified under Pontius Pilate;
He suffered, died, and was buried.
On the third day He rose again in fulfillment of the Scriptures;
He ascended into heaven and is seated at the right hand of the Father.
He will come again in glory to judge the living and the dead,
and His kingdom will have no end.
We believe in the Holy Spirit, the Lord, the giver of life,
who proceeds from the Father.
With the Father and the Son He is worshipped and glorified.
He has spoken through the Prophets.
We believe in one holy, catholic and apostolic Church.
We acknowledge one baptism for the forgiveness of sins.
We look to the resurrection of the dead,
and the life of the world to come. Amen.

The Athanasian Creed

Whosoever will be saved, before all things it is necessary that he hold the Catholic faith.

Which faith except everyone do keep whole and undefiled, without doubt he shall perish everlastingly.

And the Catholic faith is this, that we worship one God in Trinity and Trinity in Unity,

Neither confounding the Persons nor dividing the Substance.

For there is one Person of the Father, another of the Son, and another of the Holy Ghost.

But the Godhead of the Father, of the Son, and of the Holy Ghost is one: the glory equal, the majesty coeternal.

Such as the Father is, such is the Son, and such is the Holy Ghost.

The Father uncreated, the Son uncreated and the Holy Ghost uncreated

The Father incomprehensible, the Son incomprehensible, and the Holy Ghost incomprehensible.

The Father eternal, the Son eternal, and the Holy Ghost eternal.

And yet they are not three Eternals, but one Eternal.

As there are not three Uncreated nor three Incomprehensibles, but one Uncreated and one Incomprehensible.

So likewise the Father is almighty, the Son almighty, and the Holy Ghost almighty.

And yet they are not three Almighties, but one Almighty.

So the Father is God, the Son is God, and the Holy Ghost is God.

And yet they are not three Gods, but one God.

So likewise the Father is Lord, the Son Lord, and the Holy Ghost Lord.

And yet not three Lords, but one Lord.

For like as we are compelled by the Christian verity to acknowledge every Person by Himself to be God and Lord,

So are we forbidden by the Catholic religion to say, There be three Gods or three Lords.

The Father is made of none, neither created nor begotten.

The Son is of the Father alone, not made nor created, but begotten.

The Holy Ghost is of the Father and of the Son, neither made nor created nor begotten, but proceeding.

So there is one Father, not three Fathers; one Son, not three Sons; one Holy Ghost, not three Holy Ghosts.

And in this Trinity none is before or after other; none is greater or less than another;

But the whole three Persons are coeternal together and coequal, so that in all things, as is aforesaid, the Unity in Trinity and the Trinity in Unity is to be worshiped.

He, therefore, that will be saved must thus think of the Trinity.

Furthermore, it is necessary to everlasting salvation that he also believe faithfully the incarnation of our Lord Jesus Christ.

For the right faith is that we believe and confess that our Lord Jesus Christ, the Son of God, is God and Man;

God of the Substance of the Father, begotten before the worlds; and Man of the substance of His mother, born in the world;

Perfect God and perfect Man, of a reasonable soul and human flesh subsisting,

Equal to the Father as touching His Godhead and inferior to the Father as touching His manhood;

Who, although He be God and Man, yet He is not two, but one Christ:

One, not by conversion of the Godhead into flesh, but by taking the manhood into God;

One altogether; not by confusion of Substance, but by unity of Person.

For as the reasonable soul and flesh is one man, so God and Man is one Christ;

Who suffered for our salvation; descended into hell; rose again the third day from the dead;

He ascended into heaven; He sitteth on the right hand of the Father, God Almighty; from whence He shall come to judge the quick and the dead.

At whose coming all men shall rise again with their bodies and shall give an account of their own works.

And they that have done good shall go into life everlasting; and they that have done evil, into everlasting fire.

This is the Catholic faith; which except a man believe faithfully and firmly, he cannot be saved.

The Apostles Creed

I believe in God, the Father almighty,
Maker of heaven and earth;
And in Jesus Christ, His only Son, Our Lord.
Who was conceived by the Holy Spirit,
born of the Virgin Mary;
suffered under Pontius Pilate;
was crucified, died, and was buried;
He descended into hell.
On the third day He rose again from the dead.
He ascended into heaven,
and is seated at the right hand of the Father.
From thence He will come again to judge the living and the dead.
I believe in the Holy Ghost,
the Holy Catholic Church,
the Communion of Saints,
the Forgiveness of Sins,
the Resurrection of the body,
and the Life everlasting. Amen.

STATIONS OF THE CROSS

<u>The Fourteen Stations</u>

First Station—Jesus is Condemned to Death
Second Station—Jesus is made to bear His Cross
Third Station—Jesus falls the first time under his Cross
Fourth Station—Jesus meets His Mother
Fifth Station—Simon the Cyrene helps Jesus carry His Cross
Sixth Station—Veronica wipes the face of Jesus
Seventh Station—Jesus falls the second time
Eighth Station—Jesus speaks to the daughters of Jerusalem
Ninth Station—Jesus falls the third time
Tenth Station—Jesus is stripped of His garments
Eleventh Station—Jesus is nailed to the Cross
Twelfth Station—Jesus dies on the Cross
Thirteenth Station—Jesus is taken down from the Cross
Fourteenth Station—Jesus is buried in the sepulchre

[After announcing each station, genuflect and say:]
V. We adore Thee O Christ and we praise Thee,
R. Because by Thy holy Cross Thou hast redeemed the world.

[Then say the Our Father, the Hail Mary, and the Glory be to the Father]

Our Father, who art in Heaven,
Hallowed be Thy name,
Thy kingdom come, Thy will be done,
On earth as it is in heaven.
Give us this day, our daily bread,
And forgive us our trespasses,
As we forgive those who trespass against us.
And lead us not into temptation,
But deliver us from evil. Amen.

Hail Mary, full of grace, the Lord is with thee!
Blessed art thou among women, and blessed is the fruit of thy womb, Jesus.
Holy Mary, Mother of God, pray for us sinners, now and at the hour of our death. Amen.

✠ Glory be to the Father, and to the Son, and to the Holy Spirit, as it was in the beginning, is now, and ever shall be, world without end. Amen.

[After the final station, this prayer, adapted from one composed by Saint Alphonsus, might be said:]
O Jesus Christ, my Lord, with what great love you traveled the painful road, which led to your death-and how often have I, myself, abandoned you. But now I love you with my whole soul, and because I love you, I am sincerely sorry for having offended you. My Jesus, please pardon me, and permit me to accompany you on this journey. You died for love of me, and it is my wish, O my dearest Redeemer, to be willing to die for love of you. O my beloved Jesus, in your love I wish to live, and in your love I wish to die. Amen. ✠

PRAYERS AT MASS

Prayers At The Foot Of The Altar
[The Priest genuflects at the foot of the Altar, and says:]

P. ✠ In the Name of the Father, and of the Son, and of the Holy Ghost.
Server: Amen.

[The server leads the people in praying the responses aloud.]

ANTIPHON

Priest: I will go unto the Altar of God,
Server: Even unto the God of my joy and gladness.

PSALM XLIII

[In Mass for the Dead, and from Passion Sunday till Easter Eve inclusive (unless a Festival occur), the Psalm, Glory be, &c., and repetition of the Antiphon are left out.]

[Joining his hands, he says alternately with the servers]
P. Give sentence with me, O God, and defend my cause against the ungodly people: O deliver me from the deceitful and wicked man.
S. For thou art the God of my strength; why hast thou put me from thee: and why go I so heavily, while the enemy oppresses me?

P. O send out thy light and thy truth that they may lead me: and bring me unto thy holy hill, and to thy dwelling.

S. And that I may go unto the altar of God, even unto the God of my joy and gladness, and upon the harp I will give thanks unto you, O God, my God.

P. Why art thou so heavy, O my soul: and why art thou so disquieted within me?

S. O put thy trust in God; for I will yet give him thanks: who is the help of my countenance, and my God.

[Here at the "Glory be", the priest bows his head to the Cross]

P. Glory be to the Father, and to the Son, and the Holy Ghost.

S. As it was in the beginning, is now, and ever shall be, world without end. Amen.

P. I will go unto the Altar of God.

S. Even unto the God of my joy and gladness.

Versicle: Our help ✠ is in the name of the Lord.

Response: Who hath made heaven and earth.

The Confiteor

[Joining his hands and humbly bowing down the priest prays:]

I confess to Almighty God, to blessed Mary ever a Virgin, to blessed Michael the Archangel, to blessed John the Baptist, to the holy Apostles Peter and Paul, to all the saints, and to you, Brethren, that I have sinned exceedingly in thought, word, and deed,

[Here, the priest strikes his breast three times]

through my fault, through my fault, through my most grievous fault. Therefore, I beseech the Blessed Mary, ever a Virgin, blessed Michael the Archangel, blessed John the Baptist, the holy Apostles Peter and Paul, all the saints, and you, Brethren, to pray to the Lord our God for me.

PRIVATE PRAYERS BEFORE COMMUNION

<u>Prayer of St. Thomas Aquinas</u>—Before Communion

Almighty and everlasting God, behold I approach the sacrament of Thine only-begotten Son, our Lord Jesus Christ: I come as one sick to the physician of life, unclean to the fountain of mercy, blind to the light of eternal brightness, poor and in need of the Lord of heaven and of earth. Therefore, I beseech the abundance of Thine infinite bounty that Thou wouldst vouchsafe to heal my weakness, wash my uncleanness, give light to my blindness, enrich my poverty, and clothe my nakedness, so that I may receive the Bread of Angels, the King of kings, and the Lord of lords with such reverence and humility, such contrition and devotion, such purity and faith, such purpose and intention, as shall aid my soul's salvation.

Grant, I beseech Thee, not only to receive the sacrament of the Body and Blood of the Lord, but also its full reality and power. O most merciful God, grant me so to receive the Body of Thine only-begotten Son, our Lord Jesus Christ, which He took from the Virgin Mary, that I may merit to be incorporated into His mystical Body and to be numbered among His members.

O most loving Father, give unto me to behold for all eternity face to face Thine own beloved Son, whom now upon my pilgrimage I purpose to receive under a veil, who liveth and reigneth with Thee in the unity of the Holy Spirit, God, world without end. Amen.

<u>Prayer of St. Ambrose</u>—Before Communion

O gracious Lord Jesus Christ, to the table of Thy most sweet banquet do I, a sinner, approach with fear and trembling, relying in no wise upon mine own merits, but having confidence in Thy mercy and goodness. My heart and my body are defiled with many sins; my mind and my tongue are not watched over with care. Therefore, O loving God, O fearful Majesty, wretchedly caught in the midst of my extremities do I turn to Thee, the fountain of mercy; to Thee do I hasten to be healed; to Thy protection do I fly. And for Thee, before whom as Judge I cannot stand, as Savior do I yearn.

To Thee, O Lord, do I show my wounds; to Thee do I uncover my shame. I know that my sins are many and great, and for them I am fearful. I hope in Thy mercies, for of them there is no number. Therefore look upon me with Thine eyes of mercy, O Lord Jesus Christ, eternal King, God and man, crucified for man's sake.

Graciously hear me who hope in Thee; have mercy on me who am full of wretchedness and sin, Thou who ceasest never to flow as a fountainhead of mercy.

Hail, Saving Victim, offered up upon the gibbet of the Cross for me and for all men. Hail, noble and Precious Blood, flowing from the wounds of my crucified Lord Jesus Christ and washing away the sins of the whole world. Remember, O Lord, Thy creature, whom Thou hast redeemed with Thy Blood. I repent that I have sinned; I desire to amend what I have done.

Take from me, therefore, O most merciful Father, all my iniquities and my sins, so that cleansed in mind and body I may worthily taste the Holy of Holies. Grant that this holy reception of Thy Body and Blood, which I purpose to take, unworthy though I am, may bring to me pardon for my sins, the perfect cleansing of my faults, the expulsion of evil thoughts, and the renewal of good feelings, the health and efficacy of good works, pleasing unto Thee, and a most strong protection both in soul and body against the wiles of my enemies. Amen.

PRAYERS AFTER LOSS MASS

[After Low Mass, the priest kneeling at the altar steps, prays with the people the following:]

Hail Mary, full of grace, the Lord is with thee. Blessed art thou amongst women, and blessed is the fruit of thy womb, Jesus.
Holy Mary, Mother of God, pray for us sinners, now, and at the hour of our death. Amen.
[Three times]

Hail, holy Queen, Mother of mercy, our life, our sweetness, and our hope! To thee do we cry, poor banished children of Eve, to thee do we send up our sighs, mourning and weeping in this valley of tears. Turn then, most gracious Advocate, thine eyes of mercy towards us, and after this our exile show unto us the blessed fruit of thy womb, Jesus. O clement, O loving, O sweet virgin Mary.

P: Pray for us, O holy Mother of God.
R: That we be made worthy of the promises of Christ.

P: Let us pray. O God, our refuge and our strength, look down with favor upon Thy people who cry to Thee; and through the intercession of the glorious Virgin Mary, Mother of God, of her spouse, blessed Joseph, of Thy holy apostles, Peter and Paul, and all the saints, mercifully and graciously hear the prayers which we pour forth to Thee for the conversion of sinners and for the liberty and exaltation of holy mother Church. Through the same Christ Jesus our Lord. Amen.

St. Michael, the archangel, defend us in battle. Be our protection against the malice and snares of the devil. We humbly beseech God to command him. And do thou, O prince of the heavenly host, by the divine power thrust into hell Satan and the other evil spirits who roam through the world seeking the ruin of souls. Amen.

Invocation After Mass

P: Most Sacred Heart of Jesus.
R: Have mercy on us! *[three times]*

CHAPTER 8

Rites of Initiation For The New Member

I. FORMS FOR CONFERRING THE SACRAMENT OF BAPTISM

FORM FOR BAPTISM IN THE CASE OF EMERGENCY

[When an unbaptized infant or adult is in danger of dying before a Priest can arrive, any person (man, woman, or child) may administer the Sacrament of Baptism. The way to baptize in such a case of necessity is to pour common water on the head or face, and while pouring the water to say the following words:]

I baptize thee in the name of the Father, and of the Son, and of the Holy Spirit. Amen.

[A child in danger of death is not to be baptized by its father or mother if there be any other person to baptize it.]

SHORT FORM FOR CONDITIONAL BAPTISM OF A CHILD

[If there is reasonable doubt as to whether any person was baptized with water, In the Name of the Father, and of the Son, and of the Holy Spirit, (which are essential parts of Baptism), such person may be baptized in the form before appointed in this office; except that, at the immersion or pouring of water, the Minister shall use the following form:]

If thou are not already baptized, *N.*, I baptize thee In the Name of the Father, and of the Son, and of the Holy Spirit. Amen.

SHORT FORM FOR CONDITIONAL BAPTISM OF ADULT CONVERTS

P: We yield to thee our thanks, most merciful Father, that it has pleased thee to regenerate this, thy Servant, with the Holy Spirit, to receive *him* for thine own Child, and to incorporate *him* into thy holy Catholic Church. And humbly we beseech thee to grant, that *he*, being dead to sin, may live unto righteousness, and being buried with Christ in his death, may also be partaker of his resurrection; so that finally, with the residue of thy holy Church, he may be an inheritor of thine everlasting kingdom; through Christ our Lord.
R. Amen.

P: *N.*, what dost thou ask of the Church of God?
Convert: Faith.

P: Dost thou believe in God the Father almighty, Creator of heaven and earth?
C: I do believe.

P: Dost thou believe in Jesus Christ, His only Son, our Lord, who was born into this world and suffered for us?
C: I do believe.

P: And dost thou believe in the Holy Spirit, the holy Catholic Church, the communion of saints, the forgiveness of sins, the resurrection of the body, and life everlasting?
C: I do believe.

P: *N.*, dost thou wish to be baptized if thou art not validly baptized?
C: I do.

P: If thou art not already baptized, *N.*, I baptize thee in the name of the Father, and of the Son, and of the Holy Spirit.

[The ceremonies of anointing with chrism and the bestowal of the white robe and of the lighted candle are not of obligation in this case, but a matter of edification. Because of their mystic signification they ought not to be omitted if they can be carried out. The preceding rite is followed by sacramental confession with conditional absolution.]

STANDARD FORM FOR INFANT BAPTISM

Priest: *N.*, what dost thou ask of the Church of God?
Sponsors: Faith.

Priest What doth Faith bring to thee?
Sponsors: Life everlasting.

Priest If then thou desirest to enter into life, keep the commandments. Thou shalt love the Lord thy God with thy whole heart, with thy whole soul, and with thy whole mind; and thy neighbor as thyself.

[The Priest now breathes three times softly upon the face of the Infant, and says:]

P: Depart from *him (her),* O unclean spirit, and give place to the Holy Spirit, the Comforter.

[He then makes the sign of the Cross upon the forehead and breast of the child, while he says:]

Accept the sign of the Cross both on thy forehead and on thy breast ✠; receive the faith of the heavenly precepts; and be such in thy conduct, that thou mayest be the temple of God.

Let us pray:
Mercifully hear our prayers, we beseech thee, O Lord; and, with thy ever—abiding power, preserve this thy chosen servant *N.*, who has been marked with the sign of the Lord's Cross; that, observing the beginnings of the greatness of thy glory, *he* may, by keeping thy commandments, deserve to arrive at the glory of regeneration. Through Christ our Lord.
R. Amen.

[The Priest then places his hand on the head of the child, and says:]

Let us pray:
O Almighty, everlasting God, Father of our Lord Jesus Christ, deign to look upon this thy servant *N.*, whom thou hast vouchsafed to call to the rudiments of faith; drive out from *him* all blindness of heart; break all the chains of Satan wherewith *he* had been bound: open to him, O Lord, the gate of thy mercy, that, being imbued with the seal of thy wisdom, *he* may be freed from the filth of all evil

desires, and, by the sweet odor of thy precepts, may joyfully serve thee in thy Church, and advance from day to day. Through the same Christ our Lord.
R. Amen.

[The Priest now blesses a little salt, which may be reserved for the same purpose on other occasions, without being reblessed.]

The Blessing of the Salt

I exorcise thee, creature of salt, in the name of God the Father ✠ Almighty, and in the charity of our Lord Jesus ✠ Christ, and in the power of the Holy ✠ Ghost. I exorcise thee by the living God ✠, by the true God ✠, by the holy God ✠; by God ✠ who hath created thee for the preservation of mankind, and hath appointed thee to be consecrated by his servants for the people coming unto the Faith, that, in the name of the holy Trinity, thou mayest be made a salutary sacrament to drive away the enemy. Wherefore, we beseech thee, O Lord our God, that, sanctifying this creature of salt, thou wouldst sanctify it, and blessing thou wouldst bless it, that it may become unto all that receive it a perfect medicine, abiding in their hearts, in the name of the same our Lord Jesus Christ, who will come to judge the living and the dead, and the world by fire.
R. Amen.

[The Priest now puts a small quantity of the blessed salt into the mouth of the child to be baptized, saying:]

P: *N.*, receive the salt of wisdom; may it be to thee a propitiation unto life everlasting.
R. Amen.

Priest: Peace be with thee.
R: And with thy spirit.

Let us pray:
O God of our fathers, O God, the author of all truth, we humbly beseech thee, graciously vouchsafe to look upon this thy servant *N.*, now tasting this first nutriment of salt, and do not suffer *him* to hunger any longer through want of being filled with heavenly food, so that *he* may always be fervent in spirit, rejoicing in hope, always serving thy name. Bring *him*, O Lord, we beseech thee, to the laver

of the new regeneration, that, with thy faithful, *he* may deserve to attain unto the everlasting rewards of thy promises. Through Christ our Lord.
R. Amen.

P: I exorcise thee, unclean spirit, in the name of the Father ✠, and of the Son ✠, and of the Holy ✠ Ghost, that thou go out and depart from this servant of God, *N.* For He who walked on foot upon the sea, and stretched out his right hand to Peter when sinking, commands thee, accursed one. Therefore, accursed devil, acknowledge thy sentence, and give honor to the living and true God; give honor to Jesus Christ His Son, and to the Holy Ghost; and depart from this servant of God, *N.*, because God, even our Lord Jesus Christ, hath deigned to call *him* to his holy grace and blessing, and to the font of baptism.

[With his thumb, the Priest now makes the sign of the Cross on the forehead of the person to be baptized, saying:]

P: And this sign of the holy Cross ✠ which we make upon *his* forehead, do thou accursed devil, never dare to violate. Through the same Christ our Lord.
R. Amen.

[Then the Priest places his hand on the head of the child and says:]

Let us pray:
I entreat thy eternal and most just mercy, O holy Lord, Father Almighty, eternal God, Author of light and truth, in behalf of this thy servant *N.*, that thou wouldst vouchsafe to enlighten *him* with the light of thy wisdom; cleanse *him*, and sanctify *him*; give unto *him* true knowledge, that, being made worthy of the grace of thy baptism, *he* may retain firm hope, right counsel, and holy doctrine. Through Christ our Lord.
R. Amen.

[The Priest now places one end of his stole upon the child that is to be baptized, and leads it into the church, saying:]
P: *N.*, Come into the temple of God, that thou mayest have part with Christ unto life everlasting.
R. Amen.

[When they have entered the church, the Priest, as he proceeds to the font, says in a loud tone, either in Latin or in English according to the circumstances, the Apostles' Creed and the Our Father. The Sponsors may also say them with the Priest:]

P: I believe in one God, the Father Almighty, creator of heaven and earth. And in Jesus Christ, his only son our Lord; who was conceived by the Holy Ghost; born of the Virgin Mary; suffered under Pontius Pilate, was crucified, dead, and buried; he descended into hell; the third day he rose again from the dead; he ascended into heaven, sitteth at the right hand of God the Father Almighty, thence he shall come to judge the living and the dead. I believe in the Holy Ghost; the holy Catholic Church; the communion of saints; the forgiveness of sins; the resurrection of the body; and life everlasting.
R. Amen.

Our Father, who art in heaven, hallowed be thy name; thy kingdom come; thy will be done on earth, as it is in heaven. Give us this day our daily bread, and forgive us our trespasses as we forgive those who trespass against us; and lead us not into temptation, but deliver us from evil.
R. Amen.

[Before entering the Bapistry, the Priest says:]
I exorcise thee, every unclean spirit, in the name of God the Father ✠ Almighty, and in the name of Jesus Christ His Son ✠, our Lord and Judge, and in the name of the Holy ✠ Ghost, that thou depart from this creature of God *N.*, which our Lord hath vouchsafed to call unto his holy temple, that it may be made the temple of the living God, and that the Holy Ghost may dwell therein. Through the same Christ our Lord, who will come to judge the living and the dead, and the world by fire.
R. Amen.

[Then the Priest makes the sign of the Cross, on the right, and afterwards on the left, ear of the child that is to be baptized, and says once only:]
P: Ephphetha, ✠, that is ✠, Be thou opened.

[And then, signing the nostrils, he adds:]
P: For an odor ✠ of sweetness.

[Lastly, in a loud tone of voice, he says:]
P: But do thou depart, O devil; for the judgment of God will come.

[He then, by name, questions the person to be baptized, saying:]

P: *N.*, dost thou renounce Satan?
Sponsors. I do renounce him.

Priest. And all his works?
Sponsors. I do renounce them.

Priest. And all his pomps?
Sponsors. I do renounce them.

[The Priest then dips his thumb into the Oil of the Catechumens, and with it makes the sign of the Cross on the breast, and between the shoulders of the infant, saying:]
P: I anoint thee ✠ with the oil of salvation, in Christ ✠ Jesus our Lord, that thou mayest have life everlasting.
R. Amen

[The Priest now removes the oil from his thumb, and from the breast and back of the child with some cotton wool, and changes the purple stole, which he had hitherto worn, for a white one; and then, by name, questions the child as follows, and the Sponsors answer:]
P: *N.*, Dost thou believe in God the Father Almighty, Creator of heaven and earth?
Sponsors. I do believe.

Priest: Dost thou believe in Jesus Christ, his only Son our Lord, who was born into this world, and who suffered for us?
Sponsors. I do believe.

Priest: Dost thou also believe in the Holy Ghost, the holy Catholic Church, the communion of saints, the forgiveness of sins, the resurrection of the body, and life everlasting?
Sponsors. I do believe.

[Then, mentioning the name, the Priest asks:]
P: *N.*, wilt thou be baptized?
Sponsors. I will.
[Then, while the Godfather, or Godmother, or both of them (if both are present), hold the head of the child over the Font, the Priest takes some of the baptismal water into a small vessel, and from it he three times pours some of the water in the form of a cross upon the head of the child, at the same time clearly and distinctly pronouncing the form once only, saying:]

P: *N.*, I baptize thee in the name of the Father ✠,
[he pours the first time,]
and of the Son ✠,
[he pours the second time,]
and of the Holy Ghost ✠,
[he pours the third time.]

[The Priest then dips his thumb into the sacred Chrism, and anoints the child with the sign of Cross on the top of the head, saying:]
May God Almighty, the Father of our Lord Jesus Christ, who hath regenerated thee by water and the Holy Ghost, and who hath given unto thee the remission of all thy sins [he now anoints the child] himself anoint thee with the Chrism of salvation ✠, in the same Christ Jesus our Lord, unto life eternal.
R. Amen.

Priest. Peace be to thee.
R. And with thy spirit.

[Having removed the Chrism from his thumb and from the head of the child with cotton wool, or some similar substance, the Priest places on the head of the child either a small white garment or some white substitute, saying:]

P: Receive this white garment, and see thou carry it without stain before the judgment seat of our Lord Jesus Christ, that thou mayest have eternal life.
R: Amen.

[He then gives to the child, or to the Sponsors, a lighted taper, saying:]
Receive this burning light, and keep thy baptism, so as to be without blame; keep the commandments of God, that, when the Lord shall come to the nuptials, thou mayest meet Him in the company of all the Saints in the heavenly court, and have eternal life, and live for ever and ever.
R. Amen.

[Then the Priest says:]
P: *N.*, go in peace, and the Lord be with thee.
R. Amen.

II. THE RECEPTION OF ADULT CONVERTS

SHORT FORM FOR RECEPTION OF ADULT CONVERTS

[In case of grave necessity only]

I, *N.N.*, by the grace of God brought to the knowledge of the truth, sincerely and solemnly declare that I firmly believe and profess all that the Holy, Catholic, and Apostolic, Church believes and teaches, and I reject and condemn whatever she rejects and condemns. I ask to be received into the Old Catholic Church, to be guided by her goodly counsel, her Archbishop, Bishops, clergy and laity, to the greater glory of God, and as a coworker in the saving of souls. Amen.

[After this the priest says psalm 50.]

Psalm 50

V: Have mercy on me, O God, according to thy great mercy. And according to the multitude of thy tender mercies blot out my iniquity.
R: Wash me yet more from my iniquity, and cleanse me from my sin.
V: For I know my iniquity, and my sin is always before me.
R: To thee only have I sinned, and have done evil before thee: that thou may be justified in thy words and may overcome when thou art judged.
V: For behold I was conceived in iniquities; and in sins did my mother conceive me.
R: For behold thou hast loved truth: the uncertain and hidden things of thy wisdom thou hast made manifest to me.
V: Thou shall sprinkle me with hyssop, and I shall be cleansed: thou shall wash me, and I shall be made whiter than snow.
R: To my hearing thou shall give joy and gladness: and the bones that have been humbled shall rejoice.
V: Turn away thy face from my sins, and blot out all my iniquities.
R: Create a clean heart in me, O God: and renew a right spirit within my bowels.
V: Cast me not away from thy face; and take not thy holy spirit from me.
R: Restore unto me the joy of thy salvation, and strengthen me with a perfect spirit.
V: I will teach the unjust thy ways: and the wicked shall be converted to thee.
R: Deliver me from blood, O God, thou God of my salvation: and my tongue shall extol thy justice.
V: O Lord, thou wilt open my lips: and my mouth shall declare thy praise.

R: For if thou had desired sacrifice, I would indeed have given it: with burnt offerings thou wilt not be delighted.

V: A sacrifice to God is an afflicted spirit: a contrite and humbled heart, O God, thou wilt not despise.

R: Deal favorably, O Lord, in thy good will with Zion; that the walls of Jerusalem may be built up. Then shall thou accept the sacrifice of justice, oblations and whole burnt offerings: then shall they lay calves upon thy altar.

STANDARD FORM FOR RECEPTION OF ADULT CONVERTS

[In the case of a convert from heresy, inquiry should first be made about the validity of his former baptism. If after careful investigation it is discovered that the party was never baptized or that the supposed baptism was invalid, he must now be baptized unconditionally. However, if the investigation leaves doubt about the validity of baptism, then it is to be repeated conditionally, using the ceremony for baptism of adults. Thirdly, if ascertained that the former baptism was valid, reception into the Church will consist only in abjuration of former errors and profession of faith. The reception of a convert will, consequently, take place in one of the following three ways:]

[If baptism is conferred unconditionally, neither abjuration of former errors nor absolution from censures will follow, since the sacrament of rebirth cleanses from all sin and fault.]

[If baptism is to be repeated conditionally, the order will be: (1) profession of faith; (2) baptism with conditional form; (3) sacramental confession with conditional absolution.]

[If the former baptism has been judged valid, there will be only abjuration or profession of faith, followed by absolution from censures. But if the convert greatly desires that the full rites of baptism lacking hitherto be supplied on this occasion, the priest is certainly free to comply with his devout request. In this case he ought to use the form of baptism for adults, making those changes necessitated by the fact that baptism has already been validly conferred.]

[The convert kneels before him, and with his right hand on the book of Gospels makes the profession of faith as given below. If the person is unable to read, the priest reads it for him slowly, so that he can understand and repeat the words after him.]

Profession of Faith

I, *N.N.,*.... years of age, born outside the Old Catholic Church, have held and believed errors contrary to her teaching. Now, enlightened by divine grace, I kneel before you, Reverend Father..., having before my eyes and touching with my hand the holy Gospels. And with firm faith I believe and profess each and all the articles contained in the Apostles' Creed, that is: I believe in God, the Father almighty, Creator of heaven and earth; and in Jesus Christ, His only Son, our Lord, who was conceived by the Holy Spirit, born of the Virgin Mary, suffered under Pontius Pilate, was crucified, died, and was buried; He descended into hell, the third day He arose again from the dead; He ascended into heaven, and sits at the right hand of God, the Father almighty, from there He shall come to judge the living and the dead. I believe in the Holy Spirit; the holy Catholic Church; the communion of saints; the forgiveness of sins; the resurrection of the body, and life everlasting. Amen.

I firmly admit and embrace the apostolic and ecclesiastical traditions and all the other constitutions and ordinances of the Church.

I admit the Sacred Scriptures in the sense which has been held and is still held by holy Mother Church, whose duty it is to judge the true sense and interpretation of Sacred Scripture, and I shall never accept or interpret them in a sense contrary to the unanimous consent of the fathers, Sacred Apostolic Tradition and the seven Oecumenical Councils of all Christendom.

I profess that the sacraments of the New Law are truly and precisely seven in number, instituted for the salvation of mankind, though all are not necessary for each individual: baptism, confirmation, holy Eucharist, penance, anointing of the sick, holy orders, and matrimony. I profess that all confer grace, and that baptism, confirmation, and holy orders cannot be repeated. I also accept and admit the ritual of the Old Catholic Church in the solemn administration of all the aforementioned sacraments.

I accept and hold in each and every part all that has been defined and declared by the Old Catholic Church concerning original sin and justification. I profess that in the Mass there is offered to God a true, real, and propitiatory sacrifice for the living and the dead; that in the holy sacrament of the Eucharist the body and blood together with the soul and divinity of our Lord Jesus Christ is really, truly, and substantially present, and that there takes place in the Mass what the Church calls transubstantiation, which is the change of all the substance of bread into the body of Christ and of all substance of wine into His blood. I confess also that in receiving under either of these species one receives Jesus Christ whole and entire.

I firmly hold that Purgatory exists and that the souls detained there can be helped by the prayers of the faithful.

Likewise I hold that the saints, who reign with Jesus Christ, should be venerated and invoked, that they offer prayers to God for us, and that their relics are to be venerated. I firmly profess that the images of Jesus Christ and of the Mother of God, ever a Virgin, as well as of all the saints should be given due honor and veneration, as a sign of respect due to those whom the images represent. I also affirm that Jesus Christ left to the Church the faculty to grant indulgences, and that their use is most salutary to the Christian people. I recognize the Holy, Catholic, and Apostolic Church as the mother and teacher of all, and I promise and swear true obedience to the Archbishop-Metropolitan of the Church.

Moreover, without hesitation I accept and profess all that has been handed down, defined, and declared by the sacred canons and by the Oecumenical Councils of the Church. At the same time I condemn and reprove all that the Church has condemned and reproved. This same Catholic faith, outside of which none can be saved, I now freely profess and I truly adhere to it. With the help of God, I promise and swear to maintain and profess this faith entirely, inviolately, and with firm constancy until the last breath of life. And I shall strive, as far as possible, that this same faith shall be held, taught, and publicly professed by all who depend on me and over whom I shall have charge. So help me God and these holy Gospels.

[The convert remains kneeling, and the priest, still seated, says psalm 129]

Psalm 129

Out of the depths I have cried to thee, O Lord: Lord, hear my voice. Let thy ears be attentive to the voice of my supplication. If thou, O Lord, wilt mark iniquities: Lord, who shall stand it. For with thee there is merciful forgiveness: and by reason of thy law, I have waited for thee, O Lord. My soul hath relied on his word: my soul hath hoped in the Lord. From the morning watch even until night, let Israel hope in the Lord. Because with the Lord there is mercy: and with him plentiful redemption. And he shall redeem Israel from all his iniquities.

[He concludes with "Glory be to the Father."]
P: Glory be to the Father, and to the Son and to the Holy Spirit,
R: As it was in the beginning, is now, and ever shall be, world without end.
P: Amen.
[After this the priest stands and says:]

Lord, have mercy. Christ, have mercy. Lord, have mercy.
Our Father...
[the rest inaudibly until:]
V: And lead us not into temptation.
R: But deliver us from evil.
V: Save your servant.
R: Who trusts in you, my God.

V: O Lord, hear my prayer.
R: And let my cry come unto you.
V: The Lord be with you.
R: And with thy spirit.

Let us pray.
God, whose nature is ever merciful and forgiving, accept our prayer that this servant of yours, bound by the fetters of sin, may be pardoned by your loving kindness: through Christ our Lord.
R: Amen.

III. FORM FOR RELEASE FROM PENALTY OF EXCOMMUNICATION

[The priest again sits down, and facing the convert pronounces the absolution from excommunication or inhibition, inserting the word perhaps if in doubt as to whether it has been incurred:]

Prayer of Repentance

O Lord! teach us all Your commandments. By Your grace help us to live according to them. O God set guards to the open doors of our senses that the treasury of Your grace may not be detained from us.

O holy God, Your Holiness is adored by all saints. O Lord, cleanse our thoughts and make us worthy to glorify Your name like the seraphim who proclaim and glorify Your Holiness.

Release

By the authority of the Archbishop-Metropolitan which I exercise here, I release you from the bond of excommunication which you have *(perhaps)* incurred; and I restore you to communion and union with the faithful, as well as to the holy sacraments of the Old Catholic Church; in the name of the Father, and of the Son, ✠ and of the Holy Spirit. Amen.

[Lastly the priest imposes some salutary penance, such as prayers, visits to a church, or the equivalent.]

IV. INSTRUCTIONS AND DEVOTIONS FOR CONFESSION

Prayer Before Examination of Conscience

O most merciful God, I most humbly thank you for all your mercies unto me; and, particularly at this time, for your forbearance and long suffering with me, notwithstanding my many and grievous sins. It is of your great mercy that I have not fallen into greater and more grievous sins than those I have committed, and that I have not been cut off and cast down into hell. O my God, although I have been so ungrateful to you in times past, yet now I beseech you to accept me, returning to you with an earnest desire to repent, and devote myself to you, my Lord and my God, and to praise your holy Name for ever. Receive my confession, and spare me, O most gracious Lord Jesus Christ, whom I, an unworthy sinner, am not worthy to name, because I have so often offended you. Do not rebuke me in you anger, nor cast me away from your face, O good Jesus, who have said that you willest not the death of a sinner, but rather that he should be converted and live. Receive me, I beseech you, returning to you with a penitent and contrite heart. Spare me, O most kind Jesus, who did die upon the Cross, that you might save sinners. Have mercy upon me, O must gracious Lord, and despise not the humble and contrite heart of your servant. Grant me, I beseech you, perfect contrition for my sins.

Send forth your light into my soul, and discover to me all those sins which I ought to confess at this time. Assist me by your grace, that I may be able to declare them to the priest, your vicar, fully, humbly, and with a contrite heart, and so obtain perfect remission of them all through thine infinite goodness. Amen.

O most gracious Virgin Mary, Mother of Jesus Christ my Redeemer, intercede for me to him. Obtain for me the full remission of my sins, and perfect amendment of life, to the salvation of my soul, and the glory of his name. Amen.

I implore the same grace through you, O my Angel guardian; through you, my holy Patrons, *N* and *N*.; through you, O holy Peter and holy Magdalene; and through all the Saints of God. Intercede for me a sinner, repenting of my sins, and resolving to confess and amend them. Amen.

A Prayer of Repentance

Almighty and Eternal God, You do not deny Your mercy to the sinner who calls upon You. Through Your compassion and mercy, spare me from punishment and the rod of wrath. To praise You for Your mercy, grant me joyful months and prosperous years. By the glorious sign of Your cross guard me from every evil.

Lord, may I never be silent in praising you, and never cease glorifying You. Lord, do not judge me according to Your righteousness. I confess that I am a sinner, and beg You to have mercy on me. If You judge me according to my sins; I cannot hope to gain eternal life and cannot plead before You, and shall inherit fiery-hell. Therefore, according to Your mercy, pardon and forgive my sins.

Lord, when You judge me, let my sins not conceal me. When the righteous are clothed in glory, may I not be naked. I confess that I have fallen in sin, extend Your hand unto me that I may stand again. O compassionate One, who opens the door to all those who repent, have mercy on me as You forgave the thief on Cross at Your side.

Examination of Conscience

[An Examination of Conscience for those who confess their sins regularly and frequently, according to the threefold duty we owe to God, to our neighbor, and to ourselves.]

I. In Relation to God.

1. Have I omitted morning or evening prayer, or neglected to make my daily examination of conscience? Have I prayed negligently, and with willful distractions?

2. Have I been negligent in the discharge of any of my religious duties? Have I taken care that those under my charge have not wanted the instructions necessary for their condition, nor time for prayer, or to prepare for the sacraments?

3. Have I spoken irreverently of God and holy things? Have I taken his name in vain, or told untruths?

4. Have I omitted my duty through human respect or interest?

5. Have I been zealous for God' s honor, for justice, for virtue, and truth, and reproved such as act otherwise?

6. Have I resigned my will to God in troubles, necessities, sickness?

7. Have I carefully avoided all kinds of impurity, and faithfully resisted thoughts of infidelity, distrust, presumptions?

II. In Relation to Your Neighbor.

1. Have I disobeyed my superiors, murmured against their commands, or spoken of them contemptuously?

2. Have I been troubled, peevish, or impatient, when told of my faults, and not corrected them? Have I scorned the good advice of others, or censured their proceedings?

3. Have I offended anyone by injurious words or actions, or given way to hatred, jealousy, or revenge?

4. Or lessened their reputation by any sort of detraction, or in any matter of importance?

5. Have I formed rash judgments, or spread any report, true or false, that exposed my neighbor to contempt, or made him undervalued?

6. Have I, by carrying stories backward and forward, or otherwise, created discord and misunderstanding between neighbors?

7. Have I been forward or peevish towards anyone in my carriage, speech, or conversation?

8. Or taken pleasure to vex, mortify, or provoke them?

9. Have I mocked or reproached them for their corporal or spiritual imperfections?

10. Have I been excessive in reprehending those under my care, or been wanting in giving them just reproof?

11. Have I borne with their oversights and imperfections, and given them good counsel?

12. Have I been solicitous for such as are under my charge; and provided for their souls and bodies?

III. In Relation to Yourself.

1. Have I been obstinate in following my own will, or in defending my own opinion of things either indifferent, dangerous, or scandalous?

2. Have I taken pleasure in hearing myself praised, or acted from motives of vanity or human respect?

3. Have I indulged myself in too much ease and sloth, or any ways yielded to sensuality or impurity?

4. Has my conversation been edifying and moderate; or have I been forward, proud, or troublesome to others?

5. Have I spent over much time in recreation or useless employments, and thereby omitted or put off my devotions to unseasonable times?

6. Have I yielded to intemperance, rage, impatience, or jealousy?

Considerations to excite in our mind true contrition for our sins:

1. Place before yourself, as distinctly as you can, all the sins, which you are going to confess.

2. Consider who God is, and how good and gracious he has been to you, whom you have so often and so much offended by these sins. He made you—he made you for himself, to know, to love, and serve him, and to be happy with him forever. He redeemed you by his blood. He has borne with you and waited for you so long. He it is who has called you and moved you to repentance. Why have you thus sinned against him? Why have you been thus ungrateful? What more could he have done for you? Oh, be ashamed, and mourn, and hate yourself, because you have sinned against your Maker and your Redeemer, whom you ought to have loved above all things.

3. Consider the full consequences of even one mortal sin. By it you lose the grace of God. You destroy peace of conscience; you forfeit the felicity of heaven, for which you were created and redeemed; and you prepare for yourself eternal punishment. If we grieve for the loss of temporal and earthly things, how much more for those which are eternal and heavenly? If we grieve at the departure of a soul from the body, how much more at the death of a soul, which is the loss of the presence of the grace of God? "What shall it profit a man if he gain the whole world, and lose his own soul?" And "who can dwell with everlasting burnings?" Who can endure to be cast out from the presence of God forever?

4. Consider how great has been and is the love of God for you, if only from this, that he has so long waited for you, and spared you, when he might have so justly cast you into hell. Behold him fastened to the Cross for love of you! Behold him pouring forth his Precious Blood to be a fountain to cleanse you from your sins! Hear him saying, "I thirst," as it were with an ardent desire for your salvation. Behold him stretching out his arms to embrace you, and expecting you, until you should come to yourself and turn unto him, and throw yourself before him, and say, "Father, I have sinned against heaven and before you, and am no more worthy to be called your son." Let the consideration of these things touch your heart with love for him who has so loved you, and love will beget true contrition, most acceptable to God.

An Act of Contrition—I

O Lord Jesus Christ, lover of our souls, who, for the great love wherewith you have loved us, would not the death of a sinner, but rather that he should be converted and live; I grieve from the bottom of my heart that I have offended you, my most loving Father and Redeemer, unto whom all sin is infinitely displeasing; who has so loved me that you did shed your Blood for me, and endure the bitter torments of a most cruel death. O my God! O infinite Goodness! Would that I had never offended you. Pardon me, O Lord Jesus, most humbly imploring your mercy. Have pity upon a sinner for whom your Blood pleads before the face of the Father.

O most merciful and forgiving Lord, for the love of you I forgive all who have ever offended me. I firmly resolve to forsake and flee from all sins, and to avoid the occasions of them; and to confess, in bitterness of spirit, all those sins which I have committed against your divine goodness, and to love you, O my God, for your own sake, above all things for ever. Grant me grace to do so, O most gracious Lord Jesus.

Act of Contrition—II

O my God, I am heartily sorry for having offended thee and I detest all my sins, because I dread the loss of heaven and the pains of hell, but most of all because they offend thee, my God, who are all good and deserving of all my love. I firmly resolve, with the help of thy grace, to confess my sins, to do penance, and to amend my life.

Aspirations Before or After Confession

My Lord and my God, I sincerely acknowledge myself a vile and wretched sinner, unworthy to appear in your presence; but do your have mercy on me, and save me.

Most loving Father, I have sinned against heaven and before you, and am unworthy to be called your child; make me as one of your servants, and may I for the future ever be faithful to you. It truly grieves me, O my God, to have sinned, and so many times transgressed your law; but wash me now from my iniquity, and cleanse me from my sin. O loving Father, assist me by your grace, that I may bring forth worthy fruits of penance.

Oh, that, I had never transgressed your commandments! Oh, that I had never sinned! Happy those souls who have preserved their innocence: oh, that I had been so happy! But now I am resolved, with the help of your grace, to be more watchful over myself, to amend my failings, and fulfill your law. Look down on me with the eyes of mercy, O God, and blot out my sins. Forgive me what is past, and through thine infinite goodness, secure me, by your grace, against all my wonted failings for the time to come. your did come, O dear Redeemer, not to call the just, but sinners, to repentance; behold a miserable sinner here before thee: oh, draw me powerfully to Thyself.

Have mercy on me, O God, according to your great mercy; and according to the multitude of your tender mercies, blot out my iniquities. Sprinkle me with your Precious Blood, and I shall be whiter than snow. How great is your goodness, O Lord, in having so long spared such a worthless servant, and waited with so much patience for his amendment! What return shall I make for thine infinite mercies! Oh, let this mercy be added to the rest, that I may never more offend thee: this single favor I earnestly beg of you, O Lord, that I may for the future renounce my own will to follow thine. Help me, O Lord my God, and have compassion on my sinful soul. Amen.

A Thanksgiving After Confession

O Almighty and most merciful God, who, according to the multitude of your tender mercies, have vouchsafed once more to receive your prodigal child, after so many times going astray from you, and to admit me to this sacrament of reconciliation; I give you thanks with all the powers of my soul for this and all other mercies, graces, and blessings, bestowed on me; and prostrating myself at your sacred feet, I offer myself to be henceforth forever thine. Oh! Let nothing either in life or death ever separate me from you. I renounce with my whole soul all my treasons against you, and all the abominations and sins of my past life. I renew my promises made in baptism, and from this moment I dedicate myself eternally to your love and service. Oh! Grant that for the time to come I may abhor sin more than death itself, and avoid all such occasions and company as have unhappily brought me to it. This I resolve to do, by the aid of your divine grace, without which I can do nothing. I beg your blessing upon these my resolutions, that they may not be ineffectual, like so many others I have formerly made, for O Lord, without you I am nothing but misery and sin. Supply also, by your mercy, whatever defects have been in this my confession, and give me grace to be now and always a true penitent. Through the same Jesus Christ your Son. Amen.

Form of Absolution

[The Priest, wearing surplice and violet stole, after imposing the penance to be performed by the penitent shall say, with his right hand uplifted:]

May Almighty God have mercy upon you and forgive you your sins and bring you to everlasting life.
R: Amen.

Absolution

Our Lord Jesus Christ, who has left power to his Church to absolve all sinners who truly repent and believe in him, of his great mercy forgive you your offences: And by his authority committed to me, I absolve you from your sins, in the name of the Father ✠, and of the Son, and of the Holy Spirit.
R: Amen.

[The Priest may add:]
Go in peace, and pray for me.

CHAPTER 9

The Liturgy of the Old Catholic Church

The normative liturgy of the Old Catholic Church of the United States is the 1909 *Old Catholic Missal and Ritual*, also known as the "Gul-Mathew Mass". This is a modified English translation of the Tridentine Latin Mass developed for the Old Catholic Church of England under Archbishop Arnold Harris Mathew. The Ordinary of the Mass is included herein for instructional purposes. A special thanks to Bishop Elijah, of San Francisco and Dry Bones Press for reprinting the Missal in its entirety, and keeping it available.

MASS OF THE CATECHUMENS

[The Priest genuflects at the foot of the Altar, and says:]　　　　　　**KNEEL**
✠ In the Name of the Father, and of the Son, and of the Holy Ghost. Amen.

Antiphon

Priest: I will go unto the Altar of God,
Server: Even unto the God of my joy and gladness.

Psalm XLIII

[In Mass for the Dead, and from Passion Sunday till Easter Eve inclusive (unless a Festival occur), the Psalm, Glory be, &c., and repetition of the Antiphon are left out.]

[Joining his hands, he says alternately with the servers]
Priest: Give sentence with me, O God, and defend my cause against the ungodly people: O deliver me from the deceitful and wicked man.
Response: For thou art the God of my strength; why hast thou has put me from thee: and why go I so heavily, while the enemy oppresseth me?

Priest: O send out thy light and thy truth that they may lead me: and bring me unto thy holy hill, and to thy dwelling.
Response: And that I may go unto the altar of God, even unto the God of my joy and gladness, and upon the harp I will give thanks unto thee, O God, my God.

Priest: Why art thou so heavy, O my soul: and why art thou so disquieted within me?
Response: O put thy trust in God; for I will yet give him thanks: who is the help of my countenance, and my God.

Priest: Glory be to the Father, and to the Son, and the Holy Ghost.
Response: As it was in the beginning, is now, and ever shall be, world without end. Amen.

Priest: I will go unto the Altar of God.
Response: Even unto the God of my joy and gladness.

Priest: Our help ✠ is in the name of the Lord.
Response: Who made heaven and earth.

[Joining his hands and humbly bowing down the priest says the Confiteor.]
Priest: I confess to Almighty God, to blessed Mary ever a Virgin, to blessed Michael the Archangel, to blessed John the Baptist, to the holy Apostles Peter and Paul, to all the saints, and to you, Brethren, that I have sinned exceedingly in thought, word, and deed, through my fault, through my fault, through my most grievous fault. Therefore, I beseech the Blessed Mary, ever a Virgin, blessed Michael the Archangel, blessed John the Baptist, the holy Apostles Peter and Paul, all the saints, and you, Brethren, to pray to the Lord our God for me.
Response: May Almighty God be merciful to thee, and, forgiving thy sins, bring thee to everlasting life.
P. Amen.

[The server now says the Confiteor]
Servers: I confess to Almighty God, to blessed Mary ever a Virgin, to blessed Michael the Archangel, to blessed John the Baptist, to the holy Apostles Peter and Paul, to all the saints, and to you, Father, that I have sinned exceedingly in thought, word, and deed, through my fault, through my fault, through my most grievous fault. Therefore, I beseech blessed Mary, ever a Virgin, blessed

Michael the Archangel, blessed John the Baptist, the holy Apostles Peter and Paul, all the saints, and you, Father, to pray to the Lord our God for me.

[The priest joins his hands and then gives the absolution, saying,]
Priest: May Almighty God be merciful unto you, and, forgiving your sins, bring you to life everlasting.
Response: Amen.

Priest: May the Almighty and merciful Lord grant us pardon, ✠ absolution, and remission of our sins.
Response: Amen.

[He bows his head, and continues]
Priest: Thou, O Lord, being turned towards us, wilt enliven us.
Response: And thy people will rejoice in thee.
Priest: Show us, O Lord, thy mercy.
Response: And grant us thy salvation.
Priest: O Lord, hear my prayer
Response: And let my cry come unto thee.

Priest: The Lord be with you.
Response: And with thy spirit.

[First extending, and then joining his hands, the priest says audibly]
Priest: Let us pray.

STAND

[When the Priest goes up to the altar, he says:]
Priest: Take away from us our iniquities, we beseech thee, O Lord, that we may be worthy to enter with pure minds into thy Holy of Holies. Through Christ our Lord. Amen.

[When be bows before the altar, he says:]
Priest: We beseech thee, O Lord, by the merits of *[here he kisses the altar]* all the saints, that thou wouldst vouchsafe to forgive me all my sins. Amen.

[Here, at High Masses, the Priest, blesses the incense, saying:]
Priest: Mayest thou be blest in Him, in whose honor thou shalt be burnt. Amen.

[And receiving the thurible from the deacon, he incenses the altar. He then moves to the Epistle side of the tabernacle (to the right) makes the Sign of the Cross ✠, and reads the Introit, which, being variable, must be sought for in its proper place.]

Introit

Blessed be the Holy Trinity, and undivided Unity; we will praise Him because He hath shown his mercy toward us.

Ps. viii. O Lord, our God, how wonderful is thy name; even to the utmost boundaries of the earth.

V. Glory be to the Father and to the Son and to the Holy Ghost, As it was in the beginning, is now, and ever shall be, world without end. Amen.

Blessed be the Holy Trinity, and undivided Unity; we will praise Him because He hath shown his mercy toward us.

Kyrie

[The priest returns to the middle of the Altar. Joining his hands he says alternately with the server]

P. Lord, have mercy on us.	Kyrie Eleison.
C. Lord, have mercy on us.	**Kyrie Eleison.**
P. Lord, have mercy on us.	Kyrie Eleison.
C. Christ, have mercy on us.	**Christe Eleison.**
P. Christ, have mercy on us.	Christe Eleison.
C. Christ, have mercy on us.	**Christe Eleison.**
P. Lord, have mercy on us.	Kyrie Eleison.
C. Lord, have mercy on us.	**Kyrie Eleison.**
P. Lord, have mercy on us.	Kyrie Eleison.

[When the GLORIA is said, the priest stands at the middle of the Altar, extends and then joins his hands, makes a slight bow and says,]

STAND

Gloria in Excelsis

Priest: Glory be to God on high, and on earth peace to men of good will. We praise thee, we bless thee, we adore thee, we glorify thee. We give thee thanks for thy great glory. O Lord God, heavenly King, God the Father Almighty. O Lord

Jesus Christ, the only begotten Son. O Lord God, Lamb of God, Son of the Father, who takest away the sins of the world, have mercy on us. Who takest away the sins of the world, have mercy on us. Who sittest at the right hand of the Father, have mercy on us. For thou only art holy, thou only art Lord, thou only art most high, O Jesus Christ, together with the Holy Ghost, in the glory of God the Father. Amen.

[The priest kisses the altar and, turning towards the people, says:]
Priest: The Lord be with you.   Dominus vobiscum.
Response: And with thy spirit.   Et cum spiritu tuo.

[He returns to the middle of the Altar, and turning toward the people says;]
Priest: Let us Pray   Oremus.

The Collect

[Then is said the Collect. At the end of the Collect, the Server responds:]
Response: Amen.

The Epistle   SIT

[Then is said the Epistle (on the right of Altar) which is sought in its proper place. At the end of the Epistle the Server responds:]
Response: Thanks be to God.

The Gradual

[Then is said the Gradual, which is sought in its proper place.]

Munda cor Meum

Priest: Cleanse my heart and lips, O Almighty God, who didst cleanse the lips of the prophet Isaias with a burning coal, and vouchsafe, through thy gracious mercy, so to purify me, that I may worthily attend to thy holy Gospel. Through Christ our Lord. Amen.

Priest: May the Lord be in my heart, and on my lips, that I may worthily, and in a becoming manner, attend to his holy Gospel. Amen.

The Gospel

STAND

[Turning toward the book at the Gospel side (left) of the Altar, he says:]
Priest: The Lord be with you.
Response: And with thy spirit.

Priest: The continuation (or: beginning) of the holy Gospel according to, &c.
Response: Glory be to thee, O Lord.

[Seek the Gospel in its proper place, at the end of which is answered:]
Response: Praise be to thee, O Christ.

[Then the Priest kisses the book and says, in a low voice:]
Priest: May our sins be blotted out by the words of the Gospel.

SIT

The Sermon

The Nicene Creed

STAND

I believe in one God, **the Father Almighty, maker of heaven and earth, and of all things visible and invisible. And in one Lord Jesus Christ, the only begotten Son of God, and born of the Father before all ages; God of God, light of light, true God of true God; begotten, not made; consubstantial to the Father, by whom all things were made. Who for us men, and for our salvation, came down from heaven;**

GENUFLECT

and became incarnate of the Holy Ghost, of the Virgin Mary; *AND WAS MADE MA*N.

He was crucified also for us, suffered under Pontius Pilate, and was buried. And the third day he rose again according to the Scriptures; and ascended into heaven, sitteth at the right hand of the Father; and He is to come again with glory, to judge both the living and the dead; of whose kingdom there shall be no end.

And in the Holy Ghost, the Lord and giver of life, who proceedeth from the Father; who together with the Father and the Son, is adored and glorified; who spoke by the Prophets. And in one holy Catholic and Apostolic Church. I confess one Baptism for the remission of sins. And I expect the resurrection of the dead, and the life ✠ of the world to come. Amen.

[He kisses the Altar, and turning to the people says,]　　　　　　　　**STAND**

Priest: The Lord be with you.　　　Dominus vobiscum.
Response: And with thy spirit.　　**Et cum spiritu tuo.**
Priest: Let us pray.　　　　　　　Oremus.

MASS OF THE FAITHFUL

Offertory

　　　　　　　　　　　　　　　　　　　　　　　　　　　　SIT

[Here follows the Offertory, which may be found in its proper place.]

Oblation of the Host

[The bells are rung once]

[The priest takes the paten with host, and offers up the host, saying,]
Priest: Accept, O holy Father, Almighty and eternal God, this unspotted Host, which I thy unworthy servant offer unto thee, my living and true God, for my innumerable sins, offences, and negligences, and for all here present; as also for all faithful Christians, both living and dead; that it may avail both me and them unto life everlasting. Amen.

[Making the Sign of the Cross with the paten, he places the host upon the corporal. Going to the right side of the altar, the Priest puts the Wine and Water into the Chalice, saying:]
Priest: O God, ✠ who, in creating human nature, hast wonderfully dignified it, and still more wonderfully reformed it; grant that by the mystery of this Water and Wine, we may be made partakers of his divine nature, who vouchsafed to

become partaker of our nature, namely, Jesus Christ our Lord, thy Son, who with thee, in the unity of, &c. Amen.

Oblation of the Chalice

[Returning to the middle of the Altar, the priest takes the chalice and offers it to God.]
Priest: We offer unto thee, O Lord, the Chalice of salvation, beseeching thy clemency that it may ascend before thy divine Majesty, as a sweet odor, for our salvation, and for that of the whole world. Amen.

[He makes the "Sign of the Cross" ✠ with the chalice, and placing it on the corporal, he covers it with the pall. When the Priest bows before the altar.]
Priest: Accept us, O Lord, in the spirit of humility, and contrition of heart; and grant that the sacrifice we offer this day in thy sight, may be pleasing to thee, O Lord God.

[Raising his eyes and extending his hands, then he blesses the Bread and Wine.]
Priest: Come, O Almighty and eternal God, the sanctifier, and bless ✠ this sacrifice, prepared for the glory of thy holy name.

[Here, in solemn Masses, he blesses the Incense, saying:]
Priest: May the Lord, by the Intercession of blessed Michael the archangel standing at the right hand of the Altar of Incense, and of all his elect vouchsafe to bless ✠ this incense, and receive it as an odor of sweetness. Through. Amen.

[At the incensing of the Bread and Wine, he says:]
Priest: May this incense which thou hast blest, O Lord, ascend to thee, and may thy mercy descend upon us.

[At the incensing the altar, he says Ps. 140.]
Priest: Let my prayer, O Lord, be directed as incense in thy sight: the lifting up of my hands as an evening sacrifice. Set a watch, O Lord, before my mouth, and a door round about my lips. Incline not my heart to evil words, to make excuses in sins.

[On giving the Censer to the Deacon or Server, he says:]
Priest: May the Lord enkindle within us the fire of his love, and the flames of everlasting charity. Amen.

[Afterward the priest himself, the clergy, and the people are incensed]

<u>Lavabo</u>

[The priest then goes to the Epistle side of the Altar (right) and washing his hands, he says Ps. 25:6-12]

Priest: I will wash my hands in innocency, O Lord; and so will I go to Thine altar. That I may shew the voice of thanksgiving: and tell of all thy wondrous works. Lord, I have loved the habitation of thy house: and the place where Thine honor dwelleth. O shut not up my soul with the sinners: nor my life with the blood-thirsty; In whose hands is wickedness: and their right hand is full of gifts. But as for me, I will walk innocently: O deliver me, and be merciful unto me. My foot standeth right: I will praise the Lord in the congregations. Glory be to the Father, and to the Son and to the Holy Ghost, as it was in the beginning, is now, and ever shall be, world without end. Amen.

[Bowing in the middle of the altar, he joins his hands and says:]
Priest: Receive, O holy Trinity, this oblation which we make to thee in memory of the Passion, Resurrection, and Ascension of our Lord Jesus Christ, and in honor of the blessed Mary, ever a Virgin, of blessed John Baptist, the holy Apostles Peter and Paul, and of all the saints; that it may be available to the honor, and our salvation; and that they may vouchsafe to intercede for us in heaven, whose memory we celebrate on earth. Through the same Christ our Lord. Amen.

[He kisses the Altar; then turning himself towards the people, he says the first two words aloud, then faces the Altar while concluding the prayer,]

Priest: Brethren, pray that my sacrifice and yours may be acceptable to God the Father Almighty.
Response: May the Lord receive the sacrifice from thy hands, to the praise and glory of his own name, and to our benefit, and that of all his holy Church.

<u>The Secret</u>

[He then reads, joined by the new priests, in a low voice the prayer called the Secret, which may be found in its proper place, and concludes by saying aloud:]

Priest: World without end.
Response: Amen.

STAND

Priest: The Lord be with you.
Response: And with thy spirit.
Priest: Lift up your hearts.
Response: We have lifted them up to the Lord.
Priest: Let us give thanks to the Lord our God.
Response: It is meet and just.

The Preface (Proper)

[With his hands extended, he chants (High Mass) or says]
Priest: It is truly meet and just, right and available to salvation, that we should always, and in all places give thanks unto thee, O holy Lord, Father Almighty, eternal God. Who together with thy only begotten Son and the Holy Ghost are one God and one Lord: not in the singularity of one person, but in a Trinity of one substance. For what we believe of thy glory, as thou hast revealed, the same we believe of thy Son, and of the Holy Ghost, without any difference or distinction. So that in the confession of the true and eternal Deity, we adore a distinction in the Persons, a unity in the essence, and an equality in the Majesty. Whom the angels and archangels, the cherubim also and seraphim praise, and cease not daily to cry out with one voice, saying:

The Sanctus   KNEEL

[The priest again joins his hands, and bowing, says] [The Bells are rung three times]
HOLY, HOLY, HOLY, Lord God of Hosts. Heaven and earth are full of thy glory. Hosanna in the highest. Blessed is he that cometh in the name of the Lord. Hosanna in the highest.

THE CANON OF THE MASS

[The priest, bowing low over the Altar, says silently]

For The Church

Priest: We therefore humbly pray and beseech thee, most merciful Father, through Jesus Christ thy Son, our Lord, that thou wouldst vouchsafe to accept and bless these ✠ gifts, these ✠ presents, these ✠ holy unspotted sacrifices, which in the first place we offer thee for thy holy Catholic Church, to which vouchsafe to grant peace, as also to preserve, unite, and govern it throughout the world;

together with thy servant N, our Patriarch, all our Bishops, as also all orthodox believers and professors of the Catholic and Apostolic faith.

Commemoration of the Living

Priest: Be mindful, O Lord, of thy servants, men and women, *N* and *N [Here he prays silently for those for whom he intends to pray.]* And of all here present whose faith and devotion are known unto thee, from whom we offer or who offer up to thee this sacrifice of praise for themselves, their families, and friends, for the redemption of their souls, for the health and salvation they hope for, and for which they now pay their vows to thee, the eternal, living, and true God.

Invocation of the Saints

Priest: Communicating with, and honoring in the first place, the memory of the ever glorious Virgin Mary, Mother of our Lord and God Jesus Christ; as also of the blessed Apostles and Martyrs, Peter and Paul, Andrew, James, John, Thomas, James, Philip, Bartholomew, Matthew, Simon and Thaddeus, Linus, Cletus, Clement, Xystus, Cornelius, Cyprian, Lawrence, Chrysogonus, John and Paul, Cosmas and Damian, and of all thy Saints, through whose merits and prayers grant that we may always be defended by the help of thy protection. Through the same Christ our Lord. Amen.

Prayers at Consecration

[Spreading his hands over the oblation, he says:]
[The Bells are rung once]
Priest: We therefore beseech thee, O Lord, graciously to accept this oblation of our servitude, as also of thy whole family; and to dispose our days in thy peace, to preserve us from eternal damnation, and rank us in the number of Thine elect. Through Christ our Lord. Amen.

Priest: Which oblation do thou, O God, vouchsafe in all respects to bless ✠, approve ✠, ratify ✠, and accept; that it may be made for us the ✠ Body and Blood ✠ of thy most beloved Son Jesus Christ our Lord.

CONSECRATION OF THE HOST

[The Priest takes the host in his hands and says]
Priest: Who the day before He suffered, took bread into His holy and venerable hands, and with His eyes lifted up towards heaven to thee, Almighty God His Father, giving thanks unto Thee, He blessed ✠, brake, and gave to His disciples, saying: Take and eat ye all of this,

For this is My body.

[The Priest genuflects and adores the Sacred Host (Bells rung once).
Rising, he elevates it for the veneration of the faithful (Bells rung three times).
Then, placing It on the corporal, he genuflects, and adores It again (bells rung once).]

[After this he never disjoins his fingers and thumbs, except when he is to take the Host, until after washing his fingers at the ablutions after Communion.]

[Then, uncovering the chalice, the Priest says,]
Priest: In like manner, after He had supped,

[He takes the chalice with both hands]
taking also this excellent chalice into His holy and venerable hands, giving Thee also thanks, He blessed ✠, and gave it to His disciples, saying: Take and drink ye all of this,

[The Priest bends over the chalice and says slowly and without pausing,]
For this is the Chalice of My Blood of the New and Eternal Testament, the Mystery of Faith; which shall be shed for you, and for many, unto the remission of sins.

[He then says in a low voice]
As often as ye do these things, ye shall do them in remembrance of Me.

[The Priest genuflects and adores the Precious Blood (bells rung once).
Rising, he elevates the Chalice (bells rung three times)
Setting it down, he covers it and adores it again by genuflecting (bells rung three times)]

Prayers After Consecration

[With his hands held apart, the priest continues silently,]
Priest: Wherefore, O Lord, we Thy servants, as also thy holy people, calling to mind the blessed Passion of the same Christ Thy Son our Lord, His resurrection from the dead, and admirable ascension into heaven, offer unto Thy most excellent Majesty of Thy gifts bestowed upon us, a pure ✠ Host, a holy ✠ Host, an unspotted ✠ Host, The Holy ✠ Bread of eternal life, and Chalice ✠ of everlasting salvation.

To Ask God To Accept Our Offering

[Bowing down over the Altar with his hands joined on the Altar, he says,]
Priest: Upon which vouchsafe to look, with a propitious and serene countenance, and to accept them, as Thou wert graciously pleased to accept the gifts of Thy just servant Abel, and the sacrifices of our Patriarch Abraham, and that which Thy high priest Melchizedeck offered to Thee, a holy sacrifice and unspotted victim.

For Blessings

[Here, bowing profoundly with his hands joined on the Altar, he says:]
Priest: We most humbly beseech thee, Almighty God, to command these things to be carried by the hands of Thy holy angel to thy altar on high, in the sight of Thy divine Majesty; that as many as shall partake *[Here he kisses the altar.]* of the most sacred Body ✠ and Blood ✠ of thy Son at this altar, may be filled with every heavenly grace and ✠ blessing. Through the same Christ our Lord. Amen.

Commemoration of the Dead

[Extending and closing his hands, he says:]
Priest: Be mindful, O Lord, of thy servants *[N and N]*, who are gone before us with the sign of Faith, and rest in the sleep of peace. *[Here particular mention is silently made of such of the dead as he wishes to pray for.]* To these, O Lord, and to all that sleep in Christ, grant, we beseech thee, a place of refreshment, light, and peace. Through the same Christ our Lord. Amen.

[Here, striking his breast and raising his voice at the first three words, the Priest says:]
Priest: As to us sinners, thy servants, confiding in the multitude of thy mercies, vouchsafe to grant some part and fellowship with thy holy Apostles and Martyrs; with John, Stephen, Matthias, Barnabus, Ignatius, Alexander, Marcellinus, Peter, Felicitas, Perpetua, Agatha, Lucy, Agnes, Cecily, Anastasia, and with all thy saints:

into whose company we beseech thee to admit us, not in consideration of our merit, but of thy own gratuitous pardon. Through Christ our Lord.

Final Doxology And Minor Elevation

Priest: By whom, O Lord, thou dost always create, ✠ sanctify, ✠ quicken, ✠ bless, and give us all these good things.

[Here he uncovers the Chalice, genuflects, and taking the Host in his right hand, signs the Cross with it over the Chalice in his left, saying:]
Priest: By ✠ Him, and with ✠ Him, and in ✠ Him, is to thee, God the Father ✠ Almighty, in the unity of the Holy ✠ Ghost all honor and glory.

[He replaces the Sacred Host, covers the chalice, genuflects and says,]
Priest: For ever and ever.
Response: Amen.

COMMUNION

[The Priest joins his hands, saying,]   **STAND**

Priest: Let us pray. Instructed in thy saving precepts, and following thy divine directions, we presume to say:

[He extends his hands, directs his eyes towards the Sacrament and says audibly,]

Pater Noster

Priest: Our Father, who art in heaven, hallowed be thy name; thy kingdom come; thy will be done on earth, as it is in heaven: give us this day our daily bread; and forgive us our trespasses, as we forgive them that trespass against us; and lead us not into temptation.
Response: But deliver us from evil.
Priest: Amen. (Priest says in low voice)

Libera Nos

[The Priest takes the paten between his first and second fingers, saying,]
Priest: Deliver us, we beseech thee, O Lord, from all evils, past, present, and to come; and by the intercession of the blessed and ever glorious Virgin Mary,

Mother of God, and of the holy Apostles Peter and Paul, and of Andrew, and of all the Saints ✠ *[Here he makes the sign of the cross with the Paten, then places the Host upon it]*, mercifully grant peace in our days, that through the assistance of thy mercy, we may be always free from sin, and secure in all disturbance. *[Here he breaks the Host.]* Through the same Jesus Christ, thy Son our Lord, who with thee and the Holy Ghost liveth and reigneth, God,

Priest: World without end.
Response: Amen.

Priest: The ✠ peace of the ✠ Lord be ✠ always with you.
Response: And with thy spirit.

KNEEL

[He puts a particle of the Host into the Chalice, saying:]
Priest: May this mixture and consecration of the Body and Blood of our Lord Jesus Christ be to us that receive it effectual to eternal life. Amen.

Agnus Dei

[Then the Priest covers the chalice and, genuflecting; Then, bowing and striking his breast three times, he says:]
Lamb of God, who takest away the sins of the world, have mercy on us.
Lamb of God, who takest away the sins of the world, have mercy on us.
Lamb of God, who takest away the sins of the world, give us peace.

[In Masses for the Dead he says twice: Give them rest; and lastly, Give them eternal rest; and the first of the following prayers is also omitted.]

PRAYERS FOR HOLY COMMUNION

Prayer for Peace and Fidelity

[With his eyes directed toward the Sacrament, bowing, he says silently,]
Priest: O Lord Jesus Christ, who saidst to thy apostles, peace I leave you, my peace give unto you, regard not my sins, but the faith of thy church; and grant her that peace and unity which are agreeable to thy will; who livest and reignest for ever and ever. Amen.

Prayers for Holiness

[The Priest continues silently]
Priest: O Lord Jesus Christ, Son of the living God, who, according to the will of the Father, hast by thy death, through the cooperation of the Holy Ghost, given life to the world, deliver me by this thy most sacred Body and Blood from all my iniquities, and from all evils; and make me always adhere to thy commandments, and never suffer me to be separated from thee; who livest and reignest, God, for ever and ever. Amen.

Prayer for Grace

Priest: Let not the participation of thy Body, O Lord Jesus Christ, which I, though unworthy, presume to receive, turn to my judgment and condemnation; but through thy mercy, may it be a safeguard and remedy; both to soul and body; who with God the Father, in the unity of the Holy Ghost, livest and reignest, God, for ever and ever. Amen.

Communion of the Priest

[Here he genuflects, then taking the Host in his left hand, he says:]
Priest: I will take the bread of heaven, and call upon the name of our Lord.

[Striking his breast with humility and devotion, he says three times:]
Priest: Lord, I am not worthy that thou shouldst enter under my roof; but only say the word, and my soul shall be healed.

[He makes the Sign of the Cross with the Host over the paten, while saying,]
Priest: May the Body of our Lord Jesus Christ preserve my soul to life everlasting. Amen.
[Receiving reverently both Parts of the Host, and prays silently:]

[He uncovers the chalice, genuflects, collects any Fragments remaining on the corporal, and purifies the paten over the chalice, saying,]
Priest: What shall I render to the Lord for all the things that he hath rendered to me? I will take the Chalice of salvation, and will call upon the name of the Lord. Praising, I will call upon the Lord, and I shall be saved from my enemies.

[He makes the Sign of the Cross with the chalice, while he says:]
Priest: May the Blood of our Lord Jesus Christ preserve my soul to everlasting life. Amen.
[Standing reverently, he receives the Precious Blood.]

[Here the Holy Communion is administered, if there are any persons to receive.]

Administration of Holy Communion

[The Holy Communion is, if possible, to be administered during the Mass, after the Communion of the Priest.]

[One of the Communicants or the Server shall say aloud:]
Servers: I confess to Almighty God, to blessed Mary ever a Virgin, to blessed Michael the Archangel, to blessed John the Baptist, to the holy Apostles Peter and Paul, to all the saints, that I have sinned exceedingly in thought, word, and deed, through my fault, through my fault, through my most grievous fault. Therefore, I beseech the Blessed Mary, ever a Virgin, blessed Michael the Archangel, blessed John the Baptist, the holy Apostles Peter and Paul, all the Saints, and you Father, to pray to the Lord our God for me.

Priest: *[The Priest standing bareheaded, turns to them, saying in an audible voice, unless the Mass be sung:]* God Almighty have mercy on you, forgive you your sins, and bring you to life everlasting.
R. Amen.

Priest: The Almighty and most merciful Lord grant you pardon, absolution, and remission of your sins.
Response: Amen.

[The priest (elevating the consecrated Host on the ciborium or the paten)
(Bells rung three times)]
Priest: Behold the Lamb of God, Who taketh away the sins of the world.
P/C. O Lord, I am not worthy that thou shouldst enter under my roof, but speak the word only and my soul shall be healed. *(Three times.)*

[At the administration of the Communion:]
Priest: The Body of our Lord Jesus Christ preserve thy soul unto everlasting life. Amen.

Cleansing of the Vessels

[Wine is poured into the chalice, Taking the first ablution, the priest says:
Priest: Grant, O Lord, that what we have taken with our mouth, we may receive with a pure mind, that of a temporal gift it may become to us an eternal remedy.

[Wine and water are poured into the chalice over the fingers of the priest, who dries them with the purificator, saying:]
Priest: May thy Body, O Lord, which I have received, and thy Blood, which I have drunk, cleave unto my heart; and grant that no stain of sin may remain in me who have been fed with this pure and holy sacrament. Who livest and reignest world without end. Amen.

[He drinks the water and wine, and the chalice is purified and veiled.]

The Communion Verse

[He then says the Communion, which seek in its proper place.] [At the middle of the Altar, the priest says,]
Priest: The Lord be with you.   **STAND**
Response: And with thy spirit.
Priest: Let us pray.

[The Priest then returns to the Missal at the Epistle (right) side and begins the Postcommunion]

The Postcommunion

[He then says the Postcommunion, which seek in its proper place.]
Response: Amen.

[Going to the middle of the Altar, he kisses it, turns to the people and says aloud,]
Priest: The Lord be with you.
Response: And with thy spirit.

The Dismissal

Priest: Go, you are dismissed, *or* Let us bless the Lord. (or: Ite, Missa est.)
Response: Thanks be to God. (or: Deo gratias.)

[In Masses for the Dead, the priest omits the Ite, Missa est, faces the Altar and says:]
Priest: May they rest in peace.
Response: Amen.

The Last Blessing KNEEL

[Bowing before the altar, the priest says:]
Priest: Let the performance of my homage be pleasing to thee, O holy Trinity; and grant that the sacrifices which I, though unworthy, have offered up in the sight of thy majesty, may be acceptable to thee, and through thy mercy be a propitiation for me, and for all those for whom it has been offered. Through Christ Our Lord.

[He then kisses the Altar and turns himself towards the people, (except in Masses for the Dead) he gives them his blessing, saying:]
Priest: May Almighty God, ✠ the Father, Son, and Holy Ghost, bless you.
Response: Amen.

Last Gospel

[The priest goes to the Gospel (left) side of the Tabernacle, and says,]
Priest: The Lord be with you. STAND
Response: And with thy spirit.
Priest: The beginning of the Gospel according to St. John.
Response: Glory be to thee, O Lord.

In the beginning was the Word, and the Word was with God, and the Word was God. The same was in the beginning with God. All things were made by him, and without him was made nothing that was made. In him was life, and the life was the light of men; and the light shineth in darkness, and the darkness did not comprehend it.

There was a man sent by God, whose name was John. This man came for a witness, to give testimony of the light, that all men might believe through him. He was not the light, but was to give testimony of the light. That was the true light, which enlighteneth every man that cometh into this world. He was in the world, and the world was made by him, and the world knew him not. He came unto his own, and his own received him not. But as many received him, to them he gave power to be made the sons of God, to them that believe in his name, who are born, not of blood, nor of the will of the flesh, nor of the will of man, but of God.

GENUFLECT

AND THE WORD WAS MADE FLESH,

and dwelt among us; and we saw his glory, as it were the glory of the only begotten of the Father, full of grace and truth.
Response: Thanks be to God.

An Appendix of Catechetical Information

Appendix A

Ut Unum Sint
Ultrajectine Orientalium Catolicam Ecclesia

**Pastoral Letter on Catholic Unity within the Old Catholic Community
Bishop Andre' J. W. Queen, SCR, Provincial Ordinary, Western United States**

To all of our brothers and sisters in the Ultrajectine Diaspora, Greetings and Blessings In the Lord Jesus Christ.

A Call For Old Catholic Unity

In this new century, this new millennium, there is hope and anticipation of re-unification. In this hope, there is also an urgent need as well. Archbishop Arnold Mathew, of blessed memory, who wrote the historic "Prayer for Catholic Unity", eloquently expressed this hope. Today, more than ever, we have failed to achieve it.

Compromise In Faith, An Obstacle To Unity

With the proliferation of new separate communions, comes the ever-increasing difficulty of seeing unity realized. With some communions shrinking, desperation has overtaken apostolic teaching, and the Deposit of Faith has been substituted with secular political correctness and social theology. Where this has happened, despite protestations to the contrary, the historic apostolic lines of succession have already been lost, and exist only in the minds of those deceived. Surely, without a jealous protection of the spiritual gifts given the Ultrajectine Church, human folly can cause them to be lost forever. We must tenaciously cling to that faith believed always, by everyone, everywhere; or be relegated to the vast and barren wasteland, where there are no spiritual gifts to sustain us. Only human hubris can cause the loss of so momentous a gift to the Ultrajectine Church only our own weakness, folly and fear can lead us, as it did Adam, from our own spiritual Eden, into the vast wasteland.

Our Christian Inheritance

God calls us to Holiness. We are called to a spiritual station and charge, for the sake of others. We are called, both as a spiritual family under the Divine Fatherhood of God, and as the Bride of Christ, one body, to live out our baptismal vows. I ask all Old Catholics to embrace the ancient faith as one voice in unity. Let us bring all of our individual gifts to the table and offer them as one family united. Where there is valid teaching, let us cling to it; where there is innovation based in human reason apart from ancient Church teaching, let us flee far from it. Let the Bridegroom, in all things, find his Bride ready, and without spot.

The teachings given the Church are Sacred, having been breathed from the mouth of God as Christ taught the Apostles. These teachings have been passed down in the Church through both written and oral teaching, and faithfully taught throughout the ages. The Church's prohibitions are not recent, as evidenced by the Church's stance on abortion, "You shall not procure abortion, nor destroy a newborn child" which is found in the Didache of 140 A.D. Likewise the prohibitions against homosexuality, adultery and divorce are also ancient. Both Holy Writ and Sacred Tradition speak of the male-only priesthood, and the early Fathers of the Church defended this understanding of Holy Orders against pagan and heretical sects throughout the entire nearly two thousand year period of Christianity, anchoring the ordained priesthood of the New Testament, as fulfillment and completion of the Levitical Priesthood of the Old Testament, established by that perfect High Priest, who is Christ Jesus.

Holy Scripture and Sacred Tradition, Not two teachings, but one.

The validity of Sacred Tradition, written not on papyrus, but in the hearts of His people, professed in the daily life of the Church, is of co-equal dignity and sanctity with Holy Writ. Scripture and Tradition both expressions of the one true faith, having come to the Church from God, both inspired by the Holy Spirit, complement and not compete against, one another. Where would we be without Sacred Tradition? For If we lack Sacred Tradition, we lack the teaching of the Holy Trinity, the order and Rite of the ancient Liturgy, an understanding of our own Apostolic Succession, and much that lives and gives life to the fullness of Catholic faith.

Both Scripture and Tradition, having been shown of equal validity and sacred inspired character, form our Catholic faith. Our faith, having thus been firmly established by Holy Scripture and Sacred Tradition, what proper basis can there be, for adopting other teachings which are contrary to it?

The Folly Of Human Arrogance

Some secular intellectuals have argued that people have evolved and developed; That we are not as base as our earthly predecessors of two thousand years ago.

Some have even gone so far to say that the ancient teachings of the Ten Commandments, as well as the teachings of Christ Himself, do not apply today, to the modern, sophisticated society of today. Objectively, nearly two thousand years ago, Jesus Christ called us to repent from the evils of this world, and He re-affirmed the eternal and sacred law of the Ten Commandments. Have we then, done away with adultery, fornication, murder, thievery, lying, homosexuality, divorce, hypocrisy, idolatry and the like? Have we done away with even one of these terrible sinful burdens on mankind? We have not, and because we have not, although our technology has evolved from the primitive, our sinful nature has not. We have, in our intellect, minimized and marginalized God's Word, prefer-ring our own, fallible, finite wisdom, and thus mankind pays the price and reaps the result of its sinful ways.

Sexual promiscuity marginalizes the horrific loss of sexual innocence of our youth. High rates of teen pregnancy, drug use an inability to love, trust or bond with others, and teen suicide, are the legacy passed on. Adultery claims almost half of all marriages, and makes a gift of then to divorce. Arbitrary and capricious marriages make a mockery of what is a sacramental re-birth of that first marriage, of Adam and Eve anew. Through the horrific sin of abortion, the enlightened man has murdered more lives than in any war, and wreaked horrors more terrible even than the Shoah. This world has thrown away an understanding of woman-hood as blessed, and the bringing into the world of a new human being, as a sacred act, in which the blessed woman is called by God to cooperate in forming a new person who inherits, though the Blessed Virgin Mary's selfless act, the gift of her son Jesus Christ, which is salvation through Him, for all mankind. Our world has legalized so-called "same-sex marriages", and espouses homosexuality under the guise of diversity and equality, teaching children, whose consciences have yet to be formed, that such conduct is proper, appropriate and acceptable, and even that they may themselves, be so disposed. In the intellect of man, this world has not evolved, but rather devolved, to doing and enabling others to do, all that Christ taught us not to. Any Church therefore, that seeks to be socially acceptable, and politically correct, digresses into an incongruous religious social group, which sacrifices the supernatural love of God, for the unnatural lusts of this World.

Lest we believe we play no part in this widespread disease, we must bear the bur-den caused by our own complacency and nonfeasance. The Church militant can-not afford to yield even one inch in our struggle against the present evil that so grips this world. So that we may be ever ready to meet our foe in spiritual warfare, and emerge victorious in Christ, our spiritual armor, breastplate and sword must be well cared for—that is, our knowledge of our Catholic faith must be deep, founded in the written Word of God and spiritually emboldened by Sacred Tradition, which is the heart and life of the Church.

Do Not Be Deceived

Let us shun then, those who would ask to nullify sacred teaching, or worst, those who would add foreign words or phrases to the sacred texts of Scripture, forcing the divinely inspired writers to say something in them, that they never intended. We must proclaim the truth boldly, and not be meek. It is not by faith alone that we are saved, and we know that faith, without works, is dead. If our faith does not yield a heart within us that is given to proclaiming the Word of God, and a body, which does not act on that faith, then we do not live faithfully; we lie, and the Truth is not in us. It is not enough to say we are Catholic, our faith compels us to live as Catholics, struggle as Catholics, and at many times throughout history, die as a result of our Catholic faith.

True unity comes through faith, through a united profession and adherence to the one True Faith, believed always, by everyone, everywhere. True unity requires acceptance and adherence to the totality of the faith, whole and not partial. True unity requires true compassion, in which we call our brother back from the edge of the fiery pit and away from sin; instead of false compassion, which turns a blind eye to sin and classifies it as "none of my business", a twenty-first century, evolved version of "am I my brother's keeper". For as surely as Cain murdered Abel physically, we murder our brothers and sisters spiritually by allowing them to walk blissfully through the gate of Gehenna, and into its depths, when we leave them wallowing in sin.

We Are Called To Holiness

A call to unity is also a call to Holiness. It is a call to renew one's promises to God and walk the path of the Cross, ourselves. A call to unity is a call to attack, derision, hatred and loss, all for the sake of the kingdom, all because you believe. You may suffer loss for the sake of the kingdom, yet He will restore you a hundredfold. Turn away from that which causes you to compromise your faith, turn away any who would seek to draw you away from orthodox faith, not with a hand, but with blinding Truth, that is, the Word of God. Have no lot with the evil in this world, which creeps into the heart of man slowly, yet over time pollutes and claims his immortal soul. Draw near to God, and He will draw near to you.

Our friendship, companionship, kinship and communion are offered to those brethren in the faith, in the Ultrajectine Diaspora, and our true compassion for those lost in sin, who seek God's love and compassionate forgiveness.

Given at my Provincial See in the City of Chicago, on Sunday, May 18th, the Fourth Sunday after Easter, in the year 2003, in the Fifth year of my Episcopate.

Andreas Ioannes Gulielmus Regina

Appendix B

Ex Bona Fide
Ultrajectine Orientalium Catolicam Ecclesia

Pastoral Letter on the Protestant Episcopal Church of the USA
Bishop Andre' J. W. Queen, SCR, Vicar General of the Church, Provincial Ordinary, Western United States

To all of our brothers and sisters in communion with the Old Catholic Church of the United States, and all who love God, Greetings and Blessings In the Lord Jesus Christ.

Of Immediate Events

We have watched, with great dismay and disappointment, the setting aside of ancient Christian Faith, and substitution of it with the spirit of this current age. In confirming an individual who is openly part of the gay lifestyle on one day, only to follow by legitimizing the acts of diocese who have engaged in so-called "same-sex unions", the Protestant Episcopal Church of the USA has gravely departed from not only its own theological tradition, but also from Divine Revelation Itself. The PECUSA has moved further away from the Sacred Deposit of Faith, and has stepped completely outside of the entire community of ancient Apostolic Churches.

The Pain Caused

To those members of the PECUSA who recognize the grave error, we share their pain and grieve with them their definitive loss. To those who propose to stay and carve out pockets of orthodox Anglican communities, we empathize with them, however, we point out that ultimately it is not possible to *be a part of* a Communion of Churches, and at the same time, *be apart from* a Communion of Churches. That ultimately those individuals who chose orthodox Anglican faith over innovation, must make an uncomfortable but necessary choice between the comfortable confines of passive acceptance of innovation and the painful rejection of it for the greater glory of God. We are concerned and share the pain of our many friends and co-workers in Christ within the Episcopal Church, that we have known throughout the years.

We Must Sojourn In Truth

In spite of pain and dismay, we commend you to sojourn in truth, rejecting that which is false, and accepting whatever persecution befalls you, for the sake of the

Kingdom, in obedience to God. We do not ask what we do not undertake our-selves, rejecting the Spirit of this Age, which has so imprisoned the souls of many who would call themselves "Old Catholic", instead clinging to the ancient Deposit of Faith in which the Saints of God instruct and guide us, and the Word of God emboldens us.

In Good Faith

This current situation requires this Church of God to reiterate its position. We adhere and are obedient to Scripture and Tradition, which teaches us that homo-sexual behavior is contrary to God's will, and as such is gravely sinful. We further restate our adherence to Scripture in the sacramental nature of Marriage, and that Holy Matrimony is that sacramental estate involving, as proper matter, a natural man and natural woman, both being baptized Christians properly disposed to receive the sacrament. The Statement of Faith of this Church, her Constitutions and Canons do not admit of exception. In this, we stand in line with fellow sacra-mental Apostolic Churches, loving God and hating the lie.

So We Must Act

To ensure that the position of the Church is clearly understood, joint ministry activities with the Protestant Episcopal Church of the USA must cease immedi-ately, future plans for such activities are authoritatively terminated, and seminar-ians are prohibited from attending PECUSA seminaries and theological institutes. Further activities which do or may include clergy of the PECUSA, must be approved by the proper Ordinary having jurisdiction over that Diocese or Parish. While regrettable, these restrictions are necessary during these difficult times.

Our friendship, companionship, kinship and communion are offered to those brethren in the faith, in the Ultrajectine Church, and our true compassion for those lost in sin, who seek God's love and compassionate forgiveness.

Given by my Apostolic authority as Vicar General of this Church of God, at my Provincial See in the City of Chicago, on Thursday, August 7th, after the Eighth Sunday after Easter, in the year 2003, in the Fifth year of my Episcopate.

Andreas Ioannes Gulielmus Regina

Appendix C

Treatise on the Married Episcopate

AN ARGUMENT FROM TRADITION FOR ORDAINING MARRIED PRIESTS
TO THE EPISCOPATE OF THE ORTHODOX CATHOLIC CHURCH

by ✠Denis M. Garrison

Introduction

In the Orthodox Church in the New World, since early in the twentieth century, the concept of the married episcopate has been an important and urgent issue. The question has arisen with increasing frequency and force: Is it allowable to elect and consecrate married Priests to the episcopate and to allow them to persevere in the episcopate although they continue their married lives full and complete, co-habiting and maintaining their marital relations with their wives? Since the 6th Ecumenical Council, the discipline of Holy Church has been to prohibit the married episcopate, while still strongly maintaining the married diaconate and presbyterate. This discipline has been adhered to since with varying degrees of fidelity in various parts of the world, but it is fair to characterize this discipline as generally uniform throughout Holy Church.

This question came to be of particular importance after His Eminence, Archbishop Aftimios Ofiesh of blessed memory, married Miss Mariam Namey in 1933, many years after he was consecrated to the episcopate. Abp. Aftimios acted out of conviction that the married episcopate is truly Scriptural; furthermore, he was reacting to great scandals in the Orthodox Church involving the celibate clergy (such scandals are still common today). Abp. Aftimios also was moved to marry by his desire to force the issue of the married episcopate to consideration by a Pan-Orthodox Council; a wish which was thwarted then, but may yet be fulfilled. While Abp. Aftimios thereupon retired from the hierarchy of the Church, the remaining Bishops of his jurisdiction made it clear that they thought his expressed belief that the episcopate should include married men was correct and scripturally sound. Since that time, a number of Bishops succeeding after Abp. Aftimios, including several Primates, have been elected from the married presbyterate and have remained married as Bishops. This discipline, election of married Priests to the episcopate without requiring them to separate from their wives, is also followed in a number of the smaller Orthodox jurisdictions in the Americas; but the earlier discipline, prohibition of the married episcopate, is still maintained in the "main-line Orthodox Churches," as well as by traditionalist ethnic jurisdictions. It is accurate, therefore, to say that the issue of the married episcopate is controversial within Holy Church in this time and place.

I, myself, am a Bishop and a husband; I was married several years before I was ordained. I was consecrated Bishop in 1985. Since my consecration I have maintained my marital life unamended and hope to do so throughout my life. I believe that the Sacrament of Holy Orders, at any rank, cannot and must not vitiate the Sacrament of Holy Matrimony. I mention this so that the reader knows my analysis of the issues herein is inescapably tempered by my own marital and clerical status. Nevertheless, I believe my analysis to be objectively fair and accurate, or else I would not dare to publish it.

Marriage Before Ordination

"No Bishop, Presbyter, or Deacon shall put away his own wife under pretext of reverence. If, however, he put her away, let him be excommunicated; and if he persist in so doing, let him be deposed from office."—[Canon V of the Holy Apostles]

In accordance with the most ancient tradition, the consolation of the Holy Sacrament of Matrimony should not be denied to men who wish to receive the Sacrament of Holy Orders at a later date. It seems obvious that, just as a man, whether single or married to an Orthodox woman, may be tonsured and ordained as a Church Servitor, or a Subdeacon, or a Deacon, or a Priest, if he is otherwise qualified, likewise, a Priest, single or married to an Orthodox woman, should be allowed to be consecrated to the sacred episcopate, if he is otherwise qualified, in accordance with Canon V of the Holy Apostles. Membership in the episcopate ought not to be restricted to monks. In this time of great scarcity of monks, the married clergy necessarily are a resource from which the episcopate must be drawn.

"Whoever has entered into two marriages after baptism, or has possessed himself of a concubine, cannot be a Bishop, or a Presbyter, or a Deacon, or anything else in the Sacerdotal List."—[Canon XVII of the 85 Canons of the Holy Apostles]

"No one who has taken a widow, or a divorced woman, or a harlot, or a house maid, or any actress as his wife, may be a Bishop, or a Presbyter, or a Deacon, or hold any other position at all in the Sacerdotal List."—[Canon XVIII of the 85 Canons of the Holy Apostles]

A man who has married a second time cannot be ordained a Subdeacon, a Deacon, a Priest, or a Bishop, according to Canon XVII of the 85 Canons of the Holy Apostles. *"Whoever has entered into two marriages after baptism"* (Canon XVII) reflects the fact that, under the very strictest understanding, for a man to marry twice is adultery of a sort on his part. The rules about *"a widow, or a divorced woman"* (Canon XVIII) do not disparage those women's morality; rather, they were already married once, and therefore, again under the strictest understanding, to marry such a woman is adultery of a sort. (See Matthew 5:32 and 19:7-9.) While second (and even third) marriages may be allowed, for the weakness of the flesh, to the laity, the clergy are called to be irreproachable and, therefore, the clergy are not allowed to marry widows or divorced women.

We rarely use the word *"concubine"* (Canon XVII) in these days; we interpret *"concubine"* to refer to any woman with whom the man has entered into any kind of illicit sexual relationship. Also, in this modern age, we interpret *"a harlot, or a house maid, or any actress"* (Canon XVIII) to refer to any woman of infamous reputation or who is known for her moral turpitude. The occupations of domestic servants and actresses in the modern world cannot honestly be generically maligned as immoral; rather, it is marriage with any woman who is in any occupation which can honestly be characterized as immoral (for example, prostitution), which is prohibited. As Canons XVII and XVIII both plainly imply, a man who has married within these Canons and who is otherwise qualified may indeed be ordained *"a Bishop, Presbyter, or Deacon, or anything else in the Sacerdotal List."*

Marriage After Ordination

"As to bachelors who have entered the clergy, we allow only anagnosts (Readers) and psalts (Chanters) to marry, if they wish to do so."—[Canon XXVI of the 85 Canons of the Holy Apostles] (See also Canon XIV of the 4th Ecumenical Council and Canon VI of the 6th Ecumenical Council.)

Also in accordance with ancient tradition, the sacred clergy in Holy Orders should not feel free to marry at will. The Church may exercise discipline in this matter, as seems prudent and expedient at the time and place. A Church Servitor who was a bachelor when he was ordained has the right to marry an Orthodox woman, in accordance with Canon XXVI of the Holy Apostles and Canon XIV of the 4th Ecumenical Council (451 A.D.). A Subdeacon, Deacon, Priest, or Bishop who is a bachelor, once he is ordained, is not permitted marriage thereafter by Canon XXVI. Yet, traditionally, we may make exceptions: a Subdeacon or Deacon who announced before his ordination to his ordaining Bishop that he plans to marry may be dispensed from this prohibition, by the same Bishop or his successor, to marry after ordination, in accordance with Canon X of Ancyra. Thus, the principle of allowing, by the exercise of Economy, ordained clergy to marry and remain clergy is well established in ancient precedent. We respect the ancient tradition which discourages men already in holy orders from marrying and encourages special caution regarding the marriages of ordained clergy. However, in light of the permissive precedents established by Canon XXVI of the Holy Apostles, Canon XIV of the 4th Ecumenical Council, and Canon X of Ancyra, and considering a footnote to Canon V of the Holy Apostles which states that *"the custom prevailed of not letting those in holy orders marry…"*, showing that this was a custom rather than a necessary discipline, we cannot absolutely condemn marriage after ordination.

It seems to us that when Abp. Aftimios married, this very provocative act catalyzed the active reconsideration in Holy Church of this issue of the married episcopate. Prior to his marriage, the occasional married Bishop (there were some) was not publicly approved by the Church, but was tolerated and kept quiet. Once the issue was publicly raised, the discovery of the scriptural truth and the reaffirmation of the Apostolic teaching in this regard became more possible.

The continuing existence of Le Sacre Orientale Chiesa di Gesu Cristo Italo-Greca Ortodosso (the Holy Eastern Orthodox Italo-Greek Church of Jesus Christ), with its married episcopate and centuries of Orthodox witness, and the existence in the United States of its Italo-Greek Orthodox Christian Archdiocese, along with the witness of several small Orthodox jurisdictions with married Bishops, give us hope that the facade of ecumenical unanimity amongst Orthodox Churches on banning the married episcopate will one day fall away and the anomalous and anti-evangelical practice of an exclusively-monastic episcopate will be finally overthrown in Holy Church.

The Primary Issue: Married Bishops

Some of our brethren in the Eastern Churches may object to allowing married men to be consecrated as Bishops, for the discipline generally current throughout Orthodoxy at this time is that only monks may be consecrated as Bishops. It behooves us, therefore, to examine the matter of the married episcopate in the light of Holy Scripture and the Sacred Canons of the Church.

Holy Scripture—The Holy Apostle Paul gave explicit and clear directions in his epistles: *"A bishop then must be blameless, the husband of one wife…"*—(I Timothy 3:2); and again, *"ordain elders in every city…. If any be blameless, the husband of one wife,…for a Bishop must be blameless…."* (Titus 1:5-7). (The word *"blameless"* is best translated as *"irreproachable,"* according to The Rudder (Pedalion). The Orthodox Church agrees, as attested by St John Chrysostom (noted in the Interpretation of Canon XII of the 6th Ecumenical Council), that the word *"elders"* in the original means *"bishops."*) But how should Bishops deal with their wives? *"Art thou bound unto a wife? Seek not to be loosed."*—(I Corinthians 7:27) *"Defraud (deprive) ye not one the other, except it be with consent for a time, that ye may give yourselves to fasting and prayer; and come together again, that Satan tempt you not for your incontinency."*—(I Corinthians 7:5) *"Marriage is honorable in all, and the bed undefiled:…"*—(Hebrews 13:4); for a Bishop to shun his wife would make it apparent that he dishonors marriage, and that he thinks bed and intercourse to be impure, but the Apostle calls marriage *"honorable"* and bed and intercourse *"undefiled."* During His Sermon on the Mount, the Lord said, *"But I say unto you, That whosoever shall put away his wife, saving for the cause of fornication, causeth her to commit adultery; and whosoever shall marry her that is divorced committeth adultery."*—(Matthew 5:32; see also Matthew 19:7-9). The Lord also said, *"What therefore God hath joined together, let not man put asunder."*—(Matthew 19:6). By the clear testimony of Holy Scripture, a man who is married to one woman may be a Bishop, and he is in most grave error if he shuns her bed or divorces her for any reason other than fornication.

Therefore, only a hypocrite could argue that Holy Scripture forbids the married episcopate. Indeed, the manner in which the Apostle Paul writes in his epistles, I Timothy (3:2) and Titus (1:5-7), suggests that the married episcopate was even normative. Further, the other Scriptures cited above make it unmistakably clear that any married man, including a Bishop, must respect and honor his marriage, including intimate relations with his wife, and that it is grave error to divorce his wife or to entirely shun intimate relations with her. It is impossible to enforce, as having doctrinal significance, any Canon which actually contradicts the clear meaning of the Holy Scriptures. Hence, the Canons to which we subscribe are those which are most truly consistent with the Holy Scriptures.

The Sacred Canons—*The 85 Canons of the Holy and Renowned Apostles* is the first collection of Sacred Canons in the authoritative and official English-language text of the Sacred Canons, The Rudder (Pedalion). These Canons are those which are considered by many to have been promulgated by the Holy Apostles themselves (either by all of them together or perhaps only by Saint Paul and Saint Peter) through Clement, the Bishop of Rome. (*See pages lvii through lxi of The Rudder (Pedalion) for a discussion of the apostolic origin of these Canons.*) These Canons are of the highest degree of importance to us, being apostolic in origin.

First and most importantly, Canon V of the 85 Canons of the Holy Apostles, which I cited earlier, makes it explicit and clear beyond any honest argument that the ancient tradition of the Holy Church recognized, valued, and positively promoted the married episcopate.

"No Bishop, Presbyter, or Deacon shall put away his own wife under pretext of reverence. If, however, he put her away, let him be excommunicated; and if he persist in so doing, let him be deposed from office."—*(Canon V of the Holy Apostles).*

This Canon reflects the equally explicit and clear directions of the Holy Apostle Paul to Timothy and Titus. Only a hypocrite could argue that Canon V of the Holy Apostles can be interpreted, in any manner whatsoever, to forbid the episcopate to married men. A footnote to Canon V of the Holy Apostles in The Rudder (Pedalion) explicitly states: *"Please note that in old times it was permissible for bishops to have wives."* The footnote gives the following as cases in point: *"Felix, the bishop of Rome, was a son of a priest named Felix, Pope Agapetus was a son of a presbyter named Gordianus. Pope Gelasius was a son of a bishop named Valerius, and many others were sons of priests."* The footnote goes on to state that it was Canon XII of the 6th Ecumenical Council which sanctioned the custom of the married clergy except that *"bishops alone should not be allowed to have wives."*

Those who now forbid the episcopate to married men (viz., most Eastern Orthodox jurisdictions) cite other Canons as the bases for their discipline in this matter. Therefore, we must ask ourselves if Canon V of the 85 Canons of the Holy Apostles was ever rejected by the Ecumenical Councils and rendered ineffective. The answer is quite inescapable: both Canon II of the 6th Ecumenical Council and Canon I of the 7th Ecumenical Council explicitly accept and ratify all of the 85 Canons of the Holy Apostles. Moreover, Canon XIII of the 6th Ecumenical Council verifies verbatim Canon V of the 85 Canons of the Holy Apostles, but unjustifiably excepts Bishops from its applicability. Canon V of the Holy Apostles always was and still is a Sacred Canon of Holy Church.

"Whoever has entered into two marriages after baptism, or has possessed himself of a concubine, cannot be a Bishop, or a Presbyter, or a Deacon, or anything else in the Sacerdotal List."—(Canon XVII of the 85 Canons of the Holy Apostles)

"No one who has taken a widow, or a divorced woman, or a harlot, or a house maid, or any actress as his wife, may be a Bishop, or a Presbyter, or a Deacon, or hold any other position at all in the Sacerdotal List."—(Canon XVIII of the 85 Canons of the Holy Apostles)

These two Canons, XVII and XVIII, also cited earlier, both plainly imply that a man who has married acceptably can be *"a Bishop, or a Presbyter, or a Deacon, or anything else in the Sacerdotal List;"* otherwise, the prohibitions contained in the Canons would be moot and absurd with regard to Bishops.

Canon XL of the 85 Canons of the Holy Apostles directs that the difference between the property of the Bishop and the property of the Church be publicly known, and it prohibits a Bishop both from leaving the property of the Church to his wife and family and from depriving his wife and family from their rightful inheritance by leaving his own property to the Church through there being confusion as to whose the property really is. This Canon plainly takes for granted that some Bishops will have wives, whose inheritance could be at issue.

"If any Bishop, or Presbyter, or Deacon, or anyone at all on the sacerdotal list, abstains from marriage, or meat, or wine, not as a matter of mortification, but out of an abhorrence thereof, forgetting that all things are exceedingly good, and that God made man male and female, and blasphemously misrepresenting God's work of creation, either let him mend his ways or let him be deposed from office and expelled from the Church. Let a layman be treated similarly."—[Canon LI of the Holy Apostles]

This Canon LI plainly assumes that there will be men who do not abstain from marriage who will be Bishops, Presbyters, and Deacons. It is those *who have refused* to marry who are at risk of deposition from the clerical state and expulsion from Holy Church under this Canon. This Canon is an eloquent witness to the high regard that the Apostolic Church had for marriage, and explicitly for the marriage of Bishops, Presbyters, and Deacons. It witnesses to the Orthodox and unchangeable truth of the Christian Faith that *"all things are exceedingly good,"* and that it is blasphemous to misrepresent God's work of creation by holding that certain things (including lawful sexual relations, meat, and wine, which are simply those things about which errors arose early on) are in themselves unclean, and that it is blasphemous to abhor them.

What then are the true and allowable sacrifices? *"The sacrifices of God are a broken spirit: a broken and a contrite heart, O God, Thou wilt not despise."*—Psalm 51, Verse 17.

Further, the Apostle Paul calls marriage honorable and marital relations undefiled: *"Marriage is honorable in all, and the bed undefiled:...."*—[Hebrews 13:4]; and our Lord Jesus Christ sanctified marriage by His attendance at the marriage feast in Cana; thus it is un-Christian and anti-scriptural to consider bed and intercourse to be impure. Yet, despite the Orthodox Faith, and despite Canon LI of the Holy Apostles, beginning with the Council of Carthage and culminating in the 6th Ecumenical Council, the hierarchs of the Church enacted Canons which suppressed the marital relations and even the marriages of the clergy. The 6th Ecumenical Council could have condemned those in Africa who wished to suppress the marriages of the clergy, as they did with the very same situation in Rome, but they did not. Instead, they unreasonably and unjustifiably extended a ban on married Bishops throughout the world; this was obviously the result of the erroneous anti-marital sentiment which had become generally accepted since marital relations had come to be viewed, blasphemously, as unclean, particularly for a minister of the Sacraments.

The Heresy of Neo-Manichaeism

The term "Neo-Manichaeism" is more accurate and precise than the term "Puritanism," which was used in the prior edition of this Treatise.

"Neo-Manichaeism," as used herein, refers to the heretical impulse behind various erroneous doctrines which call for a more austere and rigid physical purity than is proper and correct according to the teaching of Christ our Lord and His faithful Apostles and disciples. The concept of impurity and purity as being susceptible of physical expression predated Christianity by many centuries; it appeared again in the heresies of the Manichees, Gnostics, and others.

Neo-Manichaeism refers specifically to heretical doctrines within Orthodox Catholicism which mirror the particular heresy of the Manichees, who combined Zoroastrianism, Gnostic Christianity, and pagan elements. Zoroastrianism, the pre-Islamic Persian religion, included a belief in an afterlife and in the continuous struggle of the universal spirit of good (Ormazd) with the spirit of evil (Ahriman), the good ultimately to prevail. Gnostic Christianity included this theological dualism and therefore despised the body as being evil and considered the soul to be trapped within the body.

The Manichees' fundamental dualistic theological concepts, of a spirit of good and a spirit of evil, on an essentially equal footing, that is, of two contending principles of good (light, God, the soul) and evil (darkness, Satan, the body), are antithetical to Orthodox Christianity which holds the fundamental monotheistic belief in One God, Who is all-good and all-powerful, and Who is opposed by Satan and the other fallen angels (i.e., the demons), all of whom are inferior to God in every respect. Canon LI of the Holy Apostles, cited above, confirms the Orthodox Faith: *"that all things are exceedingly good, and that God made man male and female"* and that abhorrence of marriage is a *"blasphemous misrepresentation of God's work of creation."*

The anti-Christian dualism of such *Neo-Manichaeism* demands compliance with laws of external cleanliness of the sort denounced by Jesus in the 23rd Chapter of Matthew. Jesus Christ taught us that it is not external things, but what comes from his heart that makes a man clean or unclean.

"And he called the multitude, and said unto them, 'Hear and understand: Not that which goeth into the mouth defileth a man; but that which cometh out of the mouth; this defileth a man.'" And after His disciples reported that the Pharisees were offended by this saying, Jesus said: "Do not ye yet understand, that whatsoever entereth in at the mouth goeth into the belly, and is cast out into the draught? But those things which proceed out of the mouth come forth from the heart; and they defile the man. For out of the heart proceed evil thoughts, murders, adulteries, fornications, thefts, false witness, blasphemies. These are the things which defile a man; but to eat with unwashen hands defileth not a man."—[Matthew 15:11 and Matthew 15:17-20]

This divine instruction is a hard saying for many people; it is particularly hard for a few of those who have put their feet on the path of monasticism. It seems that there are some monastics who do not know, or cannot keep in mind, that they abstain from some things (e.g., marriage, meat, wine) because they wish to mortify the flesh and grow spiritually stronger (this is truly Orthodox, to sacrificially abstain from good things). Too many believe that they abstain from things which are unclean, thus making themselves more pure for God (this is the heresy of *Neo-Manichaeism*). Such an attitude leads to erroneous anti-marital policies. This is

not Apostolic Christianity; this is the error of men. Witness the Orthodox, Apostolic Canon LI.

Neo-Manichaeism, which Canon LI reveals to be outright blasphemy, and the hypocrisy which promotes and defends it, seem to be the abiding sins of the institutional Churches, East and West, because men seek ritual purity on the basis of their own wisdom, despite the fact that God, in His wisdom, redeemed the whole world and all things are good in His eyes. *Neo-Manichaeism* is the result of the rejection of this very important and fundamental teaching of Christ. *Neo-Manichaeism is heresy!* When those who are perhaps most prone to falling into the error of *Neo-Manichaeism* are also the sole hierarchs of the Church (that is, with the exclusively-monastic episcopate which has been imposed upon Holy Church since the 6th Ecumenical Council), the danger of further distorting the Christian Faith in favor of *Neo-Manichaeism* obviously is very much increased. Of course, since virtually all Bishops have been monks for over a thousand years, the reversal of this erroneous trend will occur only by a great movement of the Holy Spirit. How, then, did a Canon forbidding the married episcopate come to be? Canon XII of the 6th Ecumenical Council is the primary basis for the currently widespread discipline of forbidding the married episcopate.

"And this too has come to our knowledge, that both in Africa and Libya and other regions the most God-beloved Presidents (Bishops) there continue living with their own wives even after the ordination has been conferred upon them, and will not abandon their wives, thus becoming an object of offense and a scandal to others. We have therefore made it a matter of great concern to us to do everything possible for the benefit of the flocks under hand, and it has seemed best not to allow such a thing to occur hereafter at all. We assert this, however, not with any intention of setting aside or overthrowing any legislation laid down Apostolically, but having due regard for the salvation and safety of peoples and for their better advancement with a view to avoiding any likelihood of giving anyone cause to blame the priestly polity. For the divine Apostle says: 'Do all everything for the glory of God. Give none offense, neither to the Jews, nor to the Greeks, nor to the Church of God; even as I try to please all men in everything, without seeking any advantage of mine own, but the advantage of the many in order that they may be saved. Become ye imitators of me, just as I also am (an imitator) of Christ.' [I Corinthians 10:32-33 and 11:1]. If anyone should be shown to be doing this, let him be deposed from office."—[Canon XII of the 6th Ecumenical Council]

Canon XIII of the 6th Ecumenical Council deals with the then current Roman discipline which required ordinands to the Diaconate and Presbyterate to *"solemnly promise to have no further intercourse with their wives."* Canon XIII cites the long tradition (discussed above) of the married clergy and decrees that the Roman discipline is an error.

"Since we have learned that in the church of the Romans it is regarded as tantamount to a canon that ordinands to the deaconry or presbytery must solemnly promise to have no further intercourse with their wives. Continuing, however, in conformity with the ancient canon of apostolic rigorism and orderliness, we desire that henceforward the lawful marriage ties of sacred men become stronger, and we are nowise dissolving their intercourse with their wives, nor depriving them of their mutual relationship and companionship when properly maintained in due season, so that if anyone is found to be worthy to be ordained a Subdeacon, or a Deacon, or a Presbyter, let him nowise be prevented from being elevated to such a rank while cohabiting with a lawful wife. Nor must he be required at the time of ordination to refrain from lawful intercourse with his own wife, lest we be forced to be downright scornful of marriage, which was insti-tuted by God and blessed by his presence, as attested by the unequivocal declaration of the Gospel utterance: 'What therefore God hath joined together, let no man put asun-der' [Matthew 19:6]; and the Apostle's teaching: 'Marriage is honorable in all, and the bed undefiled' [Hebrews 13:4]; and 'Art thou bound unto a wife? seek not to be loosed.' [I Corinthians 7:27]. We are cognizant, though, that those who met in Carthage and made provision of decency in the life of ministers declared that Subdeacons and Deacons and Presbyters, busying themselves as they do with the sacred mysteries, according to their rules are obliged to practice temperance in connection with their helpmates, in order that we may likewise keep the injunction handed down through the Apostles, and continued from ancient times in force, well knowing that there is a proper season for everything, and especially for fasting and prayer. For those who assist in the ceremonies of the sacrificial altar have to be temperate in all things at the time when they are handling holy things, so that they may be able to gain whatever they ask God for. If, therefore, anyone acting contrary to the Apostolic Canons require any person who is in sacred orders—any Presbyter, we mean, or Deacon, or Subdeacon—to abstain from intercourse and association with his lawful wife, let him be deposed from office. Likewise, if any Presbyter or Deacon expel his own wife on the pretext of reverence, let him be excommunicated; and if he persist, let him be deposed from office."—[Canon XIII of the 6th Ecumenical Council]

The omission of *"Bishop"* from the list of persons in sacred orders in Canon XIII of the 6th Ecumenical Council is very significant, reflecting Canon XII, which deprived Bishops of the rights of marriage. Thus, Canon XII commits wholesale the very offense (violation of Canon V of the Holy Apostles) for which, in the individual cases of Priests, Deacons, and Subdeacons, Canon XIII excommunicates and deposes!

In Canon XII, the 6th Ecumenical Council legislates in direct contradiction to Canon V of the Holy Apostles (while self-consciously declaring *"We assert this, however, not with any intention of setting aside or overthrowing any legislation laid down Apostolically...."*), and in direct contradiction of the Holy Scriptures [Matthew 5:32 and 19:6-9; I Corinthians 7:5 and 7:27; Hebrews 13:4; I Timothy 3:2; and Titus 1:5-7]; and then, immediately in Canon XIII, the 6th Ecumenical Council legislates precisely on the basis of Canon V of the Holy Apostles and Holy Scriptures (*"If, therefore, anyone acting contrary to the Apostolic Canons require any person who is in sacred orders.... Likewise, if any Presbyter or Deacon expel his own wife on the pretext of reverence,...."*) The kindest characterization which one might make is that Canon XII is anomalous and wholly inconsistent with the entire meaning and import of Canon XIII. One could, therefore, paraphrase Canons XII and XIII to implicitly say: *"If, therefore, anyone acting contrary to the Apostolic Canons require any person who is in sacred orders— any Bishop, we mean—to abstain from intercourse and association with his lawful wife, let him be. Likewise, if any Bishop expel his own wife on the pretext of reverence, let him be."*

Isn't that absurd? This is in direct contradiction to the Apostolic Canons and to the very arguments used by the same Council for Canon XIII! Remember, *"No Bishop, Presbyter, or Deacon shall put away his own wife under pretext of reverence. If, however, he put her away, let him be excommunicated; and if he persist in so doing, let him be deposed from office."*—[Canon V of the Holy Apostles.]

Thus, Canon XII of the 6th Ecumenical Council is an ***anti-evangelical*** and (vis-a-vis Canon V and Canon LI of the Holy Apostles) an ***anti-canonical*** attack on the marriages of Bishops.

There were two primary causes for this anomalous and illegitimate legislation.

First and most disturbing, there was a longstanding and accelerating trend of excessive disparagement of marriage (this has disturbing undercurrents of the widely held pre-Christian concept of ritual purity; remember that the Apostle Paul calls marriage honorable and marital relations undefiled: *"Marriage is honorable in all, and the bed undefiled:...."*—[Hebrews 13:4]; thus it is anti-scriptural to consider marital relations to be impure) and also of excessive exaltation of monasticism. Monastic excesses have proven to be a bitter fruit of the heresy of *neo-Manichaeism.* This was the unspoken subtext of Canon XII, and of other later Canons which suppressed the marital relations and even the marriages of the clergy. Excessive exaltation of monasticism and disparagement of marriage is an anti-evangelical error which still besets the Orthodox Churches. It is not at all overstating the case to frankly define *misagomy* (hatred of marriage) and *misogyny* (hatred of women) as both being blasphemous (as is proven by Canon LI of the Holy Apostles) and heretical (being premised on the *neo-Manichaen* tenet that the body is evil and impure). [Obviously, *misandry* (hatred of males), as held by some modern radical feminists and others, is identically blasphemous and heretical.]

The second cause for the anomalous legislation of Canon XII was the proximate cause: the scandal caused the faithful in North Africa by their married Bishops. This may have been a good reason to ban married Bishops in North Africa, but not throughout the world. Yet, this concession to the priests in Barbary, Africa was not given to the Roman clergy (see Canon XIII of the 6th Ecumenical Council) because the Romans were considered more docile regarding morals, while the African were considered to have a wild character.

The interpretation of Canon XXX of the 6th Ecumenical Council (*see below*) notes that the Africans had *"a strange notion of what constitutes good order as respecting ecclesiastical morals, according to Balsamon, and [a] lack of firmness of faith...."* Thus, the Council could have as well condemned those who were scandalized in Africa, as they did in Rome, but they chose not to.

The unreasonable and unjustifiable extension of the ban on married Bishops throughout the world obviously was the result of the Council's hidden agenda, viz., the erroneous anti-marital sentiment discussed above. Let us look beyond Canons XII and XIII of the 6th Ecumenical Council, at additional canonical evidence of this error.

"Wishing to do everything for the edification of the Church, we have decided to make concessions to priests in Barbarian churches, so that if they are seeking to circumvent Apostolic Canon V by not expelling their wife, on the pretext of reverence, and to do what is beyond the limits set by it, by coming to a private agreement with their spouses to abstain from intercourse with each other. We decree that these priests shall cohabit with their wives no more, in any manner whatsoever, so as to afford us thereby positive

proof that they are carrying out their promise. We make this concession to them, not for any other reason, but because of the pusillanimity of their thought, and the bizarre character of their ideas of morality, and the unsettled state of their mind."—*[Canon XXX of the 6th Ecumenical Council]*

Canon XXX discards the unnatural crypto-celibacy within cohabitation legislated in Canon XXXIII of Carthage (*see below*). Also, this Canon is quite clear that the Barbarian discipline was a circumvention of Canon V of the Holy Apostles. Nonetheless, the Council distorted the Tradition by allowing marriage to be dishonored amongst the Barbarians, against the clear teaching of the Holy Scriptures (not to mention Canon IV of Gangra (*see below*) and Canons V and LI of the Holy Apostles) because the Barbarians were pusillanimous and bizarre.

If the Ecumenical Council could so distort the Tradition by allowing marriage to be dishonored on the basis of applying Economy for pusillanimous and bizarre people, perhaps the Orthodox Churches of today, by Economy, might permit **us** to **honor** marriage, even amongst Bishops, in conformity with the clear teaching of Holy Scriptures and the ancient Canons.

Canon XII and Canon XXX of the 6th Ecumenical Council, and Canons III, IV, and XXXIII of Carthage (*see below*) all embody a conscious policy of appeasement of those who are demonstrably and admittedly in error. Appeasement is always and everywhere a bad policy since it seeks to mollify evil (thus belying truth) rather than to confront and overcome evil. This appeasement is hidden under a cloak of not wanting to give offense: *"We assert this, however, not with any intention of setting aside or overthrowing any legislation laid down Apostolically, but having due regard for the salvation and safety of peoples and for their better advancement with a view to avoiding any likelihood of giving anyone cause to blame the priestly polity. For the divine Apostle says: 'Do all everything for the glory of God. Give none offense,'"*—[Canon XII of the 6th Ecumenical Council]. Certainly, the selfsame 6th Ecumenical Council did not stop at offending the Romans by name in Canon XIII. But the real impetus, of course, was the hidden agenda—the growing heresy of *neo-Manichaeism*, pursuing *"ritual purity."*

"If anyone discriminates against a married Presbyter, on the ground that he ought not to partake of the offering when that Presbyter is conducting the Liturgy, let him be anathema."—*[Canon IV of Gangra (340 A.D.)]*

This is clearly the authentic Apostolic teaching! This venerable Canon condemns the heresy of the Eustathians, the Manichees, and others who forbade the married priests to celebrate the Liturgy. But see how quickly it is forgotten by the Council of Carthage:

"It has been decided that as regards these three ranks which have been conjoined by a certain bond of chastity and sacerdocy (I am referring particularly to Bishops, Presbyters, and Deacons), as befits devout Bishops and Priests of God, and Levites, and those ministering to divine institutions, they must be continent in all things, so as to be able to obtain whatever in general they ask God for, in order that we too may likewise keep what has been handed down through the Apostles and has been held ever since the early days."—[Canon III of Carthage (419 A.D.)]

"It is decided that Bishops, Presbyters, and Deacons, and all men who handle sacred articles, being guardians of sobriety, must abstain from women."—[Canon IV of Carthage]

This is precisely the erroneous Roman discipline, which required ordinands to *"solemnly promise to have no further intercourse with their wives,"* and which was completely condemned by Canon XIII of the 6th Ecumenical Council. It was carried from Rome to Africa by Bishop Faustinus of Picenum, the legate of the Pope of Rome and the man who proposed this Canon IV of Carthage. The absolute premise of these Canons is that women are unclean, a tenet which is blasphemous and heretical, as discussed above, not to mention being proof of the perpetrator's misagomy and misogyny. The reasoning follows that, if women are unclean, then to touch a woman sexually defiles a man and makes him unfit for sacred service. So much for the Word of God! So much for *Marriage is honorable in all, and the bed undefiled [Hebrews 13:4]*.

"It is decreed that Subdeacons who attend to the Mysteries, and Deacons and Presbyters, and even Bishops, on the same terms, must abstain from their wives, so as to be as though they had none; which if they fail to do they shall be removed from office. As for the rest of the Clerics, they shall not be compelled to do this, unless they be of an advanced age; but the rule ought to be kept in accordance with the custom of each particular church."—[Canon XXXIII of Carthage]

This Canon distinguishes between crypto-celibacy on the one hand, and real marriage on the other hand. It commands unnatural *crypto-celibacy*—the clergy continuing to cohabit with their wives, but doing so without having intimate relations. This promotion of unnatural marital relations is totally out of conformity with Holy Scripture. (Note that, even in such an anti-marital Canon as this one, the implication is clear that Bishops have wives: *"and even Bishops, on the same terms, must abstain from their wives…".*)

Canon XII of the 6th Ecumenical Council is, at best, anomalous. While I will not condemn Canon XII nor any jurisdiction which continues to follow that Canon, I believe we Orthodox should be permitted to follow the still-standing, never-revoked, God-pleasing Canons V and LI of the Holy Apostles, and Canon IV of Gangra, which promulgate the discipline which is consistent with the Holy Scriptures: qualified married Priests must be admitted to the sacred episcopate and must be allowed to keep their marriages whole and complete, as intended by almighty God.

Church Divorce for Episcopal Candidates

What the 6th Ecumenical Council intended for the wives of Bishops is made clear in Canon XLVIII of the 6th Ecumenical Council. That Canon provides that women who are wives of Priests about to become Bishops and their husbands must first divorce by common consent and, after his consecration, she is to enter a convent; if she is worthy, she may be ordained a Deaconess. Given the high office of the episcopate, there is real reason to expect some degree of coercion of candidates' wives to cooperate, so as not to block their advancement in the Church hierarchy. I believe that this should be considered to be the rule, rather than the exception, given the human realities of such situations.

Furthermore, remembering that our Lord said, *"What therefore God hath joined together, let not man put asunder,"* we should not actively promote this practice, lest Priests abuse the right and coerce their wives into entering convents. In fact, remembering that a married couple are *one flesh* in the eyes of God [Genesis 2:24], even truly voluntary divorces for this purpose should not be permitted to all who request them. Nonetheless, because there are those rare married couples who honestly and piously both wish to enter into the Angelic vocation, and where the prayerful discernment of the Bishop may find that, for that particular couple, such a course would more likely work toward their ultimate salvation, we ought to allow, very rarely, an exception so that husband and wife may become monastics. The Bishop examining such a case should be extraordinarily attentive to the real motivations of the wife and to the likelihood of coercion by the husband.

In summary, the hierarchy should admonish the clergy of every rank that they must keep their marriages whole and complete, honorable and undefiled, as intended by almighty God, and that they must not harm their marriages in any way on the pretext of reverence because they are *"in the Sacerdotal List."* While voluntary celibacy is a wonderful thing, the idea that marriage is in any respect unclean must be attacked whenever it arises, as the blasphemous heresy that it is.

Married Bishops—First Line of Defense Against Monastic Excesses and Heresy

It bears repeating once more: When those most prone to falling into *neo-Manichaeism* are also the sole hierarchs of the Church (that is, the exclusively-monastic episcopate), the danger of further distorting Christian Faith in favor of *neo-Manichaeism* obviously is very great. Since virtually all Bishops have been monks for over a thousand years, the reversal of this erroneous progression into heresy will occur only by a great movement of the Holy Spirit. The monastic hierarchy now teaches that the *Angelic vocation* of monasticism is superior to the vocation of marriage. This kind of excess scandalizes the faithful. Every person who knows the Scriptures knows that **the union of man and woman is God's plan** [Genesis 1:26-28; 2:21-25]. They know what the New Testament says: *"Marriage is honorable in all, and the bed undefiled" [Hebrews 13:4]; "What therefore God hath joined together, let not man put asunder" [Matthew 19:6].*

To say that the monastic vocation, invented by holy men and women inspired by Our Lord Jesus Christ, however excellent it may be, is superior to God's own plan for men and women—that is scandalous. To back up this excessive evaluation of monasticism with misagomous and misogynous arguments and offensive disparagement of women and marriage—that is scandalous. To ignore the human problems that can and sometimes do arise in the unnatural state of monastic life, such as homosexual behaviors, phobic attitudes toward women, and so forth, while extolling monasticism as superior to married life—that is scandalous. To legislate (as the sole legislators) changes from the Apostolic Church discipline to force the laity to follow ascetic monastic lifestyles (like the excessive fasting rules now in force in all traditionalist jurisdictions)—that is scandalous. To deceptively disparage married Bishops as *false Bishops and no Bishops at all*, knowing full well that the married episcopate was normative in the Apostolic Church and for centuries thereafter—that is scandalous. After so many centuries, these scandals have not been without their corrosive effect on the faithful.

The few married Bishops now remaining in the Orthodox Churches are, in fact, the first line of defense against the proponents of misagomy and misogyny, of *neo-Manichaean* heresy and blasphemy. In their persons, they and their wives embody the Christian truth, that God made man male and female and that all things God made are exceedingly good. They show what a heresy it is to say that the body is evil and that a woman defiles a man. They are witnesses of God's plan for the propagation of the race of mankind, the heterosexual relationship of man and wife; the exclusively-monastic episcopate cannot make this witness.

The issue of the married Bishops is far from being a minor matter of Church discipline, long-since resolved and no longer relevant or important. To the contrary, this is a very urgent matter of the greatest importance to the Church of Jesus Christ, for, if such a fundamental heresy as *neo-Manichaeism* cannot be overcome, if it continues to seduce the minds and hearts of most of the Orthodox episcopate, then the central Church organizations, the *visible Church*, will one day be found to be apostate. The *visible Church* will be an heretical organization, no better than the Manichees, no better than the Gnostics, fit only as a bride for Anti-Christ. The Church has been in the catacombs before, in the beginning of the Christian era, and in this century. It may go to the catacombs again, if that is the only place where genuine Christianity can survive. If we do go back to the catacombs, you can be sure that the Bishops will be married men, not careerist monks.

As I said earlier, when Abp. Aftimios married, it catalyzed the active reconsideration in Holy Church of the issue of the married episcopate. Once the issue was publicly raised, the discovery of the scriptural truth and the reaffirmation of the Apostolic teaching became more possible. This question of the married episcopate has been posed, not only academically, nor only in the context of proposals for canonical legislation, but it has been embodied and lived in sacrificial Christian witness by Abp. Aftimios and Mariam Ofiesh, and by the many Bishops and their co-suffering wives who followed in their courageous example, acting out of conviction that the married episcopate is truly Scriptural. Abp. Aftimios' desire to force the issue of the married episcopate to consideration by a Pan-Orthodox Council was thwarted in 1933, but by the grace of God, it may yet be fulfilled.

Humbly submitted by Denis M. Garrison, January 1996.

"Marriage is honorable in all, and the bed undefiled:..." [Hebrews 13:4]

"What therefore God hath joined together, let not man put asunder." [Matthew 19:6]

"No Bishop, Presbyter, or Deacon shall put away his own wife under pretext of reverence. If, however, he put her away, let him be excommunicated; and if he persist in so doing, let him be deposed from office." [Canon V of the Holy Apostles]

"If any Bishop, or Presbyter, or Deacon, or anyone at all on the sacerdotal list, abstains from marriage, or meat, or wine, not as a matter of mortification, but out of an abhorrence thereof, forgetting that all things are exceedingly good, and that God made man male and female, and blasphemously misrepresenting God's work of creation, either let him mend his ways or let him be deposed from office and expelled from the Church. Let a layman be treated similarly." [Canon LI of the Holy Apostles]

"If anyone discriminates against a married Presbyter, on the ground that he ought not to partake of the offering when that Presbyter is conducting the Liturgy, let him be anathema." [Canon IV of Gangra (340 A.D.)]

Appendix D

Archbishop Joseph Renee' Vilatte:
Our Tie to the Syrian & Indian Orthodox Churches
Cornerstone of Old Catholicism in the United States

The vignettes on the life and times of Archbishop Joseph René Vilatte, the first person to bring independent Catholicism to North America, which appear below, were written by Bishop Donald Pierce Weeks in Oakland, California. On behalf of the entire Old Catholic community, we wish to thank him for his time and dedication. A very special thanks goes out to him from us, for giving us his permission to reproduce his work here.

"Likewise Bishops, being principal pastors, are either at large or else with restraint; at large, when the subject of their regiment is indefinite and not tied to a certain place. Bishops with restraint are they whose regiment over the Church is contained within some definite local compass, beyond which compass their jurisdiction reacheth not"

Joseph René Vilatte

Joseph Rene Vilatte was a lapsed Catholic of the Latin Rite. He was the progenitor of more then twenty churches. His adventures in the ecclesiastical world of his time are worth reviewing, again and again. Vilatte was born in Paris, France, the son of a butcher, on January 24, 1854. His parents belonged to the region of La Maine, in northwest France, and belonged to "Petite Eglise" (this church had all but died out and he was baptized by a layman). His mother died shortly after his birth and his boyhood was spent in an orphanage at Paris, under the care of the Brothers of the Christian Schools. He was re-baptized conditionally and confirmed at Notre Dame Cathedral, Paris, in 1867.

During the latter part of the Franco-Prussian War he enlisted in the Garde National. After the siege of Paris and the horrors of the Commune, he decided to leave France for Canada, having been attracted by the appeals for settlers in rural districts. Soon after landing on Canadian soil Vilatte found that a teacher was needed for a school near Ottawa at some distance from the nearest Catholic Church, he acted as catechist, and on Sunday, when there was no chance of getting to Mass, he conducted a simple service for the people. One of the priests that attended the region was impressed with Vilatte and taught him Latin, he returned to France after two years. He received his "calling-up" papers for the French Military service.

Upon returning to Paris, he was informed that there would be a seven-year requirement in the army. He decided to leave his native land. From there he went to Belgium and after a few months entered the Community of Christian Brothers, at that time, a lay teaching order at Namur. He was in danger of arrest as a conscientious objector. Vilatte did not find his vocation in this institute and left Belgium in 1876, feeling that he was called for the secular priesthood. He once again sailed for Canada.

In Canada he approached the Bishop of Montreal, who sent him to the College of Saint-Laurent, conducted by the Holy Cross Fathers, where he studied for three years. About this time, he meet the famous ex-priest Chiniquy, who was devoting his time to preaching against the Roman Catholic Church. After hearing what Chiniquy had to say Vilatte left the seminary and sought the advice of a French Protestant pastor in Montreal, this pastor helped Vilatte study at McGill University for two years. After McGill University, Vilatte reconciled with Rome and entered the Clerics of Saint Viator at Bourbonnais, Illinois. Again he met Chiniquy, who convinced him to leave Illinois and go to Green Bay, Wisconsin. There he would find Belgian settlers that were waiting for conversion to Protestantism, for, as explained by Chiniquy, they were slipping from Romanism into infidelity. Chiniquy also advised Vilatte to contact Hyacinthe Chiniquy, who had been a Discalced Carmelite friar. He was excommunicated in 1869, after he married an American widow and founded Gallican Catholic Church. So in 1884, with the blessing of two unfrocked Roman Catholic priests, Vilatte went o Wisconsin to minister in the Green Bay Area. He considered himself a freelance Presbyterian missionary.

By the time Vilatte arrived at Green Bay, many French-Canadians had settles and established a fairly good fur trade business. These former Belgians had ceased to practice their religion, some had become Spiritualists. At Duval, forty families of lapsed Catholics had opened a schismatic place of worship. Vilatte to turn these people into Presbyterians.

After about a year trying to convert the Belgians on the peninsula north of the city of Green Bay, he saw that matters would not work out. On the advice of Loyson, he approached Bishop John Henry Hobert Brown, the Episcopal Bishop of Fond du Lac. He pointed out that in the northeast part of his diocese there were many hundreds of Belgian and French settles who had already lapsed from communion with Rome, and that they wanted nothing to do with a church ruled over by an Italian pope. That, here in deed was an opportunity to organize a purified Catholic church which would present the Gospel to the people as did the primitive Church, and exercise authority according to the spirit of free America. Vilatte suggesting that the Presbyterian mission should be taken over by the Diocese of Fond du Lac as an Old Catholic outpost.

Bishop Brown, who was a broad-minded High Churchman, replied that he had already heard of Vilatte's mission work, and that he would be glad to help the movement. He explained that it would help promote good relations between the Protestant Episcopal Church and the Old Catholic Churches, which in Europe were doing so much to break down the power of the papacy.

Loyson had already written to Vilatte, asking him to come to Paris, so that he could discuss the possibility of his becoming a priest by Bishop Herzog at Berne. This would be the first step at setting up an Old Catholic Church in North America.

Vilatte replied to Loyson that he did not want to abandon his flock—he also did not have the money to travel to Europe.

Bishop Brown informed Vilatte that he was willing to support the missions, but that, he must be examined by two professors at Nashotah House (Seminary) on his theological knowledge. The test being satisfactory, Bishop Brown wrote that he would consult with some of his fellow bishops regarding Loyson's advice that Vilatte should be ordained by Bishop Herzog. (Herzog, by law was not allowed by the Swiss Government to perform episcopal acts outside Switzerland, but he ordained for the Gallican Church in France, some men who were sent to him by Loyson).

Word came on May 27, 1885, that the bishops (consulted by Bishop Brown) had decided that ordination of Vilatte by the Old Catholic Church was the wisest course to follow. It was also suggested at the time, that Vilatte accept ordination of the Protestant Episcopal Church and that there orders were just as valid as the Old Catholics in Europe. Vilatte did not accept this proposal, as his followers did not want to be part of any church that may have question of orders. However, Vilatte did ask Bishop Brown for a testimonial letter and the following was written:

My dear Brother,

Permit me to introduce to your confidence and esteem bearer of this letter, Mr. Rene Vilatte, a candidate for Holy Orders in the Diocese of Fond du Lac. Mr. Vilatte is placed in peculiar circumstances. Educated for the priesthood in the Roman Catholic Church, he found himself unable to receive the recent Vatican Decrees, and for a short time associated himself with the Presbyterian communion, but at last, by the mercy of God, was led into contact with this branch of the One Holy Catholic and Apostolic Church. He resided for a while at Green bay, a city of this diocese. In the neighborhood of this place there are settled about 30,000 Belgians. Of these a large number, probably 8,000, are believed to be inclined to the principals of pure primitive Catholicism. Several delegations of these Belgians have waited Mr. Vilatte and besought him to become their priest. Mr. Vilatte's character for piety, sobriety, purity, intelligence and prudence has been attested to the satisfaction of this diocese. Our canons, however, require a longer probation as a candidate then the exigency of circumstances will bear. At the suggestion of Pere Loyson, approved by the Bishop of Connecticut and other Bishops, at the faculty of Nashotah House Seminary, and by me. Mr. Vilatte approaches you, requesting you to ordain him to the priesthood, as speedily as you can find possible that he may enter upon the great work to which he seems to be especially summoned. It has been expedient to us to send him to you that he may learn personally something of the aims and spirit of the great movement of which you are a recognized leader and to be fitted to cooperate with you in some degree in this country. Mr. Vilatte's pecuniary means are limited and he desires to be absent from this diocese as short as time as possible. I ask you to ordain him to the priesthood and attest his character, briefly but sufficiently, by saying that I am willing to ordain him, if it should not seem expedient to you to do so.

Truly a loving brother and servant,
in the Holy Church of Our Lord,

JH Hobert Brown,
Bishop of Fond du Lac.

Armed with this letter, Vilatte arranged to return to Green bay, confident that the road was clear, so he planned to sail for Europe. But the Bishop accompanied him to the railroad depot, and before the train started, said: I will ordain you a priest tomorrow, if you will be satisfied with your ordination and rest here. To this Vilatte replied: No! Old Catholic I am and Old Catholic I will be". Then came the assurance of the Bishop that he would nerve be subject to the Standing Committee of the Diocese of Fond du Lac, Even this did not satisfy Vilatte.

He was ordained deacon and priest by Bishop Herzog on June 6 and 7, 1885. According to his own statement, he did not take the oath of canonical obedience to a diocesan bishop. This was to be the cause of much trouble in the near future.

On his return to Wisconsin, Father Vilatte opened a mission church for the Belgians at Little Sturgeon (Gardner). He dedicated it to the Precious Blood in order to stress that communion was given in both species. His first parish was located between two Roman Catholic Churches. The House of Bishops of the Protestant Episcopal Church granted him permission to use the French version of the Swiss Christian Church Liturgy, issued by Bishop Herzog in 1880. The Chapel was built with money donated by Episcopalians and the priest in charge (Vilatte) was paid a salary from the funds of the Diocese of Fond du Lac also gave his imprimatur to "Catechism Catholique", compiled by Vilatte, which rejected the doctrines of Immaculate Conception and papal Infallibility, and laid down that the Sacrament of Penance was not obligatory. Not long after the mission of the Blessed Sacrament was opened in Green Bay.

For the first three years all went well for the Old catholic Missions. In September 1887 the Fond du Lac diocesan magazine referred to Vilatte as "The young pioneer priest of the Old catholic work in America, tall with a winsome countenance and enthusiastic manner, a model of a priest and pastor. A young man of energy and dignity, culture and education, he has sacrificed his life to the cause of Old catholic reform. We pray God to open the hearts and hands of all churchmen all over the land to the aid of his noble work".

In 1961 there were thirteen Roman catholic parishes in the City of Green Bay, and where Vilatte's chapel stood there is now a Franciscan friary, the original Old catholic Church (Blessed Sacrament) is listed in the Episcopal Church Annual among Episcopal Churches without qualification.

About this time, Vilatte felt that he needed an assistant. A Mr. Gauthier, a Catholic schoolmaster was sent by Bishop Brown to Switzerland and raised to the diaconate and priesthood. Upon his return to the United States he was appointed pastor of Blessed sacrament Church in Green Bay. At this time there were three

Old Catholic parishes in Northeastern Wisconsin, Green Bay, Little Sturgeon and Dykesville.

Bishop Brown died May 2, 1888, and was on November 13, succeeded as Bishop of Fond du Lac by Charles C. Grafton, who had been one of the first members of the Crowley Fathers, founded at Oxford in 1866. Grafton was a rigid High Churchman. He at first supported Vilatte in his mission and most of all, did not want any Catholics to become part of the Roman Catholic Church. Grafton and Vilatte continued with their differences throughout the rest of his stay in Wisconsin.

Twenty-one months after his appointment as Bishop, Grafton realized that the Old Catholic missions of Northeast Wisconsin were not actually under his episcopal command that they were more or less "Free Lance". The Bishop managed to persuade Vilatte to transfer the legally to the trustees of the Diocese of Fond du Lac, to be held in trust for Old Catholicism. In return for this, the trustees agreed to pay stipend to Old Catholic clergy and finance their work. This soon proved to be a fatal error on the part of Vilatte.

In 1889, Vilatte published a pamphlet entitled 'A Sketch of the Belief of Old Catholics' In it, Vilatte was still quite convinced that he had a vocation to be an Old Catholic mission priest in the United States. He also promoted the idea of a Democratic catholic church in America. Nor Roman Catholic and not Protestant Catholic, but American Catholic (This is his first mention of the American Catholic Church).

In Dykesville, Vilatte established the first Old Catholic religious order and monastery. The Society of The Precious Blood ("SPB") he and two other members made up the first members.

When Archbishop Heykamp, Old Catholic Archbishop of Utrecht, heard of the goings on in Wisconsin between Vilatte and Bishop Grafton, he wrote to Vilatte on September 19, 1889, to break off relations with the Protestant Episcopal Church (at that time the Old Catholics did not recognize the PEC orders as valid). On October 8, 1889, Bishop Dipendaal, Bishop of Deventer wrote a letter stating that the Old Catholic hierarchy of the Netherlands regarded Father Vilatte. SPB, as one of their priests, and the recognized leader of the Old Catholics in North America.

The following April, Vilatte told Bishop Grafton about the correspondence with the Church of Utrecht, and suggested that he be raised to the episcopate. Bishop Grafton wrote to Archbishop Heykamp with the suggestion that Vilatte might be consecrated Abbot-Bishop of The Society of Precious Blood and suffragan bishop of Fond du Lac, but that this action would have to emanate from the church in the Netherlands and Vilatte would have to sent back to America by their mandate. That if a consecration did take place that Vilatte and the Old Catholics would face financial cutoff from the Diocese of Fond du Lac. That is was only through his financial support that the Old Catholic Missions were able to exist. The Bishop also stated that he would remove Vilatte as pastor of the Old Catholic Missions if such a consecration took place.

What took place next, it what I have mentioned so many times in my letters on his network. When the Old Catholic Missions of Northeastern Wisconsin were used as a pawn between the Protestant Episcopal Church and The Old Catholic Church of the Netherlands, the true-vine of Old Catholicism in the United States was cut off and from that point on, there was no true Old Catholic Church in the United States. The Polish National Catholic Church entered into communion with the Old Catholic Church of the Netherlands, but they were not Old Catholic, they were Polish in every respect.

Vilatte and Grafton were determined to rid themselves of each other. At one point, Vilatte had sent letters to the Russian Orthodox Bishop of the Aleutian Islands and Alaska, seeking assistance. The final breaking point took place when Bishop Grafton started publishing statements against Vilatte in Episcopal publications and asking fellow Episcopalians to stop sending money and donations to the Old Catholic Missions of Northeastern Wisconsin. He further stated that, "Father Vilatte had been making proposals to the Roman Catholic Bishop of Green Bay, The Russian Orthodox Bishop and the Old Catholic Bishops of Holland.

Meanwhile, the Old Catholic Bishops in Europe continued their request that Vilatte discontinue any relations with the Protestant Episcopal Church and the Diocese of Fond du Lac. They assured him that there would be no problem arranging for his episcopal consecration. In September of 1890, when Bishop Grafton showed up at the Old Catholic mission with several of his clergy, for confirmation, he was informed that there were no candidates because the Old Catholic Bishops of Holland had forbidden him to accept any sacraments from a Protestant prelate.

Grafton insisted on addressing the congregation, stating that he was their true Bishop and he reminded them of his financial support (this was at Duval). The next day the same scenes took place at Little Sturgeon. Shortly thereafter, Bishop Grafton wrote to Vilatte and suggested that he give-up his work and turn everything over to the Diocese of Fond du Lac. (This included churches, houses, furniture, religious items and vestments). On September 19, 1890, Vilatte sent a letter to Bishop Grafton; he informed him that he was severing connections with the Episcopal Church.

As proof that he no longer accepted the jurisdiction of the Bishop of Fond du Lac, Vilatte opened a new mission station near Green Bay. On hearing this, Bishop Grafton inhibited him until he obtained authorization. On October 30, he informed "the free lance priest" Vilatte, that there was no chance in obtaining an Old Catholic bishop for the United States and that the Bishops in Europe had no right to interfere with polity in the United States.

After the Old Catholic Congress held in Cologne in September of 1890, the bishops had decided that it was not expedient to carry out the consecration of Vilatte as their only official representative in the United States. It was not until 1897 that they appointed Stanislas Kozlowski as the first Old Catholic Bishop for North America, however, his mandate was directed to serve scattered Poles (there was no concern for the Belgians of Northeast Wisconsin)

Realizing that he had been rejected by both the Episcopalians and the Old Catholics, Vilatte appealed to Bishop Vladimir for the second time. In his (Vladimir) reply, he stated that he would communicate at once with the Holy Synod of Moscow, and if no answer was received after a reasonable time, he would re-ordain him 'sub conditone', and receive him as a priest of the Russian Orthodox Diocese of the Aleutian Islands and Alaska.

Matters dragged on until February 20, 1891, when Bishop Grafton informed Vilatte that he had been "removed from the mission station of St. Mary's, Dyckesville". The Russian Bishop urged Vilatte to fight against the impostors who challenged the authority of the Oecumenical Councils. On March 11, 1891, the Bishop of the Aleutian Islands and Alaska dispatched the following letter:

TO THE PIOUS OLD CATHOLIC PARISHIONERS AND TRUSTEES OF THE CHURCH AT DYCKESVILLE:

in which he states that it was a great joy for them to be a branch of the great body of Jesus Christ and members of the Church of Jerusalem, Antioch, Alexandria and Constantinople, where are the seats and cathedrals of Patriarchs of the Oecumenical Orthodox Church. He asked that God help them to defend Christian truth against the errors of the papist and Protestant sectarians, who do not belong to the true Catholic Church of Christ. He asked them to defend their priest against the Bishop of Fond du Lac, other Protestants and those who could not be regarded as true brothers on Christ, because of their heresies and lack of apostolic succession.

Bishop Grafton was furious when he read the letter of Bishop Vladimir. He wrote a letter to Vilatte and stated that if he were an honest man he would do one of three things.

1) Return to a loving and loyal obedience to him
2) Take a letter of transfer to the Archbishop of Utrecht, or to Bishop Vladimir
3) Leave the Country

On April 13, 1891 Bishop Grafton suspended Vilatte for six months from all priestly ministrations of all kinds whatsoever. Vilatte merely replied that he did not recognize Grafton's authority and he refused to leave the mission. On May 9, Bishop Vladimir issued an official document which stated:

By the Grace of God, and the Authority bestowed ion me by the Apostolic Succession, I, Vladimir, Bishop of the Orthodox Catholic Church announce to all clergyman of different Christian denominations and to all Old Catholics, that The Reverend Joseph Rene Vilatte, Superior of the Old Catholic Parish of Dyckesville, Wisconsin, is now a true Old catholic Orthodox Christian, under the patronage of our Church, and no Bishop or Priest of any denomination has the right to interdict him or suspend his religious duties, except the Holy Synod of the Russian Church, and myself. Any action contrary to this action is null and void on the basis of liberty of conscience and laws of this country.

This is one of the tough parts in the history of Archbishop Vilatte. Here he has crossed over from Old Catholicism to the Eastern or Orthodox Church. In studying the theology, doctrine, tradition of both "Catholic" bodies, it is not so easy to switch from one to another.

At this point, in the life of Vilatte, he was hated by Bishop Grafton, who called him a con-man and published letters and warnings describing him as a swindler who kept bad company, and whose associates, some of whom he mentioned by name, were his equal in crime and debauchery. It was one of these friends referred to by Bishop Grafton, a clergyman named Harding, formally a member of the Oblates of Mary Immaculate, and a missionary in India, who inspired Vilatte to pursue a line of action, which might prove to his advantage then his remaining under the protection of the Russian Orthodox Bishop. The story told was as follows:

(Taken from "Bishops At Large" Peter Anson, p. 105)

"In about 1888 about 5,000 Catholics of the Latin Rite of Ceylon and South India had formed a schismatic body known as the Independent Catholic Church of Ceylon, Goa and India. The reasons for this break with the papacy were political rather then religious. From the sixteenth century there had existed a concordat between the Holy See and the King of Portugal, which allowed the latter to nominate Bishops to the diocese of Latin Rite India, as well as other colonies which had formally been Portuguese colonies. The arrangement was known as the Patrondo (Patronage). By the second half of the nineteenth century it had become obvious that it was high time for Patrondo to be abolished.

On January 2, 1887, Pope Leo XIII set up a new Latin hierarchy for India and Ceylon, with the bishops (except for the province of (Goa) directly dependent on the Congregation of Propaganda. This change aroused considerable indignation because there still existed strong sentimental link between Indian Catholics and Portugal. Many native priests were indignant at being transferred to jurisdictions of French or Italian bishops.

Thus came into being what was called the 'Patrando Association'. Its leaders petitioned King Luis I of Portugal, to use his influence at Rome to have the royal patronage restored. On February 10, 1888, A Goan priest, who had been a Brahmin, Antonio Francisco-Xavier Alvarez, was elected by the Association as first bishop of the schismatic church. He applied to Mar Dionysios V, Jacobite Metropolitan of Malankara since 1976, to consecrate him, but with no result. His appeal to Mar Ignatius Peter III, Jacobite Patriarch of Antioch was more successful.

Vilatte, realizing that there was no further hope of being raised to the episcopate by any of the Old Catholic bishops of Europe, and doubtful of an association with the Patriarchate of Moscow, Vilatte decided to write to Alvarez—who called himself 'Mar Julius I' Metropolitan of the Independent Catholic Church of Ceylon, Goa and India—asking if he would be willing to consecrate him. The answer came as following:…"

(Again from Anson)

"We from the Bottom of our hearts thank God that He has mercifully shown you the way out of the slavery of Rome; and we rejoice to see a large number of Christians making heroic efforts in the same direction as ourselves in the New World.

Alvarez was willing to come to America to consecrate Vilatte, but Vilatte replied that it would be better if he went to Ceylon, which would save the hardships of traveling to North America. In his second letter to Vilatte, Alvarez said he would be delighted to welcome the "worthy minister of God from Wisconsin".

No time was wasted. Vilatte placed his Old Catholic missions under the care of Brother Augustine (Harding) and explained to his flock the reasons for his making the long voyage to the Far East. They were the following:

1) Because the Old Catholics in America were forbidden by the Archbishop and Bishops in Holland to present their candidates to Anglican Bishops for confirmation, or to use holy oils blessed by them;

2) The fear that in case of his death, the people would be left without pastoral care, in which case he would be responsible should they have to submit to Roman Catholic bishops;

3) The long silence of the Holy Synod of Moscow, and the apparent indifference of the Orthodox Church towards the Old Catholic Movement in North America;

4) the expressed Orthodoxy of the Independent Catholic Church of Ceylon, together with the urgent invitation to go there and receive the Apostolic Succession.

THE CONSECRATION OF VILATTE

Before leaving Green Bay, Vilatte held a Synod at which he was elected bishop and begged to obtain an indisputable episcopal consecration as soon as possible. He was given $225.00 for the trip and traveled economy or third class on a steamer. He sailed from New York on July 15, 1891, and was away from North America for over one year.

After almost a year, Vilatte was consecrated in the former Portuguese Church of Our Lady of Good Death, Colombo, which now belonged to the Independent Catholic Church. Mar Julius was assisted by his own consecrator, Mar Paul Athanasius, Bishop of Kottayam and Mar George Gregorius, Bishop of Niranam. The Roman Pontifical was used. May 29, 1892.

In the Bull of His Holiness Peter III, signed and sealed from the Patriarchal Palace at the Monastery of Sapran and Mardin on the borders of Syria and Kurdistan on December 29, 1891, the consecration of Joseph Rene Vilatte was granted for the archiepiscopal dignity, Archbishop Metropolitan, in the name of "Mar Timotheos", for the Church of the Mother of God in Dyckesville, Wisconsin, United States and the Churches of the Archdiocese of America, viz. The Churches adhering to the Orthodox Faith.

On May 30, 1892, an agreement was drawn up between Alvarez and Vilatte, in which the latter acknowledged the Confession of Faith, the canons and Rules of the Syrian Jacobite Church, and rejected all the doctrines, which are declared heretical by said Church. Vilatte promised that he would be subject and obedient to the Patriarch, and to his successors in the Apostolic See of Antioch. In return for this he would receive from Antioch, the necessary supply of holy oil, which the Patriarch alone is allowed to consecrate. Vilatte also promised to remit to the Annual Peter's Pence Collection. He also stated that if he ever severed relations with the Monophysite Churches of the Antiochian Rite or diverted from their canons or rules, he would be subject to dismissal from the dignity of Metropolitan. Mar Julius signed the certificate of consecration June 5, 1892, which conferred upon him the title of the Old Catholic Bishop of America, together with the power to consecrate churches, chancels, cemeteries and all functions appertaining to Metropolitan rank. The witness to this document was Dr. Lisboa Pinto, USA Consul for Ceylon.

On returning to Green Bay he visited Holland and France. Arriving in Green Bay, he found the following deposition from the Bishop of Fond du Lac:

(From the archives of the Bishop of Fond Du Lac)

> In virtue of the authority left by Our Lord Jesus Christ to his Church of binding and loosing and of putting away every brother that walketh disorderly, we do hereby deprive the said Joseph Rene Vilatte of all privileges and powers of the ministry of the Church and Depose him from his office as Priest. And we call upon the faithful to keep themselves from any ministrations at his hands, and we do erase and blot out his name from the register of clergy of this Church, in token that if he repent not and amend, God will blot out his name from the Book of Life.

The Old Catholic Archbishop of North America also found awaiting his return to Wisconsin a report issued by the House of Bishops at the General Convention of the Protestant Episcopal Church, presided over by Bishop Drone, Bishop of Albany, which read:

> It appears that the bishops from whom M Vilatte claims to have received consecration belong to a body which is separated from the Catholic Christendom because of nonacceptance of dogmatic decrees of the Council of Chalcedon as to our Blessed Lord's Person:
>
> These bishops had no jurisdiction or right to ordain a bishop for any part of the diocese under the charge of the Bishop of Fond du Lac: M. Vilatte was never elected by any duly accredited Synod It appears that M. Vilatte, in seeking the Episcopate, made statements not warranted by the facts of the case, and seemed willing to join with any body, Old Catholic, Greek, Roman, Syrian, which would confer it upon him. More than two months before the time of his so-called consecration, he was deposed from the sacred ministry. In view of these facts, we propose the following resolutions.
>
> 'Resolved. That in the opinion of this House, the whole proceedings in connection with the so-called consecration of J. Rene Vilatte were null and void, and that this Church does not recognize that any Episcopal character was thereby conferred.'

'Resolved. That a statement of the above-recited facts be sent to the Archbishop of Utrecht, to the Old Catholics in Germany and Switzerland, and to the Metropolitans and Primates of the Anglican Communion'.

To help save the French speaking Catholics from Archbishop Vilatte, the Roman Catholic Bishop of Green Bay, sent to France for Flemish and French priests to minister to the people under the care of Vilatte. It was never determined how many parishioners or followers he had, but an estimated 500 is in the records of the Diocese of Green Bay.

I want to say something about Peter Anson and his book, 'Bishops at Large'. I first read this book at Seminary, in the 1960's. It was then, considered the "gossip" or "tell on the trash" about the Old Catholics in England and the United States. At that time, there was very limited printed material about Old Catholicism or Independent Catholics.

How I found most of the information I have shared here is: I became personal friends with Archbishops Wallace D. Maxey, Richard A. Marchenna and Robert Burns. I held a long correspondence with prelates of England and kept a record of events, times and places. Today I have several file cabinets chuck full of information.

Now, in this modern age of computer data and web pages, some of the Old Catholic Churches have beautiful and pictorial information about their particular branch of Old Catholicism. Here I am trying to bring out the facts. I believe that Vilatte was sincere in his quest to build an American Catholic Church.

In my many talks with Archbishop Maxey (ordained to the priesthood by Vilatte) he often spoke of Vilatte's desire to unite the small independent Catholic churches. There are so many situations and circumstances that must be taken into consideration in Vilatte's quest. The two main obstacles were the Roman Catholic and the Protestant Episcopal Churches. They had the resources and money to attack every effort made by Vilatte. Then too, the Old Catholics of Holland and Germany did not keep their word to Vilatte and when he looked elsewhere, they became very authoritative (like unto Rome) and joined with American clergyman against Vilatte.

There were times when Vilatte considered taking his flock back to the Roman Catholic Church, this documented correspondence can be found in the archives of the Roman Catholic Diocese of Green Bay and was made available by Monsignor Joseph A. Marx, former Vicar General of the Diocese. Msgr. Marx spent a good deal of his life researching Vilatte's career in Wisconsin.

At no time did Vilatte ever have a large following in Wisconsin. It is estimated that 500 members would be about right. Here is where Bishop Grafton is able to belittle the work of Vilatte, saying that Vilatte's followers were unlearned and did not know the truth, that they were poor and for the most part they were. Vilatte canvassed the Eastern United States among Episcopalians, seeking clothing and other creature comforts for his parishioners. Many staunch Catholics refused to have anything to do with him, even when he did offer comforts. In some places the Archbishop of North America was driven away by the Belgians.

Often Vilatte had a difficult time making ends meet. He and his monks went hungry. Bishop Grafton had managed to get hold of the property and though he said that "it was being held in trust for the Old Catholics'" when they needed the revenue, the bishop did not make the sources available. Sometimes he had to flee to avoid creditors. He did have a booth at the World Parliament of Religions in 1893, but was not officially invited to participate in any of the events.

Finding himself at the end of his rope less then two years after being consecrated, Vilatte decided that the best thing he could do for himself and his followers was to be reconciled with the Roman Catholic Church (he believed Bishop Grafton and the PEC to be Protestant).

He approached Archbishop Satolli, the Apostolic Delegate (March 26, 1894) and the archbishop informed Bishop Messmer of Green Bay, that Vilatte was ready to submit to the Roman Catholic Church. About three weeks later, he wrote to Messmer that he was preparing his people for reconciliation with Rome. Further correspondence took place between Satolli, Messmer and Vilatte. In August of 1894, Satolli advised Messmer to finance Vilatte's journey to Rome. That the Propaganda would refund the money.

Matters dragged on for almost four years. In February 1898 the Apostolic Delegate wrote to the Bishop of Green Bay that Vilatte was now quite ready to recant his errors and submit to Holy Mother Church as a layman.

While all of this was going on, Vilatte had published an Old Catholic catechism and announced the formation of a sort of religious order—The Knights of the

Crown of Thorn's—which would have a monastery in Green Bay, when money was found to build it.

In spite of the offer of a journey to Rome, at the expense of the Diocese of Green Bay or the Congregation of Propaganda, he continued to waver. Eventually both Archbishop Satolli and Bishop Messmer realized that Vilatte would not submit to Rome. At that time, Vilatte was approached by a group of Poles, who asked him to be their bishop. Bishop Messmer wrote to Archbishop Satolli "For the present, he has an asylum among schismatic Poles, who will pay him court until he will be infatuated and foolish enough to consecrate one of them for the episcopate. Then they will cast him out." This happened six years later.

Rome offered terms to Vilatte, but they did not satisfy him. After he left Wisconsin, some of his followers reconciled with Rome but most joined with the Diocese of Fond du Lac and ended their days as Episcopalians. The priests that worked with Vilatte in Wisconsin, Gauthier (a good man); Mouthy (said to have become a scamp and drunkard); Lopez (moved to New York to take care of an Italian independent Catholic congregation.

This is the end of the Old Catholic Missions in Northeast Wisconsin. This is also the end of any real Old Catholic Church in the United States—associated with the Old Catholic bishops of Holland and Germany.

Here is a time to draw a fine line. When Vilatte left Green Bay, did he leave the Old Catholic Church of Northeast Wisconsin there or did he take it in "in his pocket" so to speak? Many would say that the Old Catholic Church of Holland and Germany ended at that time. As pointed out in series #8, most of the members joined the Episcopal Church and a few were reconciled with the Roman Catholics, some scattered in other directions. We know that the Old Catholics did not depose Vilatte or excommunicate him—but he did join another branch of the catholic church and signed and swore allegiance to another bishop.

The Archbishop of Ceylon, Goa and India (independent Catholic Church) sent Vilatte back with papers saying that he was the Old Catholic Archbishop of North America. There are those who would question the authority of that appointment. None the less, Vilatte did use that title at times. The Old Catholics, for a brief time appointed a Polish priest/bishop to represent the Church, but that was not long termed and it certainly showed Vilatte that he was not their representative.

Having failed to show to many Belgians the way out of slavery of Rome, and apparently indifferent to his obligations to the Syro-Jacobite Patriarchate, Vilatte turned his attention to a much larger body of people, optimistic of gaining support from them. These were the widely spread Polish Catholics. There had been a steady immigration of Poles to the USA since about 1830, and the first Polish priest arrived in 1851. Many Poles crossed the Atlantic in the hope of making their fortunes in the New World. After the civil war, many moved to the Middle West, mainly Chicago.

After 1873 there began a series of conflicts between Polish priests and American bishops. So fused were religion and nationalism with the Poles that most of them were determined not to be integrated with other Catholics. They wanted a church of their own. Towards the end of the century, independent Polish Catholic Churches existed in Baltimore, Buffalo, Chicago, Cleveland, New York, Toledo and elsewhere. The chief leader of these Poles was Father Antoni Kazlowski, who procured episcopal consecration from the Dutch Old Catholics in Holland on November 17, 1897 (mentioned above, this was an Old Catholic consecration, but not an official Old Catholic community in the United States). This was not the Polish Old Catholic Church in the United States, like the Belgians in Northeast Wisconsin.

The first meeting between Vilatte and the Poles was in 1894, when Father Kolaszewski invited him to dedicate a church in Cleveland. After Kazlowski's consecration, Vilatte was approached by Father Stephen Kaminski pastor of the Holy Mother of the Rosary, Buffalo, New York, to raise him to the episcopate. This priest had failed to persuade the Old Catholic Archbishop of Utrecht to raise him to the episcopate.

There is rumor and gossip that Vilatte was paid $5,000 for this consecration and that the invitation stated that both Cardinal Gibbons of Baltimore and Archbishop Martinelli, the Apostolic Delegate would assist in the ceremony.

With characteristic bravado, Vilatte arrived in Buffalo on March 21, 1898, and consecrated Kaminski (in his own church), giving him the title "Assistant Bishop". However, the new bishop fled the United States to Canada because of creditors. He was excommunicated by Rome and abandoned Vilatte. He later returned to the United States and pastored his church until he died in 1911.

On October 24, 1976; Archbishop Wallace David de Ortega Maxey related the following to me, in San Francisco, California:

After the consecration in Buffalo, Vilatte sailed to England, to meet-up with Father Ignatius of Jesus, OSB, of Llanthony Monastery, in the Black Mountains of South Wales.

Vilatte became acquainted with Ignatius when he visited the USA, 1890-91, raising funds for the work in England. Ignatius claimed that he belonged to the Ancient British Church, which was the oldest after Jerusalem and Antioch.

In his book, 'Bishops at Large', Anson makes Vilatte out to be a charlatan and accuses him of going to England to get his hands on Llanthony money. We know that Vilatte sailed from New York to England and arrived three months after the Kaminski consecration. He first visited Dr. F.G. Lee, of the Order of Corporate Reunion and Bishop of Dorchester. Lee gave Vilatte a letter of introduction to Ignatius.

Vilatte arrived in the Black Mountains on July 18, and was greeted by Ignatius. He brought all of his documents and vestments and offered valid orders to any and all, including Ignatius. Explaining that he was on his way to Russia. Anson's book relates a story from one of the monks of Llanthony:

"After the Old Catholic Archbishop's arrival at Llanthony there went up to God a ceaseless stream of prayer from 5 AM to 5 PM, besides the midnight services, daily, that God's will might be done. The archbishop offered services daily. Our superior presented three objections to the Archbishop.

1) He could not follow the Old Catholics in their excessive rancor against the Church of Rome.

2) He could never be anything but a faithful son to the Church of Britain and must use the 'Filioque' until the National Church permitted its erasure from the Creed.

3) Was not the Syrian Patriarch and his Church, Monophysite?"

There is a long story about Vilatte and these monks, eventually Ignatius and others received ordination from the hands of Vilatte, using the Latin Rite. It was further stated that 'the Archbishop had great humility and gentle courtesy'

The last three days of his visit to Llanthony, Vilatte confirmed a young boy, blessed and consecrated holy oils, consecrated veils for nuns, gave his solemn benediction. There was a former monk, Bertie Cannell, whom the archbishop took long smoking walks with, was also convinced that he was called to the priesthood as was Baron Rudolph de Bertouch, then 16 years old.

Before leaving Llanthony, Vilatte blessed Ignatius as abbot. Bishop Grafton started rumor that Vilatte was given a large sum of money from Ignatius, but a member of the community Calder-Marshall states that: "A small sum of money was pressed in the hands of the archbishop" In the same letter Bishop Grafton accuses Vilatte of being a drunkard. In a letter to the Church Times, he writes:

1) I was obliged in the year 1892 to degrade Joseph Rene Vilatte from the priesthood and excommunicate him from the Church.

2) I have discovered that he is morally rotten; a swindling adventurer. He was reported to me for drunkenness, swindling, obtaining money under false pretenses and other crimes, he is a notorious liar.

3) The man has somewhat exceptional gifts as an impostor. He can preach and pray with great fervor

4) He has been surrounded by and uses for his tools, a small group of ex-Roman Catholic priests who are equal in his crime and debauchery. His late secretary is now in State prison, a Brother William is now in an insane asylum and he is accused of criminal conduct with boys."

Again, I wish to point out that Vilatte continued to have problems with Bishop Grafton, this Episcopal Bishop followed the career of Vilatte and often wrote against him, but on several occasions, he offered him a position in the Diocese of Fond du Lac if he would just submit to him. I personally believe that "submit" is the word and that because Vilatte refused Episcopal orders and Bishop Grafton believed the Episcopal orders to be the only authentic catholic orders in the United States, there remained a constant feud on the side of Bishop Grafton. The bishop did not want to be told that he was not authentic and here Vilatte, a former priest of Northeast Wisconsin, now an Archbishop.

Before he left South Wales, Vilatte stated that his next official stop would be Russia and a visit with the Holy Synod. There is no proof or documentation that he ever reached his destination when he departed in the last week of July 1898, one hundred years ago.

However there is documented proof that the archbishop was in Rome and in January of 1899, most Catholic newspapers of Europe and North America reported that Vilatte was seeking reconciliation with the Holy See of Rome, instead of the Holy Synod of Moscow. On February 2, 1899, Father David Flemming, Defender General of the Friars Minor, and Consulter of the Congregation of the Holy Office, issued a statement to the effect that Joseph Rene Vilatte had expressed his most sincere and heartfelt regret for having taught many errors and for having attacked and misrepresented the Holy Roman Catholic Church; that he withdrew any such teachings, and that he regretted that he has illicitly and sacrilegiously conferred upon others various orders. This cleric called upon others whom he ordained to submit to the Vicar of Christ. On May 25, 1899 Bishop Zardetti wrote Bishop Messmer (Green Bay) that Father Flemming had the case well in hand.

Then came reports that Vilatte had not made his final abjuration with Rome or been reconciled with the Church. It was explained that he was awaiting the result of the Process before the Holy Office. Meanwhile, the Holy Office received an eight page report from the Diocese of Green Bay, in which the Bishop laid stress on the insincerity of Vilatte in the past; suggesting that he merely wanted Rome to say that his orders were valid so that he could go to England and validate the Orders of Anglican clergyman.

By 1900, Vilatte was in France. His hosts were the Benedictine monks of the Abbey of Saint Martin, near Poitiers. He was there to make a careful study of his orders in the Syro-Malabar Church, so that he could convince the Holy Office of the validity of his episcopate. This is confirmed by Joris Karl Huysmans, a French novelist that was also visiting the Abbey. When asked in later years to comment on that visit and Vilatte. He said "He is dead now; may he rest in Peace, for his Havanas were excellent".

{Here I must point out, was a very low time for the archbishop. While he enjoyed the company of the monks of the abbey, he had no income. He waited for the slow process of the Congregation of the Holy Office to decide on the validity of his orders and yet he wanted to proceed in the building of the Church}

On April 17, 1900, Cardinal Richard of Paris circulated a warning among his clergy to be on their guard against priests who produced papers signed by Vilatte. On June 13, 1900 Roman authorities issued excommunications against two priests, Paolo Miragila Gulotti and Joseph Rene Vilatte. On May 6, 1900, Vilatte consecrated Gulotti as Old Catholic Bishop of Italy, with the title of Bishop of Piacenza. This later became known as the Italian National Episcopal Church.

After two years in Europe, Vilatte decided to once again seek refuge in Canada. He went to Saint Joseph Island (1901) and there he opened a small domestic chapel. It is said by the local Jesuit priest, that the Indians, who were used to seeing their priest in black cassock, were "overawed" to see Vilatte in his Roman purple cassock.

In the summer of 1903, Vilatte was back in South Wales and raised to the episcopacy the Rev. Henry Marsh-Edwards, with the title of Bishop of Cearleon. He was a former Anglican priest of the Diocese of Southwell. The next day both men consecrated Henry Bernard Ventham as Bishop of Dorchester. Priests were ordained that summer in both England and the Continent.

While Vilatte was in England and Europe a series of conflicts between the Church and the State of France broke out, arising from anticlerical legislation. This gave Vilatte inspiration to return to his native country. This he did in the summer of 1906.

The previous December the government passed a bill stating that they did not recognize any form of religion. Vilatte was on friendly terms with Aristide Briand, one of the leaders of this movement and the Minister of Education. There were talks of opening up a National Church on Gallican lines. The State now had the power to sequester property administered by church councils, and pass it over to welfare and charitable institutions under the control of local authorities.

Soon after his arrival in Paris, Vilatte managed to obtain possession of the Barnabite Church in Rue Legendre, which he reopened for Old Catholic services. One of his former priests from Wisconsin assisted.

{Once again, Anson has dug up stories and dirt against Vilatte. He had a difficult time paying bills and on March 2, 1907, the police in Paris took away his miters and crozier for nonpayment, but Vilatte managed to retrieve them by June 21 of the same year}

On June 21, 1907 Vilatte consecrated a former Trappist monk, Francois Giraud. Shortly after this consecration Cardinal Richard issued a warning to the people about apostate priests who were celebrating mass under cover of a pseudo American Bishop. Vilatte was then excommunicated a second time by the Archbishop of Paris. Soon thereafter Vilatte returned to the United States.

Chicago became the next home to Archbishop Vilatte. At this time, he had severed all relations with the Independent Catholic Church of Ceylon, Goa, the Syro-Jacobite Church and the Old Catholic Churches of Europe. The establishment of the Polish National Church and the consecration of Father Francis Hodur was the final blow to his to his hope of being the Old Catholic Archbishop of North America.

In 1909 he traveled to Winnipeg, Canada to ordain two monks from Llanthony Abbey—Dom Asaph Harris and Dom Goldas Taylor. The latter went on to Mexico, where for some years he worked in establishing the Mexican National Church.

It was in 1910, that Vilatte raised to the priesthood, Dom Francis Brothers, prior of Saint Dunstan's Abbey, Waukegan, Illinois. This was an Old Catholic group of men, legally incorporated in Fond du Lac (1909) by Bishop Grafton as "The American Congregation of the Order of Saint Benedict" (In 1911 the Abbey was united with the Polish Old Catholic Church).

In 1915, Vilatte founded "The American Catholic Church". It was at this time that he received Rev. Frederick Ebenezer Lloyd into the Church and on December 19, 1915 was consecrated at Saint David's Chapel on East thirty-sixth Street, Chicago. Vilatte was assisted by Bishop Paul Miragila Gulotti, formally of Italy and then of New York and working with Vilatte in the United States. During this consecration the Archbishop addressed the congregation and newly consecrated prelate saying:

It needs to prophet to foretell for you and the American Catholic Church a great future in the Province of God. The need for a Church both American and Catholic, and free from the papacy and all foreign denominations, has been felt for many years by Christians of all the denominations. May your zeal and apostolic ministry be crowned with success.

The second wife of Bishop Lloyd, Philena Peabody was an ancestor of George Peabody, the American industrialist and merchant who made his fortune in England. They were a devoted couple.

By 1914, the dynamic energy of Vilatte was diminishing and in a Synod held in Chicago on April 10, 1920, he offered to retire and named Lloyd as his successor as Primate and Metropolitan of the American Catholic Church. The clergy attending granted Vilatte the honorary title of Exarch. He lived in retirement at 4427 North Mulligan Avenue, Chicago and he did not perform any more episcopal functions until September 22, 1921 when he helped launch the African Orthodox Church. It was also at this time, that he ordained to the priesthood, Wallace David de Ortega Maxey.

This is the end of the American ministry of Archbishop Vilatte. There is very limited information about the life of Vilatte. Most printed material comes from men like Bishop Grafton or Anson—men who were out to disparage the Old Catholic movement and anyone that had anything to do with launching the Church in England or the United States.

Vilatte was a poor man but because of friends and financial help from here and there managed to survive. He had all the beautiful vestments and appointments of a bishop, many originating from Rome. They were gifts from prelates and other people that admired his work. He was a Frenchman that remained loyal to his native country and on every occasion afforded him, he returned there.

In the beginning of this history, I tell of Vilatte being born into the Petite Eglise, he was from a small non-papal Catholic Church from birth. He wanted to continue to provide France with a Church free from the papacy and when he could not do that, he made the attempt among the French settlers of Canada and the United States.

France was poor, the settlers were poor, friends offered him the money to proceed. Sometimes he lived well and other times he was so poor that he and his monks went hungry.

Do you know a missionary who has not given his life, money, cloths and other material values for the 'Love of God'. The bishop writing to me asked that I say something kind about Vilatte.

He was dedicated, he was kind and loving to his people, he traveled in the United States, Canada and Europe begging for clothing, food and medicine for the people of God that he served in Northeast Wisconsin. He humbled himself to work within the Diocese of Fond du Lac, and when his benefactor died, the buildings and churches he erected were swindled away from him. Yes, some of those buildings are there today. They are a memorial to his work. However no one in Northeast Wisconsin is working at erecting a monument or scholarship fund or any other memorial attributed to this man.

Someone suggested to me Sunday last, "Vilatte should be a Saint"—Yes he should. Bishop James Rankin pointed out that almost all of the Old Catholic and Independent prelates (including myself) of the United States have apostolic succession from Joseph Rene Vilatte. He is truly our Father in the American Catholic Church.

On June 1, 1925, Vilatte made his formal declaration before Bishop Ceretti, Apostolic Nuncio at Paris, regretting and repenting having received Holy Orders and having conferred them on others. A week later LaCroix and other newspapers announced that Vilatte, with an American boy-servant (Maxey), was staying at the Cistercian Abbey of Port-Colbert. He was there at the request of Pope Pius XI. The Holy See granted him a pension of 22,000 francs annually in recognition of his episcopal status.

On June 23, 1925, the Bayerischer Kurieg published at statement, at the orders of the Swiss Christian Catholic Church, to the effect that Vilatte had never been a priest of this body nor any other genuine Old Catholic Church. Bishop Ceretti replied to the newspaper as follows:

Archbishop Vilatte received Minor Orders and the Order of Subdeacon on June 5, 1885, The Order of Deacon of June 6 of the same year, and on the following day, June 7, 1885, the Ordination to the Priesthood. All these orders were conferred upon him by Bishop Herzog (Old Catholic Bishop) in the Old Catholic Church in Berne. This proved by documents, seals and signatures of Bishop Herzog.

Concerning his Episcopal Consecration, it took place on May 29, 1892. Archbishop Vilatte was consecrated by three Jacobite Bishops in the Cathedral of Archbishop Alvarez in Colombo (Ceylon). Archbishop Vilatte is likewise in the possession of the consecration deed in question bearing the signatures of the three above mentioned bishops and of the American Consul, who was present at the ceremony.

This letter was published in the same newspaper and Vilatte was very pleased that Bishop Ceretti believed and accepted his priesthood and consecration, even though they were irregular.

For the next three and a half years, Vilatte led a quiet and secluded life in a cottage within the Abbey grounds. He was addressed as Archbishop, but wore a soutane, he was offered to be re-ordained by Pope Pius XI, but he declined. He attended daily Mass, receiving communion on Sundays.

His end came suddenly. Archbishop Joseph Rene Vilatte died of heart failure on July 8, 1929, he was buried in simple form in the cemetery in Versailles. One of the bishops he consecrated and some of the priests he ordained were among the mourners In his lifetime, he consecrated seven bishops. Shortly after his death, most of his papers vanished.

ETERNAL REST GRANT UNTO YOU—ARCHBISHOP JOSEPH RENE VILATTE

My Relations with the Protestant Episcopal Church
by Archbishop Joseph Rene Vilatte

The Introduction to this work is given by Mar Georgius I, the patriarch of Glastonbury et al. [Mar Georgius I, (H.G. de Willmott Newman)—Joseph Renee Vilatte, Glastonbury, London, UK, 1960]

Joseph Rene Vilatte was born at Paris, France, on the 24th of January 1854, and on 7th June 1885 was ordained to the sacred priesthood by Monsignor Edward Herzog, Old Catholic Bishop of Berne, Switzerland. He was consecrated to the Episcopate on 29th May 1892 by Archbishop Antonio Francisco Xavier Alverez of the Independent Catholic Church of Ceylon, Goa and India. As Archbishop of The Old Catholics of America. Monsignor Vilatte operated in the area of Lake Michigan for some 40 years. In his old age he returned to his native land France, where he died in 1932, in communion with the Apostolic See of Rome.

So far as his Episcopal career is concerned, this I propose to deal with in a forthcoming monograph; but until I am able to complete this, and also to more or less pave the way for it, I am publishing Monsignor Vilatte's own work, which amply covers his career as a priest and at least explains, though it does not justify, some of the reasons for that relentless and persistent persecution which Monsignor Vilatte sustained at the hands of the Anglicans until the end of his days and even thereafter.

From Archbishop Vilatte the following facts emerge:

1. In March 1884, entirely upon his own authority, Vilatte, then a layman, started a mission in Green Bay, Wisconsin, among French and Belgian immigrants, of Roman Catholic antecedents.

2. About twelve months later on the suggestion of Pere Hyacinthe of Paris, he contacted the Rt. Rev. J. H. Hobert Brown, Bishop of Fond du Lac in the Protestant Episcopal Church, who became interested in his (Vilatte's) scheme for making this mission an outpost of Old Catholicism.

3. Bishop Brown, after Vilatte had been examined by two of his clergy in theology, recommended him to Monsignor Herzog, Old Catholic Bishop of Berne, for ordination to the priesthood.

4. Wilst awaiting the decision of Bishop Herzog, Bishop Brown tried to persuade Vilatte to accept Anglican ordination, which he refused. On the eve of Vilatte's departure for Europe, he made a further attempt with the same result.

5. On 7th June 1885, when Vilatte was ordained Priest by Bishop Herzog, the latter, instead of administering the Oath of Canonical Obedience the form employed by a Bishop to his Priest, he used the formula "Dost thou promise to the Bishop, thy Ordinary". In view of the fact that by so doing Bishop Herzog discluded jurisdiction over Vilatte, his obligation of obedience, in the absence of any other Old Catholic Bishop having jurisdiction, would automatically become due to the Archbishop of Utrecht, or primus inter pares in the Old Catholic Episcopate.

6. Although certain misleading statements were published in various Anglican newspapers in the years 1885/6/7 to the effect that Vilatte was under the jurisdiction of their Diocese of Fond du Lac, this could not have been the case, inasmuch as Vilatte at no time fulfilled the conditions required for incardination into the ministry of the Protestant Episcopal Church, inasmuch

as he never subscribed the Declaration provided by Article 7 of the Constitution of the Protestant Episcopal Church.

7. Notwithstanding the foregoing, Vilatte did agree to Bishop Brown including his name in the Diocesan clergy list, understanding this as an honorary distinction.

8. Vilatte did solicit donations to his missions using as his testimonial a letter from Bishop Brown, dated 16th September 1887, whereupon no mention was made of the Protestant Episcopal Church.

{Bishop Brown died May 2, 1888}

9. Bishop Brown having died 2nd May 1888, he was on 13th November, succeeded in the Anglican See of Fond du Lac by Charles Chapman Grafton, who, realizing that Vilatte's missions were Old Catholic and nothing to do with the Protestant Episcopal Church, persuaded him to transfer them to the Trustees of the Diocese of Fond du Lac, to be held in trust for Old Catholicism, in return for which the Trustees apparently financed them, and paid Vilatte a stipend. This was a fatal mistake on the part of Vilatte.

10. Monsignor Heykamp, Archbishop of Utrecht, to whom Vilatte owed canonical obedience, having been made aware of this extraordinary position and relations between Vilatte and the Diocese of Fond du Lac, wrote him on the 19th September 1889. Urging him to sever connection. By letter dated 8th October 1889, Monsignor Dipendaal, Bishop of Deventer, a suffragan of Utrecht, wrote Vilatte in similar strain. From these and subsequent letters, and also from letters from Professor Van Thiel, and other Dutch priests, it is clear the Church of Holland regarded Vilatte as their protégé, and leader of an Old Catholic movement in the USA, and not under the jurisdiction of the Protestant Episcopal Church.

11. In April 1890, Vilatte informed Grafton of the letters he had received from Holland, and during the discussion the question of his consecration first came up for particle consideration. Dr. Grafton eventually persuaded Vilatte to let him approach Archbishop Heykamp.

12. By his letter to Archbishop Heykemp, dated April 1890, Grafton commenced his attacks upon Vilatte, not scrupling to make veiled threats towards His Grace, and to tell deliberate lies.

13. By letter dates 14th April 1890, Grafton offered to transfer Vilatte to either Heykemp or Herzog; which if there had been a genuine misconception on either side, would have been the correct thing to do.

14. By letter dated 14th April 1890, Monsignor Heykemp ruled that even if Vilatte had taken an oath of obedience to Fond du Lac, as a Catholic priest, he ought to sever any relationships.

15. Grafton, meanwhile, was continuing his vilification of Vilatte, and on 8th August 1890 wrote a letter to the Russian Orthodox Church, Bishop Vladimir in an attempt to disturb the harmonious relations which existed between him and Vilatte.

16. In the interim, it had been arranged that a proposal for the consecration of Vilatte, as Old Catholic Bishop of the United States, should be considered by the forthcoming Old Catholic Congress at Cologne.

17. In September 1890, Grafton, writing to the Anglican newspapers, warned Protestant Episcopalians not to donate money to Vilatte, who on 19th September formally withdrew connection.

18. At the Old Catholic Congress at Cologne in September 1890, it was decided that it was not expedient to proceed with the proposed consecration of Vilatte.

19. Being served from Fond du Lac, and abandoned by the Old Catholics, who had encouraged him to take that step, Vilatte, through Bishop Vladimir, opened up negations with the Russian Holy Governing Synod, meanwhile being taken under Vladimir's protection.

20. By letter of 23rd October 1890, Vilatte wrote informing the Archbishop of Utrecht that he had been taken under the protection of the Russian Orthodox Church, and would therefore require nothing further from Utrecht.

21. On 20th February 1891, Grafton purported to suspend Vilatte, not with-standing that he was under the protection of Vladimir.

22. Meanwhile Vilatte had got into contact with Archbishop Alvarez of Ceylon, to whom he explained his position and difficulties; and who, by letter dated 10th May 1891 wrote offering to confer the Episcopate upon Vilatte.

23. No decision having been reached by the Russian Synod, Vilatte accepted the offer of Alvarez, and departed for Ceylon, where he remained for some months.

24. On 29th March 1892, Grafton purported to depose Vilatte from the priesthood.

25. On 29th of May 1892, Vilatte was consecrated Old Catholic Bishop of America by Archbishop Alvarez.

It is difficult to see from the foregoing record anything which can be charged to Father Vilatte's discredit. It is equally clear that it fully disposes of Grafton's claim that Vilatte was never under his jurisdiction. Accordingly Grafton had no right to depose him, or even suspend him.

That there was some sort of an informal association between the Vilatte missions and the Diocese of Fond du Lac is certain; but it was in the first instance exceedingly loose and ill-defined. It is possible that Vilatte, who for many years was not too facile with his English, might have misconstrued remarks of Bishop Brown, or that the latter may have misconstrued the remarks of Vilatte. One would prefer to think no, in order to clear Bishop Brown, who seems to have been a kindly old soul. But the position with regard to Bishop Grafton admits no question of mis-understanding. By his crafty scheme to get control of Vilatte's missions, and by various letters he wrote, he reveals his duplicity.

It is certain:

a) If Vilatte was under the jurisdiction of Fond du Lac, then Grafton would have been entitled to depose him.

b) If, on the other hand, Vilatte was not under Grafton's jurisdiction, then whosoever jurisdiction was in fact under notwithstanding, Grafton had no power to suspend or depose him.

The matter is settled for all time: Vilatte at no time subscribed the Declaration required by the Canon Law of the Protestant Episcopal Church to be subscribed by clergy ordained outside that church.

Until he did so, he could not, legally or canonically, become a Presbyter of the Protestant Episcopal Church. He was therefore, at no time under the jurisdiction of the Bishop of Fond du Lac, Consequently, Grafton had no right or power to depose him; and his propertied act of deposition was illegal, and ineffective. His persecution of Violate, therefore, lacks even the poor excuse that Vilatte had laid himself open to it by being a disloyal Presbyter of his (Grafton) diocese; and rests upon no other foundation then hatred, malice and all uncharitableness.

On this unpleasant note ends Monsignor Vilatte's relationship with the Protestant Episcopal Church; though the persecution did not end. But that is another story, which I hope to tell later.

In conclusion, I would like to say, that presenting Archbishop Vilatte's MS to the public, my duty has compelled me to make drastic criticisms of Anglicanism generally, and of Bishop Grafton in particular. So far as the latter is concerned, his letters and actions speak for themselves, and the reader will be well able to judge for himself weather or not my criticisms have been justified. Anglicanism can only be judged by the acts of its representatives. But least any should imagine that I have some deep-seated animosity against that body, I would make it clear that such is not the case.

Although the actions of Anglicanism towards Archbishops Vilatte, and Mathew, and Bishop Herford and others, have frankly disgusted me, and caused me to reverse that favorable opinion which formally I had of it; and although I have been disillusioned regarding its claims to Orders, Missions and Jurisdiction, I do not bear it any personal ill-will. Indeed, I take this opportunity to testify to the fact that had the Anglican Church failed to survive the attacks by the Puritans of the 17th century, there is still little doubt that Britain would have lapsed into ultimate agnosticism or even atheism; for whatsoever her imperfections from the Catholic standpoint, Anglicanism has kept alive some concept of a Church of Episcopacy, and of Liturgical Worship, and of the Catholic Creeds. For this we are truly indebted.

Is it to much to hope that the Anglican Communion will at long last recognize that every man is by law entitled to worship God in his own way. Without let, hindrance, attack and vilification? So far as Britain is concerned, with a population of nearly 50 million churchless souls, there is surely room in the vineyard for bishops and priests of non Ultramontane Catholicism?

+Georgius
Patriarch of Glastonbury.

MY RELATIONS WITH THE
PROTESTANT EPISCOPAL CHURCH

Archbishop Joseph Rene Vilatte

The question of my relations with the Episcopal Church in America has been the subject of correspondence, explanation and strife almost from the beginning of my work as an Old Catholic Missionary. In dealing with this question, I, in my experience with Christian Bishops, believed always that the only defense necessary was a statement of simple truth concerning the question at issue. How I have fared as a result of the following faithfully this principle, the entire world knows. When I was attacked openly by Bishop Grafton and his party I defended myself so well as I could by publishing extracts from his letters to refute the charges brought against me. He, however, when silenced on one point, would always change his position and raise a new issue. Fortunately, for myself, I had preserved every letter of importance written by persons bearing on my relations with the Episcopal Church, and the Old Catholics of Europe; and owing to my unconscious foresight, I am able to give you evidence bearing on the question, which has never been published before. I myself, at that time, on account of my unfamiliarity with the English language, was unaware of their great importance in showing how the controversy arose. I found several years ago, a friend who is not only a theologian, but also well versed in civil and church law and to whose research I am indebted for the substance of this defense.

During a short visit last October, he requested me to allow him to examine all my correspondence, beginning with the first missionary work in this country. This search took ten days to complete, and among other documents relating to this question, the once mentioned above, were found. He is studying now in detail the entire matter and has written me that when his work is completed, and given to the world, it will bring about a day of retribution for my enemies, all the more terrible because delayed so long.

To enable you to understand how the controversy arose, I will tell briefly how I became connected with the Protestant Episcopal Church. During the latter part of the Franco-Prussian War, I enlisted in the National Guard, which was defending the City of Paris. When the siege was succeeded by the 'Commune', bringing with it great suffering and want, I determined to leave my native land and sail for Canada, as numerous placards had been posted in the rural districts asking for settlers. Some weeks after arriving in Canada, I learned that a teacher was needed to take charge of a school attached to one of the missions under the direction of a French priest near Ottawa. I took the charge as parish teacher and catchiest, and as the priest visited the mission only once a month, I conducted divine Service on Sunday when the priest was absent. He was pleased with the result of my work that he began to instruct me in Latin. After about two years service I felt a desire to revisit my native land, having received besides a notice from the French Government that I was drafted for a long period of service in the army. When I presented myself to the officers in Paris, I was informed that seven years of service in the army would be required of me. But the spirit of liberty which I had imbibed in America, together with memories of the Franco-Prussian War, made me determined to leave my native land rather then reenter the army.

I went therefore to Belgium and after a few months entered the Community of Christian Brothers, a lay teaching order at Namur. After a year's stay, I felt clearly that my vocation was for the priesthood, and therefore began studying with a professor of Latin for about a year. Then being desirous of returning to Free America, I went to Montreal and presented myself to the Roman Catholic Archbishop Febre of Montreal, who advised me to enter the seminary of Saint Lawrence, where I studied for three years. The teaching of the seminary was rabidly Romanastic that all other beliefs were condemned as heresies, which brought eternal damnation to all who accepted them. During my second vocation, I learned that the famous French priest, Father Chiniquy, was devoting his life to preaching against Roman error, announced in Montreal a series of sermons against Roman error. I attended with great fear several of them and returned to the seminary with my mind much disturbed. After sometime I felt that I could not remain there longer and not knowing what course to peruse. I visited a French Protestant minister in Montreal and after disclosing my state of mind, requested him to advise me. He urged me to join a private class in theology, which he was instructing where I met a French minister who was a professor in McGill University, controlled by the Presbyterians of Canada. He became interested in me and introduced to the President who urged me to continue there my theological studies, which I did, remaining there two years.

After some time, I began to compare Roman Catholicism with Protestantism, and saw plainly that while on the one hand Romanism has added much error and corruption to the primitive faith, Protestantism has not only taken away the Roman errors but also a part of the primitive deposit of faith. Nevertheless, I sought to bring peace to my mind by beginning anew my studies in the Roman Church, and therefore entered as a novice the monastery of the Clerics of Saint Viateur in Illinois. I had been there about six months when I learned that Father Chiniquy was living near the monastery. I determined to visit him and discuss my perplexities. Father Chiniquy sympathized with me and invited me to remain with him, which I did. After several months of friendship, he advised me not to return to the monastery, but to go to Green bay, Wisconsin, and begin work as a missionary among the French people, who, who although both Protestant and Roman Catholic, were drifting into spiritualism and infidelity. Father Chiniquy also suggested my writing to the famous Father Hyacinthe of Paris, who, as a reformer and fellow Gallican would both sympathize and direct my path. Father Chiniquy wrote to the people of Green bay telling them of my state among them. There reply was a request to come, I therefore took leave of Father Chiniquy and went in March 1884 to that city to begin my labors.

Finding there nothing but factions of different forms of belief, I began visiting various families and urging them to unite and form one congregation and ignore for the present all differences of doctrine. I felt that as long as my own mind was not at rest, I could preach nothing but the simple gospel. Shortly after beginning my work, I wrote Father Hyacinthe of Paris telling him of my situation and state of mind, declaring my conviction that neither Roman Catholicism nor Protestantism would satisfy the spiritual needs of these people who had already abandoned the Roman Church, I requested him to inform me concerning his religious movement in Paris and asked whether council and aid would be given in the effort to establish in America a Catholic church without any other qualification. While waiting for an answer, I conducted Service twice every Sunday and saw my first few listeners increase to a congregation filling the chapel which was enlarged only to be filled again. Under date of September 22, 1884, Pere Hyacinthe wrote that his church held the doctrinal position of the undivided Church before the separation of the East and the West and stated his conviction that if my work were directed by the same principal it would succeed, he also requested information concerning my work in Green Bay. His letter brought peace to my mind because I realized clearly now, where the hope for the future was. I replied to his request for information by stating that there were many hundreds of French and Belgians, a part of whom had already departed the Church, and the remainder, while nominally members, were thoroughly dissatisfied with their Church and therefore I believed that there was a fruitful field for the organization of the purified Catholic Church which would present the Gospel to the people as did the primitive Church, and exercise authority accordingly to the Spirit of free America.

After some months of waiting, Pere Hyacinthe replied on March 14, 1885, by urging me at once to go to Paris to confer with him personally, in the following words:

"A mistake would be fatal to you and to the important work you propose to undertake. There is much to be said which is impossible to be said by letter. Then your ordination, which should certainly be by the Latin rite, can be easily accomplished by our Old Catholic Bishop of Berne. This is necessary if you hope for any success in the true Catholic reform. If you act with words and charity as becomes a priest of the Holy Church of Christ, you can do a great work, but if you make a false step at the beginning, you will certainly fail, and not only injure your future vocation, but do great harm to the cause of true Catholicism and religious reform. In case you cannot possibly come then you should take advice from the Bishop of the American Episcopal Church of your diocese who is a good and wise man. And you should try by the power of all Christian charity to keep the confidence and love of your people".

As it was impossible for me to leave my newly gathered congregation to consult with Pere Hyacinthe in Paris, I followed his advice by going to the American Bishop Brown, telling him of my intention of beginning a movement of catholic reform among the French speaking people of Green Bay, and showing him the letters of Pere Hyacinthe. Bishop Brown replied to me stating he had heard much concerning my work in Green Bay and would be glad to aid me in this movement. He hoped, furthermore, that in referring this matter to his Standing Committee, that they would understand my particular position, and appreciate the good relationship which would be established between the Episcopal and Old Catholic Church, through me as a medium. Several weeks later I received a letter from Bishop Brown informing me first of all I must take leave of my congregation in Green Bay, after which I was to meet him at the Episcopal Rectory in that city, furthermore that I was to be examined by two of his clergy on my theological education. The examination be satisfactory, Bishop Brown wrote me that he would consult with several of his fellow bishops regarding Pere Hyacinthe's advice that I be ordained by the Old catholic Bishop Herzog. In the meantime I was to go to their seminary at Nashotah and remain until a decision was made. Several weeks after coming to Nashotah, I wrote to Pere Hyacinthe informing him of my position, and two days later, I wrote to Bishop Herzog of Berne, requesting him to ordain me.

After one month's waiting I received the following letter from Bishop Brown, dated April 27, 1885.

"I have submitted the suggestion of Pere Hyacinthe, that you go to Berne for ordination, to the judgment and advice of our bishops and am satisfied that it is the wisest course for you and all interested to be pursued".

One week later, I received from his letter, dated May 5, 1885.

> "The Standing Committee of the diocese have just met. After full discussion of your matter they have put into my hands testimonials warranting your ordination to the diaconate immediately and to the priesthood as soon afterwards as possible. The main reason controlling the Standing Committee were the conviction that the Anglican succession off Apostolic authority is preferable to that of the Old Catholics the importance of maintaining the sufficiency of it in this country, the saving of the time and expense, and a knitting of a closer unity with the diocese from the beginning of the movement."

As soon as I received this letter I went to Fond du Lac and stated to Bishop Brown that I could not accept an Anglican ordination, because it would prevent my work securing the support from the people, that the catholic ordination would insure. For which reason I insisted that he would send at once my certificates to the Old catholic Bishop Herzog of Switzerland. Seeing plainly that I would not accept his ordination, Bishop Brown wrote the following letter, dates May 5, 1885, giving me a copy.

On May 5, 1885, Bishop Brown wrote the following letter to Bishop Herzog.

"The Right Reverend Dr. Herzog,
Bishop of Berne

My dear Brother:

Permit me to introduce to your confidence and esteem the bearer of this letter. Mr. Rene Vilatte, a candidate for Holy Orders in the Diocese of Fond du Lac. Mr. Vilatte is placed in peculiar circumstances. Educated for the priesthood in the Roman Catholic Church he found himself unable to receive the recent Vatican decrees and for a short time associated himself with the Presbyterian communion, but at last, by the mercy of God, was led into council with this branch of the One, Holy, Catholic and Apostolic Church. He resided for a while at Green Bay, a city of this diocese. In the neighborhood of this place there are now settled about 30,000 Belgians. Of these, a large number, probably 8,000, are believed to be inclined to the principals of a pure and primitive Catholicism. Several delegations of these Belgians have waited on Mr. Vilatte and besought him to become their priest. Mr. Vilatte's character for piety, sobriety, purity, intelligence and prudence has been attested to the satisfaction of the authorities of this diocese. Our canons, however, require a longer probation of a candidate the exigency of the circumstances will bear. At the suggestion of Pere Hyacinthe (Loyson) approved by the Bishop of Connecticut, and other Bishops, and by the faculty of Nashotah Seminary, and by me, Mr. Vilatte approaches you to ordain him to the priesthood, as speedily as you can find possible that he may enter upon the great work to which he seems specially summoned. It has been expedient to us to send him to you that he may learn personally something of the aims and spirit of the great movement of which you a recognized leader and to be fitted to cooperate with you in some degree in this country. Mr. Vilatte's means are limited and he desires to be absent from this diocese as short a time as possible. I ask you to ordain him to the priesthood and attest his character, briefly, but sufficiently by saying that I am willing to ordain him, if it should not be expedient to you to do so.

Truly and lovingly your brother and servant, in the Holy Church of Our Lord,

J.H. Hobart Brown
Bishop of Fond du Lac"

As my path was clear of all obstacles, I prepared myself for the journey. Bishop Brown accompanied me to the railroad station, and before leaving me said "I will ordain you a priest tomorrow, if you will be satisfied with your ordination and rest here". To which I replied. "No; Old Catholic I am and Old Catholic I will be". Bishop Brown then assured me that I should never be subject to the Standing Committee of the diocese.

During my absence the following replies to my letters arrived from Pere Hyacinthe and Bishop Herzog.

"Pere Hyacinthe charges me to write you again to say that he has written to Bishop Herzog concerning you, and that if you have made your studies in the Roman Church, and taken the minor orders as we are informed you have, and bringing with you letters of recommendation from the American Episcopal Bishop of your diocese, there is no doubt whatever that Bishop Herzog will confer the priesthood upon you, and this will imply perhaps a residence at Berne for tow or three weeks".

> From Bishop Herzog, May 7, 1885:
>
> Dear and honorable Brother:
>
> In reply to your letter of 14th of April, I must tell you that I consider as indispensable, the formal ordination by a Catholic Bishop. I will ordain you a priest with pleasure, but the position I occupy in my country and the relations in which I am placed, face to face with the Bishops of the Episcopal Church of the United States, do not permit me to proceed with your ordination, unless I am authorized formally by the Bishop of the Episcopal Church of the diocese in which your parish is situated.
>
> + Edward Herzog
> Bishop

I arrived in Berne on June 3, and presented the letter from Bishop Brown to Bishop Herzog who requested me immediately to accompany him to Dr. Charles R. Hale, an American Episcopal clergyman who was visiting Berne. Bishop Herzog asked him to examine my testimonials and state his judgment on the matter. Dr. hale replied to Bishop Herzog that of the signers of my papers he knew personally, Dr. Cole, Dr. Adams, and Professor Riley; Professor Kemper alone was a stranger to him. He felt therefore sure that everything was right, and hoped that Bishop Herzog would proceed. Bishop Herzog replied that he would.

The following day, June 4, I was examined by Bishop Herzog, assisted by three priests. On June 5, I received minor orders and the sub-diaconate, on June 6, the diaconate and on June 7, the priesthood.

Concerning my ordination to the priesthood, I wish to call your attention to the following rubrics of the Roman rite of ordination:

> "Then each one goes up again to the Bishop and kneeling places his joined hands between those of the Bishop, who says to each, if he be his Ordinary: 'Dost thou promise to me and my successors reverence and obedience'? And he answers "I promise".

> "But if the Bishop be not his Ordinary, he says to each secular Priest, while he holds their hands between his own, as aforesaid, 'Dost thou promise to the Bishop, they Ordinary and to his successors, reverence and obedience' and the answer is 'I promise'."

This promise of obedience, as is evident from the rubric, is intended to apply only to ordinations performed by one Roman Bishop for another; it could not be construed to apply to any other ordination. It cannot therefore, be construed into the oath of canonical obedience to the Bishop of Fond du Lac, as the Episcopal Bishop Grafton has stated falsely, and on which his entire contention is based, that I was an Episcopalian clergyman.

On June 13, I sailed for America and arrived at Green Bay on July 3. Soon after my return I began visiting the settlements of French people, and later I obtained a small building in Little Sturgeon which was fitted up as a chapel for regular divine service. On October 16, I was visited for the first time in my parish by Bishop Brown. About a month later Bishop Brown asked me to visit him in Fond du Lac, which I did. During the visit he asked me weather I would permit him to place my name on the Clergy List of the diocese, to which I consented immediately.

In order to enable you to understand how my relations ceased with the Protestant Episcopal Bishop Grafton, which separation resulted in controversy concerning me, with all the falsehoods, slanders and continually repeated attacks on my char acter and work, I will state briefly now the events that compelled me to take the successive steps resulting in my archiepiscopal consecration, under the Bull of His Holiness Mar Peter Ignatius III, Patriarch of Antioch and all East.

During Bishop Brown's life, my time was occupied entirely in pastoral work, establishing new missions, and soliciting contributions to the aid and support the work, using the following letters of Bishop Brown to introduce myself.

"Sept 16, 1887

The Reverend Pere Vilatte is about to leave his work at the Mission of the Precious Blood, in quest of funds for the founding and support of the Theological School at Sturgeon Bay, which seems now to be the necessary agent for the extension and perpetuation of his peculiar and most interesting work. From personal observation of Pere Vilatte's labors, I am quite confident that they are undertaken in a spirit of devotion, self-sacrifice, prudence and loyalty to the faith and Order of the Church of Our Lord, which entitles him to the sympathy and aid of loving _____ I bespeak for him a kind and patient hearing.

J.H. Hobart Brown
Bishop of Fond du Lac"

You will notice the absence of any reference to the Protestant Episcopal Church. This omission is especially noteworthy because its letter was used continually as my authority to collect contributions. While collecting in New York City, I became acquainted with Reverend de Beaumont, a priest who had left the Roman Church several years before. I explained to him the Old Catholic work in Wisconsin, as a result of which, he offered his services as the head of the seminary, the land for which had already been donated. In Chicago, I met Reverend Proth, an ex-Trappist monk, who accompanied me to Little Sturgeon, where I secured a house in the city, which could be used temporarily as a seminary and placed Reverend de Beaumont in charge. About this time, Reverend Oser, a former Swiss parish priest, who with his congregation, was one of the first to join the Old Catholic movement, and whose name was one of the three from which the Old Catholic Bishop of Switzerland was chosen, wrote and asked information concerning my work. I replied, inviting him to visit with me, which he did, remaining about a month. But when he learned of the concoction with the Episcopal diocese of Fond du Lac, he refused to take part in the work. Reverend de Beaumont was introduced by me to Bishop Brown, who after examining his ordination certificate, which I had obtained from the Roman Catholic Bishop

Healy of Portland, expressed himself as satisfied. Reverend Proth remained with me until after Bishop Brown's death, collecting money by my authority and with my certificate.

Owing to my ignorance of English, I did not know during these few busy years, that these mis-statements of relations of myself and missions, to the diocese of Fond du Lac, for which Bishop Brown, even though his intention was good, must be considered responsible, were accepted as true by the Episcopal clergy as the extracts given from church papers have shown. In this connection I will mention the oft repeated remark made to me by Bishop Brown "Dear Father: I hope to see you an Old Catholic Bishop"

After Bishop Brown's death on May 2, 1888, my constant fear was that his successor might be a Low Church bishop, who might refuse to aid me in my work. About this time, a letter of inquiry came from Herr Wormhaut, a gentleman of Delft, Holland; who having read in the Dutch paper, an account of my work in Wisconsin wrote me asking further information regarding the movement. I replied by giving him the information requested, and then stated my fears for the future, by saying that Bishop Brown's successor might be a bishop who will not understand the relation of my mission to the diocese of Fond du Lac. That by refusing aid would place insurmountable obstacles in my way, to avoid which, it is evident, we must have a bishop of our own. I stated further that this step need not necessarily in the breaking of the ties which bound us together, but that we could continue to dwell together in charity and love. I closed by requesting Herr Wormhaut to bring this matter of attention to his parish priest (Pastor Harderwyk).

Some weeks after Bishop Brown's death, a French Canadian Christian Brother named Gauthier, whom I had meet during my stat in Montreal, and with whom I had corresponded more or less, offered his services. I received him, and on his arrival, began training him, preparatory for ordination. I have given you these details of my various assistants, in order to show you how much truth there was in the reports (which Bishop Grafton circulated in Europe) of the insignificance of my work, after I, in obedience to the command of Archbishop Heycamp, refused to allow him to administer confirmation to my mission.

On November 13, 1888, Bishop Grafton was chosen to succeed the deceased Bishop Brown. I supported his nomination, believing in view of his well known catholic opinions, that I and my missions would be safe under his protection, until such time as we could secure a bishop of our own. He was consecrated April 25, 1889. {Charles Chapman Grafton, a former "Cowley Father" that is, a member of the Anglican religious order called "The Society of Saint John the Evangelist", was one of the leading High Churchman of his times. He was responsible for the bitter attacks upon Archbishop Vilatte. He died in 1912—DW}

Several weeks after this, I received the following letter from Herr Wormhaut of Delft, in answer to the one I addressed to him, after Bishop Brown's death.

"Reverend and dear Father,

Nothing in your letter please me so much as your freedom from the milk-and-water theology of Protestantism. But what I don't comprehend is your desire, even if you had the Old Catholic succession to be in perfect communion with the Protestant Episcopal Church, for you surly must be aware of the fact that the whole Catholic church, both the East and the West, including our own national branch, consider her orders exceedingly doubtful. Some of her own members, both lay and clerical, participate in this doubt, and have in England banded themselves together into a society known as the Order of Corporate Reunion, as for the doctrine of the Anglican Church, it is undoubtedly heretical, and heresy is heresy, whether found in the Book of Common Prayer or in the decrees of the Vatican".

Very soon after I received this letter, the following letter dated June 4, 1889, came from Pastor Hyderwyk.

"When you write to Herr Wormhaut that it is necessary for you to have a bishop in perfect communion with the American Episcopal Church, I must say that to such a position and proposition, I could never subscribe. For (1st) The American Episcopal Church is not Catholic in doctrine, her faith in the holy sacraments (of which the Catholic Church numbers seven) is in no wise that of the primitive church. The doctrine of the American Episcopal Church, as well as that of the Church of England, touching to the holy sacraments of the altar and the sacrifice of Jesus Christ in the Eucharist, is positively Protestant. (2nd) The Apostolic Succession and validity of the Episcopal consecration in England and America is extremely doubtful. Perhaps you will say: The Old Catholics of Germany and Switzerland are in communion with Anglicans. It is true. But I believe the prelates in Germany and Switzerland are led astray by the specious sayings of individual bishops without being at all at one with the Anglican Church in general".

Sometime after his consecration, Bishop Grafton, visited me during the summer of 1889 at Little Sturgeon, when I presented Brother Gauthier to him, and stated that I intended to have him ordained by Bishop Herzog, without consulting anyone else connected with the Episcopal diocese. Bishop Grafton consented and requested me to write to Bishop Herzog concerning the ordination, stating that he would also write to him.

In discussing the financial questions relating to the support of the missions, I stated to him that I thought it necessary to go and collect money to pay the debt of our new church, as after Bishop Brown's death, I had sold many things belonging to me, even my watch, to pay the workmen. Bishop Grafton replied: "No; I would be the beggar for Old Catholicism; donate your missions to the Diocese of Fond du Lac, and the trustees will pay your debt; for I do not wish you to make appeals yourself." But when I accessed, I gave the property to the Diocese of Fond du Lac on the condition that it should be for the use of Old Catholicism, hence it would be no more diverted to the use of the Protestant Episcopal Church then to the Methodists.

Bishop Herzog replied to Bishop Grafton's request as follows:

"Berne, August 20, 1889.

To: The Right Reverend Charles C. Grafton
Bishop of Fond du Lac

My Lord,

Accept, first of all, my cordial wishes of congratulation and benediction on your elevation to the Episcopate. The news I received of your election and consecration was an evidence to me, how peculiarly fortunate the Diocese of Fond du Lac should consider itself to have procured your person, so distinguished a successor to the memorable Bishop Brown. I thank you, too especially the kindly disposition which you manifest towards Vilatte and his work. It rejoices my heart, that in your episcopal visitation you have made satisfactory observation and regard to the movement as deserving your entire support. It will afford me great pleasure to conform to your wish to supply an assistant to ____ Vilatte by conferring priestly ordination upon the Rev. J. B. Gauthier.

Rev. Dr. Hale, Dean of Davenport, who was present at the ordination of Vilatte at Berne, has made it clear to me, why it would be advantageous that the ordination should be performed by me.

I am most worthy Bishop
Your devoted,

Edward Herzog,
Bishop

In this connection, I want to call your attention to the underlined sentence in Bishop Herzog's letter {it was not underlined "that in your Episcopal visitation you must have made satisfactory observation and regard the movement as deserving your entire support" in part 12]} which show plainly that at this time, I and the mission were not considered a part of, or under the jurisdiction of the Episcopal Diocese of Fond du Lac.

On September 6, 1889, I received a letter from Bishop Grafton containing among other things the following: "Bishop Herzog's most satisfactory and cheerful epistle shows that Brother Gauthier must depart soon to meet him. I have sent a copy of this letter to Brother Gauthier. See that this matter does not get into the papers. There is one matter that I want you and Brother Gauthier to be cheerful of. Study as to how you can keep yourselves and your affairs out of the newspapers. Don't let anything said prompt you to reply. Let the world and the Church and the Romans think we have failed and died out. Let us study how we can keep hidden for a few years. Do not let the opening of the monastery be a public matter".

It is evident to everyone that Bishop Grafton realized at this time that the proposed ordination of Brother Gauthier by Bishop Herzog, like my own, was one which by its very nature placed him beyond any canonical jurisdiction of the Bishop of Fond du Lac. If this were not so, there would be no reason for keeping the knowledge of his Church, the steps by which this ordination was obtained. This fact, is proof that Bishop Grafton realized even more clearly then did Bishop Brown, that I was, accordingly to the canon law of the Protestant Episcopal Church, independent of the Bishop of Fond du Lac.

Bishop Herzog's reply being satisfactory to all concerned, I gave Brother Gauthier the necessary money to go to Berne, and on his return, I assigned him to the mission in Little Sturgeon, as I had removed to the new mission at Duval, a few weeks before Bishop Brown's death. In answering the letter of Pastor Harderwyk of June 4, 1889, I told him among other things of the steps I had taken to have Brother Gauthier ordained by Bishop Herzog and stated that on account of our poverty, I would be unable to continue sending young men to Bishop Herzog for ordination, for which reason, if for no other, it is absolute necessary that we have a bishop as soon as possible. I concluded by saying that if the bishops of Holland preferred to consecrate one of their own priests our bishop, instead of conferring the episcopate on me, that I would be entirely satisfied.

Pastor Harderwyk replied with the following letter:

> "Delft, Holland
> September 11, 1889
>
> You must disentangle yourself from the Protestant Episcopal Church. For that reason you have acted prudently in not having Mr. Gauthier ordained priest by Bishop Grafton, who had, to say the least, a doubtful, if not invalid consecration. It is impossible for you, who are a Catholic, to remain under the jurisdiction of a Bishop (?) who is, seriously speaking, Protestant and whose apostolic succession is very doubtful. For this reason, I counsel you to separate yourself totally from the Episcopal Church. You will say then, that it is absolutely necessary for you to have a truly Catholic Bishop" he goes on to say "I do not doubt that our bishops will participate with you once you have disconnected yourself from the Protestant Episcopal Church and that the Old Catholic Church in America would be a daughter of the Church in Holland".

Some weeks before, I had written to Archbishop Heykamp of Utrecht, telling him of my movement for Catholic reform and its connection with the Episcopal Diocese of Fond du Lac. His reply to my letter, came several weeks after the last one I received from Pastor Harderwyk, and reads as follows.

> "Utrecht,
> September 19, 1889
>
> To. Reverend Rene Vilatte
> Priest over the Old Catholics in America.
>
> We received with great joy your protestation of being, and wishing, to remain free from all Protestant influences; for what is a dangerous stumbling block over which so many have fallen, when seeing the

deplorable state in which the Church of Christ is found, they have risen up against the profane novelties introduced, and opposed themselves to ultramontanism. We also note with great joy that you do not make common cause with the Anglicans, who, leaving aside the validity of their orders, at bottom are not Catholics, but Protestants. For this reason, we hope that, however painful may be your situation, you will not rest in ecclesiastical communion with them, nor ever accept from them any religious service. It is better, in the wilderness where divine providence has led us, to abandon ourselves wholly to God then to implore the spiritual succor of those who are not united with us in the same faith in the truth which is one.

The Church of Holland recognizes the Roman Church as the only true Church of Jesus Christ, and the Pope of Rome as the Center of Catholic unity. Whoever occupies the See of Rome as long as the supreme tribunal of the Catholic Church has not condemned him, the Church of Holland regards as vested with the primacy in the church. She respects the character with which he is invested, but does not obey him in that which is contrary to truth and the spirit of the holy gospel. She, by the Grace of God, remains in the Roman Church and abhors schism as the greatest crime of the Church. Thus, by unmerited grace, the Church of Holland guards a sound and correct position in the Roman Catholic Church.

I salute you and your brothers with all my heart,
Your humble and devoted servant,

John Heykamp
Archbishop of Utrecht

Bishop Grafton came to visit me about this time, and during his stay, I showed him the letters which I had received from Herr Wormbout, pastor Harderwyk, Archbishop Haykamp and Bishop Diespendaal, explaining how I came to begin the correspondence. Bishop Grafton said nothing in reply, but as the following letter from Archbishop Heykemp, dated December 21, 1889, plainly shows, he must have decided at that early time, on his plan of action; which was to make the Bishops of Holland believe that my work was so insignificant, that a bishop was utterly unnecessary.

"You may well conceive, dear Father, that we would in no manner have it understood that from the human and material assistance, you should remain in harmony and ecclesiastical relationship with a church whose faith is not Catholic, and which is, separate from the center of Catholic unity. We had thought of you as though there were certain priests who had chosen your side; we now have learned 'that they are Anglican ministers' who quitted you later on, regretting the opinions and leeks of Egypt, ie: creature comforts of the Anglican Church and not willing to share with you a more modest situation.

Whatever the future may be my dear Father, do not loose courage; the cause you have the happiness to defend this cause of God.

John Haykemp
Archbishop of Utrecht"

Early in the year 1890, I compiled and had printed our Confession of Faith, sending a copy to Bishop Grafton, to Archbishop Haykemp of Utrecht, and to Bishop Vladimir, the Russian Bishop of Alaska. I could not possibly have dared to do this, had I been at the time, or considered myself an Episcopal minister. The reason for this statement is obvious by reading Article 7 of the Constitution of the Protestant Episcopal Church.

The Following letter from Professor van Thiel, the President of the Old Catholic Seminary at Amersfoort, is very interesting.

"I am happy to assure you that the reading of your 'Sketch' has quite satisfied me. It has rejoiced me so much the more in that, while altogether respecting your apostolic zeal, I believed there was some subject for fear lest your church ran the risk of departing from the true Catholic doctrine. For firstly, I know your ministry was connected, though even so slightly, with the Anglican diocese; then, in an account of Old Catholic work, I read among other things 'although the creed or doctrine be the same, our Old Catholic ritual is entirely different from the Episcopal liturgy' nevertheless, I know that the doctrine of the Episcopal Church differs in essential points from that of the Catholic Church, But, now happily the profession of faith you have published leaves no doubt whatever, that your missionary church is altogether conformed to the ancient faith of the Catholic Church, and that she is determined to cling closely thereto. Your profession appears to me to be very clear and assuredly, as to its doctrine, we should have no difficulty subscribing to it. I understand that you will keep yourself and your students, as much as possible, in conformity with our doctrinal education and practice of the Church of Utrecht, which you like to consider as your spiritual mother; to whom you are very intimately attached, and of the Catholic purity of whose doctrine you are entirely convinced. I rejoice with all my heart in your good intention. I need not say to you that in the meantime, I am ready to give you as much aid, advice and information, as is in my power. However I pray that the Lord may bless the work of your Mission, and that nothing will prevent our Church from procuring for you very soon the spiritual aid you need. Accept the affectionate and respectful sentiments of,

Yours devotedly,

C.J. van Thiel
Amersfoort"

Appendix E

The Rule of Faith, St Vincent of Lerins, 434

From: A COMMONITORY FOR THE ANTIQUITY AND UNIVERSALITY OF THE CATHOLIC FAITH AGAINST THE PROFANE NOVELTIES OF ALL HERESIES.

CHAPTER II.

A General Rule for distinguishing the Truth of the Catholic Faith from the Falsehood of Heretical Pravity. I HAVE often then inquired earnestly and attentively of very many men eminent for sanctity and learning, how and by what sure and so to speak universal rule I may be able to distinguish the truth of Catholic faith from the falsehood of heretical pravity; and I have always, and in almost every instance, received an answer to this effect: That whether I or any one else should wish to detect the frauds and avoid the snares of heretics as they rise, and to continue sound and complete in the Catholic faith, we must, the Lord helping, fortify our own belief in two ways; first, by the authority of the Divine Law, and then, by the Tradition of the Catholic Church. But here some one perhaps will ask, Since the canon of Scripture is complete, and sufficient of itself for everything, and more than sufficient, what need is there to join with it the authority of the Church's interpretation? For this reason,—because, owing to the depth of Holy Scripture, all do not accept it in one and the same sense, but one understands its words in one way, another in another; so that it seems to be capable of as many interpretations as there are interpreters. For Novatian expounds it one way, Sabellius another, Donatus another, Arius, Eunomius, Macedonius, another, Photinus, Apollinaris, Priscillian, another, Iovinian, Pelagius, Celestius, another, lastly, Nestorius another. Therefore, it is very necessary, on account of so great intricacies of such various error, that the rule for the right understanding of the prophets and apostles should be framed in accordance with the standard of Ecclesiastical and Catholic interpretation.

Id teneamus, quod ubique, quod semper, quod ab omnibus creditum est; hoc est etenim vere proprieque catholicum. [Moreover, in the Catholic Church itself, all possible care must be taken, that we hold that faith which has been believed everywhere, always, by all.]

For that is truly and in the strictest sense "Catholic," which, as the name itself and the reason of the thing declare, comprehends all universally. This rule we shall observe if we follow universality, antiquity, consent. We shall follow universality if we confess that one faith to be true, which the whole Church throughout the world confesses; antiquity, if we in no wise depart from those interpretations which it is manifest were notoriously held by our holy ancestors and fathers; consent, in like manner, if in antiquity itself we adhere to the consentient definitions and determinations of all, or at the least of almost all priests and doctors.

CHAPTER III.

What is to be done if one or more dissent from the rest. WHAT then will a Catholic Christian do, if a small portion of the Church have cut itself off from the communion of the universal faith? What, surely, but prefer the soundness of the whole body to the unsoundness of a pestilent and corrupt member? What, if some novel contagion seek to infect not merely an insignificant portion of the Church, but the whole? Then it will be his care to cleave to antiquity, which at this day cannot possibly be seduced by any fraud of novelty. But what, if in antiquity itself there be found error on the part of two or three men, or at any rate of a city or even of a province? Then it will be his care by all means, to prefer the decrees, if such there be, of an ancient General Council to the rashness and ignorance of a few. But what, if some error should spring up on which no such decree is found to bear? Then he must collate and consult and interrogate the opinions of the ancients, of those, namely, who, though living in divers times and places, yet continuing in the communion and faith of the one Catholic Church, stand forth acknowledged and approved authorities: and whatsoever he shall ascertain to have been held, written, taught, not by one or two of these only, but by all, equally, with one consent, openly, frequently, persistently, that he must understand that he himself also is to believe without any doubt or hesitation.

The American Catholic Union, *Traditional Old Catholic Dogma,* Daniel Wells, Used by Permission, 2003.

Appendix F

The Synod of Jerusalem 1672

To the candid and lovers of truth, what hath been said will be sufficient, or rather, so to speak, more than enough to enable them to understand what is the doctrine of the Eastern Church, and that she hath never at any time been in agreement with the Calvinists in their novelties (nor in fact with any others besides herself), nor hath she recognized him whom they contend was of their party, as being so. For the complete refutation, however, and uprooting of the designs which have been formed, contrarily to the glory of God, against the sacred bulwarks of our Orthodox religion, and, so to speak, for the complete demolition of the blasphemies contained in the vaunted Chapters {of the 1629 Confession}, we have thought it right to put forth certain Questions and Chapters corresponding in number to those written by Cyril, and diametrically opposing the same, wherein he hath, as it were (as hath been supposed many times), whetted his tongue against God, {Psalm 43:4} so that they may be called a refutation and correction of the said Chapters of Cyril. And the order which is there observed will be followed in these which will be put forth by us, so that each of the Faithful may be able to compare, and judge of both, and easily know the Orthodoxy of the Eastern Church, and the falsehood of the heretics. Where, however, necessity requireth, we shall omit some things, or add some other things tending to the accurate understanding of the matter. And we shall use words, entire sentences, and periods set out there, so that we may not seem to fight against words and Orthodox sentences rather than against novelties and impious dogmas.

[THE CONFESSION OF DOSITHEUS.]

Dositheus, by the mercy of God, Patriarch of Jerusalem, to those that ask and inquire concerning the faith and worship of the Greeks, that is of the Eastern Church, how forsooth it thinketh concerning the Orthodox faith, in the common name of all Christians subject to our Apostolic Throne, and of the Orthodox worshippers that are sojourning in this holy and great city of Jerusalem (with whom the whole Catholic Church agreeth in all that concerneth the faith) publisheth this concise Confession, for a testimony both before God and before man, with a sincere conscience, and devoid of all dissimulation.

DECREE I.

We believe in one God, true, almighty, and infinite, the Father, the Son, and the Holy Spirit; the Father unbegotten; the Son begotten of the Father before the ages, and consubstantial with Him; and the Holy Spirit proceeding from the Father, and consubstantial with the Father and the Son. These three Persons in one essence we call the All-holy Trinity,—by all creation to be ever blessed, glorified, and adored.

DECREE II.

We believe the Divine and Sacred Scriptures to be God-taught; and, therefore, we ought to believe the same without doubting; yet not otherwise than as the Catholic Church hath interpreted and delivered the same. For every foul heresy receiveth, indeed, the Divine Scriptures, but perversely interpreteth the same, using metaphors, and homonymies, and sophistries of man's wisdom, confounding what ought to be distinguished, and trifling with what ought not to be trifled with. For if [we were to receive the same] otherwise, each man holding every day a different sense concerning the same, the Catholic Church would not [as she doth] by the grace of Christ continue to be the Church until this day, holding the same doctrine of faith, and always identically and steadfastly believing, but would be rent into innumerable parties, and subject to heresies; neither would the Church be holy, the pillar and ground of the truth, {1 Timothy 3:15} without spot or wrinkle; {Ephesians 5:27} but would be the Church of the malignant {Psalm 25:5} as it is manifest that of the heretics undoubtedly is, and especially that of Calvin, who are not ashamed to learn from the Church, and then to wickedly repudiate her. Wherefore, the witness also of the Catholic Church is, we believe, not of inferior authority to that of the Divine Scriptures. For one and the same Holy Spirit being the author of both, it is quite the same to be taught by the Scriptures and by the Catholic Church. Moreover, when any man speaketh from himself he is liable to err, and to deceive, and be deceived; but the Catholic Church, as never having spoken, or speaking from herself, but from the Spirit of God—who being her teacher, she is ever unfailingly rich—it is impossible for her to in any wise err, or to at all deceive, or be deceived; but like the Divine Scriptures, is infallible, and hath perpetual authority.

DECREE III.

We believe the most good God to have from eternity predestinated unto glory those whom He hath chosen, and to have consigned unto condemnation those whom He hath rejected; but not so that He would justify the one, and consign and condemn the other without cause. For that were contrary to the nature of God, who is the common Father of all, and no respecter of persons, and would have all men to be saved, and to come to the knowledge of the truth; {1 Timothy 2:4} but since He foreknew the one would make a right use of their free-will, and the other a wrong, He predestinated the one, or condemned the other. And we understand the use of free-will thus, that the Divine and illuminating grace, and which we call preventing grace, being, as a light to those in darkness, by the Divine goodness imparted to all, to those that are willing to obey this—for it is of use only to the willing, not to the unwilling—and co-operate with it, in what it requireth as necessary to salvation, there is consequently granted particular grace; which, co-operating with us, and enabling us, and making us perseverant in the love of God, that is to say, in performing those good things that God would have us to do, and which His preventing grace admonisheth us that we should do, justifieth us, and maketh us predestinated. But those who will not obey, and co-operate with grace; and, therefore, will not observe those things that God would have us perform, and that abuse in the service of Satan the free-will, which they have received of God to perform voluntarily what is good, are consigned to eternal condemnation.

But to say, as the most wicked heretics do and as is contained in the Chapter answering hereto—that God, in predestinating, or condemning, had in no wise regard to the works of those predestinated, or condemned, we know to be profane and impious. For thus Scripture would be opposed to itself, since it promiseth the believer salvation through works, yet supposeth God to be its sole author, by His sole illuminating grace, which He bestoweth without preceding works, to shew to man the truth of divine things, and to teach him how he may co-operate therewith, if he will, and do what is good and acceptable, and so obtain salvation. He taketh not away the power to will—to will to obey, or not obey him.

But than to affirm that the Divine Will is thus solely and without cause the author of their condemnation, what greater calumny can be fixed upon God? And what greater injury and blasphemy can be offered to the Most High? For that the Deity is not tempted with evils, {James 1:13} and that He equally willeth the salvation of all, since there is no respect of persons with Him, we do know; and that for those who through their own wicked choice, and their impenitent heart, have become vessels of dishonour, there is, as is just, decreed condemnation, we do confess. But of eternal punishment, of cruelty, of pitilessness, and of inhumanity, we never, never say God is the author, who telleth us that there is joy in heaven over one sinner that repenteth. {Luke 15:7} Far be it from us, while we have our senses, thus to believe, or to think; and we do subject to an eternal anathema those who say and think such things, and esteem them to be worse than any infidels.

DECREE IV.

We believe the tri-personal God, the Father, the Son, and the Holy Spirit to be the maker of all things visible and invisible; and the invisible are the angelic Powers, rational souls, and demons,—though God made not the demons what they afterwards became by their own choice,—but the visible are heaven and what is under heaven. And because the Maker is good by nature, He made all things very good {Genesis 1:31} whatsoever He hath made, nor can He ever be the maker of evil. But if there be aught evil, that is to say, sin, come about contrarily to the Divine Will, in man or in demon,—for that evil is simply in nature, we do not acknowledge,—it is either of man, or of the devil. For it is a true and infallible rule, that God is in no wise the author of evil, nor can it at all by just reasoning be attributed to God.

DECREE V.

We believe all things that are, whether visible or invisible, to be governed by the providence of God; but although God foreknoweth evils, and permitteth them, yet in that they are evils, He is neither their contriver nor their author. But when such are come about, they may be over-ruled by the Supreme Goodness for something beneficial, not indeed as being their author, but as engrafting thereon something for the better. And we ought to adore, but not curiously pry into, Divine Providence in its ineffable and only partially revealed judgments. {Romans 11:33} Albeit what is revealed to us in Divine Scripture concerning it as being conducive to eternal life, we ought honestly to search out, and then unhesitatingly to interpret the same agreeably to primary notions of God.

DECREE VI.

We believe the first man created by God to have fallen in Paradise, when, disregarding the Divine commandment, he yielded to the deceitful counsel of the serpent. And hence hereditary sin flowed to his posterity; so that none is born after the flesh who beareth not this burden, and experienceth not the fruits thereof in this present world. But by these fruits and this burden we do not understand [actual] sin, such as impiety, blasphemy, murder, sodomy, adultery, fornication, enmity, and whatsoever else is by our depraved choice committed contrarily to the Divine Will, not from nature; for many both of the Forefathers and of the Prophets, and vast numbers of others, as well of those under the shadow [of the Law], as under the truth [of the Gospel], such as the divine Precursor, {St. John the Baptist} and especially the Mother of God the Word, the ever-virgin Mary, experienced not these, or such like faults; but only what the Divine Justice inflicted upon man as a punishment for the [original] transgression, such as sweats in labour, afflictions, bodily sicknesses, pains in child-bearing, and, in fine, while on our pilgrimage, to live a laborious life, and lastly, bodily death.

DECREE VII.

We believe the Son of God, Jesus Christ, to have emptied Himself, {Philippians 2:7} that is, to have taken into His own Person human flesh, being conceived of the Holy Spirit, in the womb of the ever-virgin Mary; and, becoming man, to have been born, without causing any pain or labour to His own Mother after the flesh, or injury to her virginity, to have suffered, to have been buried, to have risen again in glory on the third day, according to the Scriptures, {1 Corinthians 15:3,4} to have ascended into the heavens, and to be seated at the right hand of God the Father. Whom also we look for to judge the living and the dead.

DECREE VIII.

We believe our Lord Jesus Christ to be the only mediator, and that in giving Himself a ransom for all He hath through His own Blood made a reconciliation between God and man, and that Himself having a care for His own is advocate and propitiation for our sins. Albeit, in prayers and supplications unto Him, we say the Saints are intercessors, and, above all, the undefiled Mother of the very God the Word; the holy Angels too—whom we know to be set over us—the Apostles, Prophets, Martyrs, Pure Ones, and all whom He hath glorified as having served Him faithfully. With whom we reckon also the Bishops and Priests, as standing about the Altar of God, and righteous men eminent for virtue. For that we should pray one for another, and that the prayer of the righteous availeth much, {James 5:16} and that God heareth the Saints rather than those who are steeped in sins, we learn from the Sacred Oracles. And not only are the Saints while on their pilgrimage regarded as mediators and intercessors for us with God, but especially after their death, when all reflective vision being done away, they behold clearly the Holy Trinity; in whose infinite light they know what concerneth us. For as we doubt not but that the Prophets while they were in a body with the perceptions of the senses knew what was done in heaven, and thereby foretold what was future; so also that the Angels, and the Saints become as Angels, know in the infinite light of God what concerneth us, we doubt not, but rather unhesitatingly believe and confess.

DECREE IX.

We believe no one to be saved without faith. And by faith we mean the right notion that is in us concerning God and divine things, which, working by love, that is to say, by [observing] the Divine commandments, justifieth us with Christ; and without this [faith] it is impossible to please God.

DECREE X.

We believe that what is called, or rather is, the Holy Catholic and Apostolic Church, and in which we have been taught to believe, containeth generally all the Faithful in Christ, who, that is to say, being still on their pilgrimage, have not yet reached their home in the Fatherland. But we do not in any wise confound this Church which is on its pilgrimage with that which is in the Fatherland, because it may be, as some of the heretics say, that the members of the two are sheep of God, the Chief Shepherd, {Psalm 94:7} and hallowed by the same Holy Spirit; for that is absurd and impossible, since the one is yet militant, and on its journey; and the other is triumphant, and settled in the Fatherland, and hath received the prize. Of which Catholic Church, since a mortal man cannot universally and perpetually be head, our Lord Jesus Christ Himself is head, and Himself holding the rudder is at the helm in the governing of the Church, through the Holy Fathers. And, therefore, over particular Churches, that are real Churches, and consist of real members [of the Catholic Church], the Holy Spirit hath appointed Bishops as leaders and shepherds, who being not at all by abuse, but properly, authorities and heads, look unto the Author and Finisher of our Salvation, {Hebrews 2:10; 12:2} and refer to Him what they do in their capacity of heads forsooth.

But forasmuch as among their other impieties, the Calvinists have fancied this also, that the simple Priest and the High Priest {Bishop} are perhaps the same; and that there is no necessity for High Priests, and that the Church may be governed by some Priests; and that not a High Priest [only], but a Priest also is able to ordain a Priest, and a number of Priests to ordain a High Priest; and affirm in lofty language that the Eastern Church assenteth to this wicked notion—for which purpose the Tenth Chapter was written by Cyril—we explicitly declare according to the mind which hath obtained from the beginning in the Eastern Church:—

That the dignity of the Bishop is so necessary in the Church, that without him, neither Church nor Christian could either be or be spoken of. For he, as a successor of the Apostles, having received in continued succession by the imposition of hands and the invocation of the All-holy Spirit the grace that is given him of the Lord of binding and loosing, is a living image of God upon the earth, and by a most ample participation of the operation of the Holy Spirit, who is the chief functionary, is a fountain of all the Mysteries [Sacraments] of the Catholic Church, through which we obtain salvation.

And he is, we suppose, as necessary to the Church as breath is to man, or the sun to the world. Whence it hath also been elegantly said by some in commendation of the dignity of the High Priesthood, "What God is in the heavenly Church of the first-born, {Hebrews 12:23} and the sun in the world, that every High Priest is in his own particular Church, as through him the flock is enlightened, and nourished, and becometh the temple of God." {Ephesians 2:21}

And that this great mystery and dignity of the Episcopate hath descended unto us by a continued succession is manifest. For since the Lord hath promised to be with us always, although He be with us by other means of grace and Divine operations, yet in a more eminent manner doth He, through the Bishop as chief functionary make us His own and dwell with us, and through the divine Mysteries is united with us; of which the Bishop is the first minister, and chief functionary, through the Holy Spirit, and suffereth us not to fall into heresy. And, therefore [John] the Damascen, {sic} in his Fourth Epistle to the Africans, hath said, the Catholic Church is everywhere committed to the care of the Bishops; and that Clement, the first Bishop of the Romans, and Evodius at Antioch, and Mark at Alexandria, were successors of Peter is acknowledged. Also that the divine Andrew seated Stachys on the Throne of Constantinople, in his own stead; and that in this great holy city of Jerusalem our Lord Himself appointed James, and that after James another succeeded, and then another, until our own times. And, therefore, Tertullian in his Epistle to Papianus called all Bishops the Apostles' successors. To their succession to the Apostles' dignity and authority Eusebius, the [friend] of Pamphilus, testifieth, and all the Fathers testify, of whom it is needless to give a list; and this the common and most ancient custom of the Catholic Church confirmeth.

And that the dignity of the Episcopate differeth from that of the simple Priest, is manifest. For the Priest is ordained by the Bishop, but a Bishop is not ordained by a Priest, but by two or three High Priests, as the Apostolic Canon directeth.

And the Priest is chosen by the Bishop, but the High Priest is not chosen by the Priests or Presbyters, nor is he chosen by secular Princes, but by the Synod of the Primatial Church of that country, in which is situated the city that is to receive the ordinand, or at least by the Synod of the Province in which he is to become a Bishop. Or, if ever the city choose him, it doth not this absolutely; but the election is referred to the Synod; and if it appear that he hath obtained this agreeably to the Canons, the Elect is advanced by ordination by the Bishops, with the invocation of the All-holy Spirit; but if not, he is advanced whom the Synod chooseth. And the Priest, indeed, retaineth to himself the authority and grace of the Priesthood, which he hath received; but the Bishop imparteth it to others also. And the one having received the dignity of the Priesthood from the Bishop, can only perform Holy Baptism, and Prayer-oil, minister sacrificially the unbloody Sacrifice, and impart to the people the All-holy Body and Blood of our Lord Jesus Christ, anoint the baptised with the Holy Myron [Chrism], crown the Faithful legally marrying, pray for the sick, and that all men may be saved and come to the knowledge of the truth, {1 Timothy 2:4} and especially for the remission and forgiveness of the sins of the Faithful, living and dead. And if he be eminent for experience and virtue, receiving his authority from the Bishop, he directeth those Faithful that come unto him, and guideth them into the way of possessing the heavenly kingdom, and is appointed a preacher of the sacred Gospel. But the High Priest is also the minister of all these, since he is in fact, as hath been said before, the fountain of the Divine Mysteries and graces, through the Holy Spirit, and he alone consecrateth the Holy Myron. And the ordinations of all orders and degrees in the Church are proper to him; and in a primary and highest sense he bindeth and looseth, and his sentence is approved by God, as the Lord hath promised. {Matthew 16:19} And he preacheth the Sacred Gospel, and contendeth for the Orthodox faith, and those that refuse to hear he casteth out of the Church as heathens and publicans, {Matthew 18:17} and he putteth heretics under excommunication and anathema, and layeth down his own life for the sheep. {John 10:11} From which it is manifest, that without contradiction the Bishop differeth from the simple Priest, and that without him all the Priests in the world could not exercise the pastorate in the Church of God, or govern it at all.

But it is well said by one of the Fathers, that it is not easy to find a heretic that hath understanding. For when these forsake the Church, they are forsaken by the Holy Spirit, and there remaineth in them neither understanding nor light, but only darkness and blindness. For if such had not happened to them, they would not have opposed things that are most plain; among which is the truly great mystery of Episcopacy, which is taught by Scripture, written of, and witnessed to, both by all Ecclesiastical history and the writings of holy men, and always held and acknowledged by the Catholic Church.

DECREE XI.

We believe to be members of the Catholic Church all the Faithful, and only the Faithful; who, forsooth, having received the blameless Faith of the Saviour Christ, from Christ Himself, and the Apostles, and the Holy Œcumenical Synods, adhere to the same without wavering; although some of them may be guilty of all manner of sins. For unless the Faithful, even when living in sin, were members of the Church, they could not be judged by the Church. But now being judged by her, and called to repentance, and guided into the way of her salutary precepts, though they may be still defiled with sins, for this only, that they have not fallen into despair, and that they cleave to the Catholic and Orthodox faith, they are, and are regarded as, members of the Catholic Church.

DECREE XII.

We believe the Catholic Church to be taught by the Holy Spirit. For he is the true Paraclete; whom Christ sendeth from the Father, {John 25:26} to teach the truth, {John 26:13} and to drive away darkness from the minds of the Faithful. The teaching of the Holy Spirit, however, doth not immediately, but through the holy Fathers and Leaders of the Catholic Church, illuminate the Church. For as all Scripture is, and is called, the word of the Holy Spirit; not that it was spoken immediately by Him, but that it was spoken by Him through the Apostles and Prophets; so also the Church is taught indeed by the Life-giving Spirit, but through the medium of the holy Fathers and Doctors (whose rule is acknowledged to be the Holy and Œcumenical Synods; for we shall not cease to say this ten thousand times); and, therefore, not only are we persuaded, but do profess as true and undoubtedly certain, that it is impossible for the Catholic Church to err, or at all be deceived, or ever to choose falsehood instead of truth. For the All-holy Spirit continually operating through the holy Fathers and Leaders faithfully ministering, delivereth the Church from error of every kind.

DECREE XIII.

We believe a man to be not simply justified through faith alone, but through faith which worketh through love, that is to say, through faith and works. But [the notion] that faith fulfilling the function of a hand layeth hold on the righteousness which is in Christ, and applieth it unto us for salvation, we know to be far from all Orthodoxy. For faith so understood would be possible in all, and so none could miss salvation, which is obviously false. But on the contrary, we rather believe that it is not the correlative of faith, but the faith which is in us, justifieth through works, with Christ. But we regard works not as witnesses certifying our calling, but as being fruits in themselves, through which faith becometh efficacious, and as in themselves meriting, through the Divine promises {2 Corinthians 5:10} that each of the Faithful may receive what is done through his own body, whether it be good or bad, forsooth.

DECREE XIV.

We believe man in falling by the [original] transgression to have become comparable and like unto the beasts, that is, to have been utterly undone, and to have fallen from his perfection and impassibility, yet not to have lost the nature and power which he had received from the supremely good God. For otherwise he would not be rational, and consequently not man; but to have the same nature, in which he was created, and the same power of his nature, that is free-will, living and operating. So as to be by nature able to choose and do what is good, and to avoid and hate what is evil. For it is absurd to say that the nature which was created good by Him who is supremely good lacketh the power of doing good. For this would be to make that nature evil—than which what could be more impious? For the power of working dependeth upon nature, and nature upon its author, although in a different manner. And that a man is able by nature to do what is good, even our Lord Himself intimateth, saying, even the Gentiles love those that love them. {Matthew 5:46; Luke 6:32} But this is taught most plainly by Paul also, in Romans chap. i. [ver.] 19, {Rather chap. ii., ver. 14.} and elsewhere expressly, saying in so many words, "The Gentiles which have no law do by nature the things of the law." From which it is also manifest that the good which a man may do cannot forsooth be sin. For it is impossible that what is good can be evil. Albeit, being done by nature only, and tending to form the natural character of the doer, but not the spiritual, it contributeth not unto salvation thus alone without faith, nor yet indeed unto condemnation, for it is not possible that good, as such, can be the cause of evil. But in the regenerated, what is wrought by grace, and with grace, maketh the doer perfect, and rendereth him worthy of salvation.

A man, therefore, before he is regenerated, is able by nature to incline to what is good, and to choose and work moral good. But for the regenerated to do spiritual good—for the works of the believer being contributory to salvation and wrought by supernatural grace are properly called spiritual—it is necessary that he be guided and prevented by grace, as hath been said in treating of predestination; so that he is not able of himself to do any work worthy of a Christian life, although he hath it in his own power to will, or not to will, to co-operate with grace.

DECREE XV.

We believe that there are in the Church Evangelical Mysteries [i.e., Sacraments of the Gospel Dispensation], and that they are seven. For a less or a greater number of the Mysteries we have not in the Church; since any number of the Mysteries other than seven is the product of heretical madness. And the seven of them were instituted in the Sacred Gospel, and are gathered from the same, like the other dogmas of the Catholic Faith.

For in the first place our Lord instituted Holy Baptism by the words, "Go ye and make disciples of all the nations, baptising them in the name of the Father, and of the Son, and of the Holy Spirit;" {Matthew 28:19} and by the words, "He that believeth and is baptised shall be saved, but he that disbelieveth shall be condemned." {Mark 16:16}

And that of Confirmation, that is to say, of the Holy Myron or Holy Chrism, by the words, "But ye—tarry ye in the city of Jerusalem, until ye be endued with power from on high." {Luke 24:49} With which they were endued by the coming of the Holy Spirit, and this the Mystery of Confirmation signifieth; concerning which Paul also discourseth in the Second Epistle to the Corinthians, chap. i., and Dionysius the Areopagite more explicitly.

And the Priesthood by the words, "This do ye for My Memorial;" {Luke 22:19} and by the words, "Whatsoever ye shall bind and loose upon the earth shall be bound and loosed in the heavens." {Matthew 18:18}

And the unbloody Sacrifice by the words, "Take, eat ye; This is My Body;" {Matthew 26:26; Mark 14:22; Luke 22:19; 1 Corinthians 2:24} and, "Drink ye all of It; This is My Blood of the New Testament;" {Matthew 26:27; Mark 14:24; Luke 22:20; 1 Corinthians 2:25} and by the words, "Except ye eat the Flesh of the Son of Man, ye have not life in yourselves." {John 6:53}

And Marriage, when, having recited the things which had been spoken thereof in the Old [Testament], He, as it were, set His seal thereto by the words, "Those whom God hath joined together, let not man put asunder," {Matthew 19:6} and this the divine Apostle also calleth a great Mystery. {Ephesians 5:32}

And Penance, with which is joined sacramental confession, by the words, "Whose soever sins ye remit, they are remitted unto them; and whose soever sins ye retain, they are retained"; {John 22:23} and by the words, "Except ye repent, ye shall [all] likewise perish." {Luke 13:3,5}

And lastly, the Holy Oil or Prayer-Oil is spoken of in Mark, {Mark 6:13} and is expressly witnessed to by the Lord's brother. {James 5:14}

And the Mysteries consist of something natural, and of something supernatural; and are not bare signs of the promises of God. For then they would not differ from circumcision—than which [notion] what could be worse? And we acknowledge them to be, of necessity, efficient means of grace to the receivers. But we reject, as alien to Christian doctrine, the notion that the integrity of the Mystery requireth the use of the earthly thing [i.e., dependeth upon its reception]; for this is contrary to the Mystery of the Offering [i.e., the Sacrament of the Eucharist], which being instituted by the Substantial Word, and hallowed by the invocation of the Holy Spirit, is perfected by the presence of the thing signified, to wit, of the Body and Blood of Christ. And the perfecting thereof necessarily precedeth its use. For if it were not perfect before its use, he that useth it not aright could not eat and drink judgment unto himself; {1 Corinthians 11:26,28,29} since he would be partaking of mere bread and wine. But now, he that partaketh unworthily eateth and drinketh judgment unto himself; so that not in its use, but even before its use, the Mystery of the Eucharist hath its perfection. Moreover, we reject as something abominable and pernicious the notion that when faith is weak the integrity of the Mystery is impaired. For heretics who abjure their heresy and join the Catholic Church are received by the Church; although they received their valid Baptism with weakness of faith. Wherefore, when they afterwards become possessed of the perfect faith, they are not again baptised.

DECREE XVI.

We believe Holy Baptism, which was instituted by the Lord, and is conferred in the name of the Holy Trinity, to be of the highest necessity. For without it none is able to be saved, as the Lord saith, "Whosoever is not born of water and of the Spirit, shall in no wise enter into the Kingdom of the Heavens." {John 3:5} And, therefore, it is necessary even for infants, since they also are subject to original sin, and without Baptism are not able to obtain its remission. Which the Lord shewed when he said, not of some only, but simply and absolutely, "Whosoever is not born [again]," which is the same as saying, "All that after the coming of Christ the Saviour would enter into the Kingdom of the Heavens must be regenerated."

And forasmuch as infants are men, and as such need salvation; needing salvation, they need also Baptism. And those that are not regenerated, since they have not received the remission of hereditary sin, are, of necessity, subject to eternal punishment, and consequently cannot without Baptism be saved; so that even infants ought, of necessity, to be baptised. Moreover, infants are saved, as is said in Matthew; {Matthew 19:12} but he that is not baptised is not saved. And consequently even infants must of necessity be baptised. And in the Acts {Acts 8:12; 16:33} it is said that the whole houses were baptised, and consequently the infants. To this the ancient Fathers also witness explicitly, and among them Dionysius in his Treatise concerning the Ecclesiastical Hierarchy; and Justin in his fifty-sixth Question, who saith expressly, "And they are vouchsafed the benefits of Baptism by the faith of those that bring them to Baptism." And Augustine saith that it is an Apostolical tradition, that children are saved through Baptism; and in another place, "The Church giveth to babes the feet of others, that they may come; and the hearts of others, that they may believe; and the tongues of others, that they may promise;" and in another place, "Our mother, the Church, furnisheth them with a particular heart."

Now the matter of Baptism is pure water, and no other liquid. And it is performed by the Priest only, or in a case of unavoidable necessity, by another man, provided he be Orthodox, and have the intention proper to Divine Baptism. And the effects of Baptism are, to speak concisely, firstly, the remission of the hereditary transgression, and of any sins whatsoever which the baptised may have committed. Secondly, it delivereth him from the eternal punishment, to which he was liable, as well for original sin, as for mortal sins he may have individually committed. Thirdly, it giveth to such immortality; for in justifying them from past sins, it maketh them temples of God. And it may not be said, that any sin is not washed away through Baptism, which may have been previously committed; but to remain, though not imputed. For that were indeed the height of impiety, and a denial, rather than a confession of piety. Yea, forsooth, all sin existing, or committed before Baptism, is blotted out, and is to be regarded as never existing or committed. For the forms of Baptism, and on either hand all the words that precede and that perfect Baptism, do indicate a perfect cleansing. And the same thing even the very names of Baptism do signify. For if Baptism be by the Spirit and by fire, {Matthew 3:11} it is manifest that it is in all a perfect cleansing; for the Spirit cleanseth perfectly. If it be light, {Hebrews 6:4} it dispelleth the darkness. If it be regeneration, {Titus 3:5} old things are passed away. And what are these except sins? If the baptised putteth off the old man, {Colossians 3:9} then sin also. If he putteth on Christ, {Galatians 3:27} then in effect he becometh free from sin through Baptism. For God is far from sinners.

This Paul also teacheth more plainly, saying: "As through one [man] we, being many, were made sinners, so through one [are we made] righteous." {Romans 5:19} And if righteous, then free from sin. For it is not possible for life and death to be in the same [person]. If Christ truly died, then remission of sin through the Spirit is true also. Hence it is evident that all who are baptised and fall asleep while babes are undoubtedly saved, being predestinated through the death of Christ. Forasmuch as they are without any sin;—without that common [to all], because delivered therefrom by the Divine laver, and without any of their own, because as babes they are incapable of committing sin;—and consequently are saved. Moreover, Baptism imparteth an indelible character, as doth also the Priesthood. For as it is impossible for any one to receive twice the same order of the Priesthood, so it is impossible for any once rightly baptised, to be again baptised, although he should fall even into myriads of sins, or even into actual apostacy from the Faith. For when he is willing to return unto the Lord, he receiveth again through the Mystery of Penance the adoption of a son, which he had lost.

DECREE XVII.

We believe the All-holy Mystery of the Sacred Eucharist, which we have enumerated above, fourth in order, to be that which our Lord delivered in the night wherein He gave Himself up for the life of the world. For taking bread, and blessing, He gave to His Holy Disciples and Apostles, saying: "Take, eat ye; This is My Body." {Matthew 26:26} And taking the chalice, and giving thanks, He said: "Drink ye all of It; This is My Blood, which for you is being poured out, for the remission of sins." {Matthew 26:28} In the celebration whereof we believe the Lord Jesus Christ to be present, not typically, nor figuratively, nor by superabundant grace, as in the other Mysteries, nor by a bare presence, as some of the Fathers have said concerning Baptism, or by impanation, so that the Divinity of the Word is united to the set forth bread of the Eucharist hypostatically, as the followers of Luther most ignorantly and wretchedly suppose, but truly and really, so that after the consecration of the bread and of the wine, the bread is transmuted, transubstantiated, converted and transformed into the true Body Itself of the Lord, Which was born in Bethlehem of the ever-Virgin, was baptised in the Jordan, suffered, was buried, rose again, was received up, sitteth at the right hand of the God and Father, and is to come again in the clouds of Heaven; and the wine is converted and transubstantiated into the true Blood Itself of the Lord, Which as He hung upon the Cross, was poured out for the life of the world. {John 6:51}

Further [we believe] that after the consecration of the bread and of the wine, there no longer remaineth the substance of the bread and of the wine, but the Body Itself and the Blood of the Lord, under the species and form of bread and wine; that is to say, under the accidents of the bread.

Further, that the all-pure Body Itself, and Blood of the Lord is imparted, and entereth into the mouths and stomachs of the communicants, whether pious or impious. Nevertheless, they convey to the pious and worthy remission of sins and life eternal; but to the impious and unworthy involve condemnation and eternal punishment.

Further, that the Body and Blood of the Lord are severed and divided by the hands and teeth, though in accident only, that is, in the accidents of the bread and of the wine, under which they are visible and tangible, we do acknowledge; but in themselves to remain entirely unsevered and undivided. Wherefore the Catholic Church also saith: "Broken and distributed is He That is broken, yet not severed; Which is ever eaten, yet never consumed, but sanctifying those that partake," that is worthily.

Further, that in every part, or the smallest division of the transmuted bread and wine there is not a part of the Body and Blood of the Lord—for to say so were blasphemous and wicked—but the entire whole Lord Christ substantially, that is, with His Soul and Divinity, or perfect God and perfect man. So that though there may be many celebrations in the world at one and the same hour, there are not many Christs, or Bodies of Christ, but it is one and the same Christ that is truly and really present; and His one Body and His Blood is in all the several Churches of the Faithful; and this not because the Body of the Lord that is in the Heavens descendeth upon the Altars; but because the bread of the Prothesis set forth in all the several Churches, being changed and transubstantiated, becometh, and is, after consecration, one and the same with That in the Heavens. For it is one Body of the Lord in many places, and not many; and therefore this Mystery is the greatest, and is spoken of as wonderful, and comprehensible by faith only, and not by the sophistries of man's wisdom; whose vain and foolish curiosity in divine things our pious and God-delivered religion rejecteth.

Further, that the Body Itself of the Lord and the Blood That are in the Mystery of the Eucharist ought to be honoured in the highest manner, and adored with latria. For one is the adoration of the Holy Trinity, and of the Body and Blood of the Lord. Further, that it is a true and propitiatory Sacrifice offered for all

Orthodox, living and dead; and for the benefit of all, as is set forth expressly in the prayers of the Mystery delivered to the Church by the Apostles, in accordance with the command they received of the Lord.

Further, that before Its use, immediately after the consecration, and after Its use, What is reserved in the Sacred Pixes for the communion of those that are about to depart [i.e. the dying] is the true Body of the Lord, and not in the least different therefrom; so that before Its use after the consecration, in Its use, and after Its use, It is in all respects the true Body of the Lord.

Further, we believe that by the word "transubstantiation" the manner is not explained, by which the bread and wine are changed into the Body and Blood of the Lord,—for that is altogether incomprehensible and impossible, except by God Himself, and those who imagine to do so are involved in ignorance and impiety,—but that the bread and the wine are after the consecration, not typically, nor figuratively, nor by superabundant grace, nor by the communication or the presence of the Divinity alone of the Only-begotten, transmuted into the Body and Blood of the Lord; neither is any accident of the bread, or of the wine, by any conversion or alteration, changed into any accident of the Body and Blood of Christ, but truly, and really, and substantially, doth the bread become the true Body Itself of the Lord, and the wine the Blood Itself of the Lord, as is said above. Further, that this Mystery of the Sacred Eucharist can be performed by none other, except only by an Orthodox Priest, who hath received his priesthood from an Orthodox and Canonical Bishop, in accordance with the teaching of the Eastern Church.

This is compendiously the doctrine, and true confession, and most ancient tradition of the Catholic Church concerning this Mystery; which must not be departed from in any way by such as would be Orthodox, and who reject the novelties and profane vanities of heretics; but necessarily the tradition of the institution must be kept whole and unimpaired. For those that transgress the Catholic Church of Christ rejecteth and anathematiseth.

DECREE XVIII.

We believe that the souls of those that have fallen asleep are either at rest or in torment, according to what each hath wrought;—for when they are separated from their bodies, they depart immediately either to joy, or to sorrow and lamentation; though confessedly neither their enjoyment, nor condemnation are complete. For after the common resurrection, when the soul shall be united with the body, with which it had behaved itself well or ill, each shall receive the completion of either enjoyment or of condemnation forsooth.

And such as though involved in mortal sins have not departed in despair, but have, while still living in the body, repented, though without bringing forth any fruits of repentance—by pouring forth tears, forsooth, by kneeling while watching in prayers, by afflicting themselves, by relieving the poor, and in fine by shewing forth by their works their love towards God and their neighbour, and which the Catholic Church hath from the beginning rightly called satisfaction—of these and such like the souls depart into Hades, and there endure the punishment due to the sins they have committed. But they are aware of their future release from thence, and are delivered by the Supreme Goodness, through the prayers of the Priests, and the good works which the relatives of each do for their Departed; especially the unbloody Sacrifice availing in the highest degree; which each offereth particularly for his relatives that have fallen asleep, and which the Catholic and Apostolic Church offereth daily for all alike; it being, of course, understood that we know not the time of their release. For that there is deliverance for such from their direful condition, and that before the common resurrection and judgment we know and believe; but when we know not.

QUESTION I.

Ought the Divine Scriptures to be read in the vulgar tongue by all Christians?

No. For that all Scripture is divinely-inspired and profitable {2 Timothy 3:16} we know, and is of such necessity, that without the same it is impossible to be Orthodox at all. Nevertheless they should not be read by all, but only by those who with fitting research have inquired into the deep things of the Spirit, and who know in what manner the Divine Scriptures ought to be searched, and taught, and in fine read. But to such as are not so exercised, or who cannot distinguish, or who understand only literally, or in any other way contrary to Orthodoxy what is contained in the Scriptures, the Catholic Church, as knowing by experience the mischief arising therefrom, forbiddeth the reading of the same. So that it is permitted to every Orthodox to hear indeed the Scriptures, that he may believe with the heart unto righteousness, and confess with the mouth unto salvation; {Romans 10:10} but to read some parts of the Scriptures, and especially of the Old [Testament], is forbidden for the aforesaid reasons and others of the like sort. For it is the same thing thus to prohibit persons not exercised thereto reading all the Sacred Scriptures, as to require infants to abstain from strong meats.

QUESTION II.

Are the Scriptures plain to all Christians that read them?

If the Divine Scriptures were plain to all Christians that read them, the Lord would not have commanded such as desired to obtain salvation to search the same; {John 5:39} and Paul would have said without reason that God had placed the gift of teaching in the Church; {1 Corinthians 13:28} and Peter would not have said of the Epistles of Paul that they contained some things hard to be understood. {2 Peter 3:16} It is evident, therefore, that the Scriptures are very profound, and their sense lofty; and that they need learned and divine men to search out their true meaning, and a sense that is right, and agreeable to all Scripture, and to its author the Holy Spirit.

So that as to those that are regenerated [in Baptism], although they must know the faith concerning the Trinity, the incarnation of the Son of God, His passion, resurrection, and ascension into the heavens, what concerneth regeneration and judgment—for which many have not hesitated to die—it is not necessary, but rather impossible, that all should know what the Holy Spirit manifesteth to those alone who are exercised in wisdom and holiness.

QUESTION III.

What Books do you call Sacred Scripture?

Following the rule of the Catholic Church, we call Sacred Scripture all those which Cyril collected from the Synod of Laodicea, and enumerated, adding thereto those which he foolishly, and ignorantly, or rather maliciously called Apocrypha; to wit, "The Wisdom of Solomon," "Judith," "Tobit," "The History of the Dragon," "The History of Susanna," "The Maccabees," and "The Wisdom of Sirach." For we judge these also to be with the other genuine Books of Divine Scripture genuine parts of Scripture. For ancient custom, or rather the Catholic Church, which hath delivered to us as genuine the Sacred Gospels and the other Books of Scripture, hath undoubtedly delivered these also as parts of Scripture, and the denial of these is the rejection of those. And if, perhaps, it seemeth that not always have all been by all reckoned with the others, yet nevertheless these also have been counted and reckoned with the rest of Scripture, as well by Synods, as by how many of the most ancient and eminent Theologians of the Catholic Church; all of which we also judge to be Canonical Books, and confess them to be Sacred Scripture.

QUESTION IV.

How ought we to think of the Holy Eikons, and of the adoration of the Saints?

The Saints being, and acknowledged by the Catholic Church to be, intercessors, as hath been said in Eighth Chapter {sic; Decree VIII above}, it is time to say that we honour them as friends of God, and as praying for us to the God of all. And the honour we pay them is twofold;—according to one manner which we call hyperdulia, we honour the Mother of God the Word. For though indeed the Theotokos be servant of the only God, yet is she also His Mother, as having borne in the flesh one of the Trinity; wherefore also is she hymned, as being beyond compare, above as well all Angels as Saints; wherefore, also, we pay her the adoration of hyperdulia. But according to the other manner, which we call dulia, we adore, or rather honour, the holy Angels, Apostles, Prophets, Martyrs, and, in fine, all the Saints. Moreover, we adore and honour the wood of the precious and life-giving Cross, whereon our Saviour underwent this world-saving passion, and the sign of the life-giving Cross, the Manger at Bethlehem, through which we have been delivered from irrationality, {In allusion to the manger out of which the irrational animals eat their food.} the place of the Skull [Calvary], the life-giving Sepulchre, and the other holy objects of adoration; as well the holy Gospels, as the sacred vessels, wherewith the unbloody Sacrifice is performed. And by annual commemorations, and popular festivals, and sacred edifices and offerings; we do respect and honour the Saints. And then we adore, and honour, and kiss the Eikons of our Lord Jesus Christ, and of the most holy Theotokos, and of all the Saints, also of the holy Angels, as they appeared to some of the Forefathers and Prophets. We also represent the All-holy Spirit, as He appeared, in the form of a dove.

And if some say we commit idolatry in adoring the Saints, and the Eikons of the Saints, and the other things, we regard it as foolish and frivolous. For we worship with latria the only God in Trinity, and none other; but the Saints we honour upon two accounts: firstly, for their relation to God, since we honour them for His sake; and for themselves, because they are living images of God. But that which is for themselves hath been defined as of dulia. But the holy Eikons [we adore] relatively since the honour paid to them is referred to their prototypes. For he that adoreth the Eikon doth, through the Eikon, adore the prototype; and the honour paid to the Eikon is not at all divided, or at all separated from that of him that is pourtrayed, and is done unto the same, like that done unto a royal embassy.

And what they adduce from Scripture in support of their novelties, doth not help them as they would, but rather appeareth agreeable to us. For we, when reading the Divine Scriptures, examine the occasion and person, the example and cause. Wherefore, when we contemplate God Himself saying at one time, "Thou shalt not make to thyself any idol, or likeness; neither shalt thou adore them, nor serve them;" {Exodus 20:4,5; Deuteronomy 5:8,9} and at another, commanding that Cherubim should be made; {Exodus 25:18} and further, that oxen and lions {1 Kings 7:29} were placed in the Temple, we do not rashly consider the import of these things. For faith is not in assurance; but, as hath been said, considering the occasion and other circumstances, we arrive at the right interpretation of the same; and we conclude that, "Thou shalt not make to thyself any idol, or likeness," is the same as saying, "Thou shalt not adore strange Gods," {Exodus 20:4} or rather, "Thou shalt not commit idolatry." For so both the custom obtaining in the Church from Apostolic times of adoring the holy Eikons relatively is maintained, and the worship of latria reserved for God alone; and God doth not appear to speak contrarily to Himself. For if the Scripture saith [absolutely], "Thou shalt not make," "Thou shalt not adore," we fail to see how God afterwards permitted likenesses to be made, even though not for adoration. Wherefore, since the commandment concerneth idolatry only, we find serpents, and lions, and oxen, and Cherubim made, and figures and likenesses; among which Angels appear, as having been adored.

And as to the Saints whom they bring forward as saying, that it is not lawful to adore Eikons; we conclude that they rather help us; since they in their sharp disputations inveighed, as well against those that adore the holy Eikons with latria, as against those that bring the eikons of their deceased relatives into the Church, and subjected to anathema those that so do; but not against the right adoration, either of the Saints, or of the holy Eikons, or of the precious Cross, or of the other things of which mention hath been made; especially since the holy Eikons have been in the Church, and have been adored by the Faithful, even from the times of the Apostles, as is recorded and proclaimed by very many; with whom and after whom the Seventh Holy Œcumenical Synod putteth to shame all heretical impudence.

Since it giveth us most plainly to understand that it behoveth to adore the Holy Eikons, and what have been mentioned above. And it anathematiseth, and subjecteth to excommunication, as well those that adore the Eikons with latria as those that say that the Orthodox commit idolatry in adoring the Eikons. We also, therefore, do anathematise with them such as adore either Saint, or Angel, or Eikon, or Cross, or Relic of Saints, or sacred Vessel, or Gospel, or aught else that is in heaven above, or aught on the earth, or in the sea, with latria; and we ascribe adoration with latria to the only God in Trinity. And we anathematise those that say that the adoration of Eikons is the latria of Eikons, and who adore them not, and honour not the Cross, and the Saints, as the Church hath delivered.

Now we adore the Saints and the Holy Eikons, in the manner declared; and pourtray them in adornment of our temples, and that they may be the books of the unlearned, and for them to imitate the virtues of the Saints; and for them to remember, and have an increase of love, and be vigilant in ever calling upon the Lord, as Sovereign and Father, but upon the Saints, as his servants, and our helpers and mediators.

And so much as to the Chapters and Questions of Cyril. But the heretics do find fault with even the prayers of the pious unto God, for we know not why they should calumniate those of the Monks only. Moreover, that prayer is a conversation with God, and a petitioning for such good things as be meet for us, from Him of whom we hope to receive, an ascent too of the mind unto God, and a pious expression of our purpose towards God, a seeking what is above, the support of a holy soul, a worship most acceptable to God, a token of repentance, and of steadfast hope, we do know; and prayer is made either with the mind alone, or with the mind and voice; thereby engaging in the contemplation of the goodness and mercy of God, of the unworthiness of the petitioner, and in thanksgiving, and in realising the promises attached to obedience to God. And it is accompanied by faith, and hope, and perseverance, and observance of the commandments; and, as already said, is a petitioning for heavenly things; and it hath many fruits, which it is needless to enumerate; and it is made continually, and is accomplished either in an upright posture, or by kneeling. And so great is its efficacy, that it is acknowledged to be both the nourishment and the life of the soul. And all this is gathered from Divine Scripture; so that if any ask for demonstration thereof, he is like a fool, or a blind man, who disputeth about the sun's light at the hour of noon, and when the sky is clear. But the heretics, wishing to leave nothing unassailed that Christ hath enjoined, carp at this also. But being ashamed thus openly to impiously maintain as much concerning prayer, they do not forbid it to be made at all, but are distributed at the prayers of the Monks; and they act thus, that they may raise in the simple-minded a hatred towards the Monks; so that they may not endure even the sight of them, as though they were profane and innovators, much less allow the dogmas of the pious and Orthodox faith to be taught by them. For the adversary is wise as to evil, and ingenious in inventing calumnies. Wherefore his followers also—such as these heretics especially—are not so much anxious about piety, as desirous of ever involving men in an abyss of evils, and of estranging them into places, which the Lord taketh not under his care. {Deuteronomy 11:12}

They should be asked therefore, what are the prayers of the Monks; and if they can shew that the Monks do anything entirely different from themselves, and not in accordance with the Orthodox worship of Christians, we also will join with them, and say, not only that the Monks are no Monks, but also no Christians. But if the Monks set forth particularly the glory and wonders of God, and continually, and unremittingly, and at all times, as far as is possible for man, proclaim the Diety, with hymns and doxologies; now singing, forsooth, parts of Scripture, and now gathering hymns out of Scripture, or at least giving utterance to what is agreeable to the same; we must acknowledge that they perform a work apostolical and prophetical, or rather that of the Lord.

Wherefore, we also, in singing the Paracletikê, the Triodion, and the Menæon, perform a work in no wise unbecoming Christians. For all such Books discourse of the Diety as one, and yet of more than one personality, and that even in the Hymns; now gathered out of the Divine Scriptures, and now according to the direction of the Spirit; and in order that in the melodies, the words may be paralleled by other words, we sing parts of Scripture; moreover, that it may be quite plain that we always sing parts of Scripture, to every one of our Hymns, called a Troparion, we add a verse of Scripture. And if we sing, or read the Thecara [Threasury], or other prayers composed by the Fathers of old; let them say what there is in these which is blasphemous, or not pious, and we with them will prosecute these [Monks].

But if they say this only, that to pray continually and unremittingly is wrong, what have they to do with us? Let them contend with Christ—as indeed they do contend—who spake the parable of the unjust judge, {Luke 28:2} how that prayer should be made continually; and taught us to watch and pray, {Mark 13:33} in order to escape trials, and to stand before the Son of man. {Luke 21:36} Let them contend with Paul, [who] in the [5th] Chapter of the First [Epistle] to the Thessalonians, and elsewhere in many places [exhorteth to pray unremittingly]. I forbear to mention the divine leaders of the Catholic Church, from Christ until us; for to put these [heretics] to shame sufficeth the accord of the Forefathers, Apostles, and Prophets concerning prayer.

If, therefore, what the Monks do is what the Apostles and Prophets did; and, we may say, what the holy Fathers and Forefathers of Christ Himself did; it is manifest that the prayers of the Monks are fruits of the Holy Spirit, the giver of graces. But the novelties which the Calvinists have blasphemously introduced concerning God and divine things, perverting, mutilating, and abusing the Divine Scriptures, are sophistries and inventions of the devil.

Unavailing too is the assertion, that the Church cannot, without violence and tyranny, appoint fasts and abstinence from certain meats. For the Church for the mortification of the flesh and all the passions, and acting most rightly, carefully appointeth prayer and fasting, of which all the Saints have been lovers and examples; through which our adversary the devil {1 Peter 5:8} being overthrown by the grace from on high, together with his armies and his hosts—the race {2 Timothy 4:7} that is set before the pious is the more easily accomplished. In making these provisions the undefiled {Ephesians 5:27} Church everywhere useth neither violence nor tyranny; but exhorteth, admonisheth, and teacheth, in accordance with Scripture, and persuadeth by the power of the Spirit.

And to what hath been mentioned a certain fellow at Charenton—we mean the beforementioned Claud—addeth certain other ridiculous objections against us, and unworthy of any consideration; but what hath been said by him we regard as idle tales; and the man himself we consider as a trifler and altogether illiterate. For from [the time of] Photius what vast numbers have there been, and there are now, in the Eastern Church, eminent for wisdom, and theology, and holiness, by the power of the Spirit. And it is most absurd [to argue] that because certain of the Eastern Priests keep the Holy Bread in wooden vessels, within the Church, but without {outside} the Bema, {sanctuary} hung on one of the columns; that, therefore, they do not acknowledge the real and true transmutation of the bread into the Body of the Lord. For that certain of the poor Priests do keep the Lord's Body in wooden vessels, we do not deny; for truly Christ is not honoured by stones and marbles; but asketh for a sound purpose and a clean heart. And this is what happened to Paul. "For we have," {2 Corinthians 4:7} saith he, "the treasure in earthern vessels." But where particular Churches able, as with us here in Jerusalem, the Lord's Body is honourably kept within the Holy Bema of such Churches, and a seven-light lamp always kept burning before it.

And I am tempted to wonder, if it may be that the heretics have seen the Lord's Body hanging in some Churches without the Bema, because perhaps the walls of the Bema were unsafe on account of age, and so have arrived at these absurd conclusions; but they did not notice Christ pourtrayed on the apse of the Holy Bema as a babe [lying] in the Paten; so that they might have known, how that the Easterns do not represent that there is in the Paten a type, or grace, or aught else, but the Christ Himself; and so believe that the Bread of the Eucharist is naught else, but becometh substantially the Body Itself of the Lord, and so maintain the truth.

But concerning all these things it hath been treated at large and most lucidly in what is called The Confession of the Eastern Church, by George, of Chios, from Coresius in his [Treatises] concerning the Mysteries, and of predestination, and of grace, and of free-will, and of the intercession and adoration of Saints, and of the adoration of Eikons, and in the Refutation composed by him of the illicit Synod of the heretics holden on a certain occasion in Flanders, and in many other [Treatises]; by Gabriel, of Peloponnesus, Metropolitan of Philadelphia; and by Gregory Protosyncellus of Chios in his [Treatises] concerning the Mysteries; by Jeremias, the Most Holy Patriarch of Constantinople, in three dogmatic and Synodical Letters to the Lutherans of Tubingen in Germany; by John, Priest, and Economus of Constantinople, surnamed Nathaniel; by Meletius Syrigus, of Crete, in the Orthodox Refutation composed by him of the Chapters and Questions of the said Cyril; by Theophanes, Patriarch of Jerusalem, in his dogmatic Epistle to the Lithuanians, and in innumerable other [Epistles]. And before these hath it been spoken most excellently of these matters by Symeon, of Thessalonica, and before him by all the Fathers, and by the Œcumenical Synods, by ecclesiastical historians too; and even by writers of secular history under the Christian Autocrats of Rome, have these matters been mentioned incidently; by all of whom, without any controversy, the aforesaid were received from the Apostles; whose traditions, whether by writing, or by word, have through the Fathers descended until us. Further, the argument derived from the heretics also confirmeth the aforesaid. For the Nestorians after the year of Salvation, 428, the Armenians too, and the Copts, and the Syrians, and further even the Ethiopians, who dwell at the Equator, and beyond this towards the tropics of Capricorn, whom those that are there commonly call Campesii, after the year of the Incarnation broke away from the Catholic Church; and each of these hath as peculiar only its heresy, as all know from the Acts of the Œcumenical Synods. Albeit, as concerning the purpose and number of the Sacred Mysteries, and all what hath been said above—except their own particular heresy, as hath been said—they entirely believe with the Catholic Church; as we see with our own eyes every hour, and learn by experience and conversation, here in the Holy City of Jerusalem, in which there either dwell, or are continually sojourning, vast numbers of them all, as well learned, such as they have, as illiterate.

Let, therefore, prating and innovating heretics keep silence, and not endeavour by stealing some sentences, [as] against us, from the Scriptures and the Fathers, to cunningly bolster up falsehood, as all apostates and heretics have ever done; and let them say this one thing only, that in contriving excuses {Psalm 140:4} for sins they have chosen to speak wickedness against God, {Psalm 74:6} and blasphemies against the Saints.

EPILOGUE.

Let us briefly suffice for the reputation of the falsehoods of the adversaries, which they have devised against the Eastern Church, alleging in support of their falsehoods the incoherent and impious Chapters of the said Cyril. And let it not be for a sign to be contradicted {Luke 2:34} of those heretics that unjustly calumniate us, as though they spake truly; but for a sign to be believed, that is for reformation of their innovations, and for their return to the Catholic and Apostolic Church; in which their forefathers also were of old, and assisted at those Synods and contests against heretics, which these now reject and revile. For it was unreasonable on their part, especially as they considered themselves to be wise, to have listened to men that were lovers of self; and profane, and that spake not from the Holy Spirit, but from the prince of lies, and to have forsaken the Holy, Catholic, and Apostolic Church, which God hath purchased with the Blood of His own Son; {Acts 20:28} and to have abandoned her. For otherwise there will overtake those that have separated from the Church the pains that are reserved for heathens and publicans; but the Lord who hath ever protected her against all enemies, will not neglect the Catholic Church; to Him be glory and dominion unto the ages of the ages. Amen. In the year of Salvation 1672, on the 16th [day] of the month of March, in the Holy City of Jerusalem:—

I, DOSITHEUS, by the mercy of God, Patriarch of the Holy City of Jerusalem and of all Palestine, declare and confess this to be the faith of the Eastern Church.

The American Catholic Union, *Traditional Old Catholic Dogma,* Daniel Wells, Used by Permission, 2003.

Appendix G

Declaration of the Catholic Congress
Munich, 1871

Conscious of our religious duties, we hold fast to the Old Catholic creed and worship, as attested in scripture, and in tradition. We regard ourselves, therefore, as actual members of the Catholic Church, and will not be deprived of communion with the Church, nor of the rights, which through this communion, accrue to us in Church and State.

We declare the ecclesiastical penalties decreed against us, on account of our fidelity to our creed, to be unjustifiable and tyrannical; and we will not allow ourselves to be daunted or hindered by these censures in availing ourselves of our communion with the Church according to our conscience.

From the point of view of the confession of faith contained in the so-called Tridentine Creed, we repudiate the dogmas introduced under the pontificate of Pius IX in contradiction to the doctrine of the Church, and to the principles continuously followed since the Council of Jerusalem, especially the dogmas of the Pope's infallible teaching, and of his supreme episcopal and immediate jurisdiction.

We rely on the old constitution of the Church. We protest against every attempt to oust the bishops from the immediate and independent control of the separate Churches. We repudiate, as in conflict with the Tridentine Canon, according to which there exists a God-appointed hierarchy of bishops, priests, and deacons, the doctrine embodied in the Vatican doctrine, that the Pope is the sole God-appointed depositary of all ecclesiastical authority and power. We recognise the primacy of the Bishop of Rome as it was acknowledged, on authority of Scripture, by Fathers and Councils in the old undivided Christian Church.

(a.) We declare that articles of belief cannot be defined merely by the utterance of the Pope for the time being, and the express or tacit assent of the bishops, bound as they are by oath to unqualified obedience to the Pope; but only in accordance with Holy Scripture and the old tradition of the Church, as it is set forth in the recognised Fathers and Councils. Moreover a council which was not, as the Vatican Council was, deficient in the actual external conditions of oecuminicity, but which, in the general sentiment of its members, exhibited a disregard of the fundamental principles and of the past history of the Church, could not issue decrees binding upon the consciences of the members of the Church.

(b.) We lay stress upon this principle that the conformity of the doctrinal decisions of a council, with the primitive and traditional creed of the Church, must be determined by the consciousness of belief of the Catholic people and by theological science. We maintain for the Catholic laity and the clergy, as well as for theological sciences, the right of testifying and of objecting on the occasion of establishing articles of belief.

We aim at a reform in the Church in cooperation with the sciences of theology and canon law, which shall, in the spirit of the ancient Church, remove the present defects and abuses, and in particular shall fulfil the legitimate decrees of the Catholic people for a constitutionally regulated participation in Church business, whereby, without risk to doctrinal unity or doctrine, national considerations and needs may be taken account of.

We declare that the charge of Jansenism against the Church of Utrecht is unfounded, and that consequently no opposition in dogma exists between it and us. We hope for a re-union with the Greco-oriental and Russian Church, the separation of which had no sufficient origin, and depends upon no insuperable difference in dogma. Whilst pursuing the desired reforms in the path of science and a progressive Christian culture, we hope gradually to bring about a good understanding with the Protestant and Episcopal churches.

We hold scientific study indispensable for the training of the clergy. We consider that the artificial seclusion of the clergy from the intellectual culture of the present century (as in the seminaries and higher schools under the sole conduct of the bishops) is dangerous, from the great influence which the clergy possess over the culture of the people, and that it is altogether unsuited to give the clergy such an education and training as shall combine piety and morality, intellectual culture and patriotic feeling. We claim for the lower order of clergy a suitable position of consideration, protected against all hierarchical tyranny. We protest against the arbitrary removal of secular priests, amovibilitas ad nutum, a practice introduced through the French Code, and latterly imposed everywhere.

We support the constitutions of our countries, which secure us civil freedom and culture. Therefore we repudiate on national and historical grounds the dangerous dogma of Papal supremacy; and promise to stand faithfully and resolutely by our respective Governments in the struggle against that ultramontanism which assumes the form of dogma in the Syllabus.

Since manifestly the present miserable confusion in the Church has been occasioned by the society called that of Jesus; since this order abuses its influence to spread and cherish among the hierarchy, clergy, and people, tendencies hostile to culture, dangerous to the State and to the nation; since it teaches and encourages a false and corrupting morality: we declare it as our conviction that peace and prosperity, unity in the Church, and just relations between her and civil society, will only be possible when the pernicious activity of this order is put an end to.

As members of the Catholic Church, to which—not yet altered by the Vatican decrees—Government had guaranteed political recognition and public protection, we maintain our claims to all the real property and legal rights of the Church.

The American Catholic Union, *Traditional Old Catholic Dogma,* Daniel Wells, Used by Permission, 2003.

Appendix H

The Fourteen Theses of the Old Catholic Union Conference, Bonn, 1874

We agree that the way in which the Filioque was inserted in the Nicene Creed was illegal, and that, with a view to future peace and unity, it is much to be desired that the whole Church should set itself seriously to consider whether the Creed could possibly be restored to its primitive form, without the sacrifice of any true doctrine expressed in the Western form.

Article I
[The Canon and Apocrypha.]

We agree that the apocryphal or deutero-canonical books of the Old Testament are not of the same canonicity as the books of the Hebrew Canon.

Article II
[The Original Text and Translations of the Bible.]

We agree that no translation of Holy Scripture can claim an authority superior to that of the original text.

Article III
[Use of the Bible in the Vernacular Tongues.]

We agree that the reading of the Holy Scripture in the vulgar tongue can not be lawfully forbidden.

Article IV
[Liturgy in the Vernacular Tongues.]

We agree that, in general, it is more fitting, and in accordance with the spirit of the Church, that the Liturgy should be in the tongue understood by the people.

Article V
[Justification by Faith working by Love.]

We agree that Faith working by Love, not Faith without Love, is the means and condition of man's justification before God.

Article VI
[Salvation not by Merit.]

Salvation can not be merited by merit of condignity, because there is no proportion between the infinite worth of the salvation promised by God and the finite worth of man's works.

Article VII
[Works of Supererogation.]

We agree that the doctrine of opera supererogationis and a thesaurus meritorum sanctorum, i.e., that the overflowing merits of the Saints can be transferred to others, either by the Church, or by the authors of the good works themselves, is untenable.

Article VIII
[Number of Sacraments.]

We acknowledge that the number of sacraments was fixed at seven, first in the twelfth century, and then was received into the general teaching of the Church, not as a tradition coming down from the Apostles or from the earliest times, but as a result of theological speculation.

Catholic theologians (e.g. Belarmin) acknowledge, and we acknowledge with them, that Baptism and the Eucharist are principlia, praecipua, eximia salutis nostae sacramenta.

Article IX
[Scripture and Tradition.]

1. The Holy Scriptures being recognized as the primary rule of Faith, we agree that the genuine tradition, i.e. the unbroken transmission—partly oral, partly in writing—of the doctrine delivered by Christ and the Apostles, is an authoritative source of teaching for all successive generations of Christians. This tradition is partly to be found in historical continuity with the primitive Church, partly to be gathered by scientific method from the written documents of all centuries.

2. We acknowledge that the Church of England, and the Churches derived from her, have maintained unbroken the Episcopal succession.

Article X
[The Immaculate Conception of the Virgin Mary.]

We reject the new Roman doctrine of the Immaculate Conception of the Blessed Virgin Mary, as being contrary to the tradition of the first thirteen centuries, according to which Christ alone is conceived without sin.

Article XI
[Public and Private Confession.]

We agree that the practice of confession of sins before the congregation or a Priest, together with the exercise of the power the keys, has come down to us from the primitive Church, and that, purged from abuses and free from constraint, is should be preserved in the Church.

Article XII
[Indulgences.]

We agree that indulgences can only refer to penalties actually imposed by the Church herself.

Article XIII
[Commemoration of the Departed.]

We acknowledge that the practice of the commemoration of the faithful departed, i.e. the calling down of a richer outpouring of Christ's grace upon them, has come down to us from the primitive Church, and is to be preserved in the Church.

Article XIV
[The Mass.]

The eucharistic celebration in the Church is not a continuous repetition or renewal of the propitiatory sacrifice offered once for ever by Christ on the Cross; but its sacrificial character consists in this, that it is the permanent memorial of it, and a representation and presentation on earth of that one oblation of Christ for the salvation of redeemed mankind, which, according to the Hebrews (ix. 11,12), is continuously presented in heaven by Christ, who now appears in the presence of God for us (ix. 24).

While this is the character of the Eucharist in reference to the sacrifice of Christ, it is also a sacred feast, wherein the faithful, receiving the Body and Blood of our Lord, have communion one with another.

The American Catholic Union, *Traditional Old Catholic Dogma,* Daniel Wells, Used by Permission, 2003.

Appendix I

The Declaration of Utrecht, 1889 of the Old Catholic Bishops of the Netherlands, Germany and Switzerland

"We, Johannes Heykamp, Archbishop of Utrecht, Casparus Johannes Rinkel, Bishop of Haarlem, Cornelius Diependaal, Bishop of Deventer, Joseph Hubert Reinkens, Bishop of the Old Catholic Church of Germany, and Eduard Herzog, Bishop of the Christian Catholic Church of Switzerland, assembled on this four and twentieth day of September, eighteen hundred and eighty-nine at the Archepiscopal residence at Utrecht, having invoked the assistance of the Holy Spirit, address the following Declaration to the Catholic Church:

Having assembled in conference in response to an invitation from the undersigned Archbishop of Utrecht, we have determined henceforward to hold consultation together from time to time on matters of common interest, in conjunction with our assistants, councilors and theologians. We deem it fitting that, at this our first meeting, we should set forth a brief declaration of the ecclesiastical principles on which we have hitherto exercised our episcopal office, and shall continue to exercise it in the future, as we have already in separate declarations repeatedly taken occasion to state.

1. We hold firmly to the ancient ecclesiastical rule formulated by St. Vincent of Lerins, 'Id teneamus, quod ubique, quod semper, quod ab omnibus creditum est; hoc est etenim vere proprieque catholicum.' For this reason we preserve in professing the faith of the primitive Church, as formulated in the oecumenical symbols and specified precisely by the unanimously accepted decisions of the Oecumenical Councils held in the undivided Church of the first thousand years.

2. We therefore reject the decrees of the so-called Council of the Vatican, which were promulgated July 18th, 1870, concerning the infallibility and the universal Episcopate of the Bishop of Rome, decrees which are in contradiction with the faith of the ancient Church, and which destroy its ancient canonical constitution by attributing to the Pope the plentitude of ecclesiastical powers over all Dioceses and over all the faithful. By denial of this primatial jurisdiction we do not wish to deny the historical primacy which several Oecumenical Councils and Fathers of the ancient Church have attributed to the Bishop of Rome by recognizing him as the 'Primus inter pares.'

3. We also reject the dogma of the Immaculate Conception promulgated by Pius IX in 1854 in defiance of the Holy Scriptures and in contradiction with the tradition of the first centuries.

4. As for other Encyclicals published by the Bishops of Rome in recent times for example, the Bulls Unigenitus and Auctorem fidei, and the Syllabus of 1864, we reject them on all such points as are in contradiction with the doctrine of the primitive Church, and we do not recognize them as binding on the consciences of the faithful. We also renew the ancient protests of the Catholic Church of Holland against the errors of the Roman Curia, and against its attacks upon the rights of national Churches.

5. We refuse to accept the decrees of the Council of Trent in matters of discipline, and as for the dogmatic decisions of that Council we accept them only so far as they are in harmony with the teaching of the primitive Church.

6. Considering that the Holy Eucharist has always been the true central point of Catholic worship, we consider it our right to declare that we maintain with perfect fidelity the ancient Catholic doctrine concerning the Sacrament of the Altar, by believing that we receive the Body and Blood of our Savior Jesus Christ under the species of bread and wine. The Eucharistic celebration in the Church is neither a continual repetition nor a renewal of the expiatory sacrifice which Jesus offered once for all upon the Cross: but it is a sacrifice because it is the perpetual commemoration of the sacrifice offered upon the Cross, and it is the act by which we represent upon earth and appropriate to ourselves the one offering which Jesus Christ makes in Heaven, according to the Epistle to the Hebrews 9:11-12, for the salvation of redeemed humanity, by appearing for us in the presence of God (Heb. 9:24). The character of the Holy Eucharist being thus understood, it is, at the same time, a sacrificial feast, by means of which the faithful in receiving the Body and Blood of our Savior, enter into communion with one another (I Cor. 10:17).

7. We hope that Catholic theologians, in maintaining the faith of the undivided Church, will succeed in establishing an agreement upon questions which have been controverted ever since the divisions which arose

between the Churches. We exhort the priests under our jurisdiction to teach, both by preaching and by the instruction of the young, especially the essential Christian truths professed by all the Christian confessions, to avoid, in discussing controverted doctrines, any violation of truth or charity, and in word and deed to set an example to the members.

8. By maintaining and professing faithfully the doctrine of Jesus Christ, by refusing to admit those errors which by the fault of men have crept into the Catholic Church, by laying aside the abuses in ecclesiastical matters, together with the worldly tendencies of the hierarchy, we believe that we shall be able to combat efficaciously the great evils of our day, which are unbelief and indifference in matters of religion."

Utrecht, 24th September 1889

+Heykamp
+Rinkel
+Diependaal
+Reinkens
+Herzog

Appendix J

A Brief Biographical Section on Mar Julius I

By John Philip Kottapparambil, Kottayam, India

Reproduced by Permission

Fr. Alwarez of Roman Catholic Church joins the Jacobite Syrian Orthodox Church of Antioch.

Fr. Alwarez was born in a Roman Catholic family at Goa. After completing his studies from the *'Real Seminary'* of Rakkol, at the age of 30 in 1860, he joined the Jesuits Missionary at Bombay. Though he remained with them for many years, he was disillusioned with their activities and so he returned to his native place. After reaching Goa, he started an orphanage and later a college. He was a known social worker. During his stay there, he published some periodicals and through this he criticized the misgivings of the Jesuit Missionaries which was a known fact at that time. On seeing these articles, Archbishop of Goa excommunicated him from the Roman Catholic Church and he was forced to leave the place due to the continuous persecution against him risen out of the vengeance. He later escaped to Travancore.

During his stay at Travancore he came to know more about the Apostolic Suriyani Church of Antioch. He was attracted towards it. Meanwhile he started a movement namely "Swathantra Catholic Mission" and through this, opposed the atrocities of the Roman Catholic Church. Later Dr. Lisbowa Pinto, a member of this movement with other like minded people of the Catholic Church started a periodical, "Independent Catholic" published from Colombo. Many others were also convinced in the Apostolic Episcopacy of the Syrian Orthodox Church. Around the time, Fr. Alwareaz who was in regular contact with the Patriarch of Antioch, met Malankara Metropolitan Mor Dionysius V (Pulikottil Thirumeni) on His Holiness request. With the permission of the Patriarch, Mor Gregorius Geevarghese (Parumala Kochu Thirumeni) consecrated Fr. Alwarez as a Ramban of the Syrian Orthodox Church. On Monday the 29th July 1889, the Ramban was consecrated as 'Metropolitan' at the Kottayam old Seminary chapel by Malankara Metropolitan *Mor Dionysius V* and assisted by other Metropolitans including our Kochu Thirumeni. The new Metropolitan Alwarez Mor Julius was given the charge of the new Mangalore and Bombay dioceses. Later many people, particularly the disillusioned Roman Catholics from other parts of India and Ceylon joined the Syrian Church. Under the influence of the new Metropolitan, many from the Old Catholic Church of America including one Rev. J Rene Vilatte, a French Priest, joined the Church.

Later on the advice of Metropolitan Alwarez Mor Julius, the Patriarch of Antioch gave permission for the consecration of Rev. Rene Vilatte as a Metropolitan. The ceremony was planned at the St. Mary's Church, Colombo. On the Ascension day (26th May) in 1892, Rev. J Rene Vilatte was elevated as a Ramban and three days later, he was consecrated as Metropolitan 'Mor Thimothious', by Kadavil Paulose Mor Athanasious of Kottayam diocese, our Kochu Thirumeni of Niranam diocese and Alwarez Mor Julius. The new Metropolitan, Mor Thimothious was appointed as the Archbishop of American diocese under the Holy See of Antioch. This was an eventful day for the Universal Syrian Church. The expense of the ceremony was shared by the representative of the American government in Colombo. In a special function that followed, the governmental authorities awarded a rare title of *"Commander of the Crown of Thorns"* to the three Metropolitans including our Kochu Thirumeni.

In all the discussions with the newly converted Metropolitans, Parumala Mor Gregorious Bawa (together with Pulikottil Thirumeni and Kadavil Thirumeni) participated as an intermediary. It was he who contacted and informed about the latest developments to the Patriarch. Many such decisions regarding Malankara Church were taken by the Patriarch Ignatius Peter III, mainly on the advice our Kochu Thirumeni. Both were in constant contact, until the last days of the Patriarch.

Appendix K

A Sketch of the Belief of Old Catholics

By The Most Reverend Joseph Rene Vilatte

Holy Scripture:

Old Catholics receive the Holy Scriptures as God's inspired Word. This precious revelation is accepted in the sense intended by the Holy Ghost, and is interpreted by the Church, to whom it pertains to judge of the true sense and the true interpretation of the Bible. They never understand or interpret the oracles of God except in accounts with the unanimous sentiments of the Fathers. Those books are read as canonical which are generally received by the Catholic Churches throughout the world. The bishops and priests of this Church have the duty and privilege of reading the Word of God upon all the faithful. In truth they do not reecho the words of Saint Boniface, when he said "Cast aside whatever my hinder you from studying the Holy Scriptures, seek therein the divine wisdom which is brighter then gold, purer then silver, more sparkling then diamonds, clearer then crystal, more precious then topaz, the young cannot seek a better guide, and the aged cannot possess a more precious book then the Holy Scripture, which directs the vessel of our soul, and brings it without shipwreck to the blessed shores of paradise, even to the of joys divine where the angels dwell.

Creeds:

We heartily believe and receive the three symbols of the Apostles Creed, the Nicene Creed and the Creed of Athanasius; for they are consonant with the teachings of the Fathers and the testimony of the Holy Scripture.

The Councils:

We accept the seven councils recognized by all Catholic Churches, namely:

First Council of Nicaea	AD 325	against Arianism
Second Council of Constantinople	AD 381	against Appolinares/Macedonians
Third Council of Ephesus	AD 431	against Nestorianism
Fourth Council of Chalcedon	AD 451	against Monophysites
Fifth Council of Constantinople	AD 553	against Nestorianism/Monophysites
Sixth Council of Constantinople	AD 680	against Monothelites
Seventh Council of Nicaea	AD 787	against Iconoclastes

The Sacraments:

We believe that the Sacraments of the 'New Dispensation' are not merely sacred signs which represent grace to us, nor the seals which confirm it in us, but that they are the instruments of the Holy Ghost which apply and confer grace upon us in virtue of the words pronounced and the act performed upon us from without, provided we do not raise any obstacle by our own bad dispositions.

Baptism:

We acknowledge Baptism as the Sacrament established by Christ to cleanse men from original sin, and to make them Christians. It is the Sacrament of the new birth, "Verily, verily, I say unto thee, unless a man is born again of water and the Holy Ghost, he cannot enter the Kingdom of Heaven".

Confirmation:

We believe that the Bishop is the ordinary minister of Confirmation and that in this Sacrament, the Holy Ghost is given with the fullness of His gifts. "For they had only been baptized in the Name of the Lord Jesus, then the Apostles laid their hands upon them and they received the Holy Ghost".

Penance:

We believe that it has please Jesus Christ to give His Church the authority to pardon those who have broken the law of the Gospel after Baptism and that every priest validly ordained has this power through the merits and in the person of Christ. "Whosoever sins you shall forgive, they are forgiven then, and whosoever sins you shall retain, they are retained".

Eucharist:

We profess that the Eucharist is both a sacrifice and a Sacrament. That is the unbloody sacrifice of the mass, which is the central rite and most essential act of public worship a Christian owes to God, there is a true, proper, propitiatory sacrifice for the living and the dead. We maintain that the Liturgy ought to be said in the tongue understood by the people to be in accordance with the Word of God and the custom of the primitive Church. We believe in the Most Holy Sacrament of the Eucharist there is truly and relay the Body and Blood of Jesus Christ. We affirm that the cup of the Lord is not to be denied to the laity; for both the parts of the Lord's Sacrament by Christ's ordinance and commandment ought to be administered to all men alike. "Verily, verily, I say unto you, except ye eat of the flesh of the Son of man, and drink His Blood, ye have no life in you".

Extreme Unction:

We believe Extreme Unction to be a Sacrament of the New Dispensation, instituted for the spiritual and corporal solace of the sick. Its efficacy and mode of administration are plainly indicated in the Catholic Epistle of Saint James. "Is any sick among you, let him bring in the priests of the Church and let them pray over him, anointing him with oil in the Name of the Lord".

Sacred Orders:

We believe that Orders is a Sacrament which confers upon those who validly receive it the power to exercise the several functions of the ministry. Bishops are the ministers of this Sacrament. The Catholic Church makes a distinction between the Minor Orders and the greater or Holy Orders; the latter being so called by reason of eminent dignity they confer and the grave obligations they impose.

Matrimony:

We believe that Holy Matrimony is a sacrament which sanctifies the lawful union of a Christian man and women. "For this reason a man shall leave his father and his mother, and shall cleave to his wife, and the two shall become one flesh. This is a great sacrament, but I speak in Christ and in His Church".

{Note of Archbishop Vilatte: None of our priests has the right to contract marriage after his ordination. But a married man having a vocation for the sacred ministry may receive holy orders notwithstanding his previous marriage contract, in accordance with the discipline which dates from the earliest ages of the faith, and is still in rigor in all the Oriental Churches}

The Church:

The visible Church of Christ is a society in which all the faithful are joined together by the profession of the same faith, and forming a body of which Jesus Christ is the Head and Source of all authority.

The Episcopate:

We believe that the Episcopate is as necessary for the life of the church, as breath is for the life of man; and that it is the common center of unity and the guardian of the deposit of divine revelation; that bishops are equal in power and authority by divine right, and that to them belongs the duty of defending the truth of Catholic tradition; to the end that, the whole church being united under their guidance, there may ever be: "O Lord, One Faith, One Baptism, One God the Father of all, who is above all, over all and in us all" Saint Paul to the Ephesians.

Monastic Life:

Old Catholics recognize that religious orders area source of strength and benediction not to be neglected, but to be cherished and developed among the Children of God. The life of sacrifice and of super-imminent love towards God and man which characterized the Apostles, ought to be initiated by elect souls in the Church, chosen by the Holy Ghost, for a free will immolation of self of one upon the altar of charity, so that thus the example of Evangelical virtues may be offered to the world. We believe therefore that voluntary celibacy is most agreeable to God, to which many are called for the glory of God, their own souls' surer salvation, and the solace of the sick and poor. "For he who is unmarried careth for the things of the Lord; he seeketh how he may please God; but he who is married busieth himself with the affairs of the world, he seeketh how he may please his wife, and is divided". Paul to the Corinthians.

Sacred Images:

We emphatically deny the accusations of our separated brethren who pretend that Catholics adore the images of Christ, The Blessed Virgin and the Saints. We venerate them as sacred things, and representing sacred persons. The Catholic Church compels no one to use sacred images or pictures in his worship. It is recommended as a pious practice, but it is neither necessary for justification nor for salvation. We furthermore believe that when it is practiced, it should be done wisely according the spirit and rules of the Universal Church, in order to avoid the abuses which they always so easy and hurtful in this matter.

The Saints:

We believe that there is but "One Mediator (of redemption) between God and man, to wit: The Man Christ Jesus" 1 Timothy 2-5. But that it is a good and useful thing to invoke the saints, who are our glorified brethren, in order that they may help us by their prayers; for if "for if the prayers of a righteous man availeth much" on this earth, how much more powerful must they not be when near the throne of God in the realms of glory. That our departed brethren pray for us we know from the universal tradition of the Church and from Holy Writ. As an example we find the Prophet Jeremias interceding for the people long after his death. "This is the lover of his brethren and the people of Israel; this is he who prayeth much for the people, and the entire holy nation, even Jeremias, the Prophet of God. II Mach.

Our Bond of Union:

We allow no dissidence in matters of faith, as already said we recognize the Seven Ecumenical Councils and the fountainhead for the unity of the faith. In them are the ways of peace, from them flow the stream of grace, which one day shall efface all divisions. Their kindly light shall lead all sects to unity by sincere return to Old Catholicism. Should any member of our Church unhappily rebel against the faith he would cease to be a member, and would be regard as a heathen and publican. For no one has the right to add to, or take away from, the defined faith.

Appendix L

The Most Reverend Arnold Harris Mathew
The Declaration of Autonomy

We the undersigned Bishop, on behalf of our clergy and laity of the Catholic Church of England, hereby proclaim and declare the autonomy and independence of our portion of the One, Holy, Catholic and Apostolic Church.

We are in no way whatever subject to or dependent upon any foreign See, nor do we recognize the right of any members of the religious bodies known as 'Old Catholics' on the Continent, to require submission from us to their authority or jurisdiction, or the decrees, decisions, rules or enactments of any of their Conventions, Synods, Congresses, or other assemblies, in which we have neither taken part nor expressed agreement.

The Venerable Church of the Netherlands, which is a British and Irish foundation, due to the apostolic labors of St. Willibrord and St. Boniface, and consolidated by the efforts of other Saints and Monks of the ancient Churches of England and Ireland, remained staunch and true to its primitive Catholic belief, traditions and customs for more than twelve centuries.

With inexpressible joy, therefore, did we, in the year 1907, receive the sacred Episcopate, to be restored to our country through the instrumentality of His Grace the most Reverend Lord Archbishop of Utrecht, Mgr. Gul, who presides over the small remnant of the ancient Dutch Church still surviving in the Netherlands. Whilst retaining our profound respect for and gratitude to this estimable Prelate, we cannot but express the deep regret we feel that our hopes should have been disappointed in the way we now describe:

We had supposed and believed that the Faith, once delivered to the Saints, and set forth in the decrees of the Councils accepted as Ecumenical no less in the West than in the East, would have continued unimpaired, whether by augmentation or by diminution, in the venerable Church of the Dutch Nation.

We anticipated that the admirable fidelity with which the Bishops and Clergy of that Church had adhered to the Faith and handed it down, untarnished by heresy, notwithstanding grievous persecution during so many centuries, would never have wavered.

Unfortunately, however, we discover with dismay, pain, and regret that the standards of Orthodoxy, laid down of old by the Fathers and Councils of the East and West alike, having been departed from in various particulars by certain sections of Old Catholicism, these departures, instead of being checked and repressed, are, at least tacitly, tolerated and acquiesced in without protest, by the Hierarchy of the Church of the Netherlands.

In order to avoid misapprehension, we here specify nine of the points of difference between Continental Old Catholics and ourselves:

(1) Although the Synod of Jerusalem, held under Dositheus in 1672, was not an Ecumenical Council, its decrees are accepted by the Holy Orthodox Church of the Orient as accurately expressing its belief, and are in harmony with the decrees of the Council of Trent on the dogmas of which they treat. We are in agreement with the Holy Orthodox Church, regarding this Synod, Hence, we hold and declare that there are Seven Holy Mysteries or Sacraments instituted by Our Divine Lord and Savior Jesus Christ, therefore all of them necessary for the salvation of mankind, though all are not necessarily to be received by every individual, e.g. Holy Orders and Matrimony. Certain sections, if not all, of the Old Catholic bodies, reject this belief and refuse to assent to the decrees of the Holy Synod of Jerusalem.

(2) Moreover, some of them have abolished the Sacrament of Penance by condemning and doing away with auricular confession; others actively discourage this salutary practice; others, again, whilst tolerating its use, declare the Sacrament of Penance to be merely optional, therefore unnecessary, and of no obligation, even for those who have fallen into mortal sin after Baptism.

(3) In accordance with the belief and practice Of the Universal Church, we adhere to the doctrine of the Communion of Saints by invoking and venerating the Blessed Virgin Mary, and those who have received the crown of glory in heaven, as well as the Holy Angels of God.

The Old Catholics in the Netherlands have not yet altogether abandoned this pious and helpful custom, but, in some other countries, invocation of the Saints has been totally abolished by the Old Catholics. Even the Angelic Salutation, **or Ave Maria**, familiar to the lips of every Christian, is no longer recited by them, and from the various newly-devised vernacular liturgies, the names of the Saints have been omitted.

(4) Although it may be permissible and, indeed, very desirable, in some countries, and' under certain circumstances, to render the Liturgy into the vernacular languages, we consider it to be neither expedient nor tolerable that individuals should compose new liturgies, according to their own particular views, or make alterations, omissions and changes in venerable rites to suit their peculiar fancies, prejudices or idiosyncrasies. We lament the mutilations of this kind which have occurred among the Old Catholics in several countries and regret that no two of the new liturgies composed and published by them are alike, either in form or in ceremony. In all of them the ancient rubrics have been set aside, and the ceremonies and symbolism with which the sacred Mysteries of the Altar have been reverently environed for many centuries, have, either wholly or in part, been ruthlessly swept away. The Rite of Benediction of the Blessed Sacrament has also been almost universally abolished among the Old Catholics.

(5) Since the time of the Venerable Bede, 'Old Rome," 'the Imperial City,' has always been regarded as the religious capital of Western Christendom, just as 'New Rome'—Constantinople—became the religious capital of Eastern Christendom.

We therefore, treading in the footsteps of our Catholic forefathers, and in accordance with the decrees of the Ecumenical Councils, regard the Bishop of Old Rome as Primate of Christendom and Patriarch of the West, and our desire is to exhibit due respect and veneration for the person of His Holiness in that exalted station.

In accordance with the primitive teaching of the Church of the Netherlands, which prevailed until a very recent date, we consider it a duty on the part of Western Christians to remember His Holiness the Pope as their Patriarch in their prayers and sacrifices. The name of His Holiness should, therefore, retain its position in the Canon of the Mass, where, as we observed at our consecration in Utrecht, it was customary, and remained so until a recent date in the present year (1910), for the celebrant to recite the name of our Patriarch in the usual manner in the Mass and in the Litany of the Saints. The publication of a new vernacular Dutch Liturgy in the present year causes us to regret that the clergy of Holland are now required to omit the name of His Holiness in the Canon of the Mass. Happily, only a small number of other alterations in the text of the Canon have, so far, been introduced. These however, include the audible recitation of the whole of the secret prayers of the Mass, and the omission of the prayer **Haec Commixtio,** and the omission of the title, 'ever Virgin' whenever it occurs in the Latin Missal.

Such alterations pave the way for others of an even more serious nature, which may be made in the future, and, as we think, are to be deplored.

Among other sections of Old Catholicism not only have all public prayers for the Western Patriarch been abandoned, but the historical position and legitimate and generally-recognized prerogatives of His Holiness have been ignored, whilst, by some a tone of bitterness and vulgar insolence has been introduced in referring to the Roman Pontiff, which is only comparable to that adopted by the most vituperative, ignorant and inveterate of the Protestant sects. This attitude we deeply regret, and entirely dissociate ourselves from it. **Caritas benigna est.**

(6) Following the example of our Catholic forefathers, we venerate the adorable Sacrifice of the Mass as the supreme act of Christian worship instituted by Christ Himself.

Since, during very many centuries, it has been the custom, throughout the Western Church, for the clergy to celebrate daily, we require our clergy to fulfill this sacred duty, exulting in the privilege and benefiting by the graces which thus become theirs.

We grieve that the Old Catholic clergy, in most countries, have abandoned the daily celebration Of Mass, and now limit the offering the Christian Sacrifice to Sundays and a few of the greater feasts.

The corresponding neglect of the Blessed Sacrament, and infrequency of Holy Communion, on the part of the laity, is marked.

(7) In accordance with Catholic custom and with the decrees of the Ecumenical Councils, we hold that the honor and glory of God are promoted and increased by the devout and religious use of holy pictures, statues, symbols, relics, and the like, as aids to devotion, and that, in relations to those they represent, they are to be held in veneration. The Old Catholics have, generally speaking, preferred to dispense with such helps to piety.

(8) We consider that the Holy Sacraments should be administered only to those who are members of the Holy Catholic Church, not only by Baptism, but by the Profession of the Catholic Faith in its integrity, by repudiation of all heresies, by rejection of any bond of union, and refusal of actual communion, with all persons and sects professing unorthodox beliefs, whether as individuals or by

formularies to which they are committed. Unhappily, we find persons who are not Catholics, of whose baptism and orthodoxy there is no certainty, and who are members of denominations professing heretical tenets, are now admitted, without even conditional baptism or confession or profession of faith, to receive Holy Communion in all the Old Catholic places of worship on the Continent. Although Communion under one species is still regarded as sufficient, non-Catholics desiring Communion under both species are thus communicated out of deference to their tenets.

Moreover, clergymen of the Anglican Communion, whose Orders are open to the gravest doubt, have been permitted to celebrate the 'Service for the Administration of the Holy Communion,' from Anglican books of devotion, entitled 'The Book of Common Prayer,' at Old Catholic altars, thus causing both Catholics and Protestants to suppose that Anglican Orders are accepted as valid by the Old Catholics in general.

(9) The Old Catholics have ceased to observe the prescribed days of fasting and abstinence, and no longer observe the custom of receiving Holy Communion fasting.

For these and other reasons, which it is unnecessary to detail, we, the undersigned Bishop, desire, by these presents, to declare our autonomy and our independence of all foreign interference in our doctrine, discipline and policy. **In necessariis unitas, in dubiis libertas, in omnibus caritas.**

Given under our hand and sealed with our seal this 29th day of December, the Feast of St. Thomas of Canterbury, in the year of our Lord, on thousand nine hundred and ten.

✠ Arnold H. Mathew

Appendix M

Bishop Mathew's Statement of Union of 1911

Bishop Arnold Mathew severed relations with the Utrecht Union. Looking for recognition from a major catholic-orthodox body, he petitioned and was received into the Syrian Orthodox Communion under Patriarch Meletios of Antioch in 1911. The "Statement of Union" that follows is the declaration Bishop Mathew submitted as part of his petition.

Statement of Faith submitted by Bishop Arnold Mathew

1. The Way of Salvation. Eternal Salvation is promised to mankind only through the merits of our Savior Jesus Christ, and upon condition of obedience to the teaching of the Gospel, which requires Faith, Hope, and Charity, and the due observance of the ordinances of the Orthodox and Catholic religion.

2. Faith, Hope and Charity. Faith is a virtue infused by God, whereby man accepts, and believes without doubting, whatever God has revealed in the Church concerning true religion.

Hope is a virtue infused by God, and following upon Faith; by it man puts his entire trust and confidence in the goodness and mercy of God, through Jesus Christ, and looks for the fulfillment of the Divine promises made to those who obey the Gospel.

Charity is a virtue infused by God, and likewise consequent upon Faith, whereby man, loving God above all things for His own sake, and his neighbor as himself for God's sake, yields up his will to a joyful obedience to the revealed will of God in the Church.

3. The Church. God has established the Holy Catholic Church upon earth to be the pillar and ground of the revealed Truth; and has committed to her the guardianship of the Holy Scriptures and of Holy Tradition, and the power of binding and loosing.

4. The Creed. The Catholic Church has set forth the principle doctrines of the Christian Faith in 12 articles of the Creed, as follows:

I believe in One God, the Father, The Almighty, maker of the heaven and earth, and all that is seen and unseen.

I believe in one Lord Jesus Christ, the only begotten Son of God, begotten of the Father before all worlds, God from God, Light from Light, true God from true God, begotten not made, of one substance with the Father. Through Him all things were made. For us and for our salvation he came down from heaven, by the power of the Holy Spirit he was born of the Virgin Mary, and became man. For our sake he was crucified under Pontius Pilate, he suffered died and was buried. On the third day he rose again in the fulfillment of scriptures, he ascended into heaven and is seated at the right hand of the Father. He will come again in glory to judge the living and the dead, and his Kingdom will have no end.

I believe in the Holy Spirit, the Lord and Giver of Life, who proceeds from the Father, who together with the Father and the Son the Spirit is worshipped and glorified, and has spoken through the prophets. I believe in one Holy Catholic and Apostolic church. I acknowledge one baptism for the remission of sins, I look for the resurrection of the dead and the life of the world to come. Amen.

This sacred Creed is sufficient for the establishment of the Truth, inasmuch as it explicitly teaches the perfect doctrine of the Father, the Son, and the Holy Ghost.

5. The Sacraments. The fundamental ordinances of the Gospel, instituted by Jesus Christ as a special means of conveying Divine grace and influence to the souls of men, which are commonly called Mysteries or Sacraments, are seven in number, namely, Baptism, Confirmation (Chrismation), the Holy Eucharist, Holy Orders, Matrimony, Penance, and Unction.

Baptism is the first Sacrament of the Gospel, administered by three-fold immersion in or affusion with water, with the words, "I baptize thee in the name of the Father, and of the Son, and of the Holy Ghost." It admits the recipient into the Church, bestows upon him the forgiveness of sins, original and actual, through the Blood of Christ, and causes in him a spiritual change called Regeneration. Without valid Baptism no other Sacrament can be validly received.

Confirmation, or Chrismation, is a Sacrament in which the baptized person, on being anointed with Sacred Chrism consecrated by the Bishops of the Church, with the imposition of hands, receives the sevenfold gifts of the Holy Ghost to strengthen him in the grace which he received at Baptism, making him a strong and perfect Christian and a good soldier of Christ.

The Holy Eucharist is a Sacrament in which, under the appearances of bread and wine, the real and actual Body and Blood of Christ are given and received for the remission of sins, the increase of Divine grace, and the reward of everlasting life. After the prayer of Invocation of the Holy Ghost in the Liturgy, the bread and wine are entirely converted into the living Body and Blood of Christ by an actual change of being, to which the philosophical terms of Transubstantiation and Transmutation are rightly applied. The celebration of this Mystery or Sacrament, commonly called the Mass, constitutes the chief act of Christian worship, being a sacrificial Memorial or re-Presentation of our Lord's death. It is not a repetition of the Sacrifice offered once for all upon Calvary, but is a perpetuation of that Sacrifice by the Church on earth, as our Lord also perpetually offers it in heaven. It is a true and propitiatory Sacrifice, which is offered alike for the living and for the dead.

Holy Order is a Sacrament in which the Holy Ghost, through the laying-on of hands of the Bishops, consecrates and ordains the pastors and ministers of the Church, and imparts to them special grace to administer the Sacraments, to forgive sins, and to feed the flock of Christ.

Matrimony is a Sacrament in which the voluntary union of husband and wife is sanctified to become an image of the union of Christ and His Church; and grace is imparted to them to fulfill the duties of their estate and its great responsibilities, both to each other and to their children.

Penance is a Sacrament in which the Holy Ghost bestows the forgiveness of sins, by the ministry of the Priest, upon those who, having sinned after Baptism, confess their sins with true repentance; and grace is given to amend their lives thereafter.

Unction is a Sacrament in which the Priests of the Church anoint the sick with oil, for the healing of the infirmities of their souls, and if it should please God those of their bodies also.

The efficacy of the Sacraments depends upon the promise and appointment of God; howbeit they benefit only those who receive them worthily with faith, and with due preparation and disposition of mind.

6. Holy Scripture. The Scriptures are writings inspired by God, and given to the Church for her instruction and edification. The Church is therefore the custodian and the only Divinely appointed interpreter of Holy Scripture.

7. Tradition. The Apostolic and Ecclesiastical Traditions received from the seven General Councils and the early Fathers of the Church may not be rejected, but are to be received and obeyed as being both agreeable to Holy Scripture and to that Authority with which Christ endowed His Church. Matters of discipline and ceremonial do not rank on the same level with matters of Faith or Morals, but may be altered from time to time and from place to place by the Authority of the Church, according as the welfare and greater devotion of the faithful may be furthered thereby.

8. The Communion of Saints. There is a Communion of Saints in the Providence of God, wherein the souls of the righteous of all ages are united with Christ in the bond of faith and love. Wherefore it is pleasing to God, and profitable to humanity, to honor the Saints and to invoke them in prayer; and also to pray for the faithful departed.

9. Religious Symbols. The Relics and representations of Saints are worthy of honor, as are also all other religious emblems; that our minds may be encouraged to devotion and to imitation of the deeds of the just. Honor shown to such objects is purely relative, and in no way implies a confusion of the symbol with the thing signified.

10. Rites and Ceremonies. It is the duty of all Christians to join in the worship of the Church, especially in the Holy Sacrifice of the Mass, in accordance with our Lord's express command; and to conform to the ceremonies prescribed by Holy Tradition for the greater dignity of that Sacrifice and for the edification of the faithful.

11. The Moral Law. All Christians are bound to observe the Moral Law contained in the Ten Commandments of the Old Testament, developed with greater strictness in the New, founded upon the law of nature and charity, and defining our duty to God and to man. The laws of the Church are also to be obeyed, as proceeding from that Authority which Christ has committed to her for the instruction and salvation of His people.

12. The Monastic Estate. The monastic life, duly regulated according to the laws of the Church, is a salutary institution in strict accord with the Holy Scriptures; and is fully of profit to them who, after being carefully tried and examined, make full proof of their calling thereto.

ORGANIC ARTICLES

1. Head of the Church. The Foundation, Head and Supreme Pastor and Bishop of the Church is our Lord Jesus Christ Himself, from whom all Bishops and Pastors derive their spiritual powers and jurisdiction.

2. Obedience. By the law and institution of our Lord Jesus Christ in the Gospel, all Christians owe obedience and submission in spiritual things to them who have rule and authority within the Church.

3. Ministerial Authority. Our Lord Jesus Christ did not commit rule and authority within the Church to all the faithful indiscriminately, but only to the Apostles and to their lawful successors in due order.

4. Apostolic Succession. The only lawful successors of the Apostles are the Orthodox and Catholic Bishops, united by profession of the self-same belief, participation in the same Sacraments, and mutual recognition and intercommunion. The Bishops of the Church, being true successors of the Apostles, are by Divine right and appointment the rulers of the Church.

In virtue of this appointment, each individual Bishop is supreme and independent in that part of the Church which has been committed to his care, so long as he remains in Faith and Communion with the united company of Catholic Bishops, who cannot exclude any from the Church save only them who stray from the path of virtue or err in Faith.

By virtue of this same Divine appointment, the supreme Authority over the whole Church on earth belongs to the collective Orthodox and Catholic Episcopate. They alone form the highest tribunal in spiritual matters, from whose united judgment there can be no appeal; so that it is unlawful for any single Bishop, or any smaller group of Bishops apart from them, or for any secular power or state, to usurp this Authority, or for any individual Christian to substitute his own private judgment for that interpretation of Scripture or Authority which is approved by the Church.

5. Church Authority. The collective body of the Orthodox Catholic Episcopate, united by profession of the Faith, by the Sacraments, and by mutual recognition and actual intercommunion, is the source and depository of all order, authority and jurisdiction in the Church, and is the center of visible Catholic unity; so that no Pope, Patriarch or Bishop, or any number of Bishops separated from this united body can possess any authority or jurisdiction whatsoever. The authority of this collective body is equally binding, however it may be expressed: whether by a General Council or by the regular and ordinary consultation and agreement of the Bishops them-selves. It is an act of schism to appeal from the known judgment of the Orthodox and Catholic Episcopate, however it may have been ascertained; or to appeal from any dogmatic decree of any General Council even though such appeal be to a future Council. For the Episcopate, being a continuation of the Apostolate, is clearly a Divine institution, and its authority is founded in Divine right. But General councils are not of themselves of direct Divine appointment; and so the Episcopate having clearly the Scriptural promise of Divine guidance into all Truth, cannot be hampered in the exercise of its authority by the necessity of assembling a General Council, which may obviously be rendered impossible through natural circumstances.

There have been seven General Councils only, which are recognized by the whole of Catholic Christendom, held respectively in Nicea (A.D. 325), Constantinople (381), Ephesus (431), Chalcedon (451), Constantinople (553), Constantinople (680), and Nicea (787).

At no other Councils was the entire body of the Orthodox and Catholic Episcopate representatively assembled; and the decrees and pronouncements of no others must of themselves be accepted as binding upon the consciences of the faithful.

The Authority of the Church can never be in abeyance, even though a General Council cannot be assembled. It is equally to be submitted to and obeyed in whatever way it may be exercised, and although it may be exercised only through the ordinary administration of their respective jurisdictions by individual Bishops.

6. Hierarchy. All Patriarchs, Archbishops and Metropolitans (that is to say, all Bishops exercising authority over other Bishops) owe that authority solely to the appointment or general consent of the Orthodox and Catholic Episcopate; nor

can they ever cease from owing obedience to the collective body of the Episcopate in all matters concerning Faith and Morals.

7. The Five Patriarchates. There are five Patriarchates, which ought to be united and form the supreme authority in the administration of the Holy Catholic Church. These are Jerusalem, Antioch, Rome, Alexandria, and Constantinople. Unfortunately, owing to disputes and differences on the one hand and to the lust for power on the other, the Patriarchs are not at present in Communion; and the welfare of Christendom is jeopardized by their disedifying quarrels, which we pray may soon have an end.

Appendix N

Metropolitan Gerassimos Messarra's Reception of Bishop Mathew

[Translation of the Document of Reception by the Syrian Orthodox Communion]

"Monsignor,

Colleague and brother in Jesus Christ, with open arms in the love of the Savior, I receive you among us, and I accept your oath of fidelity to His Beatitude the Orthodox Patriarch and his Holy Synod of Antioch, since those who hold our Faith and wish to be united with us have never been prevented from joining us.

Praying God to bless you, and not only you but all those who come to us with you, we bless you in the name of His Beatitude the Patriarch and of the Holy Synod of Antioch.

Your Colleague and Brother in Jesus Christ,

GERASSIMOS MESSARRA,
Prince Archbishop and Metropolitan,
Orthodox Church of Beyrout

5th Aug. 1911"

Appendix O

The 1931 Bonn Agreement

[Intercommunion agreement between the Continental Old Catholics and the Anglicans]

Das Bonner Abkommen

1. Jede Kirchengemeinschaft anerkennt die Katholizität und Selbständigkeit der andern und hält die eigene aufrecht.

2. Jede Kirchengemeinschaft stimmt der Zulassung von Mitgliedern der andern zur Teilnahme an den Sakramenten zu.

3. Interkommunion verlangt von keiner Kirchengemeinschaft die Übernahme aller Lehrmeinungen, sakramentalen Frömmigkeit oder liturgischen Praxis, die der anderen eigentümlich ist, sondern schließt in sich, daß jede glaubt, die andere halte alles Wesentliche des christlichen Glaubens fest.

The Bonn Agreement

1. Each Communion recognizes the catholicity and independence of the other and maintains its own.

2. Each Communion agrees to admit members of the other Communion to participate in the Sacraments.

3. Intercommunion does not require from either Communion the acceptance of all doctrinal opinion, sacramental devotion or liturgical practice characteristic of the other, but implies that each believes the other to hold all the essentials of the Christian faith.

The American Catholic Union, *Traditional Old Catholic Dogma,* Daniel Wells, Used by Permission, 2003.

0-595-34066-0

Printed in the United States
61052LVS00003B/19